D0075001

PACE UNIVERSITY LIBRARIES
3 5061 00571014 1

HV 97 .R6 F6 1988

Fosdick, Raymond Blaine,
1883-

The story of the Rockefeller
Foundation

PACE UNIVERSITY
MORTOLA LIBRARY
Pleasantville, N.Y. 10570
Telephone (914) 993-3380

TO THE BORROWER:

The use of this book is governed by rules established in the broad interest of the university community. It is your responsibility to know these rules. Please inquire at the circulation desk.

THE STORY OF THE ROCKEFELLER FOUNDATION

HV
97
.R6
F6
1988

THE STORY OF THE ROCKEFELLER FOUNDATION

Raymond B. Fosdick

With a new introduction
by
Steven C. Wheatley

Transaction Publishers
New Brunswick (U.S.A.) and Oxford (U.K.)

New material this edition copyright (c) 1989 by Transaction Publishers, New Brunswick, New Jersey 08903.
Originally published in 1952 by Harper & Brothers.

All rights reserved under International and Pan-American Copyright Conventions. No part of this book may be reproduced or transmitted in any form or by any means, electronic or mechanical, including photocopy, recording, or any information storage and retrieval system, without prior permission in writing from the publisher. All inquiries should be addressed to Transaction Publishers, Rutgers–The State University, New Brunswick, New Jersey 08903.

Library of Congress Catalog Number: 88-21152
ISBN: 0-88738-248-7
Printed in the United States of America

Library of Congress Cataloging-in-Publication Data

Fosdick, Raymond Blaine, 1883-
The story of the Rockefeller Foundation / Raymond B. Fosdick: with a new introduction by Steven C. Wheatley.
p. cm
Reprint. Originally published: New York: Harper & Row, 1952.
Bibliography: p.
Includes index.
ISBN: 0-88738-248-7
1. Rockefeller Foundation. 2. Endowments--United States.
I. Title.
HV97.R6F6 1988
361.7'632'0973--dc19 88-21152 CIP

CONTENTS

A GROUP OF SIXTEEN PHOTOGRAPHS MAY BE FOUND FOLLOWING PAGE 176.

INTRODUCTION TO THE TRANSACTION EDITION

Raymond B. Fosdick's *The Story of the Rockefeller Foundation* has been for many years the single most reliable treatment of one of the most important philanthropies in the United States, and indeed the world. Since the original publication of the book, there has been an explosion of scholarship concerning the role of foundations in American history. However, despite this new scholarship, Fosdick's book remains the one most comprehensive guide to the activities of the Rockefeller Foundation (RF) before 1950. None of the historians now laboring in libraries and foundation archives have, so far, assayed to revise or extend Fosdick's first draft of institutional history. It would certainly be a daunting task. As *The Story* makes clear, the activities of the RF have been global in scope, often arcane in method, and complex in their development. Indeed, historians have explored thoroughly only a few of the many programs which Fosdick describes.

Apart from the difficulty of analyzing those important programs and projects, any new history of the RF also would have to consider a set of socio-political questions which recent scholarship has raised. These analysts have sought to understand why the philanthropic foundation is, in Fosdick's words, "almost exclusively an American phenomenon of the twentieth century." Their answers have involved issues of power, politics and authority, issues which Fosdick only glancingly deals with.[1]

Pointing out this omission is not, however, to fault Fosdick or *The Story of the Rockefeller Foundation*. For while we may now find that it falls short of our present standards for institutional biography, its great value is that it is a much rarer contribution: an institutional autobiography, or at least as close to that imaginary species as we are likely to get. As Fosdick notes in his history, he was for twelve years the president of the RF, from 1936 to 1948, having been a trustee since 1921. During those years the Rockefeller Foundation was, almost literally, the "foundation" of institutions of advanced science and research at home and abroad. As the largest grant-making endowment in the world during that period, its influence was considerable. That influence was further magnified by the financial and organizational disruption and change of depression and war which made its aid even more critical. Fosdick's was one of the longest presidencies up to that time, and during it the Foundation finally developed a stable organizational character.

Even this brief statement of his career understates Fosdick's importance to the history of the Foundation and the Rockefeller family. Raymond B. Fosdick was to John D. Rockefeller, Jr. what Frederick T. Gates was to John D. Rockefeller, Sr.: principal colleague and chief interpreter of the outside world. Both before and after his presidency, Fosdick was Rockefeller, Jr.'s lawyer, adviser, friend, and, eventually, biographer.[2] Rockefeller, Jr. had many lawyers, but Fosdick was one of the closest to him, working out of 61 Broadway, the offices of the family and of the Rockefeller philanthropic boards. Rockefeller, Jr. had several advisers, but none whose advice he sought on as broad a range of issues as Fosdick's. Rockefeller, Jr. had very few friends. While close and mutual, his friendship with Fosdick had a formality which has passed with their generation; they never addressed each other but as "Mr. Rockefeller" and "Mr. Fosdick." As early as 1921, Rockefeller, Jr. urged Fosdick to assume the leadership of one of the several Rockefeller philanthropic boards. It was Fosdick who managed the major reorganization of the Rockefeller philanthropies in 1928 and dedicated the Foundation to supporting "the advancement of knowledge."[3] Thus, when he assumed the presidency of the RF in 1936, he stepped into a position which he had played a crucial part in designing.

Fosdick, then, was an "insider" and it was as an insider that he wrote *The Story of the Rockefeller Foundation*. Indeed, he probably undertook the task as a matter of institutional defense. The date of the book's initial publication (1952) is revealing. Unlike most "house histories" (official narratives of a foundation), it commemorates no chronological anniversary. It seems likely that publicity was deemed expedient because of a mounting political attack on the foundation community. This attack was from the right; a committee of the House of Representatives, chaired by Congressman Reece, portrayed the foundations as a subversive influence on American education and society. A history like Fosdick's might help balance the scales by laying before the public the catalogue of the Foundation's good works.

The book is therefore a deliberate self-portrait and that is its value today as an historical document. It conceals as much as it reveals and in so doing reveals a great deal about the perspective of one of the most important of the Rockefeller philanthropic managers. Even the casual reader, unfamiliar with the controversies which have surrounded the RF and the Rockefeller name, will quickly apprehend the tone of restrained pride and modulated defensiveness in which the book is written. Unlike a later generation of bureaucratic managers, Fosdik had no urge to refight old battles in print and he only most circumspectly hints at his past annoyances and at the faults of his quondam opponents.

In order to appreciate fully Fosdick's *Story*, it therefore is necessary to bear in mind Fosdick's background and the crucial issues surrounding the RF.

Raymond Blaine Fosdick

Fosdick quite self-consciously saw himself to be a transitional man. He entitled his personal autobiography, *Chronicle of a Generation*.[4] In that, he was not being immodest but rather testifying to what he felt was the unique historical experience of his age. Much of his writing-his autobiography, his history of the Foundation, his collected essays (entitled *The Old Savage in the New Civilization*),[5] even his Foundation memos-are all characterized by a consciousness of accelerating social change, by the conviction that his generation was hurtling across a very rickety bridge between the past and the future. Probably many individuals in every age feel themselves witnesses to dramatic transitions, but Fosdick has some just claim to the feeling that his experiences are noteworthy and not simply nostalgic.

He was part of a generation which lived through, and indeed effected, the transformation of America from a collection of individual communities to a mass society. The forces of urbanization, industrialization, commercialism, and globalism that had all been gathering strength throughout the nineteenth century reached during this generation a critical mass that changed not only the form but also the content of American culture and society. This was the period known as the "Progressive era." Historians have come to see "Progressivism" more as a constellation of related impulses than as a coherent point of view. Nonetheless, it was a period of great social and ideological ferment and experimentation as society strove to understand the challenges of industrial civilization. Those, like Fosdick, who embraced and sought to direct these changes shed their inherited loyalties to orthodox religion and to the religion of partisan politics to seek new commitments in the trinity of "reform"; charismatic leadership, social commitment, and organizational development.

Fosdick's life captured this era in microcosm. He grew up in western New York where his father was the broad-minded principal of a Buffalo high school. His family was rigorously Baptist and unreflectingly Republican; to them these positions were not achieved viewpoints, but premises of self-definition. His autobiography details a happy childhood where reading, thrift, wholesomeness, and highmindedness were encouraged. It was only after a difficult intellectual migration that young Fosdick discarded his received world view. That journey began during his days at Colgate University but took definite shape when he transferred to Princeton as a junior.

It was at Princeton that Fosdick met the man who was to become his guiding model: Woodrow Wilson. Wilson, who had just assumed the Princeton presidency, brought both intellectual rigor of modern scholarship and the moral force of Christian vision to bear on contemporary problems and issues. Fosdick, like many in the Progressive years-only far more personally-found in Wilson a leadership that gave plausibility to the whole idea of "reform." Others, such as Fosdick's college classmate and friend Norman Thomas, eventually sought to solve the problems of modern industrial society through wholesale renovation. But Fosdick's path was the more common one: to "reform" society through the application of new techniques and forms such as scientific research, bureaucratic management, and professional organization to the issues of the day.

After leaving Princeton (where he spent an additional year as a graduate student), Fosdick made his ways through the catalogue of reform. His *curriculum vitae* does truly suggest the courses by which the twentieth century American elite learned its role. Between 1906 and the 1920s, Fosdick's career progressed from local private philanthropy (the Henry Street Settlement House) to local government reform (City Chamberlain of New York), to national political activity (Treasurer of the Democratic Party) and then to quasi-state organizational leadership (the Commission on Training Camp Activities in World War I). There was a brief period of service in what was the closest thing to an international government (the League of Nations), before Fosdick settled for what was arguably the next best thing: the Rockefeller philanthropies dedicated, as the charter of the RF had it, to "the well-being of mankind throughout the world."

The Rockefeller Foundation

Fosdick's association with foundation philanthropy was therefore in many ways a logical culmination to his reform career. The general purpose foundation was another of the Progressive period's institutional innovations. As long as there was poverty there had been charity and the concept of a charitable endowment is of great antiquity. However, the idea that huge sums of money could be set aside for unspecified future social needs emerged only in the early twentieth century. It was when magnates such as Rockefeller and Andrew Carnegie sought to bring to their charitable donations the same managerial techniques that they had applied to their business affairs that the philanthropic foundation as we know it today achieved legal and organizational form. So, just as there grew new agencies and organizations dedicated to managing the consequences of halcyon social and economic changes, the foundations began with not only a similar objective but with the wherewithal to support that intention.

But there is an important tension here. John D. Rockefeller represented to many everything which the reforms of the Progressive era were trying to erase: irresponsible power, secretive self-seeking, the triumph of private over the public interest. The philanthropic boards which Rockefeller and other magnates developed were designed, at least in part, to vindicate American capitalism against the charge that it was incapable of dealing with the burgeoning problems of the twentieth century. So, in seeking to undertake a program of social management, the philanthropic foundations took some of the reform agenda, the reform vocabulary, and the reform personnel, such as Fosdick, as their own. Yet this politically charged tension persisted. The foundations were (and remain) suspect not simply because of the involvement of Rockefeller or individual Rockefellers, but because they were, like Rockefeller, wealthy, powerful, and not elected by anyone.

This tension has bubbled up repeatedly since the invention of the philanthropic foundation. It first became apparent when the Rockefeller foundation's attempt to receive a Congressional charter was rebuffed. President William Howard Taft, no radical, let it be known that he was opposed to the "bill to incorporate John D. Rockefeller." (A charter was eventually, and easily, obtained from New York State.) A stronger reaction came after the Ludlow massacre, an episode of violence during a labor dispute in

Rockefeller-owned mines in Colorado. The fledgling RF was then presided over by John D. Rockefeller, Jr. It was deicded, quite unwisely, that the new enterprise should involve itself in the systematic investigation of industrial relations. This was exactly the specter which haunted the critics of foundations: philanthropic wealth propagandistically whitewashing the depredations of the robber barons. In several days of fierce testimony before the Congressionally-mandated Commission on Industrial Relations, the reticent and insecure young Rockefeller was mercilessly grilled and later pilloried in the public press. As mentioned above, in the 1950s, attack came from the right and, in 1969, the foundation community was again hauled before Congress, this time to respond (and not completely successfully) to charges of abusive elitism.

In the aftermath of the first major assaults on the foundations' roles, figures like Fosdick became essential because of their value in managing this tension between the foundations' large agenda of social management and their narrow political legitimacy. These men (and they were almost entirely men) brought two vital capabilities to the foundations. Because of their reform careers they had a familiarity with both the potential and the limitations of government. By the same token, they had access to and rapport with a broader range of publics than did the donors and their associates drawn from industry and finance. Originally, philanthropists had relied upon university presidents to broaden their reach. It was from that milieu that the Rockefeller Foundation drew Fosdick's two immediate predecessors: George Vincent (from the University of Minnesota) and Max Mason (from the University of Chicago). But the new managers (Frederick P. Keppel of the Carnegie Corporation, and Frank Lowden of the Farm Foundation are other examples) brought with them an even wider array of experience. They helped solidify the legitimacy of the philanthropic foundation by creating the role of the foundation president. The president was now not only to supervise the development and management of philanthropic policies and programs. He was to do so while continually recognizing all the various publics that were legitimately, if quite variably, involved in that process: foundation staff, recipient institutions, political elites, trustees, donors, and the general public.

What these new presidents did was to get control of the foundation mechanism. Fosdick's *Story* briefly discusses the reorganization of the Rockefeller boards in 1928, but does not make clear what a major change it was. The foundations (both the cluster of

Rockefeller philanthropies and the collection of benefactions established by Andrew Carnegie) had grown up in fits and starts. When these new managers surveyed their domains, they confronted over-commitment to a large number of disparate programs and institutions. This was further complicated by the presence of some difficult personalities who maintained petty empires within larger philanthropic boards and who based their claims to autonomy on their relationships to the founders. (This was especially acute in the Carnegie boards. The Rockefellers, as a living presence, were much less easy to appropriate.)

In order that the foundations be organizations which could provide leadership across a range of issues and not just "milk cows," as Keppel put it, for established institutions, it was necessary to reconceptualize and reconstruct their purposes. The general goal-"the well-being of mankind throughout the world" or some other broad aim-remained the same, but the method changed. The formula which Fosdick promoted for the reformed Rockefeller Foundation was "the advancement of knowledge." This represented a turn away from the earlier pattern of organization-building and broad institutional support in favor of the support of research along selected lines through targeted smaller grants.

This change had important consequences for the way foundation managers saw their role and for the public rationale for the social purpose of the philanthropic foundation. Since the fight over the incorporation of the Rockfeller Foundation, foundations had searched for rhetorical justifications for their place in American society. Several emerged and Fosdick's account of the history of the Rockefeller Foundation stresses one of them: what has been called the "venture capital" theory.

That view goes something like this. The increasingly complex needs of society demand both temporary relief and permanent solution. Government and local community welfare agencies must naturally bear the burden of relieving suffering, but permanent solutions will only be arrived at through a process of research and discovery. Foundations, by virtue of their isolation from quotidian responsibilities, can take on the task of supporting the search for fundamental solutions. This research is a risk in that its products may often have no immediate utility, but with alert and flexible organizations like the philanthropic foundations superintending the process of discovery what gains there are can be quickly applied to the social benefit.

The fields of medicine and public health lent themselves most exactly to this formula of social innovation and it is therefore not surprising that much of the space and most of the vivid writing of *The Story of the Rockefeller Foundation* is devoted to them. The conquest of hookworm, the fight against the gambiae mosquito, all emphasize the social implementation (sanitation, swamp drainage) of scientific discovery (the cause of infection). The metaphor is satisfyingly capitalist because the return on the investment is so spectacular.

Such public health efforts did constitute a large part of the RF's expenditures and their results were undeniably spectacular. Indeed, work along this line was so gratifying that Frederick T. Gates eventually came to feel that the Foundation should not waste its funds on any endeavors but medical ones. Recent scholarly critics of foundation philanthropy have suggested that these efforts were motivated more by a desire to exploit economically and dominate politically the areas of the world where they were undertaken. Making the tropics safe from disease made them ripe for domination.[6] Such criticism is both exaggerated and off the point. These efforts were attractive to the foundations, especially to the Rockefeller boards for the same reason, the National Institutes of Health historically has enjoyed considerable Congressional bounty: they are politically safe and appealing programs.

There are other possible definitions of the foundations' role that Fosdick's predecessors and contemporaries put forward and applied in foundation programs. One such is a frank admission that the foundations seek to provide leadership for the organization of knowledge (a different problem than the advancement of knowledge) and for the management of social problems. This "institutional leadership" theory was the view of some of the earlier foundation leaders. Henry S. Pritchett of the Carnegie Foundation for the Advancement of Teaching pointed out that in Imperial Germany the government took it upon itself to organize for the training and employment of scientific expertise, but that in the U.S. that function had fallen to the foundations.[7] Abraham Flexner of the Rockefeller-funded General Education Board put the case more strongly: "Education broadly conceived necessarily involves organizations, systems, institutions, as well as individuals: hence, if you are going to deal broadly with education, you must have contacts with, knowledge of, and influence over, institutions and systems." He rejected the notion "that foundations dole out money to deserving organizations or institutions without attempting leadership," and felt that foundation philanthropy should be "placing at the disposal of persons dealing with local problems a broader experience and wider outlook than they usually possess or can acquire."[8]

Many of the programs of the Rockefeller Foundation and of the other Rockefeller philanthropies were based on this motive. An effort such as that Fosdick describes to construct and support the Peking Union Medical College was designed not only to provide China with western medical care and research but also to provide an institutional model and leaders for the reconstruction of Chinese education and, ultimately, Chinese society. Similarly, the RF's support in the 1930s for Southern regional studies, most significantly under Professor Howard W. Odum of the University of North Carolina, was designed at least in part to nurture and provide an ideological basis for a Southern elite that would lead the South out of its racial and economic difficulties.

However, this "institutionalized leadership" theory of the philanthropic role brings in its train just the sort of politically troubling questions which Fosdick's generation of foundation managers had been developed to avoid. People's careers (and, by extension, their lives) are in many ways defined by their relation to institutions. Therefore, to pursue the course defined by the institutional leadership theory, that is, explicitly to set about building, rearranging, and making decisions about the relative merit of a variety of institutions, is to announce the intention of becoming an important arbiter of social power. The relative success of the Rockefeller Foundation, or all foundations for that matter, in assumimg that role is another, and most interesting, question. But the point here is that while the RF has clearly played this role, to make it the center of the organization's public progam is to ignite the low-combustion political mixture which is always surrounding the Foundation.

It is for this reason that in the 1928 reorganization of the Rockefeller boards Fosdick rejected the institutional leadership model. It may also be why in *The Story* he either wholly neglects or skims over rather lightly any program that raises these questions of systemic leadership. Take his discussion of the Foundation's support for such mediating organizations as the American Council of Learned Societies and the Social Science Research Council. While these organizations originated as a result of felt needs by some of the nation's more entrepreneurial academics, foundation support was absolutely essential to their growth and survival. However, they were equally valuable to the foundations as organizations through which the RF and others could support particular activities. Their representative character and relative proximity to the scholarly community gave these organizations a legitimacy that has allowed them to make choices among programs and projects proposed by scholars, choices which if made by the foundations themselves would produce more distrust than gratitude.

Similarly, Fosdick is almost coy about the important role the Foundation played in providing the government with social, scientific, and administrative expertise at a time when the intellectual resources for policy development were almost all privately supported. He discusses in detail the Foundation's support for research that led to the development of nuclear weapons, but he is not as forthcoming in the realm of applied social science. The RF was one of the principal initiators of the Institute for Government Research (eventually the Brookings Institution) which among other things promoted the idea of the need for a federal budget and provided much of the personnel for the first Bureau of the Budget. During the 1920s, the RF was quite active in supporting Herbert Hoover's efforts to set up advisory groups on employment, housing, and recent social trends. During the New Deal, the RF-funded Committee on Economic Security helped design much of what eventually became the Social Security Act, and other groups worked in the areas of agriculture and public administration.

It is perhaps not entirely fair to fault Fosdick for not making a literary presentation of a view he already had rejected administratively. Nonetheless, there is one subject with which he was principally occupied and on which his *Story*'s silence is most regrettable. Fosdick does not give any sustained treatment to what is in many ways the most interesting problem involved in the history of philanthropy: the evolution of the internal organization of the foundation. Like almost all foundation histories, Fosdick's includes an ironic quote about the difficulty of doing good with lots of money. He also provides an abstract synopsis of the policies developed by the Foundation, but he does not connect those policies to either the RF's internal organization or to the history of its development. Given the importance of the topic its absence is sorely missed. Since the philanthropic foundation is such a conspicuous invention of modern America, an analysis of its internal history may tell us a lot about the society that spawned and sustained it. The foundation idea combines bureaucratic form (with all the precision that implies) with a highly indefinite goal ("the welfare of mankind throughout the world"), thus posing fascinating questions in organizational sociology. When you add to this formulation the peculiar requirements of the grant mechanism: that the foundation is to achieve its goals largely indirectly-that is, through stimulating other organizations-it becomes clear how complex a process thoughtful philanthropic administration must be. Yet Fosdick satisfies himself with discussing the RF's objects and not its intramural processes.

We would wish, for example, for even brief discussions of the recruitment of personnel and trustees. There was certainly no clear career path to foundation employment. The personalities, predilections, and past experiences of Foundation officers were often crucial determinants of the design not just of individual programs but of the Foundation's internal organization which in turn determimed other programs. Fosdick himself is an important example in this connection. The RF's program in psychiatry during the 1930s was vitally important in the development of that field in general and in particular to stimulating academic acceptance of psychoanalysis in the U.S. While that program had several origins, an important element of its support by the trustees was their understanding of the ravaging consequences of mental illness: shortly before he assumed the RF presidency, Fosdick's wife killed herself and their two children after years of a distrubed emotional life.

Another complex question is the relationships between the foundation officers and the programs they administer, one of the most vexing of Fosdick's presidency, yet he writes very little about it. The actual implementation of the program "to advance knowledge" involved dividing up responsibilities in way that became problematic. Research in experimental biology was the responsibility of the RF's Natural Science Division, an arrangement that produced conflict with the Medical Sciences Division, considerable confusion among recipients, and a certain amount of working at cross purposes. Nevertheless, Fosdick declines to explore the general implications of this type of problem, which he would have considered "bureaucratic." To foundation managers of his generation (as to most Americans) "bureaucracy" was a term of abuse which meant poor administration and thus explained managerial problems without analyzing them.

What, then, are we to make of *The Story of the Rockefeller Foundation* when we approach it as an institutional autobiography? Taking account of Fosdick's omissions and selected emphases is not to suggest that he was careless or fraudulent. Indeed, his earnest fairmindedness comes through. He is willing to admit, in general, that the Foundation occasionally made poor choices, serious errors, and missteps. He fully understands that the RF, like all foundations, may be the object of mistrust even as he feels such fears are exaggerated. Because, genuinely, he does not regard these subjects as important he concentrates instead on the specific achievements of particular foundation activities. As Fosdick conceived it, "politics," like "bureaucracy," was perhaps an avoidable problem and not a necessary component of foundation activity. While some RF program officers privately criticized this view as a "neurotic unwillingness" to take seriously the consequences of the Foundation's importance, Fosdick's view became established philanthropic practice beyond the RF.[9]

Fosdick's history is written from, and written to substantiate, a particular view of the role of foundations in American life. Fosdick sees the foundations as engaging in the application of scientific, technical, and organizational solutions to public problems. While he appreciates the political dimension of this work, he sees that as an subsidiary problem. It is important to understand that that view has its own history as a politically conditioned response to the RF's institutional vulnerability. A history of the RF that would more squarely consider the political questions inherent in the Foundation's record would be a much different work. But such a work has yet to be written. Until it is, Fosdick's *Story* will stand as the history of the RF and as a statement of the idea that redefined that most important institution.

Notes

1. Barry D. Karl, "Philanthropy, Policy Planning and the Bureaucratization of the Democratic Ideal," *Daedalus* 105 (1976): 129-150; Barry D. Karl and Stanley N. Katz, "The American Private Philanthropic Foundation and the Public Sphere, 1890-1930," *Minerva* 19 (1981): 236-70; Karl and Katz, Foundations and Ruling Class Elites, *Daedalus* 116 (1987): 1-41; Kathleen D. McCarthy, *Noblesse Oblige: Charity and Cultural Philanthropy in Chicago, 1849-1929* (Chicago: University of Chicago Press, 1982); Ellen Condliffe Lagemann, Private Power for the Public Good: *A History of the Carnegie Foundation for the Advancement of Teaching* (Middletown, Conn.: Wesleyan University Press, 1983); John Ettling, *The Germ of Laziness: Rockefeller Philanthropy and Public Health in the New South* (Cambridge: Harvard University Press, 1981): Robert F. Arnove, *Philanthropy and Cultural Imperialism: The Foundations at Home and Abroad* (Bloomington: Indiana University Press, 1982). Steven C. Wheatley, *The Politics of Philanthropy: Abraham Flexner* and *Medical Education* (Madison: University of Wisconsin Press, 1988).

2. *John D. Rockefeller, Jr.: A Portrait* (New York: Harper and Brothers, 1956).

3. See Robert E. Kohler, "A Policy for the Advancement of Science: The Rockefeller Foundation, 1924-29," *Minerva* 16 (1978): 480-515.

4. *Chronicle of a Generation: An Autobiography* (New York: Harper and Brothers, 1958).

5. *The Old Savage in the New Civilization* (Garden City: Doubleday, Doran, 1928).

6. E. Richard Brown, *Rockefeller Medicine Men: Medicine and Capitalism in America* (Berkeley: University of California Press, 1979).

7. Henry S. Pritchett, "How Science Helps Industry in Germany." *Review of Reviews* 33 (1906): 167-170.

8. Abraham Flexner to Charles Howland, April 13, 1927, Rockefeller Foundation Archives, Rockefeller Archive Center, Pocantico Hills, N.Y.; Abraham Flexner to Simon Flexner, January 5, 1928, Simon Flexner Papers (microfilm copy), Rockefeller Archive Center.

9. Alan Gregg to Julia M.H. Carson, January 23, 1948, Rockefeller Foundation Archives.

THE STORY OF THE ROCKEFELLER FOUNDATION

CHAPTER I

THE BACKGROUND OF THE IDEA

FREDERICK T. GATES WAS A MAN OF remarkable qualities. A former Baptist minister, he became the principal adviser in business and philanthropy of John D. Rockefeller. He combined bold imagination and large horizons with shrewd business capacity and driving energy. In a candid bit of portraiture, he described himself in 1891 as "eager, impetuous, insistent, and withal exacting and irritable."[1*] In addition it may be said that he was fearless, often fiery in his words, powerful in exhortation, with a mind that was too precipitous to be always tolerant, and with a voice that thundered from Sinai. At his last meeting as a trustee of The Rockefeller Foundation in 1923, he made a farewell speech. Shaking his fist at a somewhat startled but respectfully attentive Board, he vociferated: "When you die and come to approach the judgment of Almighty God, what do you think He will demand of you? Do you for an instant presume to believe that He will inquire into your petty failures or your trivial virtues? No! He will ask just one question: *'What did you do as a Trustee of The Rockefeller Foundation?'* "[2]

In spite of his evangelical fervor—indeed, perhaps because of it—he was one of the chief architects of that extraordinary group of foundations which Mr. Rockefeller established in the first two decades of the century.

* Superior figures refer to Notes, which will be found in a group, beginning on page 315.

One would have to search over wide areas to find two men who were so completely different in temperament. Mr. Gates was a vivid, outspoken, self-revealing personality who brought an immense gusto to his work; Mr. Rockefeller was quiet, cool, taciturn about his thoughts and purposes, almost stoic in his repression. Mr. Gates had an eloquence which could be passionate when he was aroused; Mr. Rockefeller, when he spoke at all, spoke in a slow measured fashion, lucidly and penetratingly, but without raising his voice and without gestures. Mr. Gates was overwhelming and sometimes overbearing in argument; Mr. Rockefeller was a man of infinite patience who never showed irritation or spoke chidingly about anybody. Mr. Gates summed up his impression of Mr. Rockefeller in this sentence: "If he was very nice and precise in his choice of words, he was also nice and accurate in his choice of silences."[3]

And yet these two men who worked together so intimately and understandingly for forty years shared certain strong resemblances. Both were self-made men who had come out of humble circumstances in their youth; both were inspired by deep religious conviction; both were endowed with a capacity for bold planning and large designs; each was a pioneer in his own way, adventurous in spirit, eager for new methods and new ideas, ready to drive at a gallop when the way opened ahead. Their long relationship was one of mutual respect and confidence. In his book, *Random Reminiscences of Men and Events,* Mr. Rockefeller referred to Mr. Gates as "possessing a combination of rare business ability, very highly developed and very honorably exercised, overshadowed by a passion to accomplish some great and far-reaching benefits to mankind, the influence of which will last."[4] On his side, in his autobiography, as yet unpublished, and in his private papers, Mr. Gates wrote constantly of Mr. Rockefeller's sincerity and earnestness, the superior quality of his mind, and his statesmanlike grasp of detail. Years later, he said of Mr. Rockefeller: "He was a very reserved man, admitting few confidences, and these only in times of very high nervous tension and altogether exceptional stress. His usual attitude toward all men was one of deep reserve, concealed beneath commonplace and humorous anecdotes. He had the art with friends and guests of chatting freely, of calling out others, but of revealing little or nothing of his own innermost thoughts."[5]

There was another member of this informal partnership who was destined to play a notable part in the creation and development of vast philanthropic enterprises—Mr. Rockefeller's only son, John D.

Rockefeller, Jr. Graduating from Brown University in 1897 in his twenty-third year, he entered his father's office at once. "I felt . . . that if I was going to learn to help Father in the care of his affairs," he afterward wrote, "the sooner my apprenticeship under his guidance began, the better."[6] Few father-and-son relationships have been characterized by more genuine trust or by deeper affection. For forty years they worked closely and intimately together. The younger Rockefeller had many of the qualities which his father most admired: conscientiousness, tireless industry, practical judgment, and a capacity to sift the relevant from the irrelevant. These qualities were tempered by a modesty which was characteristic of both men, for as Allan Nevins says in his biography of Mr. Rockefeller: "[He] always dealt with his wealth in humility, not in arrogance."[7]

It was this three-cornered partnership that was responsible for a group of foundations to which Mr. Rockefeller ultimately contributed nearly half a billion dollars. It was a partnership singularly equipped for its task. Mr. Gates and Mr. Rockefeller, Jr., shared in the exploration of new ideas, while the elder Rockefeller retained final decision in all large matters and worked closely with his two assistants. It was a healthy relationship of complete frankness in which both lieutenants told Mr. Rockefeller exactly what they believed. Mr. Rockefeller, Jr., had this great advantage: like all sons, he belonged to a younger generation than his father, and the relationship between the two was so intimate that he could help to explain and interpret ideas and points of view which age finds unfamiliar. Mr. Gates, who could never be anything but candid and forthright, used to thunder at the elder Rockefeller: "Your fortune is rolling up, rolling up like an avalanche! You must keep up with it! You must distribute it faster than it grows! If you do not, it will crush you and your children and your children's children!"[8] In his autobiography, Mr. Gates records: "I felt that he was entitled to my ultimate thought frankly expressed. . . . I did not consciously allow his anticipated views to control or to modify my own views in the least degree. On the contrary, when I knew there would be a conflict of view I took special pains to fortify my position instead of yielding it or concealing it. . . . I was there to present my own views, with courtesy indeed but with absolute and undeviating frankness and truth. This, therefore, I always did."

But this was precisely what Mr. Rockefeller wanted. In all his business life, his invariable practice had been to surround himself with strong characters of independent judgment; and like his son after him he wanted no "yes-men" among his advisers. A man who could work with powerful and dominating figures like John D. Archbold and H. H. Rogers and Henry M. Flagler would appreciate the value of Mr. Gates. Years later, he said of Mr. Gates: "He combines business skill and philanthropic aptitude to a higher degree than any other man I have even known."[9] Speaking of the younger Rockefeller, he remarked to the writer one day in the middle of a golf game—apropos of nothing that had previously been said: "My greatest fortune in life has been my son."

II

Critics have frequently charged that Mr. Rockefeller's benefactions were set up as a shield against public censure, in an attempt to reestablish himself and ward off the abuse to which over many years he was subjected. But this contention is not borne out by the facts.* The famous "Ledger A" which he kept in his teens when he secured his first job as a clerk in Cleveland, a job which paid him six dollars a month, shows that he gave away 6 per cent of his total wage to the Sunday school and various missions related to his church interests. The obligation to give was an inseparable part of his religious conviction; it was a philosophy with which he had been indoctrinated by his mother from his earliest youth. "From the beginning," he declared, "I was trained to work, to save, and to give."[10] Five years later, in 1860, his gifts were rising proportionately with his income, which was still, however, small. Moreover, his plan of giving had broadened. Although his interests were centered primarily in the activities of the Baptist church, by this time he was making contributions to a Methodist church, a German Sunday school, a Negro church, and "Catholic orphans."

In 1865, when he was twenty-six years old, his annual gifts mounted to $1,012.35. Four years later, they reached nearly six thousand dollars. As Mr. Nevins says in his biography: "[Mr. Rockefeller] had not waited to grow rich before he began giving. It is to be noted that save for one year his gifts constantly grew larger, and that

* The legend which has long persisted that Ivy Lee, the public-relations counsel, advised Mr. Rockefeller to create the various Rockefeller philanthropies as a method of establishing himself in public esteem has no basis in fact. Mr. Lee did not become associated with the Rockefeller interests until 1914, thirteen years after the founding of the Rockefeller Institute, eleven years after the General Education Board came into existence, and over a year after The Rockefeller Foundation finally received its charter.

by the later sixties he was giving considerable lump sums—$558.42 to Denison University, for example. In his early giving, as later in life, he freely crossed lines of creed, nationality and color."[11]

But there were other forces aside from his own ingrained habit of giving that were pressing on Mr. Rockefeller. By the turn of the century, the industrial revolution had swept the nation. Rapid expansion of industry due to the advancement of science, wide application of machinery, centralized financing, and large-scale operations had created a booming prosperity. It was the culmination of an age of economic laissez faire, of uninhibited business practices which rolled up colossal fortunes and rewarded aggressiveness and acquisitiveness with wealth and power. Mr. Rockefeller, then and later, found himself in company with men like Carnegie, Morgan, Stanford, Armour, Sage, Guggenheim, McCormick, Havemeyer, Bamberger, Huntington, Rosenwald, Duke, and a dozen others who faced the same problem of the responsibilities and duties imposed by the unexpected weight of their fortunes. Beginning around 1900, and continuing for a quarter of a century, this group made a contribution to American life whose impact and consequences it is impossible even yet to measure. Acquiring their fortunes under conditions unique in the history of the country, and not infrequently by methods which, if permissible at the time, no longer accord with social conscience or the requirements of law, they enriched the intellectual and cultural life of America with a stream of universities, foundations, institutes, libraries, and endowments without parallel in any other age.

Their motives were doubtless many and varied—genuine social vision; religious principle; sometimes, in part, a desire for social recognition or the perpetuation of a name. Mr. Rockefeller, writing in 1909, said: "As I study wealthy men, I can see but one way in which they can secure a real equivalent for money spent, and that is to cultivate a taste for giving when the money will produce an effect which will be a lasting gratification."[12] Mr. Rockefeller's position was undoubtedly influenced by Mr. Carnegie, whose essay on "The Gospel of Wealth" appeared in the *North American Review* in 1889. Its thesis was the pithy aphorism: "The man who dies rich dies disgraced"; or, as Mr. Carnegie elaborated it: "The day is not far distant when the man who dies leaving behind him millions of available wealth, which was free for him to administer during life, will pass away unwept, unhonored and unsung." One of the most cordial letters of congratulation which Mr. Carnegie received came from Mr.

Rockefeller: "I would that more men of wealth were doing as you are doing with your money," he wrote, "but, be assured, your example will bear fruits, and the time will come when men of wealth will more generally be willing to use it for the good of others."[13]

Mr. Rockefeller's point of view was frankly expressed in the principle which he repeatedly enunciated: "A man should make all he can and give all he can."[14] But with his wealth accumulating so rapidly, how could he give effectively and efficiently? For this was the invariable test by which Mr. Rockefeller always judged his contributions. Indiscriminate giving he abhorred. During the eighties, before Mr. Gates joined him, he had arrived at certain general principles which he endeavored to follow in his contributions. His money should be given to work already organized and of proven worth; it should be work of a continuing character which would not disappear when his gifts were withdrawn; the contributions, where possible, should be made on conditional terms so as to stimulate contributions by others; and finally—and to Mr. Rockefeller, most important—his money should make for strength rather than weakness and should develop in the beneficiary a spirit of independence and self-reliance.

But he was not content. He was giving to a multiplicity of small causes mostly related to his church interests—schools, hospitals, and missions. The scope obviously was not big enough for his rapidly accumulating fortune, nor was it broad enough to satisfy his growing awareness of social needs. Mr. Gates, who knew him better than most men did and who was a shrewd judge of character, described him in these words: "[He had] a taste for excellence and even for perfection in whatever he did, a taste so marked, so dominant, as to amount to a passion, and it was indeed the ruling passion of his life. If genius is the art of taking pains, then Mr. Rockefeller was a genius."[15] "I had a great talk with Mr. Rockefeller," Gates wrote to Dr. Harper in 1891, when the latter was selecting his faculty for the University of Chicago, "and he wished me to say to you positively that the best men must be had."[16] It was this passion for excellence which Mr. Rockefeller brought so conspicuously to the founding of his philanthropic trusts.

III

Mr. Gates joined forces with Mr. Rockefeller in 1892. "About the year 1890," said Mr. Rockefeller, "I was still following the haphazard fashion of giving here and there as appeals presented themselves. I investigated as I could, and worked myself almost to a nervous breakdown in groping my way, without sufficient guide or chart, through this ever-widening field of philanthropic endeavor."[17] Mr. Gates so completely changed this system that twenty-five years later Mr. Rockefeller referred to him as "the guiding genius in all our giving." Says Mr. Gates: "I gradually developed and introduced into all his charities the principles of scientific giving, and he found himself in no long time laying aside retail giving almost wholly, and entering safely and pleasurably into the field of wholesale philanthropy." To illustrate the point, Mr. Gates described what Mr. Rockefeller had been doing for the Baptist missionaries abroad:

> He had conducted a small foreign mission society, if I may so call it, of his own. . . . He was in daily receipt of appeals from individual Baptist missionaries in every region of Baptist missionary endeavor. . . . His office, his house, his table was beset with returned missionaries, each comparatively ignorant of all fields but his own. . . . We cut off every one of these private missionary appeals. We referred every applicant straight back to the missionary executives in Boston. . . . Mr. Rockefeller then gave not thousands as formerly, but hundreds of thousands, every dollar of which was expended by the experienced board.[18]

Mr. Gates had come to Mr. Rockefeller's office from the American Baptist Education Society, of which he had been the administrative head. Already the two of them had worked in close co-operation in Mr. Rockefeller's first great adventure in giving—the creation of the University of Chicago. Indeed, it was in the initiation of this project that Mr. Gates first came to Mr. Rockefeller's attention. Starting as an idea for a Baptist institution of higher learning, under Baptist auspices and control, it developed, during the twenty-one years of Mr. Rockefeller's active interest, into one of the great universities of the country. When in 1910 he made his final gift to the institution, and withdrew from all association with it, his total contribution had amounted to $35,000,000. In a Minute adopted at this time by the trustees of the University occurred this significant paragraph:

> We know of no parallel in the history of educational benefaction to gifts so munificent bestowed upon a single institution of learning. But unique as they are in amount, they are still more remarkable for the spirit in which they have been bestowed. Mr. Rockefeller has never permitted the University to bear his name, and consented to be called its founder only at the urgent request of the Board of Trustees. He has never suggested the appointment or the removal of any professor. Whatever views may have been expressed by members of the faculty he has never indicated either assent or dissent. He has never interfered, directly

or indirectly, with that freedom of opinion and expression which is the vital breath of a university, but has adhered without deviation to the principle that, while it is important that university professors in their conclusions be correct, it is more important that in their teaching they be free.[19]

IV

Mr. Gates' "passion to accomplish some great and far-reaching benefits to mankind" revealed itself at an early date in the field of medical research. Starting on his summer holiday in 1897, he took with him William Osler's massive *Principles and Practice of Medicine,* a thousand-page volume which had been published six years before. The retarded development of medicine which the book revealed stirred his imagination, and he returned to his office in New York fired with the idea that an institute for medical research, established on a permanent basis, where groups of competent men would have opportunity, on ample salaries, for uninterrupted scientific inquiry, was the answer to the challenge which he read in Osler's book. As was his custom, when he had an idea like this, he presented it to Mr. Rockefeller in a vigorously written memorandum.

While the suggestion appealed both to Mr. Rockefeller and to his son, it took time to mature. Careful preliminary studies were made in this country and abroad, and conferences were held with leading medical men across the country. It was not until 1901 that The Rockefeller Institute for Medical Research was launched in a loft building on Lexington Avenue in New York, with a pledge from Mr. Rockefeller of $20,000 a year for ten years. Dr. William H. Welch of Johns Hopkins was chosen president, and on the board were distinguished leaders of American medicine like Dr. L. Emmett Holt, Dr. T. Mitchell Prudden, and Dr. Hermann M. Biggs. The following year, Dr. Simon Flexner, professor of pathology at the University of Pennsylvania, was persuaded to join the staff as director.

The modest beginning of the Institute, characteristic of Mr. Rockefeller's caution, was soon followed by a series of contributions which established the Institute as one of the great centers of medical research in the world.

During the time that these plans were under consideration, another idea was being explored in Mr. Rockefeller's office relating to the field of education in the Southern states. Growing from the interest in Negro education of men like Robert C. Ogden and William

H. Baldwin, it soon enlisted a few outstanding leaders in both the North and South, among whom was Mr. Rockefeller, Jr. Interest in the Negro problem was a tradition in the Rockefeller family; Mr. Rockefeller himself had been brought up in the abolitionist atmosphere of pre-Civil War days, and one of the earliest gifts noted in his "Ledger A," when he was in his teens, was to enable a Negro "to buy his wife." Thereafter, for many years, he made current contributions to Baptist Negro schools and colleges through agencies like the American Baptist Education Society. When Mr. Rockefeller, Jr., joined his father's staff in 1897, the question of Negro education was one that was frequently discussed between father and son. Indeed, the son inherited the interest from both sides of his family. His mother's parents, Mr. and Mrs. Henry M. Spelman, had been actively identified with the underground railroad; and Spelman College in Atlanta—an advanced school for Negro girls—had been named after his grandmother. It was, therefore, natural that the younger Rockefeller should accept the invitation of Mr. Ogden in 1900 to join his party on a special train that visited Hampton, Tuskegee, and other significant educational developments in the South.

Stimulated by what he had seen, he called a series of private conferences in New York in which plans were laid down for an organization that would deal in a comprehensive way with the backward and baffling problem of education, not only colored but white. "We soon came to realize," said Mr. Rockefeller, Jr., at a later period, "that Negro education could not be successfully promoted in the South except as education for the whites was also promoted."[20] In 1903, two years after the Institute for Medical Research was launched, the General Education Board was incorporated by act of Congress and was started on its way with a pledge from Mr. Rockefeller of $1,000,000 to be used during a ten-year period for a greatly broadened plan of education "without distinction of sex, race or creed." Under the leadership of Mr. Gates as chairman of the board and of Dr. Wallace Buttrick, another Baptist clergyman, first as secretary and then as president, it proved to be one of Mr. Rockefeller's greatest benefactions. In 1907, shortly after Mr. Rockefeller had added to his initial gift sums totaling over $20,000,000, his son, writing to Mr. Ogden, made this acknowledgment: "Whenever I think of the work of the General Education Board and the magnificent future which is before it, I always remember that its conception and foundation were to a large extent the result of the Southern trip which I made as your guest."[21]

Out of an incident related to the work of the General Education Board in the South sprang the Rockefeller Sanitary Commission in 1909, devoted to the eradication of hookworm in the Southern states. In the course of his tireless journeys and constant canvass of possibilities in the field of Negro education, Dr. Buttrick was introduced to a zoologist and public health official who was profoundly concerned with the hookworm problem, Dr. Charles Wardell Stiles. The two men sat up nearly all one night in a hotel room and Buttrick was so deeply stirred by Stiles' description of the ravages of hookworm in the South that he rushed back to New York to tell Mr. Gates. Gates sent for Stiles and was equally aroused, saying: "This is the biggest proposition ever put up to the Rockefeller office." With Mr. Rockefeller's characteristic caution and thoroughness a year was given to a careful investigation of the disease, under the leadership of Dr. Flexner, verifying its extent and the fact that it could be cured and prevented. When the affirmative report was presented, a commission was established of which Mr. Gates was chairman and Dr. Wickliffe Rose of Nashville administrative secretary. To the commission Mr. Rockefeller made a pledge of $1,000,000, to be spent over five years.

The project, when first announced, aroused some opposition in the South. The Northern newspapers unfortunately played up the idea that one of the characteristic symptoms of the anaemic disease was lassitude or laziness—a comment which was resented by the Southern press. "Where was this hookworm or lazy disease, when it took five Yankee soldiers to whip one Southerner?"[22] asked a Georgia paper. And there were other remarks about "damn Yankees holding the South up to ridicule." But under Dr. Rose's tactful leadership the work progressed, and it was not long before co-operative arrangements had been made with the departments of health of eleven Southern states. Five years later, Rose was able to say: "The medical profession and the public now generally recognize the prevalence of hookworm disease, and regard its cure and prevention as an essential part of public health work in the South."[23]

V

In the decade between 1900 and 1910, Mr. Rockefeller had had an illuminating and fruitful experience in the creation of charitable trusts. He had established The Rockefeller Institute for Medical Research, the General Education Board, and the Rockefeller Sanitary Commission. He had proved to his own satisfaction that the most effective way of accomplishing the results he had in mind was to place funds at the disposal of independent boards of trustees, made up of the most experienced men he could find. Once chosen, these trustees were given a free hand to select their officers and carry on their work. "I have not had the hardihood," said Mr. Rockefeller in 1909, "even to suggest how people, so much more experienced and wise in those things than I, should work out the details even of those plans with which I have had the honor to be associated."[24] It is significant that he would not allow himself to be made a trustee of the Rockefeller Institute, the General Education Board, or the Sanitary Commission; and while in a formal sense he served for a few years as a trustee of The Rockefeller Foundation, he never attended a meeting.

By 1910, therefore, Mr. Rockefeller was ready for his greatest venture in the field of philanthropy. The ten years that had gone by were in a certain sense preparatory. And in that ten-year period, too, three men had been brought into active relationship with his affairs who were to have an incalculable influence not only on the boards which had already been created but on The Rockefeller Foundation: Dr. Simon Flexner, Dr. Buttrick, and Dr. Rose. No one can review the history of these enterprises without realizing what a stroke of fortune it was that linked up the ability and vision of these three extraordinary men to the work which Mr. Rockefeller and his associates were launching. Other distinguished figures were to be added in the next decade, notably Jerome D. Greene, George E. Vincent, Dr. Richard M. Pearce, and Abraham Flexner; but the initial choice of administrators was singularly providential.

All three came out of exceedingly humble circumstances. Dr. Flexner was the son of an itinerant peddler in Louisville. Apprenticed as a plumber, he failed and was discharged. After that, for some years, he was a clerk in a drugstore. With scanty preliminary education, he took a two-year course in the Louisville Medical School, and then, aided by the heroic efforts of his family, entered the medical school at Johns Hopkins. Here he came under the eyes of Dr. William H. Welch, who had an uncanny ability for detecting genius. His advancement was rapid, and after finishing his course at the Hopkins he went abroad for advanced study at Strasbourg, Berlin, Prague, and the Pasteur Institute. Returning, he joined the faculty at Johns Hopkins and then transferred to the University of Pennsylvania. Mr. Gates, years afterward, anxious that posterity should know by what inspiration the Rockefeller Institute was endowed with such distinguished leadership, wrote: "I hope it may never be forgotten that it is to Dr. William H. Welch that we owe the priceless suggestion that Dr. Flexner be made the director."[25]

With a preliminary education almost as sketchy as Flexner's, Dr. Buttrick, who became one of the great educational statesmen of his generation, served for five years as a brakeman and postal clerk on a railroad in northern New York, where he had been born. In his late twenties, at the urging of his wife, he entered the Rochester Theological Seminary. "I was scarcely literate," he used to say laughingly in later years, although the statement obviously was wide of the mark. After graduating from the Seminary, he served for twenty years in pastorates in New Haven, St. Paul, and Albany. During this period he was elected to the executive board of the American Baptist Education Society, where he met Mr. Gates; and later he became a member of the board of the American Baptist Home Mission Society, which had in its charge the Baptist schools for Negroes in the Southern states. It was Gates who introduced him to Mr. Rockefeller and who selected him to take over the administration of the newly formed General Education Board in 1903.

It was Dr. Buttrick who chose Dr. Rose to run the Rockefeller Sanitary Commission. Why the choice fell on Rose, or by what intuitive process Buttrick saw in him the making of great leadership in the field of public health on a global scale, cannot now with any degree of accuracy be answered. For Rose was not an M.D.; he was a professor of philosophy at Peabody College who lived with Kant and Hegel, and who, at the end of his career, could write: "My intellectual life began with my first contact with Aristotle and Plato; I still read them with the thrill of those early years."[26]

These were the men who blazed the trail in the development of the Rockefeller boards. In temperament and approach they were as different as three men could possibly be. Flexner was first and foremost a scientist who lived for science. His slight build, his soft voice, his gentle manner, were all in striking contrast to the steely precision of his reasoning. His mind was like a searchlight that could be turned at will on any question that came before him. He was incisive, exact, cautious, diffident, and just a little afraid of adjectives.

Buttrick, on the other hand, was no scholar but a man of sturdy judgment and massive common sense. There was an earthy tang about him, and his laughter rang through the corridors of his offices. He loved people and absorbed ideas not from books but from contacts. He had a solid kind of wisdom, enforced by manifest disinterestedness and freedom from all prejudice. Utterly without ambition for himself, counting his friends by hundreds, he was big of brain and heart, with a quick and alert understanding that penetrated to the core of his problems.

Rose was at home in any kind of intellectual field, not only because of the power of his mind, but because of its amazing clarity. When he finished speaking at a board meeting, there never seemed to be anything more that needed to be said. No officer in the Rockefeller boards ever submitted programs of work that were more carefully prepared or presented with more startling lucidity. He had a bold, fresh mind, with daring imagination and originality, combined with a practical sense of the immediately obtainable. It was always the new field that invited him. It was adventure, in terms of creative work, that tempted him. And yet he was modest to the point of shyness, and completely selfless. He wanted no credit for himself or his group. He took genuine satisfaction in anonymity.

These were the men and this was the spirit behind the new ideas that Mr. Rockefeller began to take hold of in a serious way at the end of the first decade of the century.

CHAPTER II

THE BIRTH OF THE ROCKEFELLER FOUNDATION

WHO ORIGINALLY WAS RESPONSIBLE FOR the idea of The Rockefeller Foundation it is now impossible to determine. It was probably Mr. Gates. In a carefully drafted letter which he wrote Mr. Rockefeller in 1905, he suggested the feasibility of a series of "great, corporate philanthropies" to deal with objectives which he described as the promotion of scientific agriculture, the enrichment of rural life in the United States, the development of the fine arts and the refinement of taste, the promotion of Christian ethics and Christian civilization throughout the world, the development of intelligent citizenship and civic virtue in our own country.[1]

Gates was always troubled by what he called "the destiny of Mr. Rockefeller's vast fortune." "Is it to be handed on to posterity," he asked, "as other great fortunes have been handed down by their possessors, with scandalous results to their descendants and powerful tendencies to social demoralization?" In his letter to Mr. Rockefeller in 1905, he said: "It seems to me that either you and those who live now must determine what shall be the ultimate use of this vast fortune, or at the close of a few lives now in being it must simply pass into the unknown, like some other great fortunes, with unmeasured and perhaps sinister possibilities."[2]

Gates' letter must have made an impression on Mr. Rockefeller, for late in the following year his son wrote him referring to an earlier conversation they had had about the establishment of "a large trust to which you [Mr. Rockefeller] would turn over considerable sums of money to be devoted to philanthropy, education, science, and religion."[3] The younger Rockefeller expressed a concern "whether it would be possible to get together a single group of men who could be expected to have knowledge and interest along so many different lines." But he was anxious to get the idea started in some form, and made a number of suggestions on how it might be done.

Mr. Rockefeller was not a man to be hurried into precipitate action. Careful study and long deliberation were for him invariably prerequisite to any move in an unknown field. It was two years before the idea was sufficiently matured in his mind to enable him to go forward, and during this period there were many conferences with his son and Mr. Gates. On June 29, 1909, he signed a deed of trust, turning over to three trustees—his son; Harold McCormick, his son-in-law; and Mr. Gates—72,569 shares of the Standard Oil Company of New Jersey, valued at $50,000,000, the trust to be known by the name of "The Rockefeller Foundation." The purposes of the trust as set forth in the deed were "to promote the well-being and to advance the civilization of the peoples of the United States and its territories and possessions and of foreign lands in the acquisition and dissemination of knowledge, in the prevention and relief of suffering, and in the promotion of any and all of the elements of human progress." This statement of purpose, which was to have significant consequences in the future, was obviously the work of Mr. Gates. Its broad and inclusive terms were characteristic of his imaginative thinking. "Is there not something within us," he asked in 1911, "an instinct which is the harbinger of better things, an instinct of humanity which cannot be fenced in by the boundaries of a merely national patriotism, a sympathy which transcends national boundaries and finds complete expression only when it identifies us with all humanity?"[4]

The deed of trust contained a clause by which Mr. Rockefeller reserved the right to revoke it; and this additional sentence throws light on the plan that was under contemplation: "I direct said trustees as soon as can advisedly be done, to apply to the Congress of the United States, or to the legislature of such state as they shall deem advisable, for a suitable corporate charter." In the bylaws which were drawn up at the same time, this interesting sentence appears: "As it is the desire of the Donor and also of the trustees that for the present the existence of the Foundation shall not be made public, pledges may be made in the name of John D. Rockefeller." In other words, it was believed that before announcing the creation of the Foundation, it would be advisable to secure a charter. In the meantime, the three trustees of the Foundation began to make appropriations of considerable sums, the recipients for the most part representing the special interests in religious and charitable work which Mr. Rockefeller over many years had supported. The adventurous projects which Mr. Gates had in mind, and to which Mr. Rockefeller was entirely hospitable, were postponed until the Foundation came officially into being.

In March, 1910, a bill was introduced in the United States Senate to incorporate The Rockefeller Foundation. It provided that the corporation should report annually to the Secretary of the Interior on the details of its operations and it contained this clause: "This charter shall be subject to alteration, amendment, or repeal at the pleasure of the Congress of the United States." Word for word, it was practically identical with the charter of the General Education Board which had been granted by an act of Congress seven years before; and no difficulty was anticipated. There were distinguished precedents for this kind of procedure; between 1889 and 1907, thirty-four organizations had secured incorporation by the United States, including the Carnegie Institution of Washington, the American Academy in Rome, and the American Historical Association. To Mr. Rockefeller's advisers, therefore, it seemed appropriate to follow the same course. As a matter of fact, for the general purposes which Mr. Rockefeller had in mind, he need not have gone to Congress at all, or even to a legislature. As a private citizen he had the right to direct the use of his funds as he saw fit, and a simple deed of trust could have created a foundation such as he contemplated.

But Mr. Rockefeller was not trying to escape government control. On the contrary, he seemed to be seeking it. His attorney, Starr J. Murphy, asserted, at the hearing before the Senate Committee, that

> the donor is perfectly content to leave this great foundation in the hands of Congress, that it may at any time in the future exercise its protecting power, not merely to protect his wishes, which are solely that this fund shall always be used for the public welfare and for no other purpose, but also that Congress may have the power, if at any time in the future this fund should get into the hands of men who might seek to use it for improper purposes, to exert its authority and bring this fund back again to the use for which it was intended.

In words which represented Mr. Rockefeller's often-expressed point of view, Mr. Murphy went on to say: "The charities of the fourteenth century are not the charities of the twentieth century. The charities of the twentieth century will not be the charities of the twenty-first century, and it is eminently desirable . . . that the dead hand should be removed from charitable bequests and that the power to determine to what specific objects they should be applied should be left in the hands of living men who can judge of the necessities and of the needs in the light of the knowledge which they have as contemporaries, and not that they shall find their hands tied by the will of the man who is long years dead. The wisdom of living men will always exceed the wisdom of any man, however wise, who has been long since dead."[5]

Another representative of Mr. Rockefeller, Jerome D. Greene, who also participated in the attempt to secure a federal charter, expressed in these words the purpose behind the request:

> The motive actuating the incorporation of The Rockefeller Foundation and expressed in its charter, is the desire to make this munificent gift directly to the whole American people, and forever subject to the control of their elected representatives. This provision not only possesses a sentimental advantage which the charter of a single state would not afford, but it expresses an implicit confidence in the stability of our national life and in the will of the people to deal justly now and forever with the high purposes of the proposed foundation.[6]

II

But Congress would have none of it. A storm of protest arose which kept the proposal dangling in the legislature for more than three years. After passing the committee stage, the Senate bill of 1910 was withdrawn, and an amended bill was half-heartedly presented in 1911. A House bill, introduced in 1912, was passed in 1913, but because of delaying tactics it failed to reach the calendar of the Senate before adjournment. At various stages in the debate, five principal amendments to the charter were adopted, all of which were accepted by Mr. Rockefeller's representatives:

(1) That the total property of the corporation should be limited to $100,000,000.

(2) That the income of the corporation was not to be accumulated or added to principal, but was to be currently applied to the purposes for which the corporation was created.

(3) That after the expiration of fifty years the corporation might distribute the principal as well as the income, and that after a hundred years such distribution was mandatory if Congress so directed.

(4) That the election of new trustees should be subject to disapproval within sixty days by a majority of the following persons: the President of the United States, the Chief Justice of the Supreme Court, the President of the Senate, the Speaker of the House of Representatives, and the presidents of the following universities: Harvard, Yale, Columbia, Johns Hopkins, and Chicago.

(5) That not more than one-tenth of the maximum value of property, held under the terms of the charter, could be invested in the securities of any one corporation.

During the three-year period that this bill was before Congress, it was the center of violent public controversy, and Mr. Rockefeller was maligned as he seldom had been even in his earlier years. The papers rang with such phrases as "the kiss of Judas Iscariot," "the Trojan horse," and "tainted money," and some of the speeches in Congress reflected the bitterness and distrust. But it was not alone in the Congress that opposition centered; what Mr. Rockefeller and his associates did not appreciate at the time was that Mr. Taft's administration looked upon the proposal with strong disfavor. In letters which have since been published, it appears that George W. Wickersham, the Attorney General, wrote to President Taft denouncing the proposal. "Never," he declared, "has there been submitted to Congress, or to any legislative body, such an indefinite scheme for perpetuating vast wealth as this; and personally I believe it to be entirely inconsistent with the public interest that any such bill should be passed." To this, Mr. Taft replied: "I agree with your . . . characterization of the proposed act to incorporate John D. Rockefeller."[7]

It must be admitted that Mr. Rockefeller's advisers could scarcely have chosen a less auspicious time to attempt to secure a congressional charter for such a project. Judge Kenesaw Mountain Landis' $29,000,000 fine, imposed upon the Standard Oil Company of Indiana, was still fresh in public memory, and the scandal of the letters from Archbold of the Standard Oil Company to Senator Foraker and Mark Hanna had by no means been forgotten. On top of this, the government's suit for the dissolution of the Standard Oil Company had just been won in the Federal Circuit Court, and the company attorneys filed their appeal to the United States Supreme Court five days after the bill to create The Rockefeller Foundation had been introduced in the Senate. The decision of the Supreme

Court, upholding the government and ordering the dissolution of the company, was handed down while the question of the charter was being debated in Congress. It was this unhappy but uncalculated coincidence which led Mr. Wickersham in his letter to President Taft to ask: "Is it, then, appropriate that, at the moment when the United States through its courts is seeking in a measure to destroy the great combination of wealth which has been built up by Mr. Rockefeller . . . the Congress of the United States should assist in the enactment of a law to create and perpetuate in his name an institution to hold and administer a large portion of this vast wealth?"

Public comment, however, was by no means wholly unfavorable to the proposal. "To refuse legal sanction to such an undertaking would be a national blunder," said the *Survey*. "The greater our confidence in the intelligence and in the capacity of the democracy, the more heartily will we welcome such voluntary socializing of wealth."[8] Said the *Independent*: "We would have such a noble fund allowed to do all the good it can without suspicious limitations."[9] "Generations yet undreamed of will profit by the work of this Foundation," said the Washington *Times*, "and no man is possessed of vision so clear as even to glimpse the possibilities of its service."[10] The Philadelphia *Inquirer* made this argument: "Much of the criticism is simply because of his [Rockefeller's] success, and much more of it is through an attempt to apply modern business ethics to a time when they did not exist or were not recognized. In any event, the public ought to welcome whatever good the money can produce."[11] Many papers followed the line of the Chicago *Inter-Ocean* in its comment that there were statesmen "who only waited for him [Rockefeller] to come out in favor of the Ten Commandments to ask that they be recorded as against the whole iniquitous proceeding." The editorial continued:

> It is safe to say that if Mr. Rockefeller should presume at the present time to ask Congress to sanction in some way his retirement to a monastery, or a trip to the Holy Land, or a gift of several millions to the famine sufferers in China . . . he would only be wasting his breath. At the mere suggestion of such an unheard of and outrageous proceeding, the patriots would rise with one voice and demand that the insidious, undemocratic, and dangerous proposal be thrown into the wastebasket, and that Mr. Rockefeller be duly warned that such attempts to subvert the very foundations of republican government would never deceive the statesmen of America.[12]

In such an atmosphere of controversy, hopes of federal incorporation withered away. "To defeat the present bill will not prevent the establishment of the Foundation," said Mr. Greene in a final plea in Washington. "It will merely prevent Congress from exercising any control over it."[13] But the door was closed, and Mr. Rockefeller's advisers turned to the New York State Legislature. Within two months after adjournment of Congress in 1913, an act was passed in Albany incorporating The Rockefeller Foundation. The news of the event created scarcely a ripple in the press; indeed, it passed almost without notice. The amendments to the charter which Congress had added during the course of the debate, and to which Mr. Rockefeller's associates had somewhat reluctantly acquiesced, were omitted in the legislative act; and somewhere along the line the statement of the purpose of the Foundation, which in the Congressional bill had followed the language of Mr. Rockefeller's deed of trust, had been happily shortened to the single phrase: "To promote the well-being of mankind throughout the world." This phrase was to be the guiding star of the organization. The words of Mr. Gates were destined to set the aim of the Foundation in terms of human welfare in a world without boundary lines.

III

The Rockefeller Foundation was launched in an atmosphere unhappily streaked by misgiving and distrust. With his characteristic directness and perhaps a trace of his training as a preacher, Gates said to Mr. Rockefeller: "If any man's happiness in doing good depends on human gratitude or praise, if his satisfaction is sought from any source except the silent approval of conscience, that man's sun will go down at the end amid the clouds of a disappointed and embittered life." Mr. Rockefeller's reply, according to Gates, "uttered with deliberation and unwonted emphasis, was *'Don't I know that!'* "[14]

But Mr. Rockefeller was not easily discouraged, and he was not moved by misrepresentation or calumny. For fear that its disclosure might jeopardize the chances of obtaining a federal charter, he had revoked, in November, 1910, the deed of gift of $50,000,000 which he had made a year and a half before; but in January, 1913, when the prospect of congressional incorporation was momentarily bright, he had turned over to four trustees bonds in the value of $3,200,000, to be conveyed—"or as much thereof as shall remain in the hands of the trustees"—to The Rockefeller Foundation, whenever it was created. As soon as the charter had been received from the New York State Legislature, he made a gift to the Foundation of approximately $35,000,000; and the following year, another gift of $65,000,000. His total gifts to the Foundation are listed below:

1913	$ 34,430,430.54
1914	65,569,919.46
1917	25,765,506.00
1917	5,500,000.00
1918	1,000,000.00
1919	50,438,768.50
1926	37,000.00
1927	109,856.40
	$182,851,480.90
1929 Received from The Laura Spelman Rockefeller Memorial	58,756,878.84
	$241,608,359.74

The letter which accompanied these various gifts always followed the same pattern: "It is more convenient for me to provide funds for the Foundation by a gift of these specific securities than by a gift of cash, and I believe the securities have intrinsic and permanent value which would justify you in retaining them as investments; but in order to relieve you from any uncertainty or embarrassment with regard to them, I desire to state specifically that you are under no obligation to retain any of these investments, but are at liberty to dispose of them or any of them and change the form of investment whenever in your judgment it seems wise to do so."[15]

In his early gifts Mr. Rockefeller reserved the right to make designations annually, up to $2,000,000 of the income, to such organizations and projects within the corporate purposes of the Foundation as he might see fit to choose. But the arrangement proved awkward, and Mr. Rockefeller relinquished his right in 1917.

The first trustees of the Foundation, named in the act of incorporation, in addition to Mr. Rockefeller, were John D. Rockefeller, Jr.; Mr. Gates; Harry Pratt Judson, president of the University of Chicago; Dr. Simon Flexner; Starr J. Murphy; Jerome D. Greene; Dr. Wickliffe Rose; and Charles O. Heydt. Within a few months, President Eliot of Harvard was added to the board, and A. Barton Hepburn, president of the Chase National Bank.

The trustees held their first meeting in May, 1913. Mr. Rockefeller, Jr., was elected president, and in 1917 became chairman of the board. Mr. Greene was made secretary, and the administrative responsibility was placed in his hands. "There was a brief time in my little room at 26 Broadway," wrote Greene years later, "when one secretary and one four-drawer file constituted the staff and equipment of The Rockefeller Foundation."[16] Greene was thirty-nine years old at the time. A Harvard graduate, he had served as secretary to President Eliot, and as secretary to the corporation of Harvard University. In 1911, he had been appointed general manager of the Rockefeller Institute, where his work attracted the attention of Mr. Rockefeller, Jr. Alert, poised, with a quick, imaginative mind and a creative drive, Greene brought rare talent to his new task, and his influence in shaping the early years of the Foundation was impressive.

The question which faced the trustees as they sat down to their first meeting was how the broad objective of their charter was to be implemented. What constitutes "the well-being of mankind throughout the world"? A large number of applications had already been received, and it is significant that they were all declined, including one from the Y.M.C.A. for the rehabilitation of buildings located in Dayton, Hamilton, and Marietta, which had been damaged in the recent floods along the Ohio River Valley. Mr. Gates phrased the objection: "The Rockefeller Foundation should in general confine itself to projects of an important character, too large to be undertaken, or otherwise unlikely to be undertaken, by other agencies."[17] This was in line with the emphasis which Mr. Rockefeller himself, six years earlier, had placed on what he called "finalities." "The best philanthropy," he had said, "involves a search for cause, an attempt to cure evils at their source."[18]

It was in line with this type of thinking that Greene, a few months later, presented to the trustees "a memorandum on principles and policies" which was to have a significant influence on the development of the Foundation. Based in large part on the experience of Mr. Rockefeller and Mr. Gates in the long years of their association, and reflecting the current practices of the General Education Board and the Rockefeller Sanitary Commission, it established a rough framework within which the Foundation operated, with relatively few deviations, during subsequent years. Greene's memorandum covered the following points:

(1) Individual charity and relief are excluded.

(2) Institutions or enterprises that are purely local are similarly excluded, "except as aid may be given to their establishment as models to other localities."

(3) When an institution goes into a community with the intention

of making a contribution to its welfare, "no gift of money however large, and no outside agency however wise or good, can render a service of permanent value except insofar as the gift or the agency offers the means or the occasion for evoking from the community its own recognition of the need to be met, its own will to meet that need, and its own resources, both material and spiritual, wherewith to meet it."

(4) "In general, it is unwise for an institution like The Rockefeller Foundation to assume permanently or indefinitely a share of the current expenses of an institution which it does not control. Such a continuing relation inevitably carries with it a continuing responsibility for the conduct of the institution that is aided . . . and the implied continuing approval of management tends to make the receiver subservient to the giver, thus detracting from the receiver's independence and self-respect. . . . When giving to the support of institutions or movements for which the community, whether general or local, ought to make itself responsible, the Foundation will, as a rule, assume less than half of the cost of current expenditure."

(5) The Foundation must carefully avoid the dangers incident to gifts in perpetuity. It should not hamper the trustees of other institutions by gifts in perpetuity narrowly limited to particular uses.

(6) "As between objects which are of an immediately remedial or alleviatory nature, such as asylums for the orphan, blind or cripples, and those which go to the root of individual or social ill-being and misery, the latter objects are preferred—not that the former are unworthy, but because the latter are more far-reaching in their effects."[19]

IV

Self-imposed limitations do not constitute a program, and while a framework may be essential, it is necessarily negative rather than positive. What were "the pregnant ideas"—to use Gates' term—to whose birth assistance could be given? From the very first meeting, it seemed to the trustees of the Foundation that public health ranked well toward the top.

> If science and education are the brain and nervous system of civilization [said Mr. Gates], health is its heart. It is the organ that pushes the vital fluid into every part of the social organism, enabling each organ to function, and measuring and limiting its effective life. . . . Disease is the supreme ill of human life, and it is the main source of almost all other

human ills—poverty, crime, ignorance, vice, inefficiency, hereditary taint, and many other evils.[20]

The enthusiasm with which the trustees supported the opinion of Mr. Gates was due in large part to the dramatic success which the Rockefeller Sanitary Commission was achieving, under the leadership of Dr. Rose, in eliminating hookworm in the Southern states. At their first meeting, therefore, the trustees of the Foundation recorded their opinion that "the extension of hookworm work to other parts of the world would be one of the most productive lines of activity to be undertaken," and Dr. Rose was asked to prepare a plan of operation. A month later, the International Health Board* of The Rockefeller Foundation was established, with Dr. Rose as director, "to extend to other countries and peoples the work of eradicating hookworm disease as opportunity offers, and so far as practicable to follow up the treatment and cure of this disease with the establishment of agencies for the promotion of public sanitation and the spread of the knowledge of scientific medicine."[21] The old Sanitary Commission was merged with this new organization which was launched on a career of such wide-reaching significance that even the optimism of its creators could hardly have foreseen it.

With this matter disposed of, the trustees moved swiftly in another direction. As a result of his missionary contacts, Mr. Rockefeller had long been interested in China, and in 1909, at the suggestion of Gates, he had financed a study of conditions in China made by the Oriental Education Commission, headed by Dr. Ernest Dewitt Burton of the University of Chicago. The monumental report of this commission, presented in six volumes, was a vast blueprint of the educational opportunities that lay wide open in this promising country. With the incorporation of the Foundation an accomplished fact, Gates moved to the attack, warmly supported by Dr. Eliot of Harvard who had recently returned from an extended trip in China. A conference was called in New York early in 1914 which was attended not only by the representatives of the Foundation and the General Education Board, but by the executive officers of the principal missionary boards employing medical missionaries. Mr. Rockefeller, Jr., who presided, set the matter before the meeting in these interesting terms:

* The International Health Board was first called the International Health Commission (1913-1916). Then it was christened the International Health Board; and finally, in 1927, the International Health Division.

> The Rockefeller Foundation, which I presume is the host on this occasion, is a very small child, very young and inexperienced. It has the world as its field and it has very few plans. It is planning to go very slowly in laying out its work, and our thought has been to get all the information we can with reference to the different eligible fields, so that when we do arrive at some conclusion as to a point of attack, we feel that we know all that can be known about the problem involved, and that we are acting under the best advice obtainable. . . . We are not committing ourselves to anything in China . . . We simply state that there is a great opportunity, a great need. Now let us study the situation and see whether there devolves upon this Foundation a responsibility in this particular country.[22]

The results of the discussion were considered at a later meeting of the trustees of the Foundation, with the following conclusions: (1) that any work in China should be in medicine, and (2) that whatever might be undertaken should be based on existing agencies, whether missionary or governmental. A week later, Mr. Gates presented to the trustees a plan for "the gradual and orderly development of a comprehensive system of medicine in China"—a document of such high strategic importance that it served as a guide for the activities of the Foundation in this area for many years.[23] Out of it came the Judson commission to China, the creation of the China Medical Board and the building of the Peking Union Medical College, which over the years was the outpost of modern medicine in the Far East—the symbol and synonym for high quality in professional education in China.

V

In spite of this auspicious beginning—and details of it are considered in later chapters—stormy days lay ahead of the Foundation. As Mr. Rockefeller, Jr., had said at the China conference, the Foundation was "a very small child, very young and inexperienced." It was groping its way toward a program, with no precedents to guide so large an undertaking, and without the accumulated wisdom of trial and error in the management of a vast charitable trust. In a sense, it was misled by its own early success. The International Health Board and the China Medical Board seemed to furnish a desirable pattern of action. These groups were direct agencies of the Foundation, financed and operated by the Foundation, and it was natural to assume that similar boards or divisions could in this manner effectively handle other perplexing and frequently controversial problems. Thus, in the field of mental hygiene, Dr. Thomas Salmon, one of the country's leading psychiatrists, was added to the staff of the Foundation, and it was apparently the intention of the trustees that the studies and surveys for which he was to be responsible were to be carried on by the Foundation through its own personnel, and that "the related fields of heredity, alcoholism and venereal diseases" were to be included. Similarly, in 1914, the trustees seriously considered the desirability of establishing, under the auspices of the Foundation, an organization for the study of social and economic questions, and a committee of economists, under the chairmanship of Professor Edwin F. Gay of Harvard, recommended that the subject of prices be the first study undertaken.

Difficulty immediately arose, however, when the trustees decided to use the personnel and machinery of the Foundation in a direct approach to the problem of industrial relations. Mr. W. L. Mackenzie King of Canada, who had made a distinguished record in this field, was appointed director of the project. Unfortunately, this action was taken against the background of one of the most savage strikes in the history of American industry—a strike of mine workers involving among other companies the Colorado Fuel and Iron Company, in which the Rockefellers were financially interested. The strike culminated in the tragic "Ludlow massacre," where in a pitched battle between the strikers and the state militia many were killed and injured. Federal troops finally brought the situation under control.

Although the action of the Foundation in retaining Mr. King was inspired by completely sincere motives, and by a deep desire to find a practicable solution to a thorny problem, a large section of the public was unconvinced; and once more the papers rang with abuse and vituperation. The United States Commission on Industrial Relations, a federal group headed by Senator Frank P. Walsh, began an investigation of the Foundation, and public hearings were held in which Mr. Rockefeller and most of the trustees were subpoenaed as witnesses. The insistent question was whether there was a dividing line between Mr. Rockefeller's interests and the interests of The Rockefeller Foundation. For weeks, the investigation was headline news, and apprehensions about the potential dangers from the abuse of the Foundation's power were spread across the country. In the end, more sober counsels seemed to prevail. Dr. George Kirchwey, dean of the Columbia Law School, testifying before the Commission on the charter powers of the Foundation, said that inasmuch as the concentration of enormous wealth in the hands of any individual was productive of a certain amount of discontent, he considered the situation "distinctly bettered by the transfer of that wealth from an individual to a corporation which is legally, to a certain degree at least, responsible to the public." "I should not think," he added, "that the possession of great wealth . . . by The Rockefeller Foundation . . . would be as apt to cause irritation and discontent and unrest as the possession and conspicuous use of that same wealth by Mr. Rockefeller himself."[24]

Mr. Rockefeller, in his testimony before the Commission, answered the charge as to the possible abuse of power by the Foundation in these words: "I have such confidence in democracy that I believe it can better be left to the people and their representatives to remedy the evils when there is some tangible reason for believing they are impending, rather than to restrict the power for service in anticipation of purely hypothetical dangers."[25]

And there lay the principal answer to the investigation. The United States Commission remained skeptical of the new organization that bore the Rockefeller name. The mellowing process of time, the perspective of events, the tangible proof that integrity as well as high purpose lay behind the creation of the Foundation—these developments were necessary before public judgment could be adequately informed.

To the Foundation, the impact of this investigation was deeply discouraging, but in the long run it proved to be salutary. Among the lessons that were learned—learned in a hard way—was one that was related to the central question which the trustees had earnestly been asking themselves from the beginning: What can a private foundation, endowed with large resources, wisely do, and what are the appropriate methods and techniques to be used? The answer to the latter part of the question was now obvious, certainly as far as The Rockefeller Foundation was concerned. Except for a narrow range of noncontroversial subjects, notably public health, medicine, and agriculture, the Foundation's participation in the areas it wished to assist must be limited to grants to outside agencies competently organized and staffed to carry on the work in question. In other words, the Foundation must become primarily not an operating agency but a fund-dispensing agency. This new policy obviously did not imply that the Foundation would avoid controversial questions. It meant that its approach to such questions would take the form of grants to agencies independent of Foundation control. In no other way could the objectivity of research be established beyond cavil and the projects freed from suspicion of ulterior interest. This was the new pattern which the Foundation was to follow for many years to come.

VI

While the trustees in the early years were exploring questions of policy and program, gifts were being made to a wide variety of institutions and causes. In retrospect, there seems to have been little cohesion in these first appropriations; they apparently followed the interests and needs of the moment rather than any definite design. A bird refuge in Louisiana was purchased and presented to the state; substantial grants were made to the Rockefeller Institute, to the Palisades Interstate Park, to Wellesley College, the American Academy in Rome, the Association for Improving the Condition of the Poor, the Bureau of Municipal Research, and the Institute for Government Research.

It must be remembered that the early days of the Foundation coincided with outbreak of the First World War in 1914. From the very beginning, the Foundation played a significant part in war-relief activities, and when the sum was totaled up at the end, it had spent more than $22,000,000 for this purpose. With Belgium facing a famine as a result of the German invasion, the Foundation itself chartered ships and dispatched them across the ocean loaded with food. It sent commissions of inquiry to many European nations and followed up its inquiries with supplies for countries like Poland, Serbia, Armenia, Syria, Montenegro, and Albania. It appropriated hundreds of thousands of dollars to organizations like the American Red Cross, the Commission on Training Camp Activities, and the societies that were contributing to the morale of the troops. It interested itself in the welfare of prisoners of war and in the various demonstration hospital units. It was a long, exhausting, and frequently frustrating task, and for nearly five years it overshadowed in priority and apparent importance all other activities which the Foundation undertook. Dr. George E. Vincent, who assumed the presidency of the Foundation in 1917, said later on, as he looked back on this feverish period: "I suppose we had to do it, and I suppose it was worth while, but think of the creative job we could have done with that money in a world of reason and sanity!"[26] Over the next three decades, this despondent note was to be sounded more than once by trustees and officers alike, as war and its aftermath slashed through the plans and projects of the Foundation.

With the advent of Vincent and the close of the First World War, a more promising era seemed to be opening up. Vincent himself, who came from the presidency of the University of Minnesota, was a different kind of person from any who had previously been associated with the organization. Urbane, brilliantly witty, skeptical of Gates' absolutes and finalities, he cared passionately for fairness, tolerance, and justice. "Eagles in captivity look resentful and remote," said Dr. Alan Gregg in describing him, "but if you can imagine a genial and alert eagle, attentive, spirited and eager, you would have my first and lasting impression of President Vincent."[27] One of the great public speakers of his generation, and certainly one of the wittiest, Vincent perhaps did more than any other single man to explain and interpret to America the interests and purposes of The Rockefeller Foundation. He was deeply sincere and he abhorred pretense; he loved excellence and hated everything that was shoddy and second-rate. He was constantly alert to the tendency of power to be ostentatious and of wealth to think of itself in terms of exaggerated importance. With his deep concern for rectitude and team play and the free exchange of ideas, he built up an *esprit de corps* in the Foundation, the memory of which still survives.

Under such leadership, it was inevitable that the program should take on a different emphasis, and change was already in the air. Gates was beginning to thunder against what he called "the policy of scatteration," and in the final months of the war the opinion of the trustees was swinging sharply to a more closely integrated program of work. Gates wrote:

> If I have any regret, it is that the charter of The Rockefeller Foundation did not confine its work strictly to national and international medicine, health and its appointments. . . . Insofar as the disbursements of the Rockefeller incorporated philanthropies have been rigidly confined to these two fields of philanthropy [medicine and public health] they have been almost universally commended at home and abroad. Where they have inadvertently transgressed these limits, they have been widely and in some particulars perhaps not unfairly condemned.[28]

The temperament of Mr. Gates did not permit him a great deal of leeway in his judgments between black and white, and his exact words would not, perhaps, have received the endorsement of his contemporaries. But in general this was the trend of thinking among the trustees as the war came to an end, and for the next ten years the major interest of the Foundation was to center in medical education and public health, conceived in global terms, with the whole world as a field of strategy.

CHAPTER III

THE CONTROL OF HOOKWORM

WHEN THE ROCKEFELLER SANITARY Commission, under Dr. Wickliffe Rose, was merged with the Rockefeller Foundation, it had already achieved, in the five years of its existence, an impressive record in the control of hookworm in the Southern states. Here was a widespread anemia-producing disease which sapped vitality and handicapped, crippled, and even killed millions of men, women, and children in the hot, moist regions of the world. Here was a disease, too, for which an effective remedy had already been discovered, a remedy easily administered and quick in its results. The obstacles were ignorance and lethargy, ignorance as to the existence and extent of the disease, and lethargy on the part of the medical profession and of the health authorities in taking action even when the facts were surmised.

Indeed, when Rose began his work in 1910, knowledge of the disease was confined to a relatively small minority of physicians, few of whom realized its importance as a feature of their practice. Of the laymen who had heard of it, many regarded it as a myth. And yet the disease was rampant in the South. In many of the rural schools the number of infected children ran as high as 90 per cent, and of the more than half a million children examined by Rose's associates in the five years from 1910 to 1914, 39 per cent were infected. In one school in Virginia, for example, thirty-eight of the forty children present were infected, and in addition there were forty-five other children belonging to the school who, because of the severity of the disease, were not strong enough to attend. The incidence was high even among adults. Three hundred college students were examined as a body without reference to clinical symptoms; 42 per cent had hookworm. Three regiments of state militia were similarly examined, with infection rates of 36 per cent, 58 per cent, and 32 per cent respectively.

Rose's first task, therefore, was to demonstrate to the people of the Southern states that hookworm disease was a reality, that it was a serious handicap, and that it was both curable and preventable. Probably the dramatic life story of the hookworm as a human parasite was of considerable assistance in the development of the campaign. For this blood-sucking inhabitant of the intestine does not enter the body by way of the human mouth, but through the soles of the human foot, in the form of minute and almost invisible larvae. Its well-incapsulated form gets into the blood stream and by way of the lungs and throat finally lands in the stomach, where its coating protects it from gastric juices. It passes from the stomach to the small intestine, which is its future home. From then on, all it has to do is to eat, grow, and copulate. It does not produce its young in the intestine, but it lays eggs which pass out with the stool and contaminate the soil, so that other bare feet can pick up the new larvae which hatch from the eggs.

The victims of this invading host become increasingly anemic. Strength is dissipated and growth is stunted. The familiar symptoms are emaciation, protruding shoulder blades—"angel wings"—a bloated stomach, and swollen joints. Ulcers form on the legs and are not easily healed, and the skin becomes sallow. In advanced cases, the appetite is perverted and dirt-eating is not uncommon.

And yet the remedy, developed in Italy in the latter part of the nineteenth century, was surprisingly simple—capsules of thymol and salts, taken over a period of about eighteen hours. "Feedin' capsules to my hookworms," said a patient in Georgia, "was like feedin' buckshot to frogs."[1] Once cleared of hookworm, the victims could be protected from reinfection by sanitary latrines and the wearing of shoes.

The first step of the campaign which Rose undertook was a thorough survey to determine the geographic distribution of the disease and the approximate degree of infection. Rose never would move without first getting the facts. The second stage was a battle of publicity. He had to dramatize to the people of the South the fact that hookworm disease, with its evil train of social and economic consequences, could be brought under control. By lectures, exhibits, and demonstrations, he had to gain the support of newspapers, doctors, health workers, and the general public. He had to show the startling results of the simple treatments in the lives of people.

To accomplish this purpose, a director of sanitation was appointed in each of the eleven states where the work was contemplated. Under each director was a corps of sanitary inspectors and a staff of microscopists. The work was centered around traveling dispensaries conducted for the free examination and free treatment of all persons who applied. Extensive literature was circulated and meetings were held. The support of the schools was enlisted, and the educational departments of state and county became the strongest allies in the campaign. To prevent the recurrence of the disease, over 250,000 rural homes were inspected by the sanitary personnel, and major emphasis was placed on soil pollution and the necessity of sanitary privies. Of the 1,142 counties in the eleven states, extensive operations were carried out in 653. Over 25,000 public meetings were held, with a total attendance of more than 2,000,000 people, and the number of pieces of literature distributed was in excess of 3,250,000. This was in accord with the meticulous plans which Rose had laid down at the beginning, before the work had even begun.

> The public consciousness [he wrote] will be aroused to the necessity of action by the publication of the facts as revealed by the investigation. . . . Such agencies as public health organizations, associated charities, women's clubs, school improvement leagues, ministers, teachers, and practicing physicians will be called into service in the interest of awakened and enlightened public opinion.[2]

Five years later, he was able to say in the final report of the Rockefeller Sanitary Commission:

> The work of demonstrating to the people of these eleven Southern states that hookworm disease is a reality, and that it can be cured and prevented, may be said to have been accomplished.[3]

All this immense activity represented a co-operative effort between the state and county governments on the one hand and Rose's organization on the other. The governmental units contributed to the expense in a ratio of about one to eight, but the personnel, provided largely by the Board, was at all times under state control. This was in accord with Rose's deep-seated philosophy.

> The eradication of this disease [he wrote] is a work which no outside agency working independently could do for a people if it would, and one which no outside agency should do if it could. The economic prosperity of the State, the lives and health of its people, and the education of its children are involved; if the infection is to be stamped out, the States in which it exists must assume the responsibility. An outside agency can be helpful only insofar as it aids the States in organizing and bringing into activity their own forces.[4]

II

When the work of the Sanitary Commission became a part of The Rockefeller Foundation in 1913 and was christened with the new name International Health Board, Rose embarked on a bold plan which had intrigued him from the beginning. To what extent he was influenced by Gates' vaulting imagination it is not now possible to estimate, but as early as 1911 he was beginning to gather information on the extent and range of hookworm in other countries. His inquiries, made through government agencies in Washington and abroad, brought out the fact that hookworm runs around the earth in a great belt about 66 degrees wide, extending from parallel 36-north to parallel 30-south, and that practically all countries lying within these two parallels, containing about a thousand million people, are infected. Already he had personally seen the devastating consequences of the disease in Puerto Rico, and the idea took root in his mind that the same technique which had been so successfully applied in the Southern states could be translated to a far broader area. It was undoubtedly this conception which lay behind the wording of the resolution of the Foundation trustees in establishing the International Health Board: "to extend to other countries and people the work of eradicating hookworm disease."

In preparation for his new undertaking, Rose made three trips—one to England, where he conferred with authorities of the Colonial Office; one to the British West Indies; and one to the Far East, where his inquiries took him to Egypt, Ceylon, Malaya, and the Philippines. The West Indies and Central America were also visited by members of Rose's staff, and the strategy was developed for a mass attack on hookworm infection around the world.

In the years that followed, Rose's daring enterprise was extended to fifty-two countries in six continents, and to twenty-nine islands of the seas. It followed the hookworm belt all the way from Fiji and

Samoa westward through the Antipodes and the Far East to Africa and the Mediterranean basin, and thence to the West Indies and the Americas. Literally millions of people were examined for the disease in these various regions, and millions were found infected and were treated. Following the practice established in the Southern states, the work was always carried on as a co-operative undertaking between the International Health Board and the governments of the countries that were involved. "A partner, but not a patron," was the slogan. The Board furnished the technical leadership and a graduated portion of the cost, but the countries also contributed in varying amounts, and the project was always an integral part of the machinery of government. "Demonstrations in which the authorities do not participate to a substantial degree from the inception of the project are not likely to be successful," said Rose. "The country must be sufficiently interested to risk something, to follow the plan critically, to take over the cost of the work gradually but steadily, and within a reasonable period to assume the entire burden of direction and expense."[5]

Indeed, this principle of "working through governments," to use Rose's phrase, was a conception with which he started from the beginning and from which he never varied. It was fundamental to every plan that he made. Unless the work was carried out under the authority and direction of Government—and he always used a capital G in writing the word—it had no foundation and no permanence. This conception was not only based on a shrewd and intuitive kind of wisdom; it was a direct reflection of the man himself. He was instinctively modest and he abhorred the idea of a private organization's seeking power or credit for itself. It is characteristic of his attitude that in laying down his plan of procedure at the very beginning of the hookworm campaign he should write this sentence: "The Commission will seek to hide itself behind its work and to keep to the front the local agencies through which the work is being done."[6]

It was at this period that Rose's unusual qualities of generalship and organizing ability became brilliantly clear. The extraordinary sweep of his vision and the compelling lucidity of his mind acted as a magnet to many men who later made substantial contributions to the leadership of the new public health movement that was beginning to develop around the world. Some of these men, indeed, became almost legendary figures in the saga of preventive medicine—men, for example, like Dr. Victor G. Heiser, whom Rose appointed as director of the Board's work in the Far East; Dr. S. M. Lambert, who spent his life in Fiji, Samoa and the Polynesian and Melanesian island chain; Dr. Wilbur A. Sawyer, who headed the activities in Australia; Dr. George K. Strode, who worked in Brazil; and others like Dr. John A. Ferrell, Dr. Lewis W. Hackett, Dr. Charles N. Leach, and Dr. William P. Jacocks. These men and their many associates guided the far-flung enterprise on an ever-widening international front.

As the campaign swept forward, experience and research brought new ideas to bear and techniques were improved and often modified from country to country. It was found, for example, that a temperature as low as 50° F. checks larval development in the soil, and that an area which has such a minimum nightly temperature will not have a hookworm problem. Thus in the mountainous areas of Ceylon the disease is of little consequence, although the seacoast is heavily infected. It was found, too, that where the annual rainfall is less than sixty inches, as in most parts of Mexico, the disease does not gain a foothold because the prerequisite conditions of moisture in the soil are lacking. But even when temperature and rainfall are favorable to larval development, the disease will not establish itself if the soil is unfavorable. Sandy and loam soils are required for the development of the larvae, while clay or silt soils will retard them. Thus the disease is automatically limited to areas characterized by certain soil types.

Contrary to expectations, the rice culture of the Far East does not lend itself to heavy hookworm infection, for although human excrement is used in fertilization and the conditions are thus theoretically perfect for the development of the larvae, rice cultivation is carried on under water, and the hookworm ova are unable to develop. However, the mulberry-tree workers in China connected with the silk industry, where human excrement is also employed, are severely infected.

Sometimes the new facts which developed had serious and discouraging implications. It was shown, for example, that the disease was spread by immigration. Every country importing native labor from India was bringing to its own soil a heavy stream of infection, because India had an infection rate estimated between 60 and 80 per cent of its entire population. In Assam, where six hundred newly arrived Indian laborers were examined, only one was found free of the disease. In British Guiana, where workers from India were the chief source of labor supply, an examination of all immigrants arriving during the course of a year showed an average infection of 74 per cent. By the importation of this kind of labor, the infection was also being carried into Dutch Guiana, Ceylon, the Federated Malay

States, the Straits Settlements, and Java. The health authorities at San Francisco examined a shipload of Indian workers and found an infection of about 90 per cent. Further immigration of this type was stopped, but every group of Indian laborers in the State became a center of infection from which the disease was spread.

As the work of the International Health Board developed around the world, it became customary in heavily infested tropical countries to dispense with individual examinations, and people were treated en masse without preliminary diagnosis. The plan was first tried out in Java and elsewhere in the Dutch East Indies, and was later put to extensive use in India and Siam. The primary reason for the adoption of this practice was the growing belief that in hookworm control the essential thing was not so much to aim at the absolute cure of every infected person in the community as it was quickly to remove the largest possible number of worms from the largest possible number of people, and thus to lower the severity of infection. But even this theory yielded to later ideas as new evidence was obtained.

In his earlier days, Rose and his associates spoke of the *eradication* of hookworm; indeed, the original Rockefeller Sanitary Commission used that word in its title. It is a goal that has never been reached. Social patterns and habits cannot be changed overnight, and discouraging reinfestation can occur where adequate sanitary arrangements are not maintained. Moreover, as the years went by, it began to be clear that there was a distinction between hookworm disease and a comparatively harmless hookworm infection. Laboratory investigation proved that people with a limited number of hookworms are not necessarily ill, and that a relative immunity can be acquired, due to the presence of antibodies, in which an equilibrium is reached in the number of worms, with little change thereafter, even in the presence of constant exposure to infective larvae.

Consequently, the approach to the disease was altered over the years. Mass treatments have been largely discarded, and emphasis is now placed on steadily improving sanitary arrangements, with treatment limited to the individual sick person with enough worms to do appreciable damage. It cannot be said that hookworm infection has been wiped out; it can be said, however, that as a vast public menace around the world it has been drastically limited and brought within manageable compass, so that it now joins the category of diseases like smallpox and typhoid which modern public health methods can readily control. Dr. William H. Welch summed up the verdict in these words: "The agency and the man were unique in the annals of preventive medicine, and in the light of subsequent developments and of the results achieved they were of epochal significance in the history of the public health movement."[7]

III

Ever present in Rose's mind was the conception that the attack on hookworm was important not so much because it was a disabling disease, but rather because it lent itself so readily to purposes of demonstration in disease control. It was an advance agent of preventive medicine. It served at once as an end in itself and as a convenient means to a larger end. In its nature, causes, and cure it was easily understood by the average citizen, and its effects upon his own health and the health of his community were plainly demonstrable. When he had seen this one disease treated and brought under control, he was prepared to support the control of other diseases that were less simple and less tangible.

Moreover, the same sanitary patterns and type of organization required for hookworm control were usable and necessary in relation to other endemics. Hookworm in the South lived side by side with malaria, another anemia-producing disease which had disastrous personal and social consequences. Rose found that malaria was responsible for more sickness and death than all other diseases combined. It was particularly prevalent among children, and therefore preyed most heavily upon human beings during the period of physical and mental growth. As early as 1915, therefore, Rose began a series of experimental projects to determine the degree to which malaria could be controlled within the limits of reasonable expenditure and under conditions prevailing in typical farm districts in the South. Once he had proved to his own satisfaction that simple antimosquito measures could sharply reduce the incidence of the disease at a cost well within the means of the average community, he began to dream of the possibility of a broad application of preventive measures. Malaria is perhaps the greatest handicap to the welfare and economic efficiency of the human race; to Rose and his associates, it seemed probable that the same world-wide pattern of attack—involving demonstration and education—which was being employed against hookworm could be made on this other disease. Five years of constantly widening work in the United States paved the way for the implementation of this conception, and in the period that followed, a boldly conceived and executed malaria program was projected around the globe.

Tuberculosis was another widespread malady which Rose encountered in the South; and when, in 1917, a marked increase in the disease developed in France, due to war conditions, the International Health Board was ready to accept the invitation of the French government to lead the campaign against it. The plan of operations was basically the same as the plan against hookworm: a preliminary statistical survey to determine the incidence of the disease, the establishment of dispensaries, and the carrying out of a broad campaign of popular education. "This is not an impertinent importation of scientific knowledge into the land of Louis Pasteur," wrote Dr. Vincent, but rather a "demonstration of method" and of "organized teamplay."[8]

Similarly with yellow fever, which is discussed in a subsequent chapter, the apprehension which the threat of this disease created in the Southern states led ultimately to activities which embraced three continents. Rose's thinking was invariably on a global scale. A technique once developed had to be projected wherever it was needed. When it came to preventive medicine, flags and boundary lines had no validity. "Unless public health is conceived in international terms," Rose insisted, "the strategic opportunity of our generation will be lost."[9] To the early pioneers of the International Health Board, the phrase *The well-being of mankind throughout the world,* which was written into the charter and engraved on the seal of The Rockefeller Foundation, was a living and beckoning symbol.

IV

But from the beginning Rose was after bigger game than hookworm or malaria or any other malady. The attack on these diseases was for him an entering wedge, a method by which states and nations could be induced to build up permanent machinery to take care of the whole problem of public health. This was his constant preoccupation from the day he first accepted the responsibility of leadership, and he drove toward this goal with his characteristic tenacity. He was not content with the elimination or control of a particular disease. Unless this type of activity served to demonstrate the necessity of adequate public health organizations, supported by taxation, the results would be superficial and ephemeral. Underlying all efforts to protect people from hookworm or malaria or tuberculosis, there must be official agencies, set up on a full-time basis, staffed with thoroughly trained men, and equipped with modern facilities.

This was what Rose was driving at. He wanted the International

Health Board to leave behind it, wherever it went, not only an awakened public consciousness and a growing belief in the fundamental need for preventive measures, but a determination and an ability to build the necessary machinery by which modern methods of sanitation and medical care could be enforced.

It must be remembered that when Rose began his activities, public health work not only in this country but elsewhere throughout the world was relatively undeveloped, although in this respect Great Britain and Germany were far ahead of the United States. Not only in terms of practice but in terms of knowledge, the science of preventive medicine was crude and rudimentary. Except for smallpox, there was little that could be done in the face of epidemics like cholera, typhoid, dysentery, and malaria. Boards of health were beginning to appear in the South, following their appearance elsewhere, but they were largely paper organizations, made up of physicians who served without pay. Appropriations for their work were usually so small as to make any effective action impossible. There was no permanent staff and little attempt at program. Conditions in rural areas were particularly lamentable, and while most of the states had provided for county boards of health or county health officers, there were no funds for their work and they functioned only in times of epidemic, if at all.

To Rose, this was the root of the problem. Unless this could be corrected, any beneficial results of the work of a private agency would endure only so long as the private agency was in the field. Beginning in 1916, therefore, the International Health Board undertook the systematic development and support of county health organizations in the United States. Practical demonstrations had already shown that for the task of providing adequate health protection for rural communities, the county was the most effective unit of organization, except in those parts of the country where the governmental unit is the township. The 1916 experiment began with ten counties in North Carolina, and the idea spread rapidly not only through the South but in other parts of the nation as well. It involved for each unit a full-time public health staff, consisting, as a minimum, of a physician as health officer, a sanitary inspector, a public health nurse, and an office assistant. For the support of the undertaking, the county itself guaranteed 50 per cent of the cost, the balance being met by the State Board of Health and the International Health Board, generally in equal proportions at first, but with the Board withdrawing its support when the experiment was successfully launched. Seldom did the

Board's share of the expense exceed $2,500 a year, and rarely if ever did the probationary period extend beyond three years. "Pump priming," Rose used to call this kind of activity, and he often used the homely simile of the farmer's half bucket of water to start the pump whose leather washer had dried out—a half bucket of water that made possible a continuous flow from a deep and copious reservoir.

Certainly in the case of county health organization, Rose's half bucket of water had extraordinary consequences. The idea was developed in hundreds of counties in the United States, and the International Health Board projected it around the world—in the *municipios* of Puerto Rico, Brazil, and the Philippine Islands, the *bezirke* of Austria, the *départements* of France, the *districts* of the Straits Settlements. Long after Rose retired from the leadership of the Board in 1923, this type of support was continued, as the idea of local responsibility for public health functions gained headway on an international scale. When the International Health Board withdrew from what was after all merely the demonstration of a practical and effective method, it had appropriated over $4,000,000 for the purpose. Today the method is taken for granted, and full-time rural health service has become an accepted fact. It has been adopted in most of the states of this country, for example, and the quality of service has improved to such a degree that many rural areas enjoy as adequate a system of health supervision as do the large municipalities.

Concurrently with the development of county units, the International Health Board stimulated the growth and evolution of state and national health services. Here again, the conception behind the activity was the conception of "pump priming." Where financial assistance was given, it was with the understanding that legislative appropriations would be secured to cover the cost of the work after a brief period. On this principle, such divisions as sanitary engineering, vital statistics, and epidemiology were added to many state health departments, and central public health laboratories were developed where diagnoses could be made of diseases like tuberculosis, typhoid fever, malaria, and diphtheria. As in all activities which Rose undertook, this type of aid was extended around the world, and in more than forty countries in Europe, Asia, and Latin America a demonstration was given of the necessary components that constitute the rapidly developing science of preventive medicine. Vital statistics in Colombia, public health laboratories in Costa Rica and the Philippines, a hygienic institute in Hungary, a statistical bureau in Bulgaria, a laboratory in Peking for producing biological products—these are random samples of the sweep and scope of the work.

It was this creative concern, this imaginative type of activity, that Rose had in mind when he voiced his frequently repeated aphorism: "Constructive thinking results from action and to action must return for its final criticism."

V

Rose had not gone very far in his work before he began to realize that the bottleneck was not so much a lack either of money or of organization as it was a lack of trained men. The idea that any physician qualified to practice could act as a health officer, giving part of his time to official duties, was an anachronism. Special qualifications and special training in the theoretical and practical aspects of public health administration were fast becoming necessary if preventive medicine was to keep abreast with modern conditions.

As early as 1914, Rose, with the enthusiastic backing of Dr. Buttrick, Dr. Simon Flexner, and Dr. Welch, began to develop the idea of a school of public health. At a conference attended by nineteen leading physicians and educators, with Mr. Gates in the chair, Rose made a statement which Dr. Welch admitted later "deeply stirred" him.[10] In consequence, Rose and Welch were appointed a committee to prepare a report, and Rose outlined his understanding of the conference in these words:

> The discussion seemed to develop substantial agreement on the following points: (1) that a fundamental need in the public health service in this country at the present time is of men adequately trained for the work; (2) that a distinct contribution toward meeting this need could be made by establishing at some convenient place a school of public health of high standard; (3) that such an institution, while maintaining its separate identity and autonomy, should in the interest both of economy and efficiency be closely affiliated with a university and its medical school; (4) that the nucleus of this school of public health should be an institute of hygiene; (5) that a plan for this institute should be formulated with a view to its beginning not on the scale of its ultimate character, but rather on that of its minimum requirements; that it should be given opportunity to grow within its own sphere as an institute of hygiene and to expand into full stature as a school of public health by drawing upon the medical school, the school of engineering, and the other departments of the university, and by utilizing for purposes of demonstration and practical experience all the facilities of the city and state department of health and of the U.S. Public Health Service.[11]

As a result of these deliberations, The Rockefeller Foundation built and endowed the School of Hygiene and Public Health at Johns Hopkins University, which was opened in 1918 with Dr. William H. Welch as director. Requiring of its students courses which included bacteriology, biostatistics, epidemiology, sanitary engineering, and public health administration, it provided for the first time in this country a thorough training for full-time public health officers in states, cities, and rural areas, as well as for those preparing to enter the United States Public Health Service. "The West Point of public health," Dr. Vincent called it.[12]

But other West Points soon became necessary, and this pioneering step was followed by a somewhat similar gift to Harvard in 1921. Thereafter, Rose and his successors as head of the International Health Board undertook the implementation of a bold and creative plan literally to girdle the globe with schools and institutes of public health, including public health nursing. Some were new organizations that were built from the ground up; others were developed or supported with substantial subsidies. The schools and institutes were located in Prague, Warsaw, London, Toronto, Copenhagen, Budapest, Oslo, Belgrade, Zagreb, Madrid, Cluj, Ankara, Sofia, Rome, Tokyo, Athens, Bucharest, Stockholm, Calcutta, Manila, São Paulo, and the University of Michigan. Over $25,000,000 was spent in this gigantic undertaking, with consequences, in terms of the improvement of public health around the world, that are beyond reckoning.

To make this new educational machinery doubly effective, Rose and his associates developed a system of fellowships by which promising students were brought to these institutes for graduate training. The students were selected with scrupulous care with reference to their fitness for important posts as scientists, teachers, or practical administrators in the public health service, to which in most cases they had a definite assurance of appointment on completion of their courses. The system embraced nearly every country in the world, and students were brought from Czechoslovakia and Brazil and Ceylon, for example, to study at Johns Hopkins or the London School of Tropical Medicine or the Pasteur Institute.

Moreover, men who were already trained as public health officers and teachers were given an opportunity for postgraduate work or "refresher courses" at some appropriate institute. Rose was anxious to tie these centers of public health and education together. It was part of a broad conception that as these new schools developed they could be made to stimulate and reinforce each other by interchange of experience, facilities, and men. A migration of public health personnel back and forth across national boundary lines would be an enriching experience by which the new ideas and techniques of one area could become the common property of all.

Rose thus initiated a fellowship program which later was adopted by the other divisions of the Foundation and became, over the years, perhaps the most important aspect of its work. It was an investment in leadership, an underwriting of promising talent, and its dividends defy calculation.

As one looks back on this initial period in the history of The Rockefeller Foundation, the genius of Wickliffe Rose seems to loom above the horizon of his contemporaries. Certainly he was one of the most intriguing figures of his generation. He was so modest and even shy that it is difficult to realize that he was also—in Dr. Welch's phrase—the ground breaker in this global attack on disease. Perhaps one of the secrets of his distinguished success lay in his urge to seek advice. As Dr. Wilbur A. Sawyer, who knew him well, says of him: "He took advice from authorities everywhere regarding all phases of his program. He went around the world visiting health officials and collecting suggestions."[13] As one sums up his career, the tribute paid to him at his death becomes him well: "In the heroic age of public health, he was one of the giants."[14]

CHAPTER IV

THE BROADENING PROGRAM IN PUBLIC HEALTH

WHEN IN 1923 WICKLIFFE ROSE RESIGNED from the directorship of the International Health Board to assume the presidency of the General Education Board and of the newly created International Education Board, the lines of development in the Foundation's health work had been firmly established. Effective campaigns against particular diseases like hookworm, malaria, and yellow fever had been launched on a world-wide front; the support of national, state, and rural health organizations was being rapidly developed; and the creation of schools of hygiene for the training of public health personnel was well under way. In its major outlines, this was the general pattern that was to govern the health work of the Foundation for the next twenty-five years.

Rose was succeeded by Colonel Frederick F. Russell, who had been in charge of the Division of Laboratories and Infectious Disease of the Surgeon General's Office of the United States Army. A thoroughly trained laboratory scientist, a scholar whose life had been spent in preventive medicine, he brought to his task an intimate technical knowledge of the various projects which the International Health Board was undertaking. A warm admirer and disciple of Wickliffe Rose, he adopted the ideas and techniques which had already been developed and made them his own.

But Russell and Rose came from radically different surroundings.

Russell had scientific experience and judgment, and he was at home in a laboratory; Rose was a philosopher with brilliant administrative gifts and a hard core of practical sense. It was natural, therefore, that while the outlines of the program of the International Health Board remained much the same, certain emphases should be shifted. In Rose's opinion, medical science had far outstripped its application. What was needed, therefore, in combating disease was to employ the facts already at hand. In hookworm, the remedy was not only known but its efficacy in field work had already been demonstrated by Dr. Stiles. In malaria, the mosquito carrier had been identified years before, and there remained the practical task of finding economical means either to destroy it or to protect people from its bite. Similarly in yellow fever, Reed had discovered the guilty mosquito, and Gorgas in Havana and Panama had traced out what seemed to be the epidemiology of the disease; the immediate concern, therefore, was to extend the scope of the campaign.

There was a simplicity about Rose's approach to his problems which Russell did not share. To be sure, Rose was concerned with research, but at this stage of his thinking his interest was at the practical rather than at the fundamental level. Thus Vincent, writing to Dr. Cole of the Rockefeller Institute in 1918, used these words to describe the line of demarcation between the Institute and the International Health Board: "It is the function of the Institute through research to provide the scientific knowledge of a given disease. The task of the International Health Board is to apply this knowledge in the field. While this latter work has research phases, these have to do with practical procedure rather than with fundamental inquiry."[1]

Russell was not content with this point of view. He did not believe that the field aspects and the fundamental research aspects of an offensive against a particular disease could be split between two organizations. He held unwaveringly to the point that of equal importance with the application of knowledge was the search for new knowledge, and that in any campaign against a disease the two columns had to move forward together. As early as 1925, he stated his philosophy in these words:

At first glance, it would seem a simple matter merely to distribute widely from the vast stores of scientific facts produced by the laboratories of the world; for few of the discoveries in disease prevention have been fully applied. And yet, when a specific work is undertaken, as in the control of hookworm disease or malaria, it is soon found that there are serious gaps in the knowledge essential to successful control. The lack of this information not only delays progress but prevents the application of many facts already discovered.[2]

Russell's emphasis therefore was increasingly placed on laboratory research, an emphasis which ultimately led not only to the creation of a base laboratory in New York as an organic part of the International Health Board, but to the development of field research on a scale such as Rose never contemplated. Even Vincent, who earlier had supported Rose's point of view, changed his mind. His last public report, written before his retirement as president in 1929, contained these words: "The Rockefeller Foundation, even in the attempt to apply existing knowledge to the protection of the public health, is forced into seeking further facts about the nature of certain diseases. Thus opens a vista of research in preventive medicine and hygiene."[3]

This new emphasis had a profound influence on the health work of the Foundation. The laboratory in New York, which utilized part of the buildings of the Rockefeller Institute, became a pivotal point in the far-flung program. It set the scientific tone for the work that was being carried on around the world. It not only served to advance knowledge of disease and of control methods, but it provided a training center for new appointees of the International Health Board, and an opportunity for "refresher" work for staff members returning periodically from the field. In this laboratory, scores of men have been trained for outside institutions as well as for the Foundation. Scores have been provided with an opportunity to exercise their talents and to learn the use of the scientific method. Together with the Rockefeller Institute it has become a kind of Mecca for visiting scientists from abroad, a focal point of distinguished and original research.

It was in this laboratory that Sawyer and his colleagues developed the vaccine for yellow fever which today protects millions of people around the world. It was here that Dr. Lowell Coggeshall carried on his studies of immunity in malaria which made possible a better understanding of the disease. It was here, too, that Dr. Thomas Francis, Jr., Dr. Frank L. Horsfall, and Dr. George K. Hirst broke new ground in an approach to an understanding of influenza. Similarly, research—often of an outstanding character—has been carried on in this laboratory in typhus, syphilis, yaws, streptococcal infections, rickettsial diseases, and other maladies which afflict mankind around the world. In this laboratory, high-speed centrifuges were designed and constructed, and significant advance was made in the application of these instruments to the study of viruses. It was not without justification that Russell spoke of the laboratory as "a leaven for the whole organization"; and when Sawyer, who had been the first head of the laboratory, succeeded Russell in 1935 as director of the International Health Board, which had now been rechristened as the International Health Division, fresh impetus was given to this new development.

II

During these years of wide-ranging activity, the International Health Division continued to be the one branch of the Foundation that carried on its work largely through its own personnel. It is true that it often appropriated funds to other organizations and research agencies to spend or administer, but its principal activities were handled by its own large staff of doctors, investigators, sanitary engineers, statisticians, and technicians who were assigned, on a great variety of tasks, to nearly every country in the world.

Beginning with hookworm, they took up one disease after another, diseases that represented the chief points of attack in preventive medicine. Although public health education and aid to state and local health services continued to loom large in the interests of the Board, an increasing degree of emphasis was given to the investigation and control of specific diseases. Rose initiated the program with his work in hookworm, malaria, and yellow fever; his successors added to the list a score of diseases that represent the principal hazards in public health. This activity spanned more than a quarter of a century, with ramifying consequences around the world. Experience developed a method that seemed to give maximum results: laboratory research, tested by field experimentation and demonstration under actual practice conditions. The constant interplay between field and laboratory ensured the rapid application in the field of new laboratory findings, while the studies and experiences in the field stimulated new research in the laboratory. The International Health Division was in a unique position to utilize this happy combination of services, because it was not tied to any one country or region, but could make its studies and set up its laboratories wherever necessary. Consequently, its work in specific diseases was undertaken under the most favorable conditions imaginable, and with results in terms of success and failure and of the various stages in between that are outlined in the necessarily brief paragraphs that follow.

Malaria. Next to yellow fever, The Rockefeller Foundation through the International Health Division has devoted a larger proportion of its resources to malaria than to any other single disease. A mosquito-borne malady, malaria affects millions of people in tropical, subtropical, and even temperate regions around the world. It is so widespread that the aggregate of the deaths directly and indirectly attributable to it is colossal. If it were a single mosquito that was responsible for malaria, the problem would be greatly simplified; but an entire subfamily of mosquitoes, the *Anophelines*, is involved, of which at least twenty-five species, varying greatly in peculiarities and habits, have at one place or another been found to be the transmitters of the disease. Consequently, the control of malaria is a specialized problem from country to country, and methods of control which have proved effective in one locality may be useless when tried in another.

As stated in the previous chapter, Rose's original approach to the disease had been from the economic angle; he wanted to make sure that malaria could be controlled "at costs which the average community could afford." His studies therefore began in a humble way in oiling some ponds in Crossett, Arkansas, and in a village in Mississippi. Within six years, the International Health Board was co-operating in malaria demonstrations in fifty-two towns located in ten Southern states, and the experiments had clearly demonstrated "that by simple anti-mosquito measures malaria can be controlled in the average small town at a cost well within the means of the community." In 1921, this malaria program began to cross national boundaries, first to Nicaragua, then to Brazil, then in a rapidly extending line that ran through practically every malarious region in the world, touching all the continents and many of the islands of the seas.

The objective remained constant, but the project became vastly complex. As the need developed for skilled personnel in malaria control, the Foundation aided in establishing and maintaining schools and training stations in malariology located at many strategic points all the way from Leesburg, Georgia, to Athens and Karachi. Scores of fellowships were given, both in the United States and abroad, to train men for malaria posts. The Foundation also supported the preparation of lectures and textbooks, from primers in a score of native languages to a recent two-volume malariology of 1,600 pages. Sound administrative principles and workable organizations had to be established, and thus governments, national, state, and local, were aided in setting up malaria control divisions, many of which, as in Italy and Portugal, have had outstanding success.

It soon became obvious that the control of malaria had to be based on a wider knowledge of the epidemiology of the disease. The Foundation therefore undertook extensive studies of the natural history of *Anopheles* mosquitoes in many parts of the world. It was found, for example, that where in the United States the *Anopheles* responsible for most of the malaria breeds in ponds, marshes, and quiet waters, in the Philippines the only *Anopheles* that transmits malaria develops in rapidly flowing foothill streams. In Trinidad, the malaria mosquito breeds in water that collects in the broad leaves of a plant growing in trees. It was discovered, too, that certain varieties of *Anopheles* are harmless, because they feed on animals rather than on human beings, or because they have developed other habits. This type of research, carried on with great success by malariologists like Dr. Samuel T. Darling in Georgia and Dr. Lewis W. Hackett in Italy, has pointed the way to a more accurately focused control of the offending mosquitoes.

In the course of this work many new field and laboratory techniques were developed—specially designed mosquito traps, for example; novel means of measuring the incidence and decline of malaria in a given region; methods by which *Anopheles* can be bred under artificial conditions in a laboratory, thus making possible the study of its entire life cycle. The employment of fish in the control of malarial waters, the use of Paris green for the destruction of larvae, the wholesale attack with insecticides by sanitary inspectors and search brigades—these were contributions that grew out of long years of research. In recent years, of course, the development of DDT has provided a weapon of incomparable value to malariologists, and the Foundation has made wide and successful use of it in places like Greece and Sardinia.

Not only the mosquito, but the parasite, injected by the mosquito into the human victim, is an important factor in malaria control; and the Foundation's program has included extensive studies of the life of the parasite: investigations of its metabolism and of the effects of various antimalarial drugs; and inquiries which have clarified the relationships between the parasite and the clinical disease. In some instances single workers, in other cases entire laboratories, have been supported in this type of research.

A third of a century separates the oiling of those ponds in 1916 in Crossett, Arkansas, from the use of isotopes and Geiger counters in 1950 in the International Health Division Laboratory in New York to determine how a malaria parasite grows. During this period, malaria has all but vanished from the United States, Italy, Sardinia,

Cyprus, and Greece, and it is rapidly being subdued in Venezuela, British Guiana, Brazil, and many other areas. Indeed, in the United States it is now difficult to find enough cases for clinical observation in our medical schools. Many factors and many agencies have contributed to this result. That the Foundation has played an influential part in the development can scarcely be questioned.

Typhus. "In its tragic relationship to mankind," said Hans Zinsser in 1933, "the disease of typhus is second to none—not even to plague or to cholera." In most of the major wars prior to the Second World War, more persons succumbed to typhus than fell on the battlefield, and Zinsser commented sardonically on "the relative unimportance of generals."[4]

In 1940, soon after the outbreak of the war made it clear that typhus would again be a major health problem, with results perhaps as devastating as they were in the First World War, the Laboratory of the International Health Division began a series of studies in an attempt to produce, if possible, an effective vaccine, and to test the efficacy of various insecticides which were coming into use. Basic knowledge regarding the disease was far from adequate. It was known, of course, that it was spread from person to person by means of the body louse, and that it developed rapidly when people were crowded together under unsanitary conditions and when there was a heavy louse infestation. But how best to control or eradicate louse breeding was not understood, nor was there any reliable method of immunization. Vaccines which fully protected guinea pigs failed to afford similar protection to laboratory workers, and two doctors on the staff of the International Health Division contracted the disease, although they had been vaccinated with the latest and supposedly the most effective type of vaccine.

The lack of an experimental animal which would equal man in its susceptibility to typhus, and in which the disease could be reproduced as it occurs in human beings, led the Foundation, in 1942, to switch its main attack to the carrier of the disease: the body louse. A louse laboratory was opened on the East Side in New York; a stock of lice was obtained from a Bowery casualty who had just been admitted to Bellevue's alcoholic ward; and research was begun on two problems: first, the long-range task of unraveling the biology of the louse, and second, the more immediate question of devising quick and effective means of killing the insects and thus preventing infestation.

The second problem progressed in a gratifyingly successful manner. A number of substances highly lethal for lice had already been discovered in various laboratories, but they required further testing under field conditions. The first comprehensive test was made by the Foundation in a conscientious objectors' camp in New Hampshire in 1942. Out of a large number of volunteers, eager to co-operate, thirty men were chosen for a three weeks' experiment, each man being infested with one hundred lice. Several chemical substances were tested on these men for their power to kill lice, and in general the results already noted in the laboratory were confirmed.

Another test was made in five villages in Mexico, in one of which typhus was present. Technique improved with practice, and it was shown that a village population could easily and completely be sterilized as far as insect typhus carriers were concerned.

The following year, the Foundation sent a typhus team to Algeria, where extensive epidemics were occurring. Here a new method was developed which had already had an elaborate trial in the New York laboratory. The application of insecticide to individuals had proved a cumbersome and time-consuming process. People had to remove their clothes, the clothes were then dusted by hand with the insecticide, and after all the seams had been thoroughly rubbed with powder, the clothes were donned again. The new method proved that it was possible by means of a blowing machine to apply the powder without removing the clothes. Where the former procedure took perhaps twenty minutes, the new method required two or three minutes, and careful tests showed that it was just as effective as the slower hand-powdering. Moreover, the experiments in Algeria brought out the fact that while the natives were loath to remove their clothes for treatment, they responded eagerly to this new approach.

Shortly after its capture by the Allied Armies in 1943, Naples was threatened by a serious epidemic of typhus. The number of cases was multiplying so rapidly that the situation was ripe for an explosive outburst of the disease. At the invitation of the United States Typhus Commission, the Foundation undertook the responsibility for the mass delousing of the population. Forty delousing stations were established in the city, and to these stations the people came by thousands and tens of thousands. At each station there was a staff of men dusters to care for the boys and men, and a staff of women to care for the girls and women. DDT had by this time come into use and after careful test had superseded the other insecticides. The powder was applied directly by compressed-air guns which swoshed it up trousers and skirts, down sleeves, into collars, seams, tucks, and folds, wherever the insect or its eggs might cling. More than 1,300,-

000 people were treated in a single month, and the epidemic which might have taken thousands of lives collapsed with astonishing rapidity.

There is still much to learn about typhus, but techniques of control are at hand, and the disease need never again threaten nations with wholesale tragedy and disaster as it has in the past.

Influenza and the common cold. In 1933, English scientists succeeded in isolating the causative agent of an epidemic of influenza, proving definitely that it was due to a filterable virus. This virus has come to be known as "influenza A." Three years later, the International Health Division took up influenza as a major interest. A base laboratory was established in New York, and subsidiary centers in research and epidemiology were developed in Buenos Aires and Budapest, as well as in connection with the State Health Departments of Minnesota and California. In 1940, with a grant from The Rockefeller Foundation, Dr. Thomas Francis, Jr., at New York University, isolated the virus of an explosive type of influenza in North Carolina. This virus was called "influenza B," and the two types are quite distinct.

Over the years, concentrated attention has been given by the International Health Division to this respiratory disease. New virus strains have been isolated, and new techniques for laboratory and field investigation have been developed. A promising vaccine has been produced and a greater understanding of the natural history of the disease has been gained. But the goal is still far off, and, as in all virus diseases, the wide gaps in fundamental knowledge are all too evident. An auspicious development in the approach to the problem is the concept which the new World Health Organization has adopted of a world-wide system of laboratories reporting constantly to a center in London.

Another preoccupation of the International Health Division has been the common cold, of which statisticians estimate there are annually 300,000,000 cases in the United States alone. In 1927, the staff of the Division undertook a seven months' study of this affliction in a small isolated village in a forest clearing of southern Alabama. The next year, a similar study was made in a fur-trading post in the interior of Labrador. Other intensive research was carried out in one of the most isolated of the tropical Virgin Islands and in a community within the Arctic Circle in Spitzbergen, hemmed in by the ice and darkness of the Polar winter. In addition, substantial sums were appropriated over twelve years to the pioneering research which Dr. A. R. Dochez was conducting at Columbia University.

It is a safe assumption that all this work has laid the basis for a wider understanding of the common cold; but much more information is necessary, and a far greater development of the techniques for the study of the responsible virus or viruses, before anything approaching immunization can be looked for. One of the main difficulties is the lack of a satisfactory experimental animal. The only creature known to be susceptible, aside from man, is the chimpanzee, and experimentation is cumbersome and expensive.

Tuberculosis. Mention has already been made of the tuberculosis commission which the Foundation sent to France in 1917, and of the system of tuberculosis dispensaries which was established throughout that war-torn country. Training facilities for visiting nurses were created, and graduate instruction for physicians in diagnosis and treatment was provided on a wide scale. During the period of cooperation between the Foundation and the French government, which lasted until 1925, the number of tuberculosis dispensaries increased from 22 to 600, and the number of hospital beds for patients from 8,000 to 30,000.

This work, however, was largely confined to the application of existing knowledge, and when Colonel Russell assumed the leadership of the International Health Division he began to think of tuberculosis in terms of basic research. "There is so much about this disease we do not know," he said.[5] In 1928, therefore, the Foundation, with Dr. Eugene L. Opie as a special adviser, began a broad investigation of tuberculosis. Field studies in the epidemiology of the disease were undertaken in New York City, Philadelphia, Alabama, Tennessee, on the islands of Jamaica and Puerto Rico, and in Austria. Surveys were made in both rural and urban areas. Thousands of persons were given the tuberculin test, and many of these were also examined by X-ray. Mobile X-ray diagnostic units were developed for use particularly in rural areas.

The aim of the investigation was threefold: first, to collect information concerning the character of the disease and the incidence of its various manifestations; second, to determine how the disease spreads and what the conditions are that modify its transmission; and third, upon the basis of the information thus acquired to devise preventive measures adapted to local conditions.

In general terms, it was established that tuberculosis is spread, in large part, by long-drawn-out family or household contacts in which the disease is slowly transmitted from one generation to the next. Incidence of the disease was found to be much higher in urban than in rural populations, particularly in areas where people were living in crowded, unsanitary quarters. Observations indicated that in proportion to those suffering from clinically manifest tuberculosis and known to be ill, X-ray examinations revealed an approximately equal number of persons who seemed to be well but who had relatively advanced pulmonary lesions of tuberculosis. The occurrence and slow progression of these lesions not disclosed by symptoms or physical signs are important aspects in the epidemiology of the disease. These studies also revealed that tuberculosis is a particularly grave problem for the Negro. It more frequently pursues a fatal course in the Negro race, and the average annual death rate in Negro persons exposed to the disease is from three to five times higher than in white persons.

In close co-operation with Dr. Opie's laboratory at Cornell, field trials of a heat-killed tubercle bacillus vaccine were undertaken in Jamaica. Over a period of approximately ten years, experience showed that in a particular mental hospital, tuberculosis attack and death rates were significantly lowered among the immunized group. The vaccine was also tried out in groups of the general populations, but with inconclusive results.

Dr. Simon Flexner used to say that tuberculosis was a dirt disease that would disappear "as civilization cleaned itself up." Certainly its incidence in the United States has sharply declined in recent years. Better economic conditions, better housing, more abundant supply and utilization of foods, wider recreational facilities, and less overcrowding have undoubtedly contributed to this result. But there is still much to be learned about the disease; and it will remain a public health hazard until science discovers a specific cure for it and a thoroughly reliable means of personal immunization against it.

Rabies. In the middle thirties, due to a large unimmunized dog population, rabies increased to alarming proportions in several Southern states. Impetus was given to the spread of the disease by the presence of the infection in certain wild animals, particularly foxes. In collaboration with the State of Alabama, the Foundation erected a small research laboratory near Montgomery; and over a period of nine years significant studies were carried out on the distribution of rabies among dogs as well as on methods of diagnosis and techniques of vaccination. It was found that dogs could be immunized by a single injection of a satisfactory vaccine, and the studies developed not only a broader knowledge of the characteristics and behavior of the rabies virus, but also a clearer concept of the prevention and treatment of the disease in man. An interesting footnote to this research was the discovery by the personnel of the laboratory that the paralytic disease of cattle in Mexico, called derriengue, is due to rabies transmitted by vampire bats which bite the cattle at night and suck their blood.

The influence of this novel rabies laboratory has been fairly extensive, and community control programs can now be based upon more adequate information.

Yaws. This is a dread disease which is widespread throughout the tropics. It is highly contagious, is contracted in childhood, and cripples and disfigures its victims. Although the causative agent is known, its epidemiology is not clearly understood. Over the years, the Foundation has carried on studies in this disease in Samoa, Puerto Rico, and Jamaica, combining laboratory research with extensive field surveys. As a result, an effective method of treatment has been developed, and the possibilities of controlling the disease have been satisfactorily demonstrated.

Schistosomiasis. A serious health problem in Egypt is schistosomiasis, a disease caused by the liver fluke, a small organism carried by certain species of snails living in the canals of irrigated lands. The research in this disease undertaken by the Foundation involved extensive study of snails and snail habits. Snails were grown under satisfactory conditions for examination, and untreated water from the Nile was employed in the laboratory in one aspect of the research. It was discovered that the only feasible method of reducing the incidence of the disease was by a vigorously conducted canal-clearance campaign. As a result, an economically practicable method was devised by which the waterways could be systematically cleaned in order to rid them of the offending animal.

III

Space is lacking in which to describe in any detail the ramifications of this attack on specific diseases. Scarlet fever, with Rumania as the principal center of field study; anemia in Puerto Rico; amoebic dysentery in Tennessee; undulant fever in France; oroya fever in Peru; syphilis in many countries with laboratory research centered at Johns Hopkins; dengue fever in Guam, Saipan, Samoa, Fiji, and the Marshall and Gilbert Islands; nutritional studies in Mexico, Canada, England, France, Spain, and in various parts of the United States—these are samples of the wide-ranging activities of the International Health Division over a quarter of a century.

Sometimes the results of the work were largely negative. In infective jaundice, for example, no susceptible laboratory animal could be found and the research was abandoned. In other instances, particularly in some of the virus diseases, progress lagged because it was dependent on an advance of knowledge which had not yet been made. But, by and large, it can be said with no danger of exaggeration that this global concept of the attack on disease not only introduced a new method and a new type of strategy, but added materially to the controls by which human ailments are progressively circumscribed.

During the quarter of a century since Rose relinquished his leadership of the International Health Division, the other projects which he set in motion have been vigorously expanded and developed. Around the world an investment has been made in men, ideas, buildings, and equipment. The education of doctors and scientists for public health work has been forwarded by liberal support of many postgraduate schools of hygiene of university grade; public health nurses have been trained on a global scale in institutions from Toronto and Johns Hopkins to Bangkok and Peking;* national and local health departments in sixty-eight countries have been strengthened with equipment and essential services. The work has been pioneering in spirit, sound in principle, and practical in purpose.

In recent years, under the leadership of Dr. George K. Strode, who succeeded Dr. Sawyer, the International Health Division has given attention to the problem of the economics and sociology of medical care. How can the burden of illness be equitably spread? Good health is as essential to the community as to the individual, and there should be no economic barrier to adequate medical services. No nation that values the worth built into its human population can continue to allow its citizens to die, or for that matter to be only half alive, solely because they are unable to pay for what modern medicine could give them. Public health is thus growing in its conception of responsibility. It is reaching the stature of a social science in the service of society, and has become an integral part of the social process. No organization working in this field can escape the impact of these new ques-

* The Foundation's interest in nursing goes back to 1914 when the China Medical Board began its work in the training of nurses. The interest has broadened and deepened over the years until now there are five countries in Asia, fourteen in Europe, and ten in the Americas, including Canada and the United States, which have been helped to attain higher standards in nursing, through grants from the Foundation. The Foundation's work in this field has been developed under the stimulating leadership of three able nurses: Miss F. Elizabeth Crowell, Miss Mary Beard, and Miss Mary Elizabeth Tennant.

tions, nor evade their significance in the broadening program of preventive medicine.

Effectiveness cannot be measured by money, and the amount of dollars spent in advancing the multifarious projects described in the preceding pages is by no means an indication of their merit. When we say that in the forty years following the creation of the Rockefeller Sanitary Commission, $94,000,000 was spent by that organization and its successor, the International Health Division of the Foundation, for public health around the world, we do not use the figure to gauge the results. It does give some indication, however, not only of the size of the operations but of the belief and confidence in this work of those who have guided the progress of these institutions.

CHAPTER V

THE CHALLENGE OF YELLOW FEVER

ON NO DISEASE IN THE LONG LIST OF HUMAN afflictions did The Rockefeller Foundation put greater emphasis or a larger proportion of time and financial support than on yellow fever. For over thirty years, beginning in 1915, this disease absorbed the concentrated attention of a large staff of doctors and scientists, working in Latin America and Africa, as well as in the laboratories in New York. The record of their activities is one of the dramatic installments in the developing saga of preventive medicine. It is the story of a long-sustained and far-flung campaign against a baffling enemy, who, more than once, masked his defense and struck back from unexpected quarters.

According to historical records, yellow fever first made its appearance in North America in 1668 when severe epidemics occurred in New York and Philadelphia. Thereafter, the disease was recorded from New Hampshire to Florida, as far west as Texas, and up the Mississippi River to St. Louis. Between the years 1668 and 1821, there were no less than twenty epidemics in Philadelphia, fifteen in New York, eight in Boston, and seven in Baltimore. The ravages continued during the nineteenth century; and as late as 1905, only five years before the Rockefeller Sanitary Commission began its work, yellow fever struck at New Orleans and slashed through the Southern states, with 5,000 cases of the disease and 1,000 deaths.

It is difficult to exaggerate the terror of these epidemics. The mortality rate was so high that burying parties frequently worked day and night disposing of the dead. People either fled to the country or shut themselves up in their homes. Friends avoided meeting in the streets and handshaking fell into disuse. Commerce was paralyzed and business came to a standstill. In Buffalo, during the Civil War, the rumor that Confederate sympathizers in Canada were sending across the Niagara River bundles of rags infected with yellow-fever germs caused a panic in which a substantial proportion of the population evacuated their homes. In some of the Southern cities, yellow fever was present almost continuously. In Charleston, South Carolina, deaths from the disease occurred practically every year in the nineteenth century, and there were frequent and violent epidemics in Galveston, New Orleans, and other Gulf ports. Mexico, Central and South America, and the West Indies were haunted by the disease, and it richly earned the title which it bore for three centuries: "The terror of the Western Hemisphere."

Not until the United States Army Commission under Major Walter Reed demonstrated in Cuba during the Spanish-American War that yellow fever is transmitted by mosquitoes and not by contact or by contaminated objects was any progress made in the control of the disease. The offending mosquito was identified as the *Stegomyia,* now known under the scientific name *Aëdes aegypti,* and popularly designated as the aegypti. When General W. C. Gorgas, the Chief Sanitary Officer of the United States Army in Cuba, made quick use of Reed's discovery, and by vigorous antimosquito measures in Havana caused yellow fever to disappear as if by magic, the first battle in the conquest of the disease had been brilliantly won. Three years later, by applying similar measures in Panama, Gorgas made possible the building of the Panama Canal.

When Wickliffe Rose returned from his hookworm trip to Malaya and the Philippines in 1914, he told Gorgas of the serious apprehension in the Far East over the possibility that yellow fever might be introduced into that area as a result of the opening of the Panama Canal, which was then nearly completed. Gorgas showed keen interest, and expressed the opinion that yellow fever could be "eradicated from the face of the earth within a reasonable time and at a reasonable cost,"[1] and that the Foundation could not undertake a more rewarding activity. The Foundation thereupon created a yellow-fever commission, under the chairmanship of General Gorgas, and in 1916 this commission visited suspected endemic centers in Ecuador, Peru, Colombia, Venezuela, and Brazil.

To appreciate the developments over the next decade, it is necessary to understand two assumptions which underlay the approach of the Gorgas commission to yellow fever. The first was based on Walter Reed's conclusion, which, because it had been proved in Cuba and Panama, was accepted without question: that the sole carrier of the disease was the aegypti mosquito. This mosquito is distinctly domestic in its habits. It breeds almost exclusively in and around houses, and has practically never been found in swamps, rivers, lakes, and other places where malaria mosquitoes usually breed. Consequently, the belief developed that yellow fever was largely an urban disease, depending for its maintenance upon the simple cycle, man-mosquito-man, and was spread from one point to another, either by the movement of the human host during the period of incubation, or by the accidental transportation of the infected mosquito from place to place. The second assumption—the so-called key-center theory which Gorgas and his scientific colleagues strongly held—was that endemic centers of yellow fever are the seed beds without which there can be no epidemics. If the seed beds are destroyed, the disease will disappear from all other points.

If these two assumptions had been wholly true, the story of the conquest of the disease would have taken a far different course. Unfortunately, the epidemiology of yellow fever turned out to be infinitely more complex than these simple assumptions indicated, with the result that a decade later, when the disease seemed to be almost under control if not eradicated, it suddenly struck back with savage fury.

Gorgas' commission returned from South America with the conclusion that the only endemic center existing at the time was Guayaquil in Ecuador. The commission's report contained three recommendations: to eliminate the infection from Guayaquil; to keep under observation the east coast of Brazil and the southern littoral of the Caribbean and to undertake intensive work to control yellow fever at any point in the area where it might be discovered; and finally, to extend the investigation to Mexico and West Africa, "which regions are under suspicion but have not yet been examined."[2]

II

The years that followed were years of intense activity and what seemed at first to be complete success. Gorgas was made director of the Foundation's work for the eradication of yellow fever—the word "eradication" being indicative of the high expectations of the moment —and in notifying him of his appointment the Foundation expressed the hope that it would be his privilege to write the last chapter in the history of the disease.[3] By the use of the same methods which had been employed in Havana and in Panama, Guayaquil, where for generations yellow fever had been rampant, was cleared of the disease. A staff of 125 men, working in 25 squads, rid the city of the aegypti mosquito. They screened the water-storage tanks, cleaned out the roof gutters, and cleared the courtyards and surroundings of the houses of cans, buckets, and other containers where the mosquito could breed. They drained, ditched, and oiled, and resorted to such ingenious devices as using fish to devour mosquito larvae in water barrels. In 1918, there had been 460 cases of yellow fever in Guayaquil; in May, 1919, six months after the control work began, the last case of the disease was recorded, and in the years that have followed there has been no recognized case of yellow fever in all of Ecuador. The key-center hypothesis seemed to be justified.

Thereafter, proceeding on the same theories and utilizing the same techniques, intensive campaigns were inaugurated in Mexico, Guatemala, Honduras, Salvador, Nicaragua, Peru, Colombia, and Brazil. In every case, the method used was to prevent the breeding of aegypti mosquitoes in the key-center communities. The results in the principal coastal cities were as completely successful as they had been in Guayaquil, but contrary to expectations, the disease continued to appear spasmodically in some neighboring communities and even in interior towns.

However, good news seemed to be at hand. Dr. Hideyo Noguchi, the distinguished scientist from the Rockefeller Institute, who had been a member of the earlier commission to Ecuador, isolated from the blood of six out of twenty-seven reported yellow-fever patients a spirochete which produced in guinea pigs lesions suggestive of yellow fever. To this he gave the name *Leptospira icteroides* ("slim spiral, the jaundice resembler"), and after prolonged study he came to the conclusion that it was the cause of yellow fever, in spite of the fact that, years before, Reed had traced the cause to a filterable virus. Noguchi prepared a vaccine and an immune serum, both of which were effective in animals experimentally infected with *Leptospira icteroides,* and both were thereafter frequently reported, in publications of The Rockefeller Foundation and elsewhere, as effective in the prevention and cure, respectively, of yellow fever in man.

But Noguchi was mistaken. He had not discovered the germ of yellow fever. Instead, he had isolated the germ of Weil's disease, or infectious jaundice, either erroneously diagnosed as yellow fever, or concomitant with yellow fever.

If this seems like a harsh comment, it must be remembered that earlier workers were groping in the dark, without the knowledge which later laboratory research has given us. There were—and still are—many missing pieces in the picture puzzle. For one thing, it was difficult to find experimental animals susceptible to yellow fever. It was not until the rhesus monkey was imported from India that satisfactory results could be obtained; and it was three years later before it was discovered that white mice, infinitely more convenient for laboratory purposes, could be used. In the second place, yellow fever presented great difficulties in the way of accurate diagnosis. It was this situation which led Noguchi astray. Since his tragic death in Africa, while working on the problem of yellow fever, laboratory research has provided techniques hitherto unknown. Prominent among them is viscerotomy—or liver examination—by which the disease can now be diagnosed with great accuracy in cases which have proved fatal. Another technique contributed by the Foundation's laboratory is the so-called mouse protection test. By testing the blood of individuals for its power to protect mice against injections of yellow-fever virus, it is possible to tell whether those individuals ever had the disease. One of the American soldiers who voluntarily exposed himself to yellow fever in Walter Reed's experiments in Cuba after the Spanish-American War contributed blood which protected mice against the disease thirty years after the soldier's illness. It is now possible, therefore, to chart the geographical distribution of yellow fever, and discover where it has been.

But these tools were in the future, and the hypotheses with which the campaign had started seemed to be working well. General Gorgas in 1920 had led an expedition to West Africa to determine the relationship of yellow fever in that continent to the disease in the Western Hemisphere. He died en route, but the expedition continued, and four months later submitted a report to the effect that while no authentic cases had been seen, there was strong indication of the presence of the infection in recent years.

In 1925, a second commission was sent to West Africa for a prolonged period of study. Yellow fever in the Americas was apparently rapidly diminishing and seemed to be sufficiently under control to permit the release of experimental personnel and adequate funds for the undertaking in Africa. By the end of the year, the commission was well-established in Lagos, Nigeria, with a staff of eight people, a thoroughly equipped laboratory, and five buildings brought from New York. Extensive studies were begun not only of the symptoms and pathology of yellow fever in natives and Europeans, but of the habits and distribution of the aegypti mosquito. It was shown that the African disease was identical with the disease in Latin America, thus clearing up the troublesome question whether or not the Old World yellow fever and the New World fever were the same. It was shown, too, that the aegypti mosquito was present in Africa in such numbers that the disease could easily be transmitted as it was transmitted in the Western Hemisphere. It was in Lagos that substantial advances were made in laboratory techniques, including the use of the rhesus monkey as a satisfactory experimental animal. It was here, too, that tragedy struck, and four of the scientists on the commission died of the disease whose secrets they were attempting to discover. Dr. Howard B. Cross of the Foundation's staff had already died of yellow fever in the campaign in Mexico, and the fatal infection of Dr. Paul Lewis in Brazil lay some years ahead. In the African laboratories, on the edge of the jungle, the four gallant men who gave their lives in what Pasteur called "the peaceful strife of science" were Dr. Noguchi, Dr. Adrian Stokes, Dr. William Alexander Young, and Dr. Theodore B. Hayne. When Dr. Stokes realized that he had been stricken through some unsuspected laboratory exposure, he insisted that mosquitoes be fed on him so that the disease could be passed in the natural way from a typical human case to rhesus monkeys, thus proving beyond any doubt that the experimental disease in monkeys was true yellow fever. As this generation looks back on the progress that has been made over the years in increasing our knowledge of yellow fever, and arming us with tools to control it, it can truly be said that these men did not die in vain.

Meanwhile, in Central and South America, progress in the control of the disease seemed to be completely reassuring. The reports of The Rockefeller Foundation prior to 1929 expressed the belief not only that yellow fever was fast disappearing as a human menace but that it had been practically eliminated. Indeed, in 1925, only three cases of yellow fever were reported from the entire Western Hemisphere. In the eleven months following April, 1927, no cases were reported, and it was assumed that the battle, which had cost the lives of research workers and millions of dollars, was practically won. "The disease seems almost banished from the Western World," wrote Dr. Vincent in his President's Review of 1927. Then, almost without warning, yellow fever erupted from its hidden and hitherto unknown home in the jungle of South America, and struck for the coastal cities. Rio de Janeiro, which had been free of the disease for twenty years, had an epidemic in 1928 with 144 cases, and a mortality rate in excess of 50 per cent. Other epidemics of undetermined numbers were reported from the hinterland, forcing a re-examination of the hypotheses which had been so carefully developed over the years, and a complete overhauling of the epidemiological concepts behind the campaign.

III

From the perspective of the present it is easy to see the oversimplification of the earlier underlying assumptions. In the first place, Walter Reed's idea that the aegypti mosquito is the sole carrier of the disease was based on inadequate information. The aegypti is perhaps the principal carrier, but there are other carriers, too, and yellow fever can occur, and frequently does occur, in areas where there are no aegypti mosquitoes. In earlier days, this was considered an impossibility. Indeed, in 1916, General Gorgas in his survey of Muzo, Colombia, where yellow fever had been reported, declared that the disease did not exist and had not recently been present because no aegypti mosquitoes or their larvae could be found—and this in the face of the fact that five cases with two deaths had been reported as yellow fever within the year, and that locally there was a general belief that the disease existed permanently in the region. This belief has since been adequately substantiated.

In the second place, the key-center theory that the destruction of a few so-called "seed beds" would cause yellow fever to disappear became untenable as the research of the ensuing years proved that the disease had a permanent home in the tropical forests of the vast hinterland of South America and Africa. Existing under these conditions, it is called "jungle yellow fever," but it is the same disease as that carried by aegypti mosquitoes in urban communities. The damage to the liver is identical, and the virus when inoculated into mice or monkeys gives the same results as the urban virus. A person infected in the jungle may, when entering a community where there is heavy aegypti breeding, serve as a source of infection for the mosquitoes, and thus initiate an epidemic of yellow fever of the classical urban type.

Although the clinical picture of yellow fever is the same whether the infection develops in the town or in the jungle, the epidemiology of the two types is quite different. Aegypti-transmitted yellow fever is generally acquired indoors; it tends to involve all nonimmunes of all ages living in infected houses. Jungle yellow fever, on the other hand, is usually acquired in or at the edges of the forest during working hours by those whose occupation takes them to the woods. It does not tend, in the absence of aegypti, to involve other members of the household living under the same roof with infective cases.

This new knowledge did not come all at once. It took almost twenty years of research to develop it, and the work is still continuing, because there are many questions as yet unanswered. During this period, The Rockefeller Foundation had three laboratories working on the problem—one in New York, one in West Africa, and one in Bahia, Brazil. Research posts were established in seven localities, four of them in South America and three in Africa. The main South American posts were at Rio de Janeiro and Bogotá, with substations at Ilhéus in Brazil and Villavicencio in Colombia. The African work stretched across the continent from Lagos in Nigeria to Entebbe in Uganda, with an additional field station in Bwamba Forest in Western Uganda. Field expeditions also constituted an important instrument in the intensified research.

As a result of the fresh knowledge which this wide-flung effort has developed, the old cycle of man-mosquito-man in the transmission of the disease has had to be modified. While this is still the pattern under urban conditions, in the jungle the infection spreads without relation to routes of human travel, indeed, it may be said, without relation to men. It was obvious, therefore, that the disease was transmitted by unknown carriers and through hosts other than man.

As a first step, all available forms of insect life in the jungle, whether blood-sucking or otherwise, were collected, divided into broad groups such as mosquitoes, ticks, etc., and then ground, centrifuged, and filtered. The filtrates were inoculated into white mice and rhesus monkeys. By these methods, the presence of yellow-fever virus was demonstrated in several species of mosquitoes—notably the *sabethine, Aëdes lencocelaenus,* and *Haemagogus* in South America, and the *Aëdes africanus* and *Aëdes simpsoni* in Africa. In spite of repeated attempts to isolate the virus from many classes of insects, no virus has been found in any form of insect life other than mosquitoes.

The next step was to determine the susceptibility of jungle animals to yellow-fever virus. In Villavicencio alone, located in an endemic yellow-fever region, more than 2,000 animals were trapped, ranging all the way from mice to wildcats, and from birds to snakes and other reptiles. Each was tested to see whether it had acquired immunity to yellow fever, or, if not, whether it responded to inoculation with the virus. Two species only showed positive results—the monkey and the opossum. That is, antibodies against yellow fever were found in the blood streams of these two species—evidence that at some time in the past they had had the disease. At Ilhéus, a sick monkey, a marmoset, was trapped, and in its blood stream was discovered not antibodies, but the active virus of yellow fever. The animal soon died, and exhaustive laboratory tests showed conclusively that it had died of yellow fever. Similarly at the stations in East Africa, much supporting evidence has been found to substantiate the belief that monkeys, whose population in this area is estimated at 400 per square mile, are the principal hosts of yellow fever. The species of monkey peculiarly susceptible is the redtail, and the mosquito vector is the *Aëdes africanus,* which lives in trees and at night bites the redtail as he sleeps there. The redtail is a notorious raider of banana gardens, where he is bitten by another mosquito, the *Aëdes simpsoni*. Contaminated originally by the *africanus* mosquito, the monkey in turn contaminates the *simpsoni* mosquito, which in its turn relays yellow fever to the human victim.

The result of all these investigations seems to justify the generalization that yellow fever is primarily a disease of jungle animals, transmitted by jungle mosquitoes. The classical form, involving transmission from man to man by the aegypti mosquito, is more of a secondary cycle depending largely upon conditions of population concentration and of mosquito breeding created by man himself. However, the existence of a vast permanent reservoir of infection in the jungle, which has no relationship to aegypti mosquitoes, paradoxically increases the necessity of anti-aegypti control measures in cities and towns. The new discoveries do not minimize the significant part which this classical mosquito plays in the distribution of the disease among human beings. It is not too much to assert that if in urban areas this insect were brought under control as it has been in Brazil, the world could avoid the threat which in these days of fast transit might so easily develop into a cataclysm in India, and even in the Orient, should the virus of yellow fever break through the barriers of quarantine and medical vigilance.

IV

In all this work in yellow fever carried on by The Rockefeller Foundation, the high point was the development of a vaccine by which people can now be protected against the disease as successfully as they are protected against smallpox or typhoid. Worked out in the New York laboratories of the Foundation by Dr. Wilbur A. Sawyer and his associates, it has become the outstanding weapon in the fight against yellow fever. Sheer necessity was the spur in this development. The deaths and illnesses of the early laboratory workers and the apparent impossibility of applying the ordinary techniques of mosquito control to jungle yellow fever made it imperative to try to find a method of immunization, although the hazard of the attempt was all too clear. It is significant that during the years that this study was under way, Dr. Sawyer himself and six of his associates contracted the disease in the laboratory, despite the adoption of every conceivable precaution. So great was the anxiety of Dr. Russell, the director of the International Health Board, that more than once he came close to ordering the discontinuance of the work.

The vaccination project progressed in three stages. In the first stage, a living virus, derived from a strain first transferred from man to monkey and thence to mice, was employed with immune human serum. This form of vaccination accomplished its immediate purpose of preventing further cases of the disease among investigators, both in the field and in the laboratory, but it was not practicable for large-scale use in yellow-fever control. In the second stage, people were vaccinated with a virus strain cultivated in tissue culture. This strain, however, was not sufficiently reduced in virulence to permit its use without immune serum. The third and final stage involved the development of a modified virus strain of exceedingly low virulence which could be used without any immune serum whatever. This was the famous virus known scientifically as 17D, and from this single strain practically all vaccines for yellow fever now employed around the world have been derived, although the French neurotropic strain has been used extensively in French Africa.

Starting in 1937, the laboratories of the International Health Division of The Rockefeller Foundation began the production on a large scale of the new vaccine. By the end of the year, 40,000 people in Brazil and Colombia had been successfully vaccinated, including the international flight personnel of the aviation companies. The following year, a million more were vaccinated. Postvaccination tests during this period proved that more than 90 per cent of those vaccinated had developed demonstrable immunity. When the war broke out, the demand for the vaccine was so great that the Foundation had to double both its laboratory space and the number of its technicians. The armed forces of America, Great Britain, and many of their allies were vaccinated for yellow fever, and the soldiers, sailors, and airmen deployed in endemic areas in Africa and Latin America were thus fully protected from the disease. Indeed, it is doubtful whether without this protection military contingents could have been detailed to certain sectors which they occupied. Experience in endemic centers of yellow fever over many decades proves that this disease can upset the best-planned military operations. From 1942 to 1946, approximately 34,000,000 doses of vaccine were manufactured and distributed without cost to governments, health agencies, and other official units. At the end of this period, the Foundation discontinued its operations in this field; the demonstration had been successfully made, and the responsibility for future manufacture and distribution was passed on to the United States Public Health Service, government agencies in Brazil and Colombia, and other institutes in England, South Africa, and India.

The significance of this new weapon against yellow fever can hardly be overestimated. The whole approach to the disease is now built around it, just as the approach to typhoid or diphtheria begins with individual immunization. The fact that it was the culmination of years of planned research, directed toward a single goal, surrounds the entire achievement with high distinction.

Three footnotes to the vaccination project perhaps deserve attention. The first relates to an outbreak of jaundice early in the war among the armed forces, an outbreak which appeared to be associated with certain definite lots of the yellow-fever vaccine. In the preceding years a total of nearly eight million vaccinations had been successfully administered without any disturbing consequences whatever. Army and navy experts joined The Rockefeller Foundation staff in intensive research of this unanticipated difficulty, and the result showed that the jaundice was due to a virus contained in the human-blood component employed in making the vaccine. Oddly enough, at the same time, cases of jaundice were appearing among British and Russian troops, following the administration of vaccines or serums which were manufactured in those countries for measles and mumps and which also contained a human-blood component. The discovery opened up medical problems which have not yet been fully solved, but a method was evolved by which the yellow-fever vaccine could be successfully made without the use of human serum, and the risk of jaundice was definitely eliminated. During the brief period of its existence, this jaundice earned the nickname among the troops of "Rockefeller's disease."

The second footnote is the curious fact that the scientists in the

Foundation laboratory have never been able successfully to repeat the long series of tissue cultures which culminated in the 17D virus strain. Somewhere in the chain of subcultures an unknown mutation occurred which has thus far defied duplication. A humorist in the Foundation has suggested that perhaps during the course of the protracted research a steamboat whistled in the East River, thus causing a precipitation in a test tube which cannot now be reproduced. The matter has no practical importance because the 17D virus strain can be indefinitely multiplied, and material for successful vaccination will always be available. It is, however, an interesting sidelight on the baffling intricacies of scientific research.

The third footnote is a matter of symbolic interest. It has to do with the fact that the 17D strain of virus goes back to a blood specimen taken in 1927 in West Africa from a black native named Asibi who was sick with yellow fever. This specimen was inoculated into a rhesus monkey which had just been received from India. Asibi recovered, but the monkey died of the disease. Practically all the vaccine manufactured since 1937, both by The Rockefeller Foundation and by governmental and other agencies as well, derives from the original strain of virus obtained from this humble native. Carried down to the present day from one laboratory animal to another, through repeated tissue cultures and by enormous multiplication, it has afforded immunity from yellow fever to millions of people in many countries. Through the creative imagination of science, the blood of one man in West Africa has been made to serve the whole human race.

V

The hope of General Gorgas that he could have the privilege of writing the last chapter in the history of yellow fever was not fulfilled. Problems which he and his associates did not dream of still remain to be solved, and continuing research is necessary to overcome the limitations of existing knowledge. For example, at least two aspects of the epidemiology of jungle yellow fever require further clarification: first, a more accurate delineation of the forested areas in both Central and South America and in Africa where yellow-fever virus may exist; and second, additional information on the persistence of the virus in forests during the periods when the known mosquito vectors are very scarce. It may also be added that, as with many other virus diseases, there is no effective treatment for yellow fever after symptoms have appeared. The work of the Foundation has been concerned with prevention rather than with cure.

But as a result of the undiscouraged activities of the last three decades, yellow fever has been pushed back to a position of secondary importance. It is still a potential menace, capable of violent outbreak, but there are techniques at hand today by which it can far more readily be brought under control. When yellow fever broke out in Panama in 1948, impressive measures were marshaled for its suppression. Two hundred and fifty thousand doses of vaccine were flown by airplane from the United States and Brazilian government laboratories, and trained personnel was immediately dispatched from half a dozen countries. Within a short time, 150,000 persons in the danger area were vaccinated, and control measures that had been tested over the years were instituted. As a result, the fire was stamped out before it had time to spread, whereas a generation or more ago it might easily have been a catastrophic disaster.

In this development, the work of The Rockefeller Foundation has been of outstanding significance. It has broadened the area of knowledge in relation to the disease. It has added fundamental techniques of control. Its staff of experts has carried on research in the two great endemic areas, from Senegal in West Africa to the upper reaches of the Nile, and from the Amazon valley in South America, north to the Rio Grande and south to the Argentine. Through its fellowship system it has trained men all over the world who now occupy positions of leadership in the campaign. It has created permanent yellow-fever institutes at strategic points in the endemic regions. If the function of a privately endowed foundation in the field of health is to blaze a trail, to try out techniques, to experiment with fresh methods, to pass back to the permanent authorities of the state the new ideas that are captured, then The Rockefeller Foundation has lived up to its standards in meeting the challenge of yellow fever.

CHAPTER VI

INVASION FROM AFRICA

IF ORSON WELLES IN HIS FAMOUS BROADCAST had announced, not that the Martians had landed in New Jersey, but that a certain mosquito from Africa had arrived on the American continent, there would have been no public alarm. Indeed, it is doubtful if there would have been any public interest. But the mosquito *Anopheles gambiae* is potentially a much more dangerous invader than the Martians would have been. H. G. Wells' Martians, it will be remembered, were unable to adjust themselves to life on this planet and quickly died. But when this mosquito invaded Brazil from Equatorial Africa in 1930, it proceeded to make itself very much at home.

Who was this new invader of the Western Hemisphere and how did it get here? Anopheles mosquitoes are malaria carriers; the *Anopheles gambiae* is the most dangerous member of a dangerous family. Although the species has hitherto been reported from Algeria and Morocco, and from Southern Arabia as well, its principal home is the African tropical belt, extending from the southern border of the Sahara Desert south to the Zambesi River. It is the scourge of Central Africa, a carrier of a serious and often fatal type of malaria, sometimes complicated by the so-called "black-water" fever.

A mosquito cannot fly across the Atlantic Ocean, and until 1930 this insect had never been seen in the Western Hemisphere. In that year, however, or shortly before, it crossed the ocean. It did not invade like an army; a single fertilized female may have been the cause of all the misery that followed. This tiny enemy alien was able to enter America because of modern methods of rapid intercontinental travel. An airplane, perhaps, which a few hours before had left West Africa, landed on the coast of Brazil, and when its door was opened the unwanted immigrant flew forth undetected, to begin the colonization of a new continent. Far more likely, the stowaway took passage on one of the fast destroyers which at that time were working in connection with the air lines between Dakar in West Africa and Natal in Brazil, and drifted to shore from the deck of the anchored vessel.

It was Dr. Raymond C. Shannon, an entomologist on the staff of The Rockefeller Foundation's yellow-fever service, who in 1930 first discovered the insect. On a Sunday morning in Natal, with idle time on his hands, he took a busman's holiday and went out to catch mosquitoes. Dipping his net in a shallow pool near the railroad station, he dredged up a number of them, which in routine fashion he placed in a bottle for later examination. Although he had never personally seen a gambiae mosquito, his examination convinced him that one of the mosquitoes in the morning's catch belonged unmistakably to that species, and knowing the danger that was involved, he reported his finding to the New York office by cablegram.

The cablegram caused consternation, but it was hoped that the invasion might be localized by natural conditions unfriendly to the invader. These hopes were disappointed. In 1930 and 1931, an outbreak of malaria occurred in the vicinity of Natal whose severity was unprecedented in the annals of the city.

By 1931, gambiae mosquitoes, following prevailing winds, had traveled up the coast 115 miles. The great drought of 1932 and 1933 seemed to check the invasion, and several years passed without further startling evidence of its presence. Then, with the return of normal rainfall, the onward flight started again. It crept slowly up the coastal plain at an average speed of about forty miles a year, and it is likely that the insect was often carried by boats from point to point along the shore. The interior of the State of Rio Grande do Norte in this section is extremely arid at all times and the mosquito failed to penetrate it; while the flat alluvial shelf, along which it succeeded in breeding its way, is in several places so narrow that fifteen or twenty men could have stopped the progress of gambiae at any time during these early years, had the geographical direction and goal of the insect been understood.

That gambiae did not spread southward from Natal during these first years was a piece of good fortune not easy to explain. It is true that the prevailing winds are in the opposite direction, but the mosquito might have made progress against the wind in cars, boats, and trains.

By 1937, the invader had reached the well-populated valleys to the northwest and calamitous epidemics followed in 1938 in localities two hundred miles from Natal. In the Jaguaribe Valley alone, over 50,000 cases of malaria developed during the year. Ninety per cent of the population was affected, with mortality in certain districts estimated at 10 per cent. So disabling and widespread was the epidemic that, in some places, crops were not planted and salt production was greatly reduced because of lack of labor. It was estimated that as a result of the ravages of this mosquito, nearly every person in these affected areas would be on government relief in 1939. Consternation spread not only in Brazil but in Latin and North America. Public health men knew all too well the hazard involved in the possibility of gambiae continuing its invasion and striking into new territory in an irresistible march. Dr. M. A. Barber, the distinguished American malariologist, expressed the alarm in these words: "This invasion threatens the Americas with a catastrophe in comparison with which ordinary pestilence, conflagration and even war are but small and temporary calamities. Gambiae literally enters into the very veins of a country and may remain to plague it for centuries. Even the penetration of yellow fever into the Orient might be a lesser evil."[1]

II

Dr. Vincent, the former president of the Foundation, in one of his early reports made this interesting observation: "It has been said that a good malaria fighter must learn to think like a mosquito. He must ask: Which of many kinds of anopheline mosquitoes shall I try to imagine myself to be? How far is it possible to fly? When and where is food to be had? Which blood is to be preferred, human or animal? How can one get into a screened house? Where shall one rest after a good meal? Where is the best place to deposit eggs? Is the water of the right kind and temperature? Is it stagnant or flowing? Is there vegetable growth to protect eggs and larvae from fish?"[2]

Fortunately, through the work of malariologists in Africa, much was known about the gambiae. It breeds prolifically and rapidly, requiring only seven or eight days to develop from egg to adult, a fact that makes breeding possible in very temporary water collections. It has variable breeding habits, but seems to prefer stagnant, sunlit water. It has a high infection rate. During the outbreak in the city of Natal in 1930, almost two-thirds of the 172 specimens of gambiae caught and dissected were found to be infected with malaria, a rate higher than anything hitherto known in the Americas. This mosquito seems to prefer human to animal blood; of over a thousand specimens tested in 1931, 82 per cent contained human blood. It is a domesticated insect; it usually bites indoors, not outdoors; fairly reliable flight records show that it can cover a distance of four and a half miles.

Late in 1938, representatives of the Brazilian health service and The Rockefeller Foundation staff investigated the infected area in North Brazil. They visited São Gonçalo and Baixa Verde, both of which had heavy outbreaks of malaria following the introduction of gambiae to the region. They also went up the Jaguaribe River to Lavras. This visit confirmed the seriousness of the situation. Once the gambiae gets into a river valley, it spreads up the valley unless blocked at some point by natural or artificial barriers.

With the assistance of The Rockefeller Foundation an antigambiae service was organized. Since the necessary expenditures were far beyond the resources of the areas invaded, the national government of Brazil together with the Foundation assumed the financial responsibility. The Malaria Service of the North East (of Brazil) was created by government decree and began the task of organizing a field force. Dr. Fred L. Soper, representative of the Foundation in Brazil, was placed in charge of the direction and administration of the offensive; Dr. D. B. Wilson, also of The Rockefeller Foundation, was his chief associate; and a staff of over two thousand doctors, technicians, scouts, inspectors, guards, and laborers recruited from Brazil was enlisted in the campaign.

This affiliation between government and a private agency made available the wide experience of a well-trained group of men accustomed to working under discipline. Except for the distribution of quinine and atabrin by field personnel working in infested districts, the Malaria Service did not assume responsibility for medical care of the sick in dispensaries or otherwise. The purpose of the service was to confine the gambiae to the relatively arid areas it occupied, and if possible to exterminate it there. It was realized that, if the mosquito broke through to the well-watered Parnahyba and São Francisco River valleys, further efforts to prevent its spread to a large part of South, Central, and perhaps even North America might be unavailing. The Parnahyba Valley is five hundred miles from Natal; the gambiae mosquitoes were already nearly halfway there.

The organization of the counterattack necessarily involved a period of delay, but the interval was utilized by the Foundation's representatives in scouting the terrain of the approaching battle. The mosquito was still rapidly on the march, and had now spread over three hundred miles to the west and had infested an area of 12,000 square miles.

The first results in the 1939 campaign were frankly disappointing. The organization of the Malaria Service of the North East coincided with the beginning of the rainy season, during which the gambiae naturally makes its maximum progress, and apparent results were not forthcoming. Widespread epidemics of malaria kept occurring, and in the early months of the Service some 114,000 persons were treated for the disease. During this discouraging period, the only tangible consequence of the broad effort was a lowering of mortality from malaria through medication of acute cases. The rainy season that year was unusually prolonged, but by July appreciable results began to appear. The further spread of gambiae in the frontier districts seemed to be minimized, and the incidence of the mosquito was reduced in certain heavily infested sections to a point where careful surveys repeatedly failed to reveal the presence of either larvae or adults.

The campaign was revealing that both climate and physical geography were indispensable allies. Gambiae is a mosquito which breeds mainly in residual rain-water pools, shallow, open to the sun, and without vegetation. Generally speaking, it does not lay its eggs in permanent or deep water, in running, salty, or shaded water, or in water supporting aquatic vegetation. On the other hand, it takes advantage of every little depression in the ground, such as wheel tracks or hoofprints, no matter how shallow or small, which can present a water surface for eight or nine days. During the four months' rainy season, from February through May, with its almost daily showers, gambiae becomes a formidable antagonist. But for eight months of the year, the heat of the tropical sun, the strong, continuous trade winds, and the low humidity combine to dry up all shallow surface waters and to make life precarious and of short duration for the gambiae. Potential breeding places are reduced to disconnected pools in the beds of the large rivers, none of which maintains a flow in summer. Most of the higher rolling country back from the coast is practically noninfectible by gambiae. Its arid, stony soil supports a scrub vegetation composed of a resistant, thorny bush mingled with cactus. The region is without water for larvae, and without shelter for gambiae adults.

III

The strategy of the campaign was like the strategy of the Battle of the Bulge. The enemy had first to be contained within the area he had seized, and then surrounded and annihilated. The process of containment involved the establishment of an outside line, defined by fumigation posts on all the outgoing roads. Every automobile and train leaving the infested area had to be stopped, inspected, and fumigated. A maritime service was organized at points along the coast to disinfect every boat or plane bound for clean ports. In addition, a ten-mile zone, beyond the gambiae's farthest limit of advance, was kept noninfectible, which from the mosquito's point of view represented the "scorched earth" policy. Within this zone, as well as within the area already infested, all breeding places of the mosquito were treated with Paris green. The most critical parts of the region were mapped from the air so that no pools, ponds, or other collections of water would be overlooked. The adult mosquitoes were sought and killed in houses with insecticide sprays to diminish the chances of their laying eggs and thus perpetuating the species in the region. It was a war in a very real and grim sense. Unlike other types of war, its purpose was the preservation of human life.

By December, 1939, the invader had been pushed back to its central strongholds in the main river valleys and on the narrow coastal shelf. If it could be held within those limits during the wet season of 1940, those in charge of the campaign began to hope that it might eventually be eradicated from the entire region. This, of course, would mean extermination of the last surviving pair. And as in all campaigns, accidents might determine the issue. Thus, in one case, the mosquito was transported many miles into previously uninfected territory in an old automobile which followed an improvised wagon road through the jungle and thus avoided the fumigation post on the main thoroughfare. In another case, the defense line was broken when in an unguarded moment a small fishing boat carried the mosquito up the coast. If the war was to be won, it was realized that victory would come only through continued vigilance. The wet season of 1940 would be the test.

That the test was successfully met, with dramatic results beyond expectation, was due to the *esprit de corps* and effective striking power of Dr. Soper's army. During the critical wet season, the mosquito was pushed back on all sides, so that by the beginning of the dry season it had been practically restricted to the lower

Jaguaribe Valley. This made possible the concentration in this area of a large number of workers for the final onslaught beginning in July. By the end of the year it was possible to report that no larvae or adults had been found in the lower Jaguaribe Valley since the first week in September. A small additional focus lying some thirty-five or forty miles beyond the known infested area was discovered in October, but it yielded to attack and was apparently clean by the middle of November. During the last forty-seven days of 1940, no evidence of gambiae was found in all Brazil. Even in areas of earlier infestation where control measures had been progressively discontinued, there was no sign of the mosquito. In the Icó field laboratory alone, microscopic examination of some two million anopheline larvae, collected during the last eight months of 1940 from areas where control measures had been suspended, failed to reveal any evidence of surviving gambiae infestation.

The critical phase of the campaign was over. Certain mopping-up operations might be necessary, but the battle had been won. The invader had brought death and suffering to thousands of people; it had laid waste an entire section of a nation; its defeat had involved immense effort and the expenditure of over two million dollars. But the Western Hemisphere was free—at least for the moment.

The price of freedom is eternal vigilance, whether the threat is mosquitoes or the evil intentions of men. Airplanes are crossing the South Atlantic with increasing frequency. Three years after the original incursion of the gambiae had been stamped out in Brazil, mosquitoes of this species were found on a plane coming from Accra and Dakar in Africa to Natal. Even more disturbing was the news that five live gambiae had been discovered in dwellings near the Natal airport. Incoming planes from Africa are, of course, fumigated before they leave Africa and before they land in Brazil, but a few mosquitoes were evidently able to stow away safely in the modern, complicated airplanes.

Thanks to the efforts of the Brazilian authorities, the immediate situation is now in hand. But it poses a problem of larger significance which cannot be evaded. Around the ports of Africa and deep within the hinterland lie the breeding centers of the gambiae. The safety of the Western Hemisphere, which is now within a few hours' flight across a narrow ocean, can no longer be left to the uncertainties of a spray-gun campaign. Modern airplane travel has made old methods and ideas of quarantine completely obsolete. If the Americas are adequately and permanently to be protected, the breeding of gambiae, wherever in Africa or elsewhere it may occur, must be eradicated. The campaign must be carried to the sources of infestation. It can no longer be defensive; it must be offensive.

IV

This story has a sequel. In 1942, the gambiae started on another invasion from its home in Africa—this time in a different direction. It struck north through the Nile Valley in Upper Egypt, pushing its attack to within two hundred miles of Cairo, and causing in this and in the following year the most serious epidemic of malaria recorded in Egyptian history. In 1944, a committee of investigation appointed by King Farouk reported that 135,000 people in the infested area had died of this gambiae-transmitted disease. The military battle of North Africa was still at its height, and the matter had to be handled with the utmost secrecy.

A few months later, the Egyptian Government requested the assistance of The Rockefeller Foundation, and a plan of campaign was developed under which the Government financed the entire cost of the project, while the Foundation assumed the responsibility for its direction. The Ministry of Health already had at its disposal, in its mosquito-control organization, an army of more than four thousand men, and this group was made available to Dr. Soper and his associates on the Foundation staff, who had been in charge of the campaign in Brazil. The Egyptian Government also provided insecticides, headquarters, field stations, and extra funds for emergency needs.

The plan of campaign followed the Brazilian experience and involved the extermination of the gambiae in the infested area. There is no such thing as partial success in species eradication. Estimates of progress based on the traditional methods of the malariologist, such as spleen rates, blood parasite rates, clinical attack rates, infant infection rates, become invalid and subordinated to the simple question: Is the species under attack still present in the area being worked? This was the test in both the Brazilian and the Egyptian campaigns, and it was pushed to its logical conclusion, i.e., the extermination of the last surviving pair of the disease-carrying mosquitoes.

In Egypt, as in Brazil, Paris green was the principal insecticide, and it was applied in the marshy regions, water holes, and other potential breeding places, following the technique used in Brazil.

Pyrethrum was also used, and half a ton of DDT was employed in the spray-painting of railroad cars, automobiles, and river boats that might serve to harbor and transport the insects from one region to another. An elaborate control and inspection system was developed to confine the gambiae within the area occupied and then to exterminate it in house-to-house warfare.

By February, 1945, the gambiae had completely disappeared from the infested area. Careful search failed to discover any of this species, even during the autumn floods when pools and other breeding places multiply and the worst epidemics are apt to occur. The danger was over, and for the moment at least this public health battle had been won.

Thus in two countries a demonstration was made of what modern public health practices can accomplish not only in repelling the carriers of disease, but in creating a rallying point of unity in an international atmosphere too often clouded by suspicion and distrust. Public health work has become one of the techniques of international cohesion. It provides a new language by which Brazil can speak to Egypt, and the knowledge and experience of one nation can be available to all.

CHAPTER VII

"THE JOHNS HOPKINS OF CHINA"

HISTORICALLY, CHINA SHARES WITH THE International Health Division in being one of the two oldest interests of The Rockefeller Foundation, and the Foundation has spent more money in that country than in any other country except the United States. It was, as usual, Mr. Gates who initiated the development, although his ideas were undoubtedly influenced by his long contact with Mr. Rockefeller's interests in church missions in the Far East. The plan, as Mr. Gates first conceived it, before The Rockefeller Foundation was established, involved the creation of a great university in China, dedicated to higher education. He was prompted in this idea by the successful launching of the University of Chicago, and he believed that with an expenditure of something like ten million dollars, a similar venture, with similar results, could be initiated in China. "I thought," he wrote a few years later, "that we might ourselves perhaps establish in China a University, teaching no religion, but hospitable to all faiths, a University in fact and not in name only, teaching all that is taught in Western universities, offering itself as a model for the Chinese government and raising up teachers for the new Chinese education."[1]

It was partly to explore this idea that Gates induced Mr. Rockefeller to finance the Oriental Education Commission, headed by Dr. Burton, which, as we have seen in a previous chapter, made an extensive study in China in 1909. The report of the Commission convinced Mr. Gates that his plan of a great university was "a dream not then possible of realization."

> The missionary bodies at home and abroad [he wrote] were distinctly and openly, even threateningly hostile to it as tending to infidelity. On the other hand, not even Mr. Rockefeller's promise of ten million dollars for an endowment could tempt the Chinese government to tolerate our proposed institution, freed though it was from all religious bias, unless we would consent that it be controlled and run by appointees of the Chinese government. The study by the Commission of the sort of schools China was actually trying to establish disclosed incompetence so universally, and dishonesty so frequently, as to make any considerable Chinese influence in the conduct of the proposed institution out of the question. Thus were we awakened in 1911 from our dream of a great Chinese university with a foundation of ten million dollars.[2]

Two years later, Rose's spectacular demonstration of what could be done with hookworm, and the extension of his campaign on a world-wide scale, started Gates on a fresh line of thinking. "Our plans for the spread of scientific medicine and sanitation," he wrote, "give our interest in China a new and more promising direction. Might we not do in medicine in China what we failed in our attempt to do in Chinese education?"[3]

Under the stimulus of Gates, warmly supported by President Eliot of Harvard, who had had much to do with the establishment of the Harvard Medical School in Shanghai in 1911, the newly organized Rockefeller Foundation began to explore the possibility of developing modern medicine on a significant scale in China. As was customary in all enterprises in which Mr. Rockefeller was concerned, action was preceded by long and careful study and by seeking advice both from technical experts and from those familiar with conditions on the ground. To President Eliot there was no better subject than medicine to introduce to China the inductive method of reasoning which lies at the basis of all modern science. He thought it would be the most significant contribution that the West could make to the East.[4] Dr. Paul Monroe of Columbia University stressed the same motive, and pointed to the lack in China of any training in the spirit and method of observation and induction by which knowledge of the conditions of life around us is acquired, tested, and put to use. The principal difference between contemporary China and Western peoples, he said, was that China had at hand for immediate employment the legacy of developments in the natural and social sciences which it had taken Western civilization four hundred years to accumulate.[5]

Many of those consulted felt that medicine would avoid the entanglements in religious, political, and social issues involved in other approaches. The missionaries would welcome it, and the Chinese government would be hospitable. The lack of stability in China was, if anything, an added argument for acting at once. "If we wait until China becomes stable," said Dr. John R. Mott, "we lose the greatest opportunity that we shall ever have of dealing with the nation." "The old Arab proverb comes to my mind," he added, "that 'the dawn does not come twice to awaken man.' "[6] The general consensus was summed up by Professor Burton of Chicago: "To promote the development of China along right lines is not to benefit China only or this generation only, but to make an important contribution to the welfare of the world for a future of indefinite extent."[7]

II

With these high hopes and in this spirit the work was undertaken. At Gates' suggestion, the first step was a survey "on the ground," and a commission, headed by President Harry P. Judson of the University of Chicago, was sent to China to determine where and in what manner "medicine, surgery and public health" could effectively be introduced. If the Burton commission of 1909 can be called the first commission, this was the first *medical* commission. Roger S. Greene, United States Consul at Hankow, and a brother of Jerome D. Greene, the secretary of the Foundation, was a member of it, as was Dr. Francis W. Peabody of the Harvard Medical School. Traveling by way of the trans-Siberian railroad, the commission visited seventeen medical schools and ninety-seven hospitals in China. Visits were also made to universities and secondary schools, both missionary and governmental. Conferences were held with the leading officials of the central government and of the various provinces, and with scores of medical missionaries. Of the eighteen provinces in China, the commission visited eleven.

This detail is necessary to understand the scope of the study and its determining effects on the later actions of the trustees of the Foundation. It outlined the method of approach and the medical and social background against which the work would be done. The recommendations of the Commission involved five principal points. First, it confirmed the idea that medicine was the most effective approach that could be made to China. "The need is great beyond any anticipation, and the opportunities for progress in all lines are equally great." Second, it emphasized the point that the work should be undertaken "on a large scale with the understanding that it will involve a long time," and that it should be "on the highest practicable standard." Third, it strongly recommended that the project should be started at two points: in Peking and Shanghai. Fourth, it proposed that the teaching in the new medical schools, "for the present and for some time to come," should be in English as the main language, because of the lack of any body of medical literature in the Chinese tongue, and the impracticability of translations. Fifth, it suggested the immediate institution of a system of fellowships which would enable selected Chinese graduates in medicine to prosecute further study abroad, and thus be prepared to assume responsibility in the new schools.[8]

Less than a month after the receipt of the Judson report, the trustees of The Rockefeller Foundation established the China Medical Board as an integral part of the Foundation structure, analogous to the International Health Board which had already been created. At the suggestion of Gates, Dr. Wallace Buttrick of the General Education Board was made director, a position which he reluctantly accepted on a part-time basis. The choice was a happy one. "No one can do what he can do to make it a go," said Judson,[9] and Dr. Welch later spoke of "the rare good fortune in capturing Dr. Buttrick to give his wisdom, personality and wonderful executive ability to the work of the China Medical Board."[10] At the same time, Roger S. Greene was appointed resident director of the Board in China, another happy choice which brought to the service of the Foundation a former State Department official who had a wide and intimate knowledge of the Far East.

One of the initial problems was the relationship of the proposed new activity in China to the medical missionary organizations which were already in the field and which were doing the best work then being done. Protestant missions alone were maintaining over three hundred hospitals in China. Dr. Eliot, who had studied their activities at first hand, was impressed by their ideals and devotion, "but their resources were always inadequate," he wrote, "and under such conditions both men and women are overworked, deteriorate in their own technique, and become callous to the disastrous conditions under which they are compelled to treat their patients."[11] As the news of the plans of the Foundation in China began to spread, it was inevitable that uneasiness should develop in some of the missionary bodies. It was at this point that the tact and judgment of Dr. Buttrick showed to the greatest advantage. He knew intimately the personnel of the missionary societies, and in many long conferences, both in the United States and in England, he was able to persuade them that the proposed development of medicine in China was in harmony with the common aims which they all shared. It was not intended to supersede but to supplement what was already being done. Indeed, the plans of the China Medical Board involved, as an integral part of the program, the idea of direct financial assistance to promising medical enterprises in China; and beginning with Buttrick's administration, and continuing through the administration of Dr. Vincent, who succeeded him as director of the Board in 1918, aid was given over many years to strategically situated medical schools and hospitals, for the most part under missionary auspices, to improve their buildings and equipment and to increase the number of their doctors and nurses. In addition, a system of fellowships was developed by which capable medical missionaries could return to the United States for further training in institutions like Johns Hopkins, Harvard, and the Mayo Clinic. Later, a similar fellowship plan brought missionary doctors to the Peking Union Medical College.

It is not too much to say that all this varied auxiliary assistance, which amounted to approximately $1,500,000, helped to sharpen and unify medical missionary effort in China. It stimulated at many points higher standards of medical practice, and thus increased in hospital constituencies the level of support for more adequate medical care.

But in the early days there seem to have been anxious moments in the relationships with missionary groups. One missionary body in a public statement declined to accept aid "until it could be determined whether the Rockefeller assistance would in any way interfere with the complete control of [our] institutions."[12] Buttrick, writing to Roger Greene in Peking, commented philosophically: "I do not worry much about this, because the General Education Board has been suspected of unworthy motives through all the years of its existence. . . . People have always suspected Greeks bearing gifts, and they will continue to do so until the end of time."[13] Nevertheless, a little later, Buttrick wrote to Gates: "I would give several pairs of old shoes—and that is a real sacrifice—if you were here now. . . . I need support."[14]

The main objective of the China Medical Board, however, was

not to scatter its aid over a wide area, but by establishing its own medical institutions to concentrate its efforts in a convincing demonstration. In 1915, therefore, after long negotiations, it purchased from the London Missionary Society the ground and buildings of the Union Medical College, which the Society owned and operated. It was around this center and on this site that the great Peking Union Medical College was erected.

Buttrick, however, was not satisfied that the technical aspects of the project had been fully canvassed, and later in the year a third commission consisting of Dr. Simon Flexner, Dr. Welch, Dr. Frederick Gates (a son of Mr. Gates), and Dr. Buttrick himself spent five months in China, "examining the situation on the ground." While the conclusions of this commission were in harmony with the general plan of work already adopted, much valuable light was obtained on concrete aspects of the work to be done, and a more adequate estimate of the magnitude of the task was made possible.

For one thing, it was discovered that if a first-class institution was to be established, provision would have to be made for the training of premedical students. Coming from their own universities, Chinese students were not prepared for the first-year work of a modern medical school. Out of this consideration developed an extensive operation by which, for many years, the China Medical Board financed premedical education not only in Peking and Shanghai, but in other Chinese centers as well. An unforeseen by-product of this operation was its widespread influence in raising the standards of science teaching in the colleges of China.*

Another point that the commission underscored related to one of the objectives of the new institution: it must aim to put the responsibility for medical education in the hands of the Chinese themselves at the earliest possible moment. As Dr. Welch observed, the speed with which the Chinese accepted scientific medicine as their own, and the rapidity with which the Board's importance in the field diminished, would be the measure of success.[15]

The commission also returned with a renewed emphasis on quality. The job must be superlatively well done. The training that was offered must compare favorably with the training given by the best

* It should be noted that between 1929 and 1935 the Natural Sciences division of the Foundation contributed to Chinese universities and institutions sums totaling a little under a million dollars to support the teaching of the sciences related to premedical training. This was supplementary to the work of the China Medical Board.

European and American medical schools. "We must create the Johns Hopkins of China," said Dr. Flexner.[16] And in a public address which Buttrick made shortly after his return, he said:

> Our best service will not be rendered by aiding a large number of schools . . . to train men imperfectly for the immediate needs of China. The greatest service we can render is by establishing these two schools [at Peking and Shanghai] on such a high plane scientifically and educationally, that there shall emerge young men and women capable of studying the medical problems of China, of producing a medical literature, and themselves becoming the teachers of the next generation of Chinese in the very best that modern medicine can offer. To that task we propose to set ourselves.[17]

III

Meanwhile, the building operation in Peking was moving forward. The interruption of the First World War created discouraging complications, but by 1921 the vast plant was completed at a cost of $8,283,000. It comprised fifty-nine buildings located on twenty-five acres. The project included laboratories for anatomy, physiology and chemistry, a pathology building, a hospital with 225 teaching beds and provision for thirty private rooms, a nurses' training school, a large out-patient department, a hospital administration unit with quarters for resident physicians and internes, an auditorium, an animal house, dormitories for students, and faculty residences grouped in two walled compounds. Besides those structures devoted to school and hospital purposes, it had been necessary to supply facilities which are ordinarily connected with the operation of a municipality: sewerage, water supply, and electric light. While the interiors of the buildings were planned to afford maximum convenience and the latest improvements in arrangement and equipment, the exterior was designed to be in harmony with the best traditions of Chinese architecture. The high, graceful, curved Chinese roof of jade-green glazed tiles, made in the factory that once supplied the tile for imperial palaces, had already given the college the name of "the Green City." Gray brick was used in the structure, similar to that in the Great Wall, and the eaves were embellished with conventional Chinese decorations, painted by native artisans. All this elaborate and somewhat expensive design was employed—against Gates' strong protests—as a symbol of the desire of the Board to make the College not something imposed from an alien source, but an agency which would fit naturally and harmoniously into the picture of a developing Chinese civilization. It reflected, too, the anxiety of the Board, in this first gesture to the Far East, to give China nothing but the best. It must be recorded, however, that in protest against what he called its "extravagance and folly," Gates resigned from the board.[18]

The dedication ceremonies were held in September, 1921, although the school had been opened two years earlier while construction was still under way. It began with a student enrollment of 140, and a teaching staff of sixty-seven, of whom seventeen were instructors in the premedical school. Twenty-five per cent of the teaching staff was Chinese, almost all of whom had been trained in the United States or in Europe. The balance of the staff was recruited from countries all over the world and represented the best that Western experience could produce. From the very start, the school did not aim to turn out numerous doctors and nurses—Chinese institutions had to assume that task—but to train leaders in medicine and nursing who would serve as teachers and investigators in Chinese medical schools, hospitals, and health organizations. The institution, moreover, was from the beginning far more than an undergraduate medical school. It was a center of medical training and research carried on in the modern scientific spirit by well-trained men and women from many parts of the world. Here graduate students, Chinese physicians, and medical missionaries on furlough from their stations pursued special studies, often with fellowships supplied by the China Medical Board. From time to time, too, intensive courses were organized in medicine, surgery, the clinical specialties, and the fundamental laboratory sciences, for groups of doctors who wished to keep abreast of recent progress. In this manner, ideas, standards, and techniques were seeded all over China. Visiting professors from America and Europe shared in these courses as well as in other teaching, and brought to the institution the stimulus of their ability, experience, personality, and prestige. Men of the caliber of Dr. Walter B. Cannon, Dr. Alfred E. Cohn, Dr. David Edsall, Dr. L. Emmett Holt, Dr. W. G. MacCallum, Dr. Eugene Opie, and Dr. Canby Robinson—to mention only a few from the American list—shared in the undertaking, and helped to make the Peking Union Medical College a rallying point for medical training and research for the entire Far East. Many of the younger American doctors who served in Peking returned to the United States to positions of influence and widening usefulness.

Meanwhile, the plans for a similiar institution at Shanghai had been reluctantly abandoned. A site for the new school had been purchased there in 1916, and a group of trustees had been chosen to administer the enterprise. But the First World War upset the calculations with steeply rising costs of materials and supplies. Experience in Peking showed that the Shanghai budget could not be kept within the limits planned. Indeed, the Peking school had already cost more than three times the combined amount of the original estimates for both projects, and with the annual budget at Peking running close to $700,000 a year, the Foundation felt that another school would represent too great a drain. Moreover, the difficulty of finding an adequate staff for a second school began to be more evident; and when this difficulty was added to the fact that the high standards of the Peking College were absorbing the total number of properly trained premedical students, and that Peking, therefore, would be able to provide for all qualified applicants for many years to come, the impracticability of the Shanghai plan became obvious.

IV

The main emphasis of the China Medical Board, therefore, was centered on Peking, although contributions, in modest amounts, continued to be made to other medical enterprises throughout China. The Peking Union Medical College had been granted a provisional charter by the Regents of the University of the State of New York, and functioned under its own board of trustees, with the China Medical Board acting in a supervisory capacity.

Up until 1928, the China Medical Board was merely a subdivision of The Rockefeller Foundation. In that year, at the instance of the Foundation, the Board was dissolved and a new corporation was established under the name of China Medical Board, Inc., to serve as an independent American organization for holding and distributing funds for the promotion of medical education in the Far East or in this country. The land and buildings in Peking were transferred from the Foundation to the ownership of the new Board, and the Foundation gave the Board $12,000,000 as an endowment fund for the support, in its discretion, of the Peking Union Medical College or for other indicated purposes related to medical education. This action was prompted by the desire of the Foundation to lodge the ultimate responsibility for the financing of the Peking College in an organization separately incorporated and wholly outside the Foundation. While it was foreseen that annual grants from the Foundation might for a number of years be necessary to supplement the income of the

China Medical Board, Inc., so that it could adequately support the Peking institution, it was frankly hoped that other sources, perhaps Chinese, could be found for this purpose.

These hopes were not realized. The invasion of China by the Japanese in the thirties and particularly the tragic consequences of the Second World War completely altered the situation. Immediately following Pearl Harbor, the Japanese seized the plant of the Peking school, and it was not recovered until 1945. During these years, Dr. Henry S. Houghton, the director of the college, who had been associated with it from early days, was imprisoned by the Japanese in Peking together with another officer of the institution. The faculty and student body were widely dispersed throughout China. The School of Nursing was reopened in West China Union University in Chengtu, and some of the medical students continued their work in the same institution. Medical education was also carried on in other places in the area, and during this confused and unhappy period the China Medical Board, Inc., appropriated $1,822,000 to the National Institute of Health and to thirteen government and mission schools to maintain the traditions of medicine in China and repair where possible the broken links of the chain of training and professional skill.

With the close of the war and the return of the plant in Peking, serious questions were presented. Although the buildings had suffered no material structural damage, considerable equipment had disappeared, and the lack of maintenance and upkeep over the years had resulted in serious deterioration. Moreover, the country was torn by a civil war, with little immediate prospect of stability. In 1946, therefore, The Rockefeller Foundation joined with the China Medical Board in sending to China a commission under the chairmanship of Dr. Alan Gregg of the Foundation staff. The commission reported early in 1947, and as a result of its recommendations the Foundation made a final grant of $10,000,000 to the China Medical Board, Inc., thus bringing its endowment fund to a total of $22,000,000. Including this endowment, the Foundation's total expenditures for the erection and maintenance of the Peking Union Medical College and the stimulation of medicine in China have been $44,944,665—the largest contribution which the Foundation ever made to a single objective.

Commenting on this latest grant, the President of the Foundation in his annual review of the work for 1947 made this comment:

> It may seem an odd moment in the history of the world, and particularly in the history of China, to make a fresh investment in the development of modern medicine in that unhappy country. But the graduates

of the Peking Union Medical College . . . are bringing their healing techniques not only to needy men and women but in a deeper sense to a human society that is desperately sick. In dark hours like these it takes perhaps a leap of faith to believe that medicine can be one of the bridges across the gulf that separates this frightened present from a saner and better-balanced future. We shall, of course, need other bridges, but modern medicine, bringing us a conception of common human need that overrides our irrational and suicidal differences, can surely help.[19]

Meanwhile, the China Medical Board, Inc., now a completely independent organization, with its own trustees and officers, is empowered by its charter to extend financial support not only to the Peking Union Medical College, but to other like institutions in the Far East, or even, indeed, in the United States.

V

Since 1947, of course, even darker hours than were anticipated have come to China and to the rest of the world. The Communist government of China has taken over the responsibility for the school in Peking, and reports as of this writing seem to indicate that it is receiving adequate financial assistance. Whether its high standards will be maintained or along what lines it will be developed, no one, of course, can foretell. In attempting to estimate its usefulness during the three decades of its existence, it can be said with assurance that it had a profound effect on the development of modern medicine in China. In the first twenty years of its operation, until it was closed by the Japanese, it became one of the leading centers of medical training in the world. It was the outpost of teaching and research in the Far East—a symbol of high quality and objective approach. Indeed, in helping to establish the value of scientific method and inductive reasoning it represented perhaps the most acceptable gift which the West could offer the East.

During this period it became an integral part of the intellectual life of China. It was welcomed with unstinted enthusiasm. Over forty years ago, in a lecture at Stanford University, William James said that a college should be a place of "intellectual ferment." That phrase describes with vivid accuracy the institution in Peking. Up until Pearl Harbor, less than ten of all its graduates had gone into private practice; all the others were absorbed in medical teaching, in hospital posts, or governmental medical positions. They had been exposed to an intellectual ferment, and they had a new gospel to preach across the length and breadth of China. It was the gospel of modern medicine and the conception of what it could do for a people who had never known it. A survey made late in the forties indicated that six of the national medical schools of China were under the leadership of graduates of the Peking institution, and six other medical schools were headed by individuals who, although not graduates of the college, spent many years as members of its staff.

Another significant development in the years after 1921 was the rapidity with which highly trained Chinese doctors had been able to take over the responsibility for the teaching positions of the Peking College. When the college opened, as we have seen, only 25 per cent of the teaching and administrative staff was Chinese. By 1927, the figure had risen to 67 per cent. By 1947, it was practically 100 per cent. With two or three exceptions, all the important posts, in medicine and surgery alike, were filled by fully competent and experienced Chinese.

What was true of the technical staff was true also of the board of trustees of the College, which, with funds provided by the China Medical Board in New York, had the complete responsibility for the administration of the institution. When the college board was first created in 1916, it did not contain a single Chinese. This situation was due in part, at least, to the fact that the early promoters of the work had no acquaintance with personnel in China. In 1947, with the exception of two or three foreigners who were resident there, the board was completely Chinese, chosen on a self-perpetuating basis, and the full responsibility for the management of the institution was in its hands. Dr. Welch's test of the measurement of success, mentioned on an earlier page—the speed with which the Chinese accepted modern medicine as their own—had been largely met.

The troubled fortunes which have swept over China in recent years have clouded perspective and given rise to deplorable recrimination. We hear much of "Western imperialism" and "American colonialism" and "the greedy interests of capitalism" and all the well-worn labels of abuse. Perhaps in some less hysterical day, with clearer visibility, the Peking Union Medical College will appear as it really was: the best that Western civilization had to offer to a people whom it profoundly admired and in whose future it deeply believed. It was a gift inspired by no motive other than a desire to promote the welfare of men. The point of view of The Rockefeller Foundation was expressed in the statement it made on the occasion of its final grant to medicine in China in 1947: "The Trustees of the Foundation are proud to have been associated in the founding of an institution whose contribution has been so significant and whose continuance means so much to the future; and they would take this occasion to rededicate it to the new generation of China in the firm belief that the light which it started in modern medicine will not be allowed to die out."[20]

CHAPTER VIII

MEDICAL EDUCATION IN THE UNITED STATES

IT WAS NOT ALONE IN CHINA THAT THE Foundation helped in the development of modern medicine. In a series of bold moves in many countries around the world, it lifted the problem of medical education to a new plane. Here again, as in the development of the Foundation's public health work and in its China program, it seems to have been Mr. Gates who first initiated the undertaking. It was what he called a "pregnant idea," and he threw his influence behind it with all his characteristic enthusiasm and intensity. "The time was," he wrote some years later, "—and we can all remember it—when medicine was under such difficulties and in such darkness that the enthusiastic young men who committed themselves to it pretty soon found themselves in one of two categories: either confirmed pessimists, disappointed and chagrined, or else mere reckless 'pill-slingers' for money."[1]

Just as Osler's book on the *Principles and Practice of Medicine* had stirred Gates' imagination and had led to the creation of The Rockefeller Institute for Medical Research, so it was another book, *Medical Education in the United States and Canada,* that now captured his alert and eager mind. The book was written in 1910 by Abraham Flexner as a result of a study he had made for the Carnegie Foundation for the Advancement of Teaching, and it was one of the great landmarks in the history of modern medicine in the United States.

Mr. Flexner, himself not a doctor, was the brother of Dr. Simon

Flexner, head of the Rockefeller Institute, and he had the keen, razorlike mind that characterized that remarkable family. The boldness of his thinking and the tenacity of his opinions frequently created antagonism, but he had an intellectual energy and drive that were to have profound consequences on contemporary medicine. He had personally investigated all the medical schools in the United States and Canada, 155 of them, and in his book he described them one by one with an objective frankness, letting the reader draw the necessary inferences. Not more than half a dozen of the schools were able to give their students anything approaching an adequate medical education. Many of them were nothing more than casual associations of local physicians. All that such schools required, Flexner pointed out, were a few practitioners to serve as professors and a few bones. Laboratories were either nonexistent or unsatisfactory. Clinical facilities, in the rare instances where they existed at all, were too often limited to precarious relations with hospitals, "the appointments to which were made on almost any basis except education and science."

To make matters still worse, there were low entrance standards or practically none at all. Of the 155 schools, 16 required two or more years of college work for entrance; 50 demanded a high-school education or its "equivalent"; 89 asked for "little or nothing more than the rudiments or the recollection of a common school education." In the majority of the schools, students' fees went directly to the instructors and the curriculum was apt to be short and ungraded. Dr. Simon Flexner, describing the medical school he entered in 1887, reported:

> It was a school in which the lecture was everything. Within the brief compass of four winter months the whole medical lore was unfolded in discourses following one another in bewildering sequence through a succession of long days; and lest the wisdom imparted should exceed the student's power of retention, the lectures were repeated precisely during a second year, at the end of which graduation with the degree of Doctor of Medicine was all but automatic.[2]

In his introduction to Flexner's report, Dr. Henry S. Pritchett, President of the Carnegie Foundation for the Advancement of Teaching, made this comment:

> For twenty-five years past there has been an enormous over-production of uneducated and ill-trained medical practitioners. This has been in absolute disregard of the public welfare and without any serious thought of the interests of the public. . . . Over-production of ill-trained men is

due in the main to the existence of a very large number of commercial schools, sustained in many cases by advertising methods through which a mass of unprepared youth is drawn out of industrial occupations into the study of medicine. . . . The inadequacy of many of these schools may be judged from the fact that nearly half of all our medical schools have incomes below $10,000, and these incomes determine the quality of instruction that they can and do offer.

The Flexner report produced an immediate and profound sensation. It touched off a reform movement which was already in the making. Several years earlier, the American Medical Association had set up a Council on Medical Education which was working persistently to improve standards; and even before the Flexner report appeared, the growing demand for more adequate laboratory instruction was cutting drastically into the profits of the poorer schools. Moreover, increasing recognition was being given to the value of having medical schools attached to universities as fully integrated departments. As Pritchett said in his introduction to Flexner's report:

> In the future the college or university which accepts a medical school must make itself responsible for university standards in the medical school and for adequate support for medical education. The day has gone by when any university can retain the respect of educated men, or when it can fulfill its duty to education, by retaining a low-grade professional school for the sake of its own institutional completeness.

The conception of the medical school that had slowly developed at the few good institutions like Johns Hopkins and Harvard involved a four-year graded course, the first two years devoted to laboratory subjects: anatomy, physiology, and pathology; the last two years to clinical subjects such as medicine, surgery, and obstetrics. For satisfactory results from the first two years of such a graded course, three things were necessary: adequate facilities, well-trained teachers devoting their full time to their work, and a competent student body already equipped with knowledge of biology, physics, and chemistry. For the "clinical years"—the last two of a four-year graded course—the need of adequate hospital facilities was being increasingly recognized. Adequate, in this connection, meant that the hospital should be readily accessible to the medical school, that it should be equipped and organized as a teaching hospital, and that the staff should be under university control, and selected with some measure of participation by the university.

II

It was at this turning point in the development of the American medical schools that Flexner's book fell into the hands of Gates. The story goes—perhaps apocryphal—that Gates invited Flexner to his office and asked him what he would do for medical education in the United States if he had a million dollars. Flexner replied instantly that he would give it to Dr. Welch at Johns Hopkins. No answer could have suited Gates better, for he had been a partner before with Dr. Welch in the planning of the Rockefeller Institute and the Rockefeller Sanitary Commission, and he was a great admirer of Welch's shrewdness, courage, and judgment. In any event, Flexner was borrowed from the Carnegie Foundation and was dispatched to Baltimore to make a survey on the ground.

Complicated events were to occur between this simple assignment and the results which ultimately followed, but the trip to Baltimore launched the General Education Board and The Rockefeller Foundation on a program in medical education in the United States to which in the end the two boards contributed more than $100,000,000, and which, although at times it caused vigorous controversy, altered the pattern of medical teaching across the country. It was the General Education Board that took the initiative in the project, and most of the money came from its funds rather than from the Foundation. In 1913, Flexner joined the staff of the Board on a permanent basis, and thereafter the leadership of the program in the United States was largely in his hands.

The approach to the problem which Flexner developed with Gates and Welch was outlined in the fall of 1913 in a formal resolution that the General Education Board "address itself in the first place to the establishment of full-time clinical departments in selected institutions possessing adequate facilities for the inauguration of this innovation."[3] The term "full-time," as strictly construed under this resolution, was to mean that the clinical departments in the last two years of the medical-school curriculum were to be under the administrative control of physicians or surgeons who would give all of their time on a university basis to teaching, to research, and to the care of patients in the teaching hospital. If, in order to further their teaching or their research, they saw private patients, the fees for such service would go to the university.

In the fall of 1913, when an application was received from Dr. Welch for funds to make possible this completely new type of clinical teaching at Johns Hopkins, a sum was voted which would provide a yearly income of $65,000. The undertaking was frankly called an experiment. Ever since its founding in 1893, the Johns Hopkins Medical School had run its laboratory departments—anatomy, physiology, pathology—on a "university basis" with instructors giving full time to their work. Under the new plan, now to be put in operation, the full-time scheme was to be tried in the clinical branches. These at first involved only medicine, surgery, and pediatrics. Later, a number of other subjects were added, including obstetrics, psychiatry, ophthalmology, the history of medicine, preventive medicine, and radiology.

The launching of this new type of medical instruction created a furor not only in the ranks of the medical profession but in the lay press. Emphatic protests were voiced that this scheme would deprive the public of the skill of outstanding doctors. Nor was the plan installed at the Hopkins without some internal difficulty. As Dr. Welch observed, the full-time experiment involved "such radical changes in conditions which now exist and have always existed in medical schools both here and in Europe that entire agreement of opinion as to the wisdom of the change is not to be expected. Nor can the plan be carried out without some hardship to individuals and some disturbance of personal relations."[4]

By and large, however, the enthusiasm of those backing the undertaking ran high. More than satisfied with the promise of this initial venture at Johns Hopkins, the Board over a period of six years voted funds for similar reorganizations on a full-time basis of the medical schools at Washington University in St. Louis, at Yale, and at Chicago. All its contributions in this field were invariably conditioned on specific funds being raised from other sources for the same purpose. This was the approach to Nashville, Tennessee, where with Chancellor Kirkland's statesmanlike co-operation, the Board developed at Vanderbilt an outstanding medical school to serve the South. As Flexner later stated, the first appropriation to Vanderbilt of four million dollars (later increased to seventeen and a half million) acted like a "depth bomb," hastening the mortality of inferior schools, while those that were determined to survive made rapid plans to enlarge their resources and elevate their aims.

Before this last large-scale plan came into full operation, however, the Board's scope in the area of medical education was vastly increased by new gifts from Mr. Rockefeller. Up to this time, the Board had financed this program from its general funds. Between 1919 and

1921, Mr. Rockefeller gave the General Education Board $45,000,000 earmarked for medical education in the United States.

III

With resources thus augmented, the Board enlarged its area of work. The Annual Report for 1919-1920 reiterated the view that the full-time scheme had been undertaken in an experimental spirit. Its cost had been found to be very great. It would be a serious mistake to leap to the conclusion, cautioned the report, that the scheme should be universally adopted at that time. And the report added: "While experience thus far sustains the presumption based on *a priori* consideration that the system is worth the price, it still remains to be objectively proved that teaching, care of the sick and scientific production are all so much better under the full-time scheme that universities generally should move to its adoption." The Board indicated that while aid would be continued to institutions already in the lead, attention would also be given to other schools. It was felt that medical education in all sections of the country needed to be stimulated and improved. And it frankly recognized that there was useful work to be done in helping communities strengthen the best their medical schools provided.

Regional needs were given particular consideration. "In the East," the officers pointed out to the Board soon after the 1919 gift had been received,

> medical education is altogether in the hands of privately endowed institutions of learning. With the exception of some eight or ten schools, medical education in the West and South is in the hands of state universities. The Board has found it practicable to cooperate with endowed institutions in developing their medical schools. It has had thus far no experience with state or municipal institutions in this field. It is evident, however, that if Mr. Rockefeller's benefaction is to be made generally effective, cooperation with state and municipal universities is necessary.[5]

In line with this thinking, Flexner brought before the Board a proposal to assist the University of Iowa in moving its medical plant across the river to a site where a new teaching hospital with its necessary laboratories could be built. Without such help, it was believed that years would elapse before the state could be persuaded to undertake so ambitious a plan, and consequently medical education in this key section of the Middle West would be greatly retarded. The proposal, which involved $2,250,000, to be contributed jointly by the

General Education Board and The Rockefeller Foundation, met with Gates' determined opposition. In one of the stormiest meetings of any of the Rockefeller boards, he fought the proposal single-handed with all his characteristic intensity. With passionate gestures and with his white hair in disarray, he seemed like an old lion at bay. The state universities, he declared, were creatures of politics, subject to dictation on economic and scientific questions. It would be against public policy for a cent of Mr. Rockefeller's money to be given to them; the best service which could be rendered them would be "to protect them in freedom of teaching by throwing around them in every state a cordon of strong, free, privately endowed colleges and universities."[6] This was in 1923, and Gates did not understand the progressive forces which, even as he spoke, were converting the great state universities into the social and scientific laboratories they have become. Flexner's point in rebuttal was conclusive: "We are fortunate in this country in having two types of institutions—one under private and one under state management. We not only escape bureaucratic uniformity, but we obtain a wholesome competition." On the medical side of the question, his argument was this: "We are trying to aid in the development of a country-wide, high-grade system of education in the United States. If we confine our cooperation to endowed institutions we can practically cooperate only in the East."[7]

It was one of Gates' last appearances at a board meeting. As an expression of protest, he resigned from the executive committee, and although he was not the type of man to allow differences of opinion to affect his personal relationships, thereafter he had little confidence in Flexner. One of the last thoughts he confided to his private papers before his death was about "bureaucratic officers, usurping the power of the Board."[8]

Following the grant to the University of Iowa, similar gifts, although in smaller amounts, were made to other state medical institutions, including the University of Colorado, the University of Oregon, the University of Virginia, and the University of Georgia. An appropriation was also made to the University of Cincinnati, a municipally controlled institution. In each of these cases the purpose of the Board was to expedite developments which undoubtedly would have occurred in time, but which might have been unconscionably delayed. In the difficult art of giving, to hasten the arrival of the inevitable is sometimes the height of statesmanship.

Because the Board had always been interested in Negro education, one of the major questions with which it was now confronted was how to provide the most effective opportunities for the training of Negro doctors. Over a period of years it extended liberal support to the medical school of Howard University in Washington, D. C., a private corporation receiving a large proportion of its aid from the federal government. But it was to Meharry Medical School in Nashville, Tennessee, that it finally gave its chief co-operation and help. A private organization, supported for many years by the Freedman's Aid Society of the Methodist Church, Meharry seemed to be the most promising center for a significant development. Consequently, with Board funds, a new site was purchased close to Fisk University, and new buildings and laboratories were erected. The Board hoped that some kind of an affiliation would be established between Fisk and Meharry and, as part of its medical program, it strengthened the science courses at Fisk through grants for that purpose. As a matter of fact, affiliation was not achieved, but proximity and daily association resulted in co-operation with regard to such matters as laboratory and library facilities. Even more significant was the strengthened stimulus felt by each institution of scholarly standards and of the scientific spirit.

The Board's aid to Meharry totaled more than eight million dollars, and the school not only achieved a stable high rating but developed into a wide regional center for the professional preparation of Negroes in medicine, public health, dentistry, and nursing.

But it was to the development of the full-time plan in key institutions that the Board devoted the major part of its resources. "Obviously," said the officers, "all medical schools could not be substantially assisted; obviously money would have to be massed at strategic points. . . ."[9] This was in accord with a policy which ran back to the days of Mr. Rockefeller's personal philanthropy—a policy of building on strength rather than on weakness. "Make the peaks higher," Rose used to say, by which he meant that as the standards in first-class institutions were progressively raised, the radiating effect would spread not only through an entire region but across an entire country. The influence of a Johns Hopkins or a Chicago would in the end reach every campus and every medical school in the United States.

Consequently, in the years following Mr. Rockefeller's new gift, the General Education Board, occasionally with the participation of the Foundation, concentrated its efforts in medical education in places like Harvard, Columbia, Cornell, Tulane, Western Reserve, and Rochester. Incidental aid, sometimes in substantial amounts, was given to many other institutions like Duke University, Emory University, and the Memorial Hospital in New York. But the major policy of the Board was to avoid scattered assistance, and to mass its support behind strength or potential promise.

In the midst of these activities it became increasingly clear that, compared to the importance of the trained man for teaching and research, endowment, buildings, and equipment were merely "accessories." As schools raised their teaching standards, the demand for qualified men was rapidly increasing. For years, a similar need had been felt at the Rockefeller Institute, where Dr. Simon Flexner was deeply concerned that men should be found and developed who would continue the Institute's scientific leadership. His views were shared by Board and Foundation officers who were working for improved medical education. Competent men were not going into academic medicine because they were financially unable to support themselves during the prolonged period required to equip teachers and investigators. To meet this need, therefore, as far as it could be met, appropriations were made by both the Board and the Foundation to the National Research Council for a system of fellowships to aid men qualified for academic careers in medicine. These fellowships have been maintained to this day; and their influence on the development of the medical sciences in America has been attested over and over again.

IV

Surveying the General Education Board's experience in medical education over the decade and a half (1913-1929) in which the program was in active operation, it is evident that "full-time" was the point upon which opinion continued to be sharply divided. Undoubtedly, insistence on university standards for clinical departments served to swing the pendulum away from low and timid educational practices. It did more. It helped swing the whole movement for improved medical training into top-flight effort. At the same time, there were those who felt that insistence on strict full-time was an unjustified intrusion on university policy; and several trustees of the Foundation and of the General Education Board, as well as outsiders, were deeply disturbed. Dr. Eliot wrote to Buttrick on the subject, referring to

> the policy of the Board which I heard stated with great distinctness by Mr. Gates when I first joined the Board and have often heard since . . . not to interfere with the domestic management of an institution aided,

except as regards its prudent financial management. I observe in the memorandum you handed me . . . a desire or purpose to condition a gift from the General Education Board to the Harvard Medical School on the acceptance by the School of one method of introducing the full-time policy. This condition does not seem to me consistent with what I have always believed to have been the wise and generally acceptable policy of the Board. . . .[10]

Buttrick's reply was based on a distinction between grants for general endowment and for specific kinds of work:

In making appropriations to colleges and universities for general endowment no restrictions have been imposed other than that the sums contributed by us should be preserved inviolate as endowment; in making appropriations upon the requests of colleges and universities for specific departments or kinds of work, the Board has naturally, and I think wisely, so made its appropriations as to insure the carrying out of the programs under which and for which the contributions were made.[11]

And it cannot be doubted that many thoughtful people besides Buttrick and Flexner felt that the only sure way to attain the high standards for which the Board was aiming was to insist on strict full-time as a condition of aid.

Nevertheless, the policy came under increasing criticism. Anson Phelps Stokes in his capacity as a Board trustee wrote in the summer of 1924:

It is not a question of whether we are right or wrong in our opinions regarding the university or full-time basis of medical education. I think that where adequate funds are available we are absolutely right in favoring this policy, and I am very proud of what has been accomplished by the Board under Mr. Flexner's leadership in the field of medical education. But it is a question of whether or not we can psychologically and morally afford—in view of public opinion and our great wealth as a board—to be imposing, or at least requiring, detailed conditions regarding educational policy in medicine in elaborate contracts which can only be amended with our consent. . . . Personally, I think this policy unwise and fraught with serious dangers. . . .[12]

Taking all these points of view into consideration, the Board modified its policy in 1925, authorizing the revision of contracts with medical schools to permit such modification as educational and scientific experience might, in the judgment of each school, justify. Some schools to which the Board had given money continued on a strict full-time basis; others modified the plan. As these modifications were developed, they generally took the form of what is now called "geographical full-time." Under this plan, the school or hospital provides the professor or physician with his office, rent free, and there he conducts all his consultation work and practice. This has a considerable advantage in centralizing his work and the work of the department to which he belongs. A staff member on geographical full-time is either paid a fairly substantial salary and allowed to keep an amount equal to this salary out of the fees he collects (the surplus being turned over to the university); or he is paid a small nominal salary, and allowed to keep all his fees.

Dr. Alan Gregg, reviewing the whole situation in 1950, made these three points:

> (1) By its emphasis on planned professional teamwork, full-time clinical teaching has paved the way for an important form of practice today, group practice, with its economical use of costly diagnostic and therapeutic machines and instruments. (2) By diminishing the obligation of young professors, while teaching, to build up an extensive local private practice, the full-time system has opened to them a much larger choice of posts over the country, and has thus favored the growth, advancement and dissemination of able young men. Entire regions of the country can benefit from talent that otherwise would have stayed in Eastern metropolitan centers. (3) Few, if any, young men trained in full-time departments would now vote for the part-time teaching system, and what young men prefer has vitality for the future.[13]

The decision to work for improved medical education brought the Board and the Foundation into contact with new educational techniques. "We ourselves never pretended to have an original idea," said Flexner later, "but we knew educational strategy. The revolution thus accomplished brought American medicine from the bottom of the pile to the very top."[14] And indeed it was a revolution. It was a vast pump-priming operation, geared to an ambitious idea. The hundred million dollars contributed by the two Rockefeller boards, matched many times over by the generosity of scores of citizens like Rosenwald in Chicago, Eastman in Rochester, and Harkness in New York, took the teaching of medicine in the United States from the discreditable position it occupied in 1910 and gave it a status which it shares with only a few other countries in the world.

As controversy arose over theories and methods, the two boards clarified and broadened their own thinking. Maintaining an inquiring and flexible point of view, they adapted their procedures to developments that their own initiative and experimenting helped to bring about. But their fundamental aim remained always the same—to throw their weight behind the improvement of medical education in the United States. This involved difficult policy decisions as well as ingenuity, resourcefulness, and persistence. Intent on helping to "develop the best," it is fair to say that the Foundation and particularly the General Education Board had a firm hand also in defining and strengthening what the best might be.

Although, at the close of the twenties, not one university in the United States possessed what could be called a complete medical school offering all the specialties, the General Education Board felt that such substantial progress had been made in medical education over the period that its efforts would thenceforth have greater significance in other fields. Before this time came, however, the Foundation was to extend the drive to improve the training of doctors until it touched many of the leading centers of the world.

CHAPTER IX

MEDICAL EDUCATION AROUND THE WORLD

IN THE DEVELOPMENT OF MEDICAL education in the United States, the Foundation, as we have seen, played a role secondary to the General Education Board. The decision to use the Board's resources for this purpose was due to the fact that when the idea was first brought to Gates' attention, the Foundation had not yet been incorporated, while the Board had funds and a policy adaptable to the development of such a program. Only as the program grew to sizable proportions was the Foundation called in to help. Any extension of the project beyond the boundaries of the country the General Education Board could not have undertaken, because under its charter it was limited to work within the United States. Consequently, in the second stage of the program, i.e., the work overseas, it was the Foundation that took the lead.

It was a lead which for some years Rose had been planning, because he had long since come to realize that unless basic medical education could be greatly improved, there was little promise for public health in many of the countries in which he was working. It was this apprehension that led him in 1916 to ask Dr. Richard M. Pearce, professor of pathology and research medicine at the University of Pennsylvania, to undertake a survey of medicine in Brazil. So successful was this project that soon after his return, Pearce was appointed adviser to the International Health Board in medical education; and in 1919 the Foundation established a separate Division of Medical Education with Pearce as Director. The objective of the

Division, as defined by Vincent, was to help "strategically placed medical schools in various parts of the world to increase their resources and to improve their teaching and research."[1]

For this task Pearce was admirably equipped. Lacking, perhaps, in Flexner's intensity and verve, he was a man of uncompromising thoroughness, deeply concerned with education. Gregg, who served as his assistant, said of him that he brought to the Foundation "the blunt if regretful candor of the pathologist";[2] and Vincent recalled that "his observations were incisive, sometimes surgical, but always aseptic."[3] But like Rose, whom he most admired, he was a man of infinite modesty; and as Vincent noted, "with millions in the background he studiously avoided the very appearance of dogmatism or dictation."[4] Until death overtook him in midstride ten years later, he threw his great capacities as administrator, teacher, and scientist behind the idea of improving the quality of medical teaching, and he developed it in a series of bold strokes around the world.

The Foundation's basic policy of knowing the facts before going into action was nowhere more scrupulously followed than in this new field of medical work. Surveys were vigorously pushed on a broad front to determine how doctors were trained and what the possibilities were of improving their education. This was a large and ambitious undertaking. To investigate the chief medical schools of the world took time. It was a matter of miles and manpower. The miles can be figured on any map, for the medical schools of North and South America were all covered, as were those of Europe and Asia, except for a few in Russia. In Africa, medicine, as defined by Western standards, was not taught except in Egypt and South Africa, and the schools of these two areas were included in the survey. In the Far East, as we have seen, China was already a major undertaking of the Foundation, but the new surveys included Japan, the Philippine Islands, Siam, the schools of Singapore and Hongkong, Java, New Zealand, and Australia.

The manpower available for this undertaking never totaled more than four at any one time, and usually not more than one or two. Dr. Pearce covered a great deal of the ground himself; Dr. Alan Gregg handled the principal projects in Continental Europe, while Dr. William S. Carter covered much of the Far East and South African territory. Since, with such a limited staff, these surveys had to be a continuing mission for several years, they necessarily coincided with the development of major projects. In fact, in the matter of timing, of deciding what to do first and where to do it, a policy of realistic opportunism played a large part in the undertaking.

In many of the places thus surveyed, the Foundation did not engage in active work. However, to decide not to participate often necessitated the same degree of careful consideration involved in positive co-operation. Having only limited funds to use for the promotion of better medical training, the Foundation had to weigh carefully the claims of one place against the claims of others. Many factors were decisive in reaching negative decisions. They included the extreme poverty of some countries; the serious backwardness of premedical education in others; the grave uncertainty as to whether there existed in a given area sufficient conviction as to the value of medical education to insure the continuation of any school the Foundation might assist; complacent conservatism among local doctors, or by government personnel or the people generally; doubt as to whether various units would pool their interests with enthusiasm and genuine co-operation so that one medical school might serve as a leader for an entire region.

These problems, however, and many others, were to become apparent only as the work moved forward. Dr. Pearce's first focal point of concern as he took office at the close of 1919 was the British Isles. Much of the Foundation's public health work outside the United States was being carried on in British dominions and colonies. It was natural, therefore, that early consideration should be given to England, Scotland, and Wales, where outstanding schools were located, and where fruitful ideas might be obtained for application elsewhere.

II

There was, perhaps, an element of presumption in the attempt of the Foundation to improve the quality of medical education in other lands. For at the end of the second decade America was by no means pre-eminent in this field. Much, of course, had been accomplished in the development of university medicine, and the proprietary schools which had been such a scandal ten years before were rapidly disappearing. But German medical science, which between 1870 and 1914 had achieved the leadership of the world, was still, in spite of the setback of the war, a powerful and inspiring influence; and Sweden, Denmark, Holland, and Switzerland kept up creditably with the German pace. Indeed, in 1921, Flexner, in commenting on the reported decision of the German government to abolish the medical schools at Marburg and Giessen, made this remark: "It is no exaggeration to say that there is at this day no medical school in the United States which possesses under complete university control clinical facilities as extensive as these two smallest and weakest of the German universities which are about to be discontinued."[5]

British and French medicine, too, had their points of excellence, particularly in the importance which they attached to opening the hospital wards freely to medical students. Writing from Paris, Pearce referred to the French method of actual bedside instruction as "impressive—no . . . magnificent! In no other country," he added, "does the student as an undergraduate live so constantly with the patient. And though the student has little chance to use laboratory methods himself, they are used for demonstration in relation to a given patient, most thoroughly. . . . The French emphasize the disease and bring every fact in the science and art of medicine to bear on the problem of the patient."[6] But in both France and England, unlike Germany, medical education had developed outside the universities rather than inside them, the laboratory sciences were not closely or systematically integrated, and teaching was apt to be subordinate to practice in the life of many a professor. Even so, the average standard of medical education in Great Britain and France in 1920 can fairly be described as superior to that obtaining in the United States.

Under these circumstances, what pattern did the Foundation have in mind in its attempt to assist the teaching of medicine around the world? Vincent stated that the Foundation "offers no one model for universal imitation; it has no inflexible program. It recognizes that each type of medical school has developed under certain conditions, racial, economic, governmental, social. . . . Obviously each country has something to contribute to a common fund of practical experience."[7] This statement was literally correct, but it is obvious that the ideal which the Foundation pursued in the decade in which this program was in operation was the ideal of university medicine as it had originally been developed in Germany and transplanted to a few American institutions like Johns Hopkins and Harvard. This ideal was based on the belief that medicine, developed under the auspices and influence of a university, places deliberate and acknowledged emphasis upon adding to knowledge and transmitting it, rather than merely applying and demonstrating what is already known, even if the latter is ever so impressively done. If fairly complete medical schools could be established on such principles in the leading centers of the world, it was believed that the best possible results would ensue.

This was the ambition and the objective which Pearce took with him to London, in the closing days of 1919. To his surprise, as he reported later, he "discovered that all medical London was talking about the new 'Unit' system of clinical teaching, to be attempted . . . in four of the London schools, with the understanding that if successful it would be extended to other schools of London and the provinces."[8] This Unit system was similar to the full-time scheme being tried out in the United States. It involved, as Sir William Osler said, not only the inclusion of clinical teaching within the sphere of the university, but the adaptation of certain hospitals "to meet the demands of the scientific study of disease and the scientific training of students."[9] It had been recommended, after long study, by a Royal Commission on University Education, and it is perhaps significant that Abraham Flexner, on one of his visits to London, had appeared by invitation as a witness before the Commission. "There can be no question," wrote Pearce, "that Mr. Flexner's testimony focussed attention on the possibilities of a full-time scheme and that he was responsible for the final recommendations of the Commission as to true university professors in clinical subjects and the adoption of the principle of the hospital Unit."[10]

Of the four schools in London where the project was under consideration, only one—the University College Hospital School—had been built to give a university faculty a hospital for teaching purposes; the other three had been developed around hospital staffs. Pearce, therefore, decided that University College offered the best opportunity for developing a medical school which might serve as a model for the whole English-speaking world outside the United States. On his recommendation, strongly supported by Rose and Vincent, the Foundation appropriated five million dollars toward building and equipment, and endowment for the support of teaching. "The finest moment we have known since the Armistice," said the London *Morning Post*.[11] The building program included an Institute of Anatomy, a biochemical building, a new obstetrical unit, laboratory facilities in close connection with hospital wards, the remodeling of the hospital itself, a new home for nurses, and new quarters for resident physicians. "It is inconceivable," said King George V, in dedicating the new plant in 1923, "that Englishmen should decline to welcome this generous challenge from our kinsmen across the Atlantic to a friendly rivalry in medical skill, devotion and beneficence."[12]

Five years later, looking back on the experiment, Pearce commented: "My feeling is that we have realized here everything we had in mind, and although progress during the last eight years has been slow, the ultimate plan has worked out to greater advantage. It can truly be said to be the most compact and complete school in Britain."[13]

From London, where other grants, in smaller amounts, were made to the medical schools of St. Bartholomew's Hospital, St. Thomas's Hospital, and the London Hospital, Pearce moved on to Oxford and Cambridge. Because of their outstanding work in the premedical sciences, these two institutions had a wide influence on the development of medicine. Indeed, it was stated at the time of Pearce's visit that of the leaders of medicine in England, upward of 80 per cent had had their training either at Oxford or Cambridge or at the Scottish universities. Pearce was impressed by the necessity which both institutions faced for new buildings and endowment in the fundamental sciences, and in furthering this purpose the Foundation made appropriations to Cambridge for pathology and to Oxford for biochemistry. At the same time, a grant was given to the Welsh National School of Medicine at Cardiff, a unique and promising institution which in Pearce's opinion seemed to combine some of the best features of Johns Hopkins, Oxford, and Cambridge.

It was Edinburgh, however, that specially drew Pearce's attention and intrigued his interest. Its medical school had been famous for generations, and in point of its radius of influence its faculty was perhaps the most important in the British Empire. Its graduates were scattered around the world wherever the Union Jack was flown, and its work, in Pearce's words, was characterized by "rigorousness of standards, influence upon teaching and research, and intelligence and effectiveness of inner organization."[14] What could The Rockefeller Foundation do to aid the work of so eminent an organization? As a matter of fact, the initiative came from Edinburgh, with a plan to provide "increased facilities for teaching and research work along most modern lines."[15] After prolonged study and negotiation, in which Pearce took a leading part, a new and modified proposal was elaborated, based on the improvement of facilities for teaching laboratory subjects, the establishment of true university clinics, and the bringing together of these two developments into a close relationship with teaching and research. Toward these proposals the Foundation appropriated sums in excess of half a million dollars.

An incident occurring after the funds had been voted throws a side light on the attitude of the Foundation toward the full-time proposal, which had stirred up opposition in Great Britain just as it had in the United States. It had been the plan that the professor of surgery at Edinburgh should be on a full-time basis. It was now proposed by the University that he be allowed to devote Wednesday afternoons and Saturdays to private practice. Pearce strongly urged approval of the modification on the grounds that if the Foundation demurred, it would put itself in the position of forcing a hard and fast plan, rather than supporting a wise and progressive change in the method of teaching. The two Flexners objected, but Vincent threw his weight behind Pearce, and the modification was agreed to. "The proposed change is in accordance with the general principle by which we have been guided," said Vincent, "namely, rendering the kind of aid in a given situation which will mark an appreciable change over the existing status."[16]

In Edinburgh, as in other centers in Great Britain, and indeed in all countries where the Foundation pushed its work in medical education, Pearce used a technique which Rose had developed, i.e., to bring the leaders of the medical schools to the United States, to Canada, to France, to Germany, wherever new ideas were at work or stimulating innovations were under way. This process of cross-fertilization, of exposing the medical men of one country to the thinking and practice of another, was employed by the Foundation on an increased scale as the work developed around the world.

III

It is impossible within the limits of a chapter to discuss in detail the Foundation's far-flung operations in medical education. The necessarily brief paragraphs which follow contain an outline of certain further activities in the principal centers where the work was carried on.

Strasbourg and Lyon

The tactics of Pearce and his associates in planning this world-wide campaign centered around two main points: British medicine and Latin medicine. If these two great systems could be thoroughly permeated with modern ideas and techniques, it would have a far-ranging effect around the globe. Latin medicine centered, of course, in France, with Paris as its stronghold. But, as we shall see later, there were difficulties in connection with a direct approach to the medical situation in Paris which could not easily be overcome.

In the meanwhile, opportunities developed in Strasbourg and Lyon of which Pearce was quick to take advantage. Though the French regarded Strasbourg, with its separate laboratories and clinics built on the German plan, as something of a foreign institution, the government was anxious in the delicate days that followed the First World War to avoid any criticism that an excellent plant had been allowed to deteriorate. Consequently, the school had been given a budget equal to that of Paris and greater than that of any other faculty in France. This circumstance, together with various departures from French methods and the interest of Strasbourg clinicians in the full-time approach, was not conducive to cordial feeling toward the institution by other medical faculties.

But it was precisely this diversity which interested the Foundation. Flexner, visiting Strasbourg in 1922, was most enthusiastic. He felt that in the superb plant, where Alsatians with German training and French teachers from Paris and Nancy were already "working very harmoniously in the hope of producing something that may influence medical education throughout France,"[17] the best of each might be combined, with the new developments in England and America also making a contribution. To encourage the strengthening of this point of view, a commission of medical leaders from Strasbourg was invited to visit the United States and Britain as guests of the Foundation; and in 1925 a sizable grant was made by the Foundation for the development of the Strasbourg medical school.

Except for Strasbourg, the most important medical faculty after Paris was at that time considered to be Lyon. The city was known to be progressive and interested in its hospitals. When it was brought to the Foundation's attention that the city was building a new hospital, interest was expressed in contributing to a plan by which the medical school might be moved to a new site adjoining the hospital, and a modern medical center developed. "Together with Strasbourg," Pearce wrote, "it might possibly influence the University of Paris, which, after all is said, is the final arbiter in medicine in France."[18]

To this end, the Foundation invited the dean of the medical school of Lyon, two of his professors, and an architect to visit England and the United States to familiarize themselves with modern methods in construction and organization. As one immediate result of this visit, the dean put into effect what the Foundation considered "a most surprising change"[19]—a rearrangement of courses by which during the first year the student gave his entire time to instruction in the medical school without getting prematurely into clinical work. This was so radical a move that it was considered in itself evidence of the intention of the dean and his faculty to bring about fundamental changes at Lyon. More than a million and a half dollars were contributed by the Foundation toward this newly constructed medical center.

Brussels

The medical school of the University of Brussels, supported by grants from the municipality and by private gifts, seemed to both Pearce and Rose to offer a unique opportunity in developing modern ideas of medical teaching. "While Liège, Ghent and Louvain each has some point in its favor," wrote Pearce, "the first and second are state-controlled and the third is a church-controlled institution, and they do not have the freedom of Brussels to try new things."[20] When, therefore, in 1920, a delegation from the University came to the United States to solicit Foundation aid for a substantial reorganization of the medical program, the proposals which it presented received immediate consideration.

After long study by both the University authorities and the Foundation, plans of a wide, sweeping character were matured. They involved, first, the physical concentration on a new site of the clinical hospital, the medical school institutes, and the school of nursing; and second, the development of the teaching and research staff, placing the teaching of the laboratory sciences on a full-time basis, and introducing certain full-time teachers and workers into the clinical branches. Not everything that Pearce desired in this connection could be obtained, but as he said, his motto was: Not the whole way, but the next step in the right direction. Toward this development the Foundation contributed sums in excess of $4,500,000, paid over a period of years.

When after long delays the new plant was ready for dedication in 1930, representatives of the Foundation were invited to come to Brussels for the ceremony. Vincent, in declining, summed up the Foundation's policy in these characteristic words:

> [The Foundation] wishes to do its work with a minimum of ostentation. It prefers to keep in the background and to avoid the exploitation of itself and its officers. To be present at the opening of buildings to which the Foundation had contributed is almost to invite public praise. It seems in better taste to avoid such situations.
>
> Furthermore the spirit of the Foundation's activities is not nationalistic. While it is an American organization in origin, personnel and funds, it does not wish to be regarded as an instrument of national policy, or as an expression of American philanthropy. We realize that harm has been

done in certain quarters by a rather complacent emphasis over here upon a generosity which the United States is said to have shown to Europe. We desire to avoid any aggravation of the feeling that Americans are too ready to admit their own virtues. . . .[21]

São Paulo

During the early twenties, extensive surveys were made of medical education in all the Latin-American countries, but it was only in Brazil that conditions were found that seemed to justify Foundation assistance. Pearce had hoped that the notable receptivity of the Latin-American countries to progressive practices in public health might be stabilized through improvements in medical education, and São Paulo, the progressive city in Southern Brazil, proved to be the most promising place to begin. A commission of local medical leaders visited the outstanding institutions of Europe and the United States, and a series of forward-looking steps were taken at the University of São Paulo to improve the quality of medical training, including full-time teaching in all laboratory subjects, the limitation of the number of students to accord with laboratory and clinical facilities, and, finally, the concentration of the medical plant on a single site. Toward the consummation of this development the Foundation appropriated nearly a million dollars. São Paulo retains to this day a leading place among the medical schools of Latin America.

Canada

When in 1919 Mr. Rockefeller made his final gift of $50,000,000 to the Foundation, he included these sentences in his letter of transmittal: "The Canadian people are our near neighbors. They are closely bound to us by ties of race, language and international friendship, and they have without stint sacrificed themselves—their youth and their resources—to the end that democracy might be saved and extended. For these reasons, if your Board should see fit to use any part of this new gift in promoting medical education in Canada, such action would meet with my very cordial approval."[22]

With the advice of the Canadian medical personnel and of other citizens whose views the Foundation was anxious to obtain, a Dominion-wide policy was developed; and seven medical centers, strategically located and of maximum promise, were selected for assistance: Dalhousie at Halifax, Toronto, McGill at Montreal, Manitoba at Winnipeg, British Columbia at Vancouver, a school for the French Canadians at Montreal, and a school for Northwestern Canada at

Edmonton, Alberta. Of these seven, British Columbia alone could not be considered in connection with the gift because its plans were not sufficiently developed. Negotiations were subsequently carried on with the other six and sums ranging from several hundred thousand dollars to a million and a half were appropriated to each institution.

Beirut

The medical school of the University of Beirut has long enjoyed an enviable reputation. It serves a wide area in the Near East, including not only Syria, but Greece, Asia Minor, Mesopotamia, Persia, Palestine, and Egypt. Pearce was greatly attracted by the potential promise of this school when he visited it in 1924, and plans were immediately initiated for a fellowship program to help train future members of the faculty. Forging steadily ahead, the school adopted the suggestions which Pearce made in relation to the raising of a certain amount of endowment from other sources, construction of various buildings, establishment of an interne year, reorganization of the hospital and the appointment of some full-time teachers. Toward this general development the Foundation contributed for building, equipment, and endowment some two and a half million dollars.

"You have given us all," President Bayard Dodge wrote to Pearce, "the courage to rebuild our school on the basis of high standards and to insist upon first-class methods, rather than to be content with the sort of work which other schools in the Near East are putting up with. Your long experience has kept us from making mistakes and has given us a vision of medical education which would not have been possible otherwise."[23]

Southeast Asia and the Antipodes

Although the Peking Union Medical College was in active operation, Pearce believed that the Hongkong Medical School, affiliated with the University, represented an opportunity to serve a wide area. The school had always maintained high standards, and it was the medical center not only of Hongkong itself, but for the Straits Settlements and of Penang. Some of its students were also drawn from India, Siam, Sumatra, and the Philippines. The British Unit System was beginning to influence the development of the school, and to assist in this progress the Foundation endowed the chairs of medicine, surgery, and obstetrics on an essentially full-time basis.

Another institution of strategic importance was the King Edward VII Medical School at Singapore, founded to provide the inhabitants of the Malay Peninsula with local medical practitioners trained in European medicine. Essentially a government institution, it was supported in part by public subscription. Although it could not be ranked with the school at Hongkong, its importance as a center in the Far East was obvious, and the Foundation endowed two full-time lectureships, one in biochemistry and the other in bacteriology.

It was in Siam, however, that the Foundation engaged in an ambitious undertaking. It was nothing less than the establishment of a first-grade medical school in Bangkok with American professors serving as directors of departments for an interim period while Siamese were being trained for these positions through fellowships. Built around the existing Royal Medical School, the plan involved its complete reorganization, the strengthening of premedical work, the development of Siriraj Hospital into a modern plant, and the provision of extensive equipment. It was a co-operative arrangement between the Foundation and the Siamese government, and in carrying out the plan the Siamese contributed more than their expected share of the building costs.

The project was a demonstration in this part of the world of what a modern medical school means, and what it involves in preliminary education, buildings, equipment, personnel, hospital facilities, and nursing. When the Foundation's aid came to an end in the early thirties, substantial progress had been made, but it must be admitted that plans for so extensive a series of developments should have allowed for more time to mature. Rapidly moving political and economic events cut across the expected pattern of growth; and in the death of Prince Mahidol Songkla, himself a graduate of the Harvard Medical School, the Siamese lost their wisest patron and leader of modern medical education, and the Foundation lost an extraordinarily able collaborator.

South of the Equator, in Australia and New Zealand, the Foundation surveys found medical education in a relatively satisfactory condition. At Otago University, New Zealand had a medical school which, apart from a few fellowships and travel grants, required no large-scale assistance from the Foundation; and the three schools of Australia, supported generously by the state as well as by private gifts, had always maintained high standards of medical education and medical licensure. However, a promising opportunity developed at the University of Sydney, where a local citizen had recently given large sums toward the establishment of several full-time chairs. The Foundation's gift of £100,000 toward building and equipping clinical laboratories at Sydney was made in the belief that it would "produce in Australia decided results both in the way of an admirable school and in influence in the Dominion."[24]

The South Pacific Islands

One of the most interesting and perhaps significant of the Foundation's undertakings in medical education was in connection with the development of a school in Fiji to serve the vast chain of islands in the South Pacific under the jurisdiction of the British, Australian, and New Zealand governments. In a strict sense, it was hardly a medical school at all—at least by accepted Western standards. It was an attempt to train native practitioners, mostly Polynesians and Melanesians, in the rudiments of rural medicine and public health. It gave them the basic essentials of the control of hookworm, soil pollution, and diseases like malaria and yaws. They learned obstetrics, how to set broken bones, how to perform relatively minor operations, and what to do with the fevers and hazards of the sea and jungle. They acquired a background of anatomy, pathology, and bacteriology. They would have been out of place at Johns Hopkins or at the University College Hospital School in London, but their training was admirably adapted to the practical and immediate needs of their own environment.

The idea of enlisting The Rockefeller Foundation behind this somewhat primitive type of preparation was born in the mind of an extraordinary man, Dr. Sylvester M. Lambert, who, for nearly a decade, had represented the International Health Division of the Foundation in the South Pacific. In his campaigns against hookworm, yaws, and malaria he had come to know the islands and the people as few of his contemporaries knew them. He had traveled the South Seas from the Pacific atolls to the dense Papuan jungles, on trading vessels, in dugouts, or on trails that wore out hobnails in a day. He saved life abundantly and he lived it abundantly—this "doctor with a million patients." His long and intimate experience brought him to the conclusion that the natives could never obtain satisfactory care through white physicians trained in Western medicine. "In the first place," he said, "their cost makes an adequate number prohibitive. Secondly, they fail to answer their full purpose from ignorance of the language and customs. Thirdly, they cannot and will not stand the hardships which medical work entails in these islands." He had nothing but scorn for the average white doctor he met. "He comes out to the islands often with no knowledge of tropical medicine," he said, "frequently an alcoholic, usually a medical cripple of some sort."[25]

Lambert's answer to the problem, as he said repeatedly and with emphasis, was to train native doctors, "who understand native languages and customs, and above all, the native mind, as a white man never does." There was already a school of sorts at Suva on Fiji, established by the British government. Lambert's idea was to enlarge it and make it a center for the training of nurses and practitioners (he never called them doctors) who would serve a wide-flung need.

But Pearce and the New York office of the Foundation would have none of it. Lambert said in disgust that it gave them "almost physical nausea."[26] The yellowing pages of the records relating to this episode are studded with Pearce's disapproving and sometimes caustic comments: "[These are] not doctors but men of the type of hospital stewards or hospital assistants. Lower grade practitioners. . . . [We] must stick to the policy of aiding only Class A schools. . . . [We are] not prepared to enter into any program which would give less training than that required to practice in this country."[27]

Pearce, when aroused, was a fighter, but in Lambert he met a man who cared nothing for conventional relationships and rode roughshod over red tape. In one sense, it was a drawn battle. Pearce refused to recommend the project as far as his own Division of Medical Education was concerned, and after considerable delay, support was given by the Foundation's International Health Division. Not until after Pearce's death did his successor, Dr. Alan Gregg, recognize the project as a legitimate part of medical education. Support from the Foundation continued for nearly a decade until the maintenance of the school was assumed completely by government agencies. The purpose of the school and Lambert's enthusiasm for it seem to have been amply justified. It made available a medical and health service to native people at low cost and in a form that was most easily assimilable by their society. More than that, it provided a pattern which is perhaps applicable under similar circumstances to other areas.

Emergency Program in Europe

The chaos of the First World War had affected so deeply the countries of Europe, particularly of Central and Eastern Europe, that in many cases the only type of medical aid that could be given was of a temporary nature—something, as Pearce said, that would "keep the status of medicine in any given institution from slipping too rapidly,"[28] something that would, if possible, reconstitute the broken links in the chain of medical education and practice. Unfavorable exchange had cut institutions off from foreign literature and laboratory materials; lack of economic security was discouraging research; and intense nationalistic prejudices were rapidly affecting the influence and importance of certain centers. Unless the situation was to get completely out of hand, emergency measures were necessary, and the Foundation embarked on such a program.

Three general types of activity were undertaken: (1) furnishing medical literature to important medical centers; (2) providing laboratory equipment to make possible the continuance of research; (3) arranging resident fellowships, especially in Germany. The area in which this work, or some part of it, was carried on included most of the countries of Continental Europe, with particular emphasis in Eastern Europe. It was the kind of program that Pearce was inclined to consider a necessary evil—something unavoidable, but which cut across the broad lines of creative development in which he was primarily interested. He referred more than once to being "worried to death by the routine details of the emergency aid we are now giving";[29] and the size as well as the complexity of the program troubled him.

Technically, these emergency devices came to an end in December, 1926. Actually, much of the same work continued after that date. The distribution of literature became part of a program for research aid; scientific equipment was provided for returned fellows not only in Europe but in all parts of the world; and the principle of resident fellowships was incorporated in a later program. All this was merely a shift in purpose, the aim after 1926 being, not the salvaging of a situation, but the use of these aids as adjuncts to constructive and forward-looking plans.

IV

In a world-wide program as sweeping as this, disappointments and failures were inevitable. To Pearce, whose whole life was dedicated to the problem, the inability of the Foundation to establish a broader base for modern medicine in Latin America was discouraging. Equally in South Africa, the breakdown of negotiations with the government seemed a highly unfortunate setback. Both the Capetown and the Johannesburg medical schools had been closed to the

Negro population, and natives were forced to go to the British Isles for their medical education. The Foundation offered to contribute £70,000 for buildings, equipment, and teaching facilities if the government would maintain a medical school for Negroes at the University of Witwatersrand at Johannesburg, with the understanding that the teaching should be of the same standard as that for Europeans, and lead to the same degree. The proposal included also a three-year course for training health assistants who would be sanitary inspectors; a three-and-a-half year course for native nurses; and a temporary two-year course for nurses' aides. While the proposal was never officially rejected by the government, strong anti-native feeling and serious race riots prevented the possibility of favorable action, and the Foundation finally withdrew the offer.

It was in relation to the French medical situation in Paris, however, that the Foundation encountered its major setback. From its early interest in the University of São Paulo in Brazil, all its efforts in the Latin countries, or in countries which might influence them, had had as an ultimate goal a substantial change in the center of French medicine as represented in Paris. Aid to Strasbourg, Lyon, Brussels, Beirut, Brazil, and French Canada had always in view the possibility of eventual influence on the University of Paris, the chief stronghold of Latin medicine.

In 1927, the long looked-for opportunity seemed to be opening. Aid was requested by the University of Paris for independent institutes of experimental medicine and hygiene. Officers of the Foundation, meeting with representatives of the medical faculty, pointed out the advisability of considering a larger fundamental program rather than the piecemeal help then being sought. It was indicated that the Foundation might be prepared to help with a truly significant scheme at the University, if soundly conceived.

Further investigation revealed the fact that there existed in Paris a site occupied by the Halle aux Vins which from every point of view would be eminently desirable as the location for a medical center. This property, containing about forty-two acres, belonged to the city of Paris, but was occupied by wine merchants who used it largely for storage purposes. The main advantages of the site for a medical center were several: adequate space for the laboratories and hospitals of the proposed institutes; nearness to the main buildings of the University; proximity to some of the largest hospitals in the city which were used by the faculty for clinical teaching; and, finally, the possibility of bringing together on the same site the laboratory sciences of the medical faculty, the biological sciences of the University, and the large biological facilities of the Jardin des Plantes.

Actually, three problems were involved in the Paris situation: land; buildings and maintenance; and the question of some type of reorganization of the teaching. Vincent and Gregg felt that securing the land was of paramount importance, and Gregg was opposed to complicating it with any suggestion for reorganization. He believed that the acquisition of this site could be "a clean-cut procedure against which there would be very little opinionated resistance. Indeed," he said, "I imagine, to the majority such a site seems too good to be true as well as too expensive to be realized."[30] Pearce, on the other hand, was inclined to put more emphasis on reorganization and his point of view was the one that was accepted by his trustees. The Foundation authorized a contribution of six million dollars toward the acquisition of a site and the erection of the necessary buildings "upon condition that, for the Medical School, clinical facilities controlled by the University shall be provided, and that for both the medical and biological sciences such arrangements shall be made as shall secure the full time and effort of the heads of the fundamental scientific branches."[31] A further sum of six million dollars was set aside for the development of the project once the primary program had been achieved.

The initial reception in France of the offer of the Foundation was extremely favorable, but soon the tide began to flow in the opposite direction. Delay followed delay and complications became more evident. While some of the medical faculty undoubtedly welcomed the conditions suggested by the Foundation, others did not. Lack of unanimity was in the air and in some quarters, unfortunately, a pervading anti-Americanism. The fall of Tardieu's ministry, which had been favorable to state aid to the city in acquiring the site, was a further unsettling factor, as was the assassination of President Doumier, who had welcomed the plan. Delays grew longer, inertia itself became an active force, and the alerted wine merchants, tenacious of their holdings, closed their ranks in opposition. By 1932, even the strongest advocate of a medical center at the Halle aux Vins site admitted that the project was dead. There was nothing more to be done, and the Foundation with great regret rescinded its $12,000,000 pledge.

Pearce died in 1930. But the work which he had set for himself a decade earlier was finished, and already the activities of his division were being shifted in another direction. He had always thought of the Foundation's undertakings in medical education in terms of a ten-year program, "looking toward expenditures which . . . would at the end of that time pretty well clear up the important schools of medicine and public health that might be expected to receive large contributions from the Foundation."[32] Actually, his directorship covered almost exactly that period of time.

In spite of his avowed gradualism and his stressing of the aphorism, "not the whole way but the next step in the right direction," Pearce was at heart a perfectionist, with an undisguised dislike of what seemed to him the second-rate and the next best. It is perhaps idle to speculate on the possible extent to which this ingrained perfectionism may have handicapped the development of the work to which he gave his life. The question might conceivably be asked whether in a world like this a wider and more pragmatic advance in the teaching of medicine could have been made with a policy which did not adhere so uncompromisingly to the rigorous standards of the best. But there is much to be said on the other side of the question. The lifting power of the ideals which Pearce represented affected medicine in every quarter of the world. Under his leadership, the Foundation appropriated literally scores of millions of dollars to improve the quality of medical teaching; and at the end of what might be called an incredible decade it had left an imprint of high standards and a belief in excellence which even the ravages of the Second World War have not erased.

CHAPTER X

MEDICAL RESEARCH AND PSYCHIATRY

DURING THE EARLY TWENTIES, AS WE HAVE seen, the Foundation's interest in medicine was concentrated on its relation to university teaching. It rigorously excluded not only independent research institutions, but the ancillary fields of physics, chemistry, and biology, as well as clinical activities unrelated to laboratory effort. As early as 1925, however, Pearce began to take a serious interest in such centers as Kraepelin's Institut in Munich, the Kaiser Wilhelm Institut for Brain Research in Berlin, and the Pasteur Institute at the Collège de France in Paris.

> I am quite convinced [he wrote to Gregg] that in the greater part of Southeastern and Central Europe, certainly outside of Germany and Austria, we can do nothing significant on the clinical side in the ordinary medical school. I do believe, however, that we can help advancement through stimulating work in certain research institutes which can train a higher type of men as graduate. . . . I should be prepared to do [this] . . . somewhere in Europe for psychiatry, neurology and pediatrics, if we could find the right concatenation of circumstances.[1]

He called this "the germination of a new program," and during the remaining years of his life the idea was implemented by the Foundation in substantial grants to the Institutes of Pharmacy and Physiology at Utrecht, the Institute of Physiology at Copenhagen, the Institute of Hygiene at Nancy, Kraepelin's Institut at Munich, and the Kaiser Wilhelm Institut (Vogt's Institute) in Berlin.

It is significant, however, that at this stage of the development of of the Foundation's program in medicine, its interest in pure research was not yet an end in itself, but was still qualified by the relationship of research to graduate training. As Pearce told the trustees: "It is time to depart from the older policy and to aid research as such when in exceptional circumstances it is possible to foster an institute which shall be of value in the training of medical teachers and investigators in addition to the avowed object of research itself."[2] It was not until Gregg succeeded Pearce in 1930 that the bridge was completely crossed, and the activities of the Foundation in this branch of its work were concentrated largely on extending the boundaries of knowledge.

With this new objective, which, as we shall see in the next chapter, was officially effected by the trustees in an extensive reorganization of the whole program of the Foundation's work, the Division of Medical Education became the division of Medical Sciences, and the older interest in the training of competent practitioners was in large part superseded by a drive to widen the horizons of understanding in relation to unexplored or unsolved problems. In the years that followed, research was supported in many directions. A new form of assistance was the so-called "fluid research fund," granted to various institutions in the United States, including Johns Hopkins, Oregon, Rochester, Stanford, Utah, Vanderbilt, and Yale. These were unassigned sums for allocation by the authorities of the medical schools, and it was hoped that in providing such funds for a limited period, research might be so stimulated that the value of the practice and the necessity of maintaining it could be demonstrated.

Even greater emphasis was placed on the direct support of promising lines of research. These involved multifarious projects including such subjects as infectious diseases, drug addiction, otology, tropical medicine, physiology, industrial medicine, medical economics, psychology, and human heredity. These various projects were undertaken at different times over a long period, and while the list covers wide and apparently diverse fields, in reality it represented a highly selective and imaginative approach. Occasionally, the subject opened the door to a new adventurous technique. Thus the grant to Dr. Leonard Colebrook of Queen Charlotte's Hospital in London developed the high clinical usefulness of a drug called prontosil. This drug had been discovered in Germany, oddly enough in connection with the commercial dye industry. In 1935, a German scientist, Dr. Gerhard Domagk, published the results of his experiments with mice, showing the extraordinary effect of prontosil on streptococcus. The Pasteur Institute in Paris then picked the matter up, and found out that the activity of the drug was localized in one particular part of its molecular structure. The useless part of the molecule was subtracted, and the result is what we now call sulfanilamide. At this point, Dr. Colebrook, with the Foundation's grant, made one of the first clinical applications of the reconstructed drug; it was tried on women suffering from streptococcal infection associated with puerperal or childbirth fever, with results so startling that sulfanilamide and its many ramifications and developments have now become an indispensable part of the world's medicine.

Equally adventurous was the work of Dr. Elton Mayo of the Harvard School of Business Administration in what he called "the clinical approach" to human relations in industry. Under his leadership, the Harvard project pioneered new studies in industrial psychology, studies that used business operations like the Western Electric Company as laboratories, and brought to light new ideas on such subjects as the effects of fatigue, and variations in air, temperature, and light, on human well-being and working efficiency. Supported initially by The Laura Spelman Rockefeller Memorial, this ramifying research was aided over many years by the Medical Sciences division.

Another trail-blazing type of research which the Foundation supported was carried on by Adelbert Ames of Dartmouth in physiological optics. This was a case where the primary attraction was the man and the quality of his mind rather than the particular field of study. He gave the name "aniseikonia" to a new-found defect in vision resulting from the inequality of the two lenses of a pair of eyes, in consequence of which the images received by the retinas are of unequal size. But he did not stop there, and his studies have run the gamut from physics to metaphysics, through physiology and psychology. "I think Ames will be rediscovered in future years," wrote Gregg, "as often as anyone the Medical Sciences division has aided; for I am almost sure that neither he nor anyone else as yet understands all the ideas he has put forth on optics, vision, perception, and the effect of past experience on the understanding of our current experiences."[3]

In a similar spirit of adventure, the Foundation approached the fields of endocrinology and human heredity. Most readers are familiar with the names of such internal secretions as insulin and adrenalin, and with the fact that the pituitary, the thyroid, the adrenals, and other endocrine glands produce internal secretions, small in amount, but large in effects and complicated in both structure and action. Indeed, so intricate and relatively obscure is the subject of endocrinology, and so intimately related to the growth and function of body and mind, that the Medical Sciences division, beginning in Pearce's regime, gave long-continued support to a few investigators who have possessed an unusual blend of chemical knowledge, tenacity of purpose, enthusiasm, and critical judgment. The recent encouraging developments in this field are based, in part at least, on the fundamental substructure which these scientists built—men, for example, like Charles A. Stockard of Cornell, Herbert M. Evans of the University of California, Fuller Albright of the Massachusetts General Hospital, and Bernardo Houssay, formerly of the University of Buenos Aires.

The interest of the Foundation in the allied field of human heredity began in 1932 with grants for the studies of human identical twins. Progress in this field is necessarily slow, for human matings cannot in any way be comparable to the geneticist's experimental crosses, and no one investigator would be likely to live long enough to be able to study as many as four generations of human subjects. But indirect approaches are possible, and over the years the Medical Sciences division of the Foundation has maintained a lively interest in this field.

A project related, indirectly at least, to both endocrinology and human heredity is the work of a special committee of the National Research Council—the Committee for Research on Problems of Sex. The Foundation in the second quarter of the century gave well over a million dollars to this work, and the wide sweep of the investigation has involved biology, physiology, psychology, psychopathology, sociology, and other disciplines. Among the projects supported by the Committee with Foundation funds have been the case-history studies in human sex behavior carried on by a group working under Dr. Alfred C. Kinsey, Professor of Zoology at Indiana University. Publication of the analyzed results of his survey began in 1948 with an initial volume entitled *Sexual Behavior in the Human Male*. In his preface to Kinsey's book, Dr. Gregg wrote:

> Certainly no aspect of human biology in our current civilization stands in more need of scientific knowledge and courageous humility than that of sex. The history of medicine proves that in so far as man seeks to know himself and face his whole nature, he has become free from bewildered

fear, despondent shame, or arrant hypocrisy. As long as sex is dealt with in the current confusion of ignorance and sophistication, denial and indulgence, suppression and stimulation, punishment and exploitation, secrecy and display, it will be associated with a duplicity and indecency that lead neither to intellectual honesty nor human dignity.

In all this support of research in various fields, the Foundation did not entirely neglect the appeal of medical education which had enlisted its interest in the early days. In addition to its work along these lines in psychiatry and neurology, of which we shall speak later, it is significant that even when the older program had been largely abandoned, the Medical Sciences division, under Gregg's leadership, paid for the pioneering costs of the Department of the History of Medicine at Johns Hopkins, the Chair of Clinical Science at University College, London, the Department of Legal Medicine at Harvard, and the Departments of Dermatology at Harvard and the University of Pennsylvania. The policy leading to these decisions was undoubtedly opportunistic, but the opportunities were too challenging to let slip. "Sometimes we began with fellowships or exploratory grants in aid," said Gregg, "but it was always pioneer work and pathfinding. We didn't add to what was already a substantial nucleus; our gift created the nucleus complete or provided an indispensable fraction of it."[4]

II

But it was in the broad field of psychiatry that the division of Medical Sciences placed its major concentration as the century rounded into its third decade. In a sense, it was not a new interest for the Foundation, although no emphasis of this dimension had hitherto been attempted. In 1913, shortly after its creation, the Foundation began a co-operative relationship with the National Committee for Mental Hygiene, and for many years supported its activities and studies of the institutional treatment of mental diseases. It was during the early part of this period that Dr. Thomas W. Salmon was engaged by the Foundation as its adviser in matters relating to mental hygiene, his services being placed at the disposal of the National Committee. Under this arrangement the work continued to expand, with emphasis increasingly on the problem of the individual. Out of Dr. Salmon's recommendation that all criminals sentenced to state prisons should first be sent to psychiatric clinics for classification grew the clinic established at Sing Sing in 1916, the first of its kind in the country.

Dr. Salmon resigned from the Foundation in 1921 to take the professorship of psychiatry at Columbia University, but the Foundation's contributions to the general expenses of the National Committee for Mental Hygiene and for its successor organization, the National Mental Health Foundation, have continued up to the present time. During this period, The Laura Spelman Rockefeller Memorial became interested in psychiatry and in the related areas of child psychology and industrial psychology, both in Canada and the United States. The most ambitious undertaking of the Memorial in this field led to the creation of the Institute of Human Relations at Yale. Over the years, the various Rockefeller boards contributed very substantial sums to this Institute, and while even a broad definition of psychiatry would not cover all that was done there, the major part of the support was for use in this field.

The activities which the Foundation began in 1933, however, were launched on a far more comprehensive scale. Officially, the program in psychiatry was initiated by a report made by Dr. David L. Edsall, Dean of the Harvard Medical School, who was also a trustee of the Foundation. This report became at once both the charter and the point of departure for the new venture. "Psychiatry," said Dr. Edsall, "has been distinctly separated from general medical interests and thought, to such a degree that, to very many medical men, it seems a wholly distinct thing with which they have little relation."[5] Indeed, when Dr. Edsall wrote his report, psychiatry was —and to a large extent still is today—the most backward, the most needed, and potentially the most fruitful field in medicine. The number of hospital beds devoted to the care of mental cases exceeds in many countries the number of hospital beds for all other diseases put together. It is estimated that eight million persons, about 6 per cent of the population of the United States, are suffering from some form of mental disease or personality disorder. If there were any way of knowing the number of hospital patients whose apparent bodily illnesses are the result or concomitant of mental disorders, the picture would expose even more vividly the discrepancy in our effectiveness against "diseases of the mind" as contrasted with "diseases of the body." Our tragic lack of knowledge in this backward field may be deduced from the economic, moral, social, and spiritual losses occasioned by the feeble-minded, the delinquents, the criminally insane, the emotionally unstable, the psychopathic personalities, and—less dramatic but far more widespread—the preventable anxieties, phobias, tantrums, complexes, and anomalous or unbalanced behavior of otherwise normal human beings.

In 1933, when The Rockefeller Foundation began to concentrate in this field, it can fairly be said that teaching in psychiatry was poor, research was fragmentary, and application was feeble.* Some American medical schools had no departments at all in psychiatry, neurology, and allied specialties; some had primitive and inadequate departments; and a few had departments which, though fairly well organized, were incomplete or isolated from the other activities of the school. Traditionally, psychiatry had dealt with major mental disease, and its practice frequently concerned itself only with the commitment and custodial care of the incapacitated. Little attention was paid by either the professional psychiatrist or the practitioner in other branches of medicine to the interplay of body and mind in every illness.

This was the situation which the Foundation, with imagination and a degree of audacity, set out to correct insofar as its relatively limited funds permitted. The recommendation bringing the matter before the trustees was candid: "Psychiatry cannot be said to be the most promising of immediate results, nor the field in which the finest minds are now at work, nor the field intrinsically easiest for the application of scientific method. But it would be unwise to conclude that for such reasons no effort should be made."[6] The objective of the Foundation, frankly stated, was to infuse medicine with psychiatry, to help make this discipline a headland of medicine, instead of an isolated island of speculation and terminologies. Its argument was that the physician with his inadequate training was treating specific physical symptoms but not the whole man, and that just so far as medicine failed to encompass the whole man, it failed to understand him. Body and mind cannot be separated for purposes of treatment; they are one and indivisible. Whether he will or no, the doctor's office is a confessional of spiritual as well as physical disability. With all its wisdom, if medicine neglects what integrates and harmonizes the functions and organs, its picture will be out of focus and its comprehension incomplete. "Man's eternal cry is for release, and the physician must answer it with something more than a test-tube."

* While psychiatry became the major emphasis of the division of Medical Sciences in 1933, approximately $4,000,000 had been expended in this field before that date.

Although the Foundation labeled its program psychiatry, the term was always thought of as broadly inclusive. It embraced neurology and psychology, and had its fringes in the social sciences and even in ethics. There was really no single word to cover the fields proposed for this major interest. "I should not be satisfied with the definition of psychiatry as that specialty in medicine which deals with mental disorders," said Gregg. "Like a bad newspaper headline, such a definition confines while condensing and misrepresents by oversimplifying. Psychiatry deals also with the emotional and social life of man. . . . [Its] province is the conduct of man, his reactions, his behavior as an indivisible sentient being with other such beings."[7]

The approach of the Foundation to this new field of interest was direct and clean cut. It had been outlined by Dean Edsall in his report. He had suggested two "perfectly reasonable lines of expenditure for the purpose of improving psychiatry": one, the development of good teaching in a few medical schools with the integration of psychiatry into the regular medical curriculum; and two, the support of scientific research.

With drive and spirit, Gregg proceeded to implement the program. The University of Chicago, which had no department of psychiatry, was provided with one. McGill University in Montreal was given an institute for neurology and neurosurgery, under the distinguished leadership of Dr. Wilder Penfield. The teaching of psychiatry at Tulane, Duke, McGill, and Washington University in St. Louis, previously primitive or almost entirely lacking, was put on a satisfactory basis with full-time teachers and adequate teaching material. The teaching of psychiatry at Harvard, formerly confined to the problems encountered in state hospitals, was broadened by the establishment of a department devoted to mental disease as it appears in general hospital practice. Departments of psychiatry, previously incomplete, were rounded out or extended at Johns Hopkins, Yale, the Universities of Colorado, Michigan, and Tennessee, and the Institute of the Pennsylvania Hospital. This same type of support for improved teaching in psychiatry was extended across the ocean to institutions in Europe, notably in Great Britain.

Concurrently with the program for the development of university and hospital departments, the Foundation maintained a steady stream of fellowships for advanced training in psychiatry, neurology, neurosurgery and related subjects. It also supported a few enterprises not directly within the university fold: for example, the Institute of

Psychoanalysis in Chicago and the American Psychiatric Association, the latter grant having as its purpose the stimulation of psychiatric nursing.

In the field of psychiatric research, grants were made, among many others, for mental case studies at the Worcester State Hospital in Massachusetts, for neuroanatomy at Northwestern University, for brain chemistry at Tufts, Columbia University, and McGill University, for epilepsy at Harvard, for neurophysiology at Cornell, for carbohydrate metabolism in relation to mental disease at the University of Toronto, for schizophrenia and epilepsy at the University of Illinois, for studies of the genetic factors of intelligence and emotional variation in mammals at the Roscoe B. Jackson Memorial Laboratory, and for an investigation at Columbia of the genetic factors in nervous and mental diseases. While special mention is perhaps invidious, the general high quality of this research can be illustrated by the work of Dr. W. G. Lennox of Harvard, under whose leadership the electro-encephalographic method of studying epilepsy was developed and additional effective drugs were found for the control of seizures.

This type of support was by no means confined to the United States and Canada. The Foundation aided significant research activities in Great Britain, France, Holland, Belgium, Germany, Sweden, Norway, and Switzerland. In Great Britain, for example, research grants were made for neurosurgery and psychiatry at the University of Edinburgh and the London Hospital, for neurophysiology at Cambridge University and the Burden Neurological Institute at Bristol, for human heredity at the Galton Laboratory of the University of London, for psychiatry at Tavistock Clinic in London. In addition, a substantial sum was given to the National Hospital for Diseases of the Nervous System at Queen Square, London, for building and for the endowment of research.

III

The bare skeleton of the program which we have just outlined, and into the construction of which The Rockefeller Foundation, and other foundations as well, put many millions of dollars, cannot reveal the true measure of accomplishment or the influences that were set in motion. Only with longer perspective than is available at the moment can an adequate appraisal be made. It is significant, however—whether due to the Foundation activities or otherwise—that psychiatry today occupies a position far different from that it occupied in the early thirties. It is no longer a stepchild, acknowledged, but not understood and really not wanted. While it has by no means paralleled the development of other branches of medicine, and while it has not yet been accepted on the same terms as, for example, surgery, it is slowly developing a body of knowledge and a trained personnel of high promise. There are at least a score of medical schools today which every year graduate a group of students far better oriented toward nervous and mental disorders and their role in human life than was the case in 1933. Meanwhile, research in psychiatry has become reputable, and in neurophysiology it occupies an advanced position.

The exigencies of the Second World War undoubtedly revealed the need for this development. Indeed, no greater vindication of the early decision of the Foundation to work in the field of psychiatry could have been provided than the experiences through which this country passed after Pearl Harbor. The need of psychiatric knowledge and personnel became suddenly acute in relation to the selection of draftees, their training, and the strains of active service. For medical men, the greatest unpleasant surprise of the war was the unexpected importance of psychiatry. No experience could have revealed more effectively the irrationality of isolating it from the rest of medicine. Dr. William C. Menninger, Chief Consultant in Neuropsychiatry to the Surgeon General of the Army, reported: "Of all men examined, 12 per cent were rejected because of neuropsychiatric difficulties, which amounted to 38 per cent of all rejections." Regarding hospitalization he added: "There were approximately 1,000,000 admissions to hospitals for neuropsychiatric disorders, representing 6 per cent of admissions for all causes."[8]

Since the war, the medical schools in the United States have given much more time to psychiatry than formerly, and they have spread the subject more effectively through the four years of instruction. Although university-secured support for psychiatry is still far less than the subject calls for, it is significant that the government, through the United States Public Health Service, is moving steadily along lines which the Foundation helped develop, and the sums at its disposal for psychiatric work are impressive.

During the war, Gregg served as an official consultant in neuropsychiatry to the Surgeon General of the Army. Dr. Menninger wrote him one day when the pressure of his own job made him desirous of reassurance as to directions. "What are the most important benefits psychiatry has to give?" he asked. The reply which Gregg made delineates the atmosphere in which the Foundation's program in psychiatry evolved. By indirection, it highlights some of the achievements to which the Foundation's work contributed, both in lay understanding of psychiatry and in its explicit scientific development.

First [he wrote] psychiatry along with the other natural sciences leads to a life of reason. It explains what must otherwise excite fear, disgust, superstition, anxiety, or frustration. It breaks the clinches we otherwise get into with life and all the unnecessary, blind infighting.

In the second place, by showing us the common rules, the uniform limitations and liberties all human beings live under because they are human, psychiatry gives us a sort of oneness-with-others, a kind of exquisite communion with all humanity, past, present, and future. It is a kind of scientific humanism that frees us from dogma and the tyranny of the mind, a relief from the inhuman strait jacket of rigid finality of thought.

Third, psychiatry makes possible a kind of sincere humility and naturalness I've never received from any other study or experience. . . . It provides the material for a sympathy that is honest and eager. . . .

I didn't mention the rewards research offers to human curiosity. Nor the satisfaction of being of help to poor, battered, dependent, frightened people and the justice of giving them the breaks just for once. Nor the immense economy of patching lives to a point of meeting life's demands. Nor the hope that we may understand what disease connotes as well as what it denotes. Nor the possibility that through psychiatric understanding our successors may be able to govern human politics and relationships more sagely.[9]

Gregg's last sentence holds out a hope, dim as it may sometimes seem, for a more rational future. The mentally ill merely present in exaggerated and dramatic form aspects or properties of human nature which must be taken into account by all who are responsible for the functioning of the modern world and the design of its institutions. Fear, hate, guilt, and aggressiveness, so clearly demonstrated by the disintegrated personality, are the same forces which bring about the disintegration of human society.

Psychiatry as a science is still primitive and imperfect, but enough has been accomplished to justify the application of some of its principles to wider fields than the treatment of the mentally ill. Most of the pressing questions which confront us today, from the settlement of strikes to the formation of a world order, are fundamentally problems in human relations. The search is for institutions which will provide satisfaction for man's needs while compensating and controlling his ineradicable defects. The old method of allowing these institutions to grow out of a struggle of opposing forces is no longer possible when the power at our command is so easily capable of destroying everything we have inherited. In the future, we shall have to provide social arrangements through conscious planning and mutual agreement. Such processes may reasonably look for help from those who make a profession of studying the impulses and frustrations of individual human beings. Psychiatry is a tool of evolving importance in building a new kind of stability in human society.

CHAPTER XI

THE FOUNDATION ENTERS NEW FIELDS

DURING THE TWENTIES, IN ADDITION TO THE Rockefeller Institute for Medical Research, four Rockefeller boards were in active operation: The Rockefeller Foundation, the General Education Board, the International Education Board, and The Laura Spelman Rockefeller Memorial. Each of these boards was an independent corporation, each with its own funds, under its own trustees. The Rockefeller Foundation, as we have seen, was placing its major emphasis on public health and medical education. In addition to those two branches of its work, a Division of Studies had been created under Edwin R. Embree to which were assigned several miscellaneous interests, including the training of nurses, aid to dispensaries, the human aspects of biology, and anthropology. That the trustees did not consider themselves rigidly bound by the restrictions of a program is shown in such appropriations as were made to the Shakespeare Memorial Theatre in Stratford on Avon, and for the purchase of the new site for the University of London ($1,-943,000). But these, generally speaking, were exceptions to the rule, and the rule for the most part was medical education and public health.

The General Education Board, in addition to its work in medical education in the United States, was engaged in promoting the effectiveness of the public school system, primarily in the South. It also was carrying on a program in the arts and the humanities. Moreover, under the leadership of Dr. Rose, who had resigned from the

International Health Division to accept the presidency of the Board in 1923, extensive support was being given to research in the physical and biological sciences at the university level.

The International Education Board, which, as we have seen, was created by Mr. Rockefeller, Jr., in 1923, owed its inception to Rose, who had been reluctant to assume the presidency of the General Education Board, with its charter limiting its operations to the United States, unless some way could be found by which he could carry his educational ideas overseas. In his work with the International Health Division, Rose had seen the effectiveness of ideas promulgated on an international scale, and he was accustomed to ranging the whole world as his parish. The charter of the General Education Board had been secured by act of Congress, and it was thought that the creation of a new organization would involve less difficulty than an attempt to secure amendment. Through the instrumentality of this new board, therefore, Rose, during the twenties, was giving powerful impetus to the development of the physical and biological sciences, to agriculture, and to humanistic research.

The Laura Spelman Rockefeller Memorial, founded in 1918 in memory of Mrs. Rockefeller, Sr., had originally been planned with the idea of supporting projects and causes which had claimed her personal interest. When the funds at the disposal of the trustees exceeded these limited opportunities, a wider objective was sought in the welfare of women and children. Later, larger sums given by Mr. Rockefeller to the Memorial made even this objective too narrow; and in 1923, under the directorship of Beardsley Ruml, the Memorial embarked upon a broad plan to support research in the social sciences.

II

It was inevitable that these four foundations would encounter difficulties in their relationships with each other. Established at different times and for different purposes, they had developed various programs of activity often intimately related. At least, they were separated parts or sections of a larger and more general program. These parts, however, were headed up under different sets of officers and different boards of trustees, and while the four boards worked together in an admirable spirit of co-operation, the more or less fortuitous distribution of programs unfortunately caused some degree of confusion, not only as between the boards themselves but also in the public mind.

For example, medical education was divided geographically between the General Education Board and The Rockefeller Foundation. The natural sciences were found in the General Education Board, the International Education Board, and, in some aspects, in The Rockefeller Foundation. The humanities and arts were dealt with by both the General Education Board and The Laura Spelman Rockefeller Memorial. The social sciences, while confined to The Laura Spelman Rockefeller Memorial, had certain bearings upon the college and university policies of the General Education Board. Public health in its government relations was a function of the Foundation, while the Memorial, in co-operating with private health agencies, also had some relation to this field. The subject of mental hygiene lay in the field of both the Foundation and the Memorial. Agriculture and forestry were related to both the General Education Board and the International Education Board, although these organizations, because of identity of administrative personnel, worked without overlapping or duplication.

"It is axiomatic," said an adviser of Mr. Rockefeller, "that if we were today considering the creation of machinery necessary to carry on certain general programs in medicine, health, education and the other activities of the four Rockefeller boards, we would not set up the rather confusing organization which we now have."[1] And Mr. Rockefeller, Sr., said in a letter to his son, dated May 4, 1926: "If the whole thing were to be done today, you have rightly understood me as feeling that it should be done and doubtless could be done through a single organization."

After an extended study, a committee of trustees representing the four boards came to the conclusion that while a single organization might be ideally preferable, there were legal and other practical difficulties which seemed insurmountable. Said the committee: "Considerations of tradition and established practice and the momentum of activities in actual operation must be given due weight, and we cannot build today as if nothing had happened, and we were erecting a completely new structure."

The plan that was adopted in 1928, therefore, had as its core the idea that all the programs of the four Rockefeller boards *relating to the advance of human knowledge* should be concentrated in The Rockefeller Foundation. This involved transferring to the Foundation the following activities:

(a) The natural sciences from the General Education Board and the International Education Board.

(b) The social sciences from the Memorial.

(c) The humanities and arts from the General Education Board.

(d) The medical sciences from the General Education Board.

(e) Agriculture and forestry from the International Education Board and the General Education Board.

To effect these transfers, The Laura Spelman Rockefeller Memorial was consolidated with the Foundation; and while the International Education Board continued for a short time, its funds had largely been spent and it was soon liquidated. This left two Rockefeller organizations in the field (exclusive of the Rockefeller Institute), i.e., the Foundation and the General Education Board; and the new organization of the Foundation included five divisions: the International Health Division, which was left untouched, and the divisions of the Medical Sciences, the Natural Sciences, the Social Sciences, and the Humanities.

III

There remained the question whether a board of trustees could be constituted which was sufficiently qualified to pass on the merits of projects in such widely sweeping fields. Was any single group competent to give judgment on the intricate questions involved, for example, in medicine and the humanistic studies? This, it will be remembered, was the identical question which Mr. Rockefeller, Jr., had asked twenty years earlier in a letter to his father while the plan of the Foundation was under consideration. "Would it be possible," he had said, "to get together a single group of men who could be expected to have knowledge and interest along so many different lines?"* It was on this point, too, that Gates later developed strong reservations, and in his confidential autobiography, written probably in the early twenties, he said emphatically that he believed that the various parts of the Foundation's work, such as its activities in health and medicine, "and perhaps others, might better have been incorporated and endowed independently."

But the reorganization of 1928 was predicated—and in the author's opinion successfully predicated—on a different principle. It was the principle of the centralization of ultimate responsibility, com-

* See Chapter II, p. 15.

bined with a marked decentralization in function. The problem was given searching study, and the solution lay along three lines.

(1) The board of trustees insisted on a thoroughly competent technical staff of officers for each of the five divisions of the Foundation's work—officers of such caliber and chosen with such care that their recommendations to the trustees in their specialized fields would carry an initial weight of authority and responsibility. This principle had already been successfully demonstrated in health and medicine; and in Rose, Russell, Pearce, and their associates and assistants the trustees had had contact with judgment, competence, and specialized knowledge upon which they could completely rely. The task now was to extend this same principle to the three new fields which had been added to the Foundation's operations.

(2) In special areas, covering complex operating functions, a board of scientific directors, representing the best professional talent obtainable, was interposed between the trustees and the officers, and the proposals and recommendations of the officers were screened through this new device. This occurred only in those areas where the Foundation was engaged in direct field operations under its own management and control, i.e., in its public health work and in its later work in agriculture in Latin America. The boards of scientific directors were appointed by the trustees and met periodically. At all times, however, the ultimate control of the function rested with the trustees.

(3) Further to aid the trustees in their consideration of the proposals of the officers, an occasional specialist was added to the board. In principle, the Foundation's board is a lay board, and over the years, in choosing trustees, emphasis has been placed on general ability, balance, level-headedness, and wide intellectual sympathies. The special contribution, however, which in the early days a trustee like Dr. Simon Flexner was able to make to the intelligent discussion of items in medicine brought the trustees to the realization that while a board composed exclusively of specialists would defeat its own purpose, an occasional specialist, in a group of from nineteen to twenty-one, would add to the confidence of the trustees in their own judgments. The distinguished contributions of men like Dr. David L. Edsall, Dean of the Harvard Medical School, Dr. Alfred N. Richards of the University of Pennsylvania, Dr. George H. Whipple of Rochester—to mention three who are no longer connected with the board—more than justified the decision of the trustees to vary their general principle of choice.

It was in this fashion, therefore, and with these administrative devices, that The Rockefeller Foundation assumed responsibility in 1928 for a far wider range of activity than had been earlier contemplated. Its work literally embraced the globe, and its branch offices in Paris, London, and the Far East reflected its augmented interests.

IV

The new program was defined in broad terms under the heading of the advance of knowledge—later redefined to include the dissemination and application of knowledge. This became the objective that the Foundation was to follow for many years. There was a sense, therefore, in which 1928 marked a turning point in the thinking of the trustees. This was in part due to the fact that they had come to the end of an era in philanthropy, an era that was reflected in many other foundations as well. Huge sums had been spent in the endowment of medicine, public health institutes, and programs in higher education. Apart from the Foundation's contributions, the General Education Board had given over fifty million dollars on a matching basis to raise the endowments of American colleges and universities, and over ninety million for American medical schools. This type of giving could not continue without involving the rapid liquidation of the Rockefeller boards. Moreover, after the depression of 1929, it became increasingly clear that the decline in interest rates and the mounting difficulty in inducing other donors to match foundation funds made appropriations for endowments an uncertain and dubious technique. The interest rates of four and five per cent, which in the twenties and earlier could be confidently relied upon, were slashed to a point where perhaps double the amount of principal was required to maintain incomes of any fixed figure; and indeed fixed figures grew increasingly unpredictable in terms of purchasing power. A new orientation of target, program, and technique became, therefore, a vital necessity as the twenties drew to a close.

The decision of the trustees to concentrate the work of the Foundation on the extension of knowledge was based on a growing conviction that the margin between what men know and what they use is much too thin. Psychiatric institutes can be created and medical schools strengthened, but as one professor expressed it, "we haven't enough that we can confidently teach." Unless research is constantly maintained, the stock pile of knowledge becomes much too low for safety. There is a sense in which the practical applications of knowledge are the dividends which pure science declares from time to time.

When pure science lags, or is interrupted by a cataclysm like war, then it is necessary to pay these dividends out of surplus; and obviously this process cannot long continue.

This, of course, was not an original idea, nor was it new as far as Foundation practice was concerned. Although never so sharply defined before, the advance of knowledge had always enjoyed a conspicuous place in the organization's program. As we have seen, Pearce had made research an integral part of his medical strategy, and Russell as head of the International Health Division had breasted heavy opposition to establish the laboratory approach to field work in public health. These influences were strongly marked in the thinking of the Foundation, and they were given powerful support by Wickliffe Rose when he assumed the presidency of the General Education Board and the International Education Board in 1923. Rose brought to his new posts a profound conviction that human progress in the long run is dependent upon the extension of knowledge, although in his early days with the International Health Division this conviction had not been pronounced. But somewhere along the road he had seen a new light.

> All important fields of activity [he now said] from the breeding of bees to the administration of an empire, call for an understanding of the spirit and technique of modern science. . . . Science is the method of knowledge. It is the key to such dominion as man may ever exercise over his physical environment. Appreciation of its spirit and technique, moreover, determines the mental attitude of a people, affects the entire system of education, and carries with it the shaping of a civilization.[2]

It is true that Rose was interested largely in the natural sciences. He was not too confident that any direct approach could be made through ordered knowledge to the intricate problems of social control. He looked with some misgiving upon Ruml's attempt to stimulate basic research in economics and sociology through The Laura Spelman Rockefeller Memorial. Supremely confident of the interrelation of knowledge, he believed that the development of mathematics, physics, and chemistry, where precision and laboratory experiment are definitely established, was the best contribution that could be made to what he reluctantly called the social sciences. He almost seemed to feel that there was some process of osmosis by which the aims and something of the mood of the fundamental sciences would by diffusion be transferred to problems of social control. It was characteristic of his intellectual honesty that he was the one man in all the Rockefeller group who opposed the reorganization of 1928.

That year, however, he reached the retirement age, and he left the organization with the veneration and affection of his colleagues. Vincent retired the following year, and his departure was equally lamented. New faces, a new leadership, took over the management. Dr. Max Mason, who succeeded Vincent as president, spoke for the trustees when he said:

> The advance of knowledge is the sailing direction given the officers by the Board. We would like to feel that not too great rigidity is implied. In fundamental facts there must be research in the narrow sense; but the advancement of knowledge demands also an interest in educational processes, and in many cases the demonstration or application of existing fundamental knowledge. . . . Knowledge is gained by applying it, and sanity and value are thus brought to research.[3]

It was Mason, too, who emphasized the structural unity involved in the new orientation of program. It was not to be five programs, each represented by a division of the Foundation; it was to be essentially one program, directed to the general problem of human behavior, with the aim of control through understanding.

This was the essential goal of the reorganization of 1928. Redefined and reinterpreted over the years in the light of new experience, and reshaped in some of its outlines by the necessities of the Second World War, it has served over two decades in giving to the general purpose of the Foundation as stated in its charter the meaning and significance which the times seemed to call for.

V

Throughout this period, however, the trustees were always aware that research, which was the technical tool of the new program, could, in some fields at least, become sterile. They wanted to be sure that facts were tested by practical application. Some of them felt that under the impetus of the scientific method, scholarship was inclined to become overinterested in the collection of facts for their own sake, and underinterested in the problem of the philosophy implied by the facts. Those trustees wanted to be certain that the Foundation did not lose sight of what Professor Whitehead called "totality of vision" —a capacity for synthesis and integration, an ability not only to enumerate and describe but to evaluate. In a letter to one of the officers, the president of a prominent college expressed the opinion that nine-tenths of the money that foundations spent for research did not come to grips with public need. This fraction, of course, was a guess on his part, but some of the trustees were uneasy, and one of their committees reported its opinion that "large amounts of money are spent by foundations and universities alike on research projects that are unrealistic, unproductive, and often unrelated to human aspiration or need."[4]

Another question that was raised by the trustees as the third decade of the century grew ominously black was whether the civilization which we are building can utilize the knowledge which it has. The growth of propaganda as an instrument of education, the rise of dictatorships, the arbitrary challenge to democracy as a method of social control—it was phenomena of this type which gave pause to those who believed that the primary need of our age was more knowledge.

It is interesting to note how often, during this period, the trustees gave expression to this doubt. What special branches of knowledge should be enlarged? they asked. Is all knowledge equally important? Is anybody wise enough to determine the relative significance of different types of knowledge in a social order struggling for equilibrium? In 1934, a committee of trustees, appointed to survey the work of the Foundation, made this comment:

> The end of knowledge is, among other things, the better understanding of the world. That goal will not be reached by the mere multiplication of men able to collect more facts, but by the increase of those who know, first, what facts ought to be collected, and, second, what value those facts have when assembled. . . .
>
> The possession of funds carries with it power to establish trends and styles of intellectual endeavor. With the best will in the world the trustees of a foundation may select unwisely or place emphasis where it should not be placed or initiate movements which serve only to close men's eyes to more promising avenues. To guard against these evils requires critical judgment, common sense, wide understanding and eternal vigilance. . . .
>
> In making this comment we would say again that we are by no means suggesting that research be omitted from the Foundation's activities. We assume that the Trustees will continue to be interested in explorations in the various fields of knowledge, and research will continue to be an effective weapon.[5]

The doubt was never entirely resolved and the question was never completely answered. It was agreed that vigilance was necessary, and a dozen years later the author of this history, who had succeeded Mason as president in 1936, undoubtedly voiced the opinion of the trustees when he wrote in the Annual Review:

The answer does not lie in trying to curb science or fix boundaries beyond which intellectual adventure shall not be allowed to go. Such a course, even if it could succeed, would return us to an animal existence in which mere survival was the only goal. The search for truth is, as it always has been, the noblest expression of the human spirit. Man's hunger for knowledge about himself, his environment and the forces by which he is surrounded, gives human life its meaning and purpose, and clothes it with final dignity.[6]

It was this point of view that unmistakably underlay the thinking of the trustees in the two decades following the reorganization of 1928.

CHAPTER XII

THE NATURAL SCIENCES

ONE OUTCOME OF THE REORGANIZATION OF 1928 was the establishment of a Natural Sciences division, and thereafter the promotion of fundamental science became a primary concern of The Rockefeller Foundation, co-ordinate with its interest in public health, the medical sciences, the social sciences, and the humanities.*

In turning its attention to this broad area of human endeavor, the Foundation was not entering unfamiliar fields. Indeed, the creation of the divisional organization in 1928 simply systematized and extended an interest that already had been active for a number of years, first, in a tentative way, in The Rockefeller Foundation itself, and later in the General Education Board and the International Education Board. The present program resulted from bringing together these three earlier streams.

The interest of the Foundation in the natural sciences seems to have derived from its early concern with health and medicine. Shortly after the First World War, Dr. Simon Flexner of the Rockefeller Institute, who was also a trustee of the Foundation, began to express his growing concern over the lack of an adequate background in physics and chemistry among medical researchers. The physical sciences—

* The trustees attempted to avoid divisional demarcations by passing a resolution that directors be appointed for "groups of subjects" rather than for specific fields like natural sciences, social sciences, etc. (Rockefeller Foundation Minutes, January 3, 1929, p. 29036). It was a well-intentioned gesture which had no effect.

and he stressed mathematics as well as physics and chemistry—are so intimately related to the advance of medicine that no organization concerned with the latter can neglect the former. His first idea was the establishment of an institute for research in physics and chemistry, analogous to The Rockefeller Institute for Medical Research. After considerable study this idea was abandoned, and in its place a proposal made by the National Research Council in Washington was adopted. This Council, which had been set up during the war to make the services of American scientists available to the government, represented all branches of science, and its membership included the nation's leading investigators and research directors. They now came forward with the suggestion that the most critical need was the recruitment and training of an adequate succession of young scientists versed in the techniques and standards of modern research. It was thereupon jointly decided to offer a stated number of annual fellowships, The Rockefeller Foundation to provide the funds, the National Research Council to select the fellows and administer the program.

The outcome of this decision was the launching of the National Research Fellowships, and that event in 1919 marks the beginning of Foundation aid to the natural sciences. Thirteen fellowships were awarded the first year, six in physics and seven in chemistry. In 1923, the scope of the fellowships was broadened to include mathematics and biology as well, and later astronomy, geology, and geography were added. Although it was started immediately after the First World War, there has never been any interruption of Foundation support of the National Research Fellowships, and they have continued as a consistent backdrop to all other activities in the natural sciences. By 1950, a total of 1,107 persons had been trained under these fellowships, and the appropriations for support of the program over the thirty-two years had mounted to more than four million dollars.* Today, former fellows occupy top positions in the faculties of the leading universities, others are key men in government-supported research, and three have received Nobel Prizes.

In his *Autobiography,* Robert A. Millikan, who was one of the early advisers and architects of the National Research Fellowship program, characterizes it as "the most effective agency in the scientific development of American life and civilization that has appeared on the American scene in my lifetime,"[1] and as "the most vital influence

* These fellowships are not to be confused with the National Research Council fellowships in medicine established by the Foundation and mentioned in Chapter VIII, p. 101.

in the development of the United States into a country whose scientific output is now comparable to that of other leading scientific countries."[2]

This auspicious beginning was not immediately followed by any systematic development of the field of the natural sciences, such as Rose was inaugurating in public health and Pearce was later to inaugurate in medicine. Gates was interested in the field only as it related to medicine, and President Vincent was at heart too much of a humanist to be deeply concerned. However, it was due to Vincent that the Foundation made a grant of half a million dollars to the Marine Biological Laboratory at Woods Hole, which remains today one of the world's chief centers of biological research. Following this came another grant ($756,000) to finance *Biological Abstracts* for ten years, a bit of pioneering that was to result in one of the most useful bibliographical tools of science.

But apart from a few minor grants in biology, the field was not further developed. Vincent's regime was committed to medicine and public health, and deviations from program were the exception rather than the rule.

II

The transfer of Wickliffe Rose in 1923 from the International Health Division to the leadership of the General Education Board and the newly created International Education Board furnished another and conclusive reason why the Foundation should not then move into the field of the natural sciences. For Rose moved into it with all his characteristic vigor and enthusiasm, pre-empting the natural sciences as far as the Rockefeller boards were concerned, and staking out a claim that would have discouraged the Foundation even if it had had any special interest in the area.

Within a few weeks after assuming the presidency of both boards, he produced for his own guidance a comprehensive summary of his ideas under the title: "A Scheme for the Promotion of Education on an International Scale." He made it clear, however, that he was not thinking of education in the conventional pedagogical sense—not the routine instruction of youth and adults through schools, colleges, extension courses, and lectures. Such undertakings could be left to the governments and private agencies already concerned with them. What concerned him was that the International Education Board should be useful in "fields of educational activity that may be regarded as germinal," and by this he meant the fostering of education in its twin roles of discovery (the increase of knowledge) and diffusion (the extension of knowledge among mankind).

Guided by this principle, the International Education Board selected two areas as its principal fields of interest: the *natural sciences* and *agriculture*. Actually, of course, agriculture is directly dependent on the natural sciences. Indeed, it may be defined as the application of botany, biochemistry, biophysics, genetics, and related specialties to plant improvement and production. Thus, in a quite literal sense, Rose was focusing the whole program in the direction of the natural sciences.

"Promotion of the development of science in a country is germinal," he declared. "It affects the entire system of education and carries with it the remaking of a civilization." But, he observed, "the nations now cultivating the sciences are but a small minority of the peoples of the world," and he concluded that "it should be feasible to extend the field for the cultivation and the services of science almost indefinitely."[3]

But how should the Board proceed? Rose wrote down his guiding principles in these words:

> Begin with physics, chemistry, and biology; locate the inspiring productive men in each of these fields; ascertain of each of these whether he would be willing to train students from other countries; if so, ascertain how many he could take at one time; provide the equipment needed, if any, for operation on the scale desired.
>
> Provide by means of fellowships for the international migration of select students to each of these centers of inspiration and training; students to be carefully selected, and to be trained with reference to definite service in their own countries after completion of their studies.[4]

This "scheme" became the dominating interest of Rose's life. The program and staff of the General Education Board were for the moment deeply involved in their medical and Southern interests, and so he was able to devote the major part of his time to getting the International Education Board established on its course. Toward the end of 1923, he left for Europe on a tour that occupied five months and took him to fifty universities and other research institutions in nineteen countries. In each, he sought out the leading scientists, usually calling on them in their laboratories, where he was able to meet their staffs, see their equipment, and inquire into their problems. It was an extraordinary and heartening experience for these European scientists, just emerged from the war, many of them still suffering from its privations, to have this prophet of education on an international scale come with his understanding solicitation and offer of help. "Ground harrowed by the war," Rose called Europe—"ready for new seed." He also conferred with government scientists and officials on the needs in agriculture; and the idea of a co-operative program to assist and extend education in scientific agriculture won many favorable responses. When Rose returned to New York, he had established working relations in eighteen European countries and had prospects for co-operation in four others. He proceeded to organize a staff, borrowing from Princeton its professor of physics, Augustus Trowbridge, to serve as director for the natural sciences, and from Cornell its dean of the College of Agriculture, Albert R. Mann, to serve as director for agriculture. Before the end of 1924, the program was rapidly moving into action.

Even earlier, while Rose was still in Europe, applicants for fellowships were appraised and the first appointments made. Trowbridge established an office in Paris, and it immediately became the clearinghouse for this unprecedented international exchange of young biologists, chemists, mathematicians, physicists, and other natural scientists. W. E. Tisdale, who had been associated with the National Research Fellowship program in Washington, was appointed to assist in extending the idea, and he roved over most of Europe, interviewing candidates who had been proposed for fellowships. Never before had the search for superior brains been prosecuted over so wide and diverse an area, and many young people of inherent brilliance and talent were discovered. Two of them (Fermi of Italy and Heisenberg of Germany) later received Nobel Prizes. Altogether, in the years during which the International Education Board was active, 509 fellows in the natural sciences were selected from thirty-five nations, most of them going to other countries to spend their fellowships under favorite teachers.

One of the truly great teachers in physics was Niels Bohr, at the University of Copenhagen. His Institute for Theoretical Physics there was already cramped for space, and one of the first appropriations of the International Education Board was to finance an addition to the Institute building. This enlargement not only facilitated Professor Bohr's scientific work but made it possible to extend his teaching to a wider circle, and soon young men from other lands were traveling to Copenhagen on Board fellowships to spend a year with Bohr.

In the same way, Rose and his associates picked other strategic centers of research and training, where leadership was strong but equipment or other facilities were inadequate, and by the judicious distribution of an appropriation here, a grant-in-aid there, and a traveling professorship in another place, they gave these institutions a greater usefulness.

At no time was any consideration given to the idea of weighing the claims of one country against another and dividing the assistance on a basis of geographical balance. Always, the criterion was ability: which man, which institution, which locality offered the greater opportunity for the advancement of knowledge? One of the most promising places, in Rose's belief, was the University of Copenhagen. In addition to the Institute for Theoretical Physics, it included an Institute of Physical Chemistry under J. N. Brönsted and a Department of Physiology under August Krogh, both of which enjoyed world-wide renown and attracted graduate students from many countries. But both were hampered by overcrowded quarters and limited equipment. Here was an opportunity to strengthen teaching and research, not in one science only, but in three. So, at the same time that the grant was made to enlarge Professor Bohr's Institute for Theoretical Physics, another was voted to assist the development of Professor Krogh's Department into an Institute of Physiology, and four years later a third grant was made for the construction and equipment of a building to house the Institute of Physical Chemistry. The Danish government and other donors, both local and outside, joined in the effort to upbuild and integrate Copenhagen's facilities in the natural sciences, and subsequent grants by the Foundation have raised the total of Rockefeller assistance to $800,000. Copenhagen became one of the first universities to work out a close correlation of research effort between biology and chemistry and physics. Many important results have come from the juxtaposition of the three institutes—notably, early applications of the use of isotopes to physiological research.

Another center that offered multiple opportunities was the University of Göttingen. It was particularly strong in its physics department, which occupied an obsolete building known as the Physical Institute; and its mathematical faculty, though inconveniently scattered among various buildings, was one of the most brilliant in Europe. The Board's grant to Göttingen enabled the University to enlarge the quarters and improve the laboratory equipment of the Physical Institute and to erect nearby a Mathematical Institute which provided spacious housing both for mathematical research and teaching and for close collaboration with the physicists. Thereafter, Göttingen became more than ever before a world center for graduate study in these fields. Many of America's leading mathematicians and mathematical physicists were trained there, some of them on Rockefeller fellowships.

The world's resources in mathematics were further enhanced by a substantial contribution to the University of Paris. This assisted the building of the mathematical center known as the Institut Henri Poincaré and endowed a new professorship. With these improved facilities and enlarged faculty, Paris shared popularity with Göttingen as a place for the advanced study of mathematics and theoretical physics.

> The meeting of the Board at which Dr. Rose presented the mathematical projects for Göttingen and the University of Paris stands out in the memory of all who attended it [recalls a trustee who was present]. For Rose reported, with the aid of elaborate charts and diagrams, not on Mathematics at Göttingen or Paris alone, but on mathematics in every leading institution around the world. He was reporting on where man had arrived in his mathematical thinking, and where the opportunities for progress seemed brightest. His performance was characteristic of the immense pains and thoroughgoing analysis with which he scanned every recommendation he brought before his trustees. Göttingen and Paris were preferred in his judgment because of all the places in the world at that time they represented the peaks in mathematical science.[5]

The Board's projects in physics included grants to the University of Leiden for low-temperature research, to a Norwegian Committee for the erection of the Institute of Cosmical Physics at Tromsö, and to the Jungfrau High Altitude Institute for an observatory and laboratory later built on the Sphinx, the lofty promontory which flanks the Jungfraujoch in Switzerland. Funds given the Spanish Junta for the Extension of Research and Scientific Investigations built the Institute of Physics and Chemistry in Madrid, a planting of great promise whose early flowering was blighted by Spain's civil war.

Several important contributions were made to chemistry. A grant to the University of Upsala aided The Svedberg's experiments which resulted in the development of an improved type of ultracentrifuge, an apparatus which today is an indispensable tool of research in biochemical laboratories all over the world. A larger grant to the University of Stockholm completed a fund to build a modern laboratory for Hans von Euler's studies, and this Stockholm Biological Institute is an important center of research in enzyme chemistry.

In biology, the International Education Board provided numerous items of material assistance: a biological laboratory for Harvard; buildings and endowment for biological laboratories at the University of Edinburgh and Cambridge University; a herbarium building for the Jardin des Plantes in Paris; an enlargement of facilities for the Marine Biological Station at Plymouth, England; support for the Zoological Station at Naples; a gift toward endowment of the Botanical Conservatory at Geneva; and library funds for the Society of Biology at Paris.

Astronomy was not mentioned in Dr. Rose's plan to "begin with physics, chemistry, and biology," but opportunities in this field were presented for consideration, and several received favorable action. A grant to the Harvard College Observatory enabled it to move its southern station from Peru to a more satisfactory site in South Africa and provided the new outpost with a 60-inch reflecting telescope. Smaller funds were given to the National Academy of Sciences in Washington to finance a bibliography of planets, and to the University of Lyons in France for its study of variable stars. Finally, in the last year of the Board's active life, a few weeks before Dr. Rose retired, the largest gift and the most magnificent venture of the entire natural-science program was voted: six million dollars to the California Institute of Technology for the construction and installation of a 200-inch telescope. The details of this venture are discussed in a subsequent chapter.

III

While the International Education Board was thus putting Rose's "scheme" into effect on a global scale, the General Education Board, under Rose's leadership, was pursuing a parallel course within the United States. To be sure, the international program itself included several projects in this country—e.g., the great telescope and the biological laboratory at Harvard—but Rose's principal agency for operation in the homeland was the General Education Board.

For many years, as we have seen, this board had been making grants for general endowment; and by 1925 its gifts for that purpose had totaled sixty million dollars distributed among more than two hundred American colleges and universities. In most of these institutions, the natural sciences, along with the other faculty departments, benefited from the increased endowment; but until Rose became president, there had been no systematic program within the Rockefeller boards specifically to help them, such as had been designed for the medical sciences. Under Rose's leadership, the Board expressed its conviction that "on the whole, the progress of civilization coincides with the increase of accurate knowledge and the spread of the objective and dispassionate spirit of scientific inquiry."[6] On the basis of this conviction it announced that "the General Education Board is now definitely undertaking to cooperate in improving the situation of the physical and biological sciences."

The first fruits of this decision were a series of notable grants made in 1925 to institutions reaching across the continent. One appropriation went to the California Institute of Technology, toward endowment of its teaching and research in the physical and biological sciences; another to Vanderbilt, which was endeavoring to lift its other departments to the high level attained by its recently reorganized School of Medicine. A third gift was to Princeton, to reinforce its resources in mathematics, physics, astronomy, chemistry, and biology. Finally, the Marine Biological Laboratory at Woods Hole, which had just completed its new building, was provided with funds to finance the purchase of books and periodicals for its library.

It is significant that every one of these institutions received continuing support from the Board. Rose had carefully selected them as key centers of teaching and research, strategically placed geographically, and marked for strengthening. Subsequent grants voted by the General Education Board within the next four years brought the total of its assistance to the California Institute of Technology to two and a half million dollars, to Vanderbilt to more than a million, to Princeton to two million, and to the Woods Hole laboratory to half a million.

In the year 1927, the General Education Board began a series of appropriations to the University of Chicago for science departments. By 1930, these gifts had mounted to more than two and three-quarter million dollars, providing the university with additional facilities in physics, chemistry, and biology, including new buildings for the departments of hygiene, bacteriology, and anatomy.

Physics was advanced by a grant to Harvard for a new research laboratory, the building now known as the Lyman Laboratory. Biological investigation was the beneficiary of a six-year grant to the University of Texas. At Stanford, graduate work in physics, chemistry, biology, and mathematics was aided by a series of appropriations extending over several years. The erection of science buildings was assisted at Radcliffe College, Hendrix College in Arkansas, and Randolph-Macon Woman's College in Virginia, while improved facilities for research and teaching were provided at Wellesley. Grants to the National Academy of Sciences aided publications in mathematics and biology, and a special appropriation to the Academy financed a survey of the status of oceanographical research in the United States. Grants to the National Research Council enabled a committee of the Council to evaluate studies of the effects of radiation on living material.

Again and again in his annual reports as president of the two boards, Rose declared his faith in science. On one occasion he felt moved to justify the support of research.

> In the first place [he reasoned], the scientific spirit, characterized by the objective and disinterested search for facts, is gradually invading other fields—industry, politics, law. The more solid and adequate the basic sciences become, the greater authority will scientific method win in realms not yet subdued; the more completely the world of physical, chemical, and biological phenomena can be described and accounted for, the more prestige does the scientific attitude require as respects other fields.

And in the second place:

> Whether we will or no, civilization has become increasingly a matter of applied science. To be sure, science can be and is misapplied, but this is not to be laid at the door of science. Health, transportation, food, education—these are realms of activity that cannot be properly managed until more is known. The increase of knowledge upon which human welfare depends comes largely from the laboratories dealing in the most fundamental fashion with the physical and biological sciences. In cultivating these, universities make, therefore, a notable contribution not only to knowledge, as such, but to the art of living.[7]

In the summer of 1928, Rose resigned from both Boards. He had reached the retirement age of sixty-five, and his work was done. "I want to climb a mountain and go fishing," he wrote in a letter to a friend. His story has significance because of its background. In an interlude between two great world catastrophes, a man of singular intellectual power, whose name was scarcely known even by his contemporaries but who had already made a monumental contribution to public health, was suddenly possessed by the faith of Aristotle that the salvation of mankind lay in the extension of knowledge. Moreover, he was fortunate enough to find financial backing for his faith so that in his lifetime he had the chance of putting it to the test in many practical forms around the world.

As he was fortunate in his life, so he was fortunate in his death. He did not live to see the days when the intellectual wealth of Europe, to which he had himself made so strategic a contribution, would be scattered and dissipated. He died happy in the belief that human intelligence could master the difficulties ahead and that the growing extension of knowledge across boundaries would provide both the tools and the atmosphere in which a new kind of future could be built. In the end, social forces of which he was unaware tore his ordered world of mathematics and physics to pieces, and by a bitter irony used as instruments in the destruction the very sciences upon which he based his faith.

Of course, this is not the final conclusion of the story, nor can the moral of Rose's life end on a pessimistic note. His far-ranging experiment for promoting the natural sciences lives on in the lives of many people, and in ways which neither he nor his contemporaries could have understood, his philosophy may yet be justified.

CHAPTER XIII

EXPERIMENTAL BIOLOGY

DESPITE ITS HERITAGE OF EXPERIENCE from the preceding boards, the Foundation's new program in the natural sciences did not spring into action at once. Time was required to mature it. The years 1928-1932 represented a period of transition during which the Natural Sciences division was forming its organization, getting its bearings, and experimenting with a variety of undertakings. The projects which were sponsored touched a wide area, both geographically and scientifically. They ranged from studies of the aurora borealis in Alaska to measurements of the velocity of light in California, and from providing funds for the erection of a physics research laboratory in Germany to the building, equipping, and endowing of an oceanographic institute in Massachusetts. Paleontological research was assisted in China, astrophysical research in The Netherlands, the Transvaal, Norway, and the United States. There is hardly a major segment of the natural sciences that did not receive some aid during these interim years.

Max Mason, mathematical physicist and former president of the University of Chicago, was the first director of the Natural Sciences division; but even as the appointment was being made in 1928, it was realized that his directorship would be temporary, for Dr. Mason had already been chosen by the trustees to succeed Dr. Vincent as president of the Foundation. Herman A. Spoehr was then appointed director; but the fascination of research as a plant physiologist reasserted its claim, and toward the end of 1931 Dr. Spoehr decided to return to his former work at the Carnegie Institution's Laboratory of Plant Research at Stanford. Finally, in 1932, the Foundation called upon Warren Weaver to take charge of its natural-science interests. Dr. Weaver came from a professorship at the University of Wisconsin, where he had been head of the department of mathematics. The program which was developed, and which will be the subject of this chapter, is largely the creation of his vision and leadership.

II

The first act of the new director was an appraisal of opportunities and objectives. It is not enough to support projects "merely because they are science, or even because they are outstandingly good science," he noted in a memorandum.

> A highly selective procedure is necessary if the available funds are not to lose significance through scattering. In the past, this selection has consisted chiefly of a choice of scientific leaders, among both men and institutions, although there has always been some selection on the basis of fields of interest. It is proposed, for the future program, that interest in the fields play the dominant role in the selection process. Within the fields of interest, selection will continue to be made of leading men and institutions.[1]

Several considerations were set up as guideposts to the satisfactory selection of an area for concentration. First, it must be the one that contributes in a basic way to the welfare of mankind; second, it must be sufficiently developed as a science to merit support, but so incompletely developed as to need support; and finally, the field should be one in which strategic assistance given at this stage might play a critical role in stimulating the advancement of knowledge—a result which, without such aid, would hardly occur within a reasonable time.

Measured by these criteria, the choice fell on the life sciences rather than the physical sciences. This was Weaver's line of reasoning: "The welfare of mankind depends in a vital way on man's understanding of himself and his physical environment. Science has made magnificent progress in the analysis and control of inanimate forces, but it has not made equal advances in the more delicate, more difficult, and more important problem of the analysis and control of animate forces. This indicates the desirability of greatly increasing the emphasis on biology and psychology, and on those special developments in mathematics, physics, and chemistry which are themselves fundamental to biology."[2]

It was on the basis of this recommendation that the trustees, in the spring of 1933, voted to make experimental biology the field of primary interest. This did not mean that only biological projects would be supported. "No person or group of persons is sufficiently wise to specify, even for a short time, all desirable activities. The program should always be kept flexible. Provision should be made in the budget to care for the unpredictable and unquestionable opportunities."[3] But biology would come first in the thinking and planning, and requests for the support of projects in physics, chemistry, and other physical sciences would be weighed in relation to the help such studies might contribute to the advancement of knowledge in the biological sciences.

The new interest was not entirely new, because both the public health work, with which the Foundation began its activities, as well as its support of medical education and research, reflected a fundamental preoccupation with the life sciences. Indeed, in a sense, medicine and hygiene are particular applications of biology. But the new program represented in the natural sciences a sharpening of focus and concentration of effort beyond anything that had previously been attempted. It was conceived, moreover, as being closely linked with other aspects of the Foundation's program, notably the program in psychiatry of the Medical Sciences division and the social-science program in human relations. Biology is important because it has the potentiality of contributing to the problem of understanding ourselves, and the three programs—in widely separated fields—could be thought of as a unified endeavor to stimulate research in the sciences underlying the behavior of man.

The behavior of man is conditioned biologically by such factors as heredity, nutrition, endocrine balance, neurological integration, and other elements of the body's internal economy. Each of these is a subject of intricate complexity, but fortunately all animal life embodies similar or related basic mechanisms, and thus the experimental method becomes available to biology. One would have to be extremely naïve to expect to elucidate these mysteries through experiments with human beings.

> Before we can be wise about so complex a subject as the behavior of a man [observed Weaver], we obviously have to gain a tremendous amount of information and insight about living organisms in general, necessarily starting with the simpler forms of life. Experimental biology is the means for such exploration. It furnishes the basis necessary for progress in solving the sequence of problems which begins with the strictly biological and moves through the mental to the social.[4]

In a deeper sense, then, the program is new. For, although man remains the measure of all the ends that are being sought, the road toward those goals is determined, not by its classification as human biology, but by its ability to contribute fundamental knowledge of the vital processes which underlie human biology.

III

Weaver started his work with an emphasis on the application of the quantitative techniques of mathematics, physics, and chemistry to biological problems. He was interested in classical biology, but his special enthusiasm related to the borderlands where the physical sciences overlap biology. It is significant that whereas in the first year of the new program there was not a single project in biochemistry listed as such, and only one in biophysics, two years later the annual report carried a heading, "the application of physical and chemical techniques to biological problems," and enumerated more than a dozen studies. They represented grants to such widely separated universities as Oxford, Stockholm, Upsala, Utrecht, and Copenhagen in Europe; and McGill, Columbia, Michigan, and Chicago on this continent.

The biophysical projects included studies of the effects of radiation on living things, the nature of nerve conduction, brain waves, heart waves, and other electrical properties of life; and among the biochemical projects were experiments with the mechanism of nutrition, the functions of internal secretions, and chemical mediators of nervous action. These problems were already under investigation in university laboratories in many countries. The Foundation policy did not start a trend, but it gave strong impetus to a movement already under way, and the effects of its aid to biologists, chemically and physically minded, multiplied rapidly.

The trend toward collaboration shows conspicuously in the history of certain institutional projects. The California Institute of Technology presents a striking example. In 1933, the Foundation made two grants to the Institute, one for biological research under Thomas Hunt Morgan, the other for chemical research under Linus Pauling. Dr. Morgan, the well-known leader in genetics, was one of the great experimental biologists of his day, and any request from him was bound to command attention. Dr. Pauling, on the other hand, had no direct interest in biology at that time. He was a physical chemist absorbed in studying the forces which hold molecules together. Despite his apparent remoteness from biology, the grant was voted, primarily because of the fundamental nature of the chemical problem and the brilliant record the young chemist had already made as a researcher. There was also in the background of Weaver's recommendation the thought that these physicochemical studies might eventually bring information concerning the structure of substances important to biology. And this surmise turned out to be correct. For in the course of exploring the electrical forces which bind the inorganic molecules, Pauling was led to test his theories in the more complicated realm of the organic, and this brought him to experiment with hemoglobin, the red pigment of blood. From that, he passed to antibodies, and finally to a study of immunization. Thus, in the course of a few years, he had bridged the gap from purely physical chemistry to the most humanly significant biochemistry. The early grants had been labeled "for research in structural chemistry," but in 1938 they began to be designated "for the development of chemistry in relation to biological problems." From then on, the collaboration between the departments of chemistry and biology at the California Institute became progressively more direct, and, instead of appropriating separately to each, the Foundation began the practice of giving funds for the joint use of the two departments. In recent years, Pauling and George W. Beadle (who succeeded Morgan as head of biology) have been working with a large and essentially unified team of chemists, biochemists, biophysicists, geneticists, and other biologists in a combined attack on fundamental problems of the nature of living matter, and since 1945 the Foundation has contributed $800,000 toward this chemical-biological collaboration.

It is impossible within the compass of a chapter to follow the technical details of this expanding research in the application of the powerful techniques of the physical sciences to biological problems. The hybrid sciences of biophysics and biochemistry have witnessed a degree of proliferation almost unparalleled in any other branch of knowledge. Biochemistry has isolated vitamins, identified hormones, and traced out some of the indispensable functions of these two groups of body chemicals. It has spotted enzymes and unveiled many of their mediations in the complex catalysis of the living processes. It has illuminated the chemical nature of viruses, the protective offices of antibodies, and has made a start toward understanding proteins and nucleoproteins, those two related classes of substances which seem to constitute the crucial stuff of life. In all these areas, the Foundation has been interested in seeking out competent and imaginative workers, in assisting their training, equipping their laboratories, and supporting their research. Indeed, in the field of enzymology alone, the Foundation has given aid to thirty-five universities and research centers, with grants totaling over $1,600,000.

Some of the masters of modern biochemistry have participated in this research, but we have space to mention only a contribution made shortly before the Second World War by a German refugee in England. This was Hans Adolph Krebs, who had been forced by political reasons to leave the University of Freiberg and had gone in 1933 to Cambridge University on a Rockefeller fellowship. He was only thirty-three years old, but he had already been working some years on the problem of respiration, trying to piece together a rational picture of the processes by which a cell burns its various fuels. In the quiet of prewar England he completed a great work. His experiments told him that the sequence of respiratory reactions could not be in a straight line. What happened was a cycle, like the turning of a wheel, with the last reaction providing the material for the cycle's next revolution. He was able to work out the successive changes at each turn of the wheel, showing where fresh carbon is taken in and where the waste product carbon dioxide is discarded with release of energy, each of the more than twenty chemical reactions being assisted by an enzyme or a team of enzymes. The Krebs Cycle, as it is called, has become a landmark in biochemistry, providing data which have assisted other investigators in the pursuit of their biochemical problems. As this book is going to press a new grant is being made to assist Dr. Krebs.

IV

While the new orientation of physics, biology, and chemistry was synthesizing new fields of study, interest in classical fields did not slacken. Many unexplained phenomena of physiology remained primary objectives of the program. Indeed, the idea was to bring up the most powerful available artillery for the attack on them. This meant the use of spectroscopy, X-ray diffraction, chromatography, and a score of other techniques and instruments which had been invented, for the most part, by chemists and physicists. These ingenious tools recommended themselves to experimental biologists because of what they could contribute to the task of extracting the secrets of living processes.

An example of a physicochemical discovery turned to the use of experimental biology is the application of isotopes as tracers. In this technique, a radioactive or heavy isotope of some biologically important element, like carbon or phosphorus, is incorporated into a nutrient which is then fed (or injected into) the experimental animal or plant. The isotope thereafter serves as a tag by which the experimenter is able to identify the location of the nutrient as it travels through the living system; and by this means many of the minute processes of digestion, respiration, and other phases of metabolism have been worked out.

The Foundation has fostered the development of tracer technique in numerous ways, both through grants and fellowships and especially through its support over the last two decades, of the work of George Hevesy. Professor Hevesy was the originator of the tracer method. He used it first to study the way in which the atoms of one block of lead wander off into another block of lead when the two are placed in contact. Then in 1923 he used a radioactive species of lead to study certain problems of plant physiology, and his continued service in perfecting and extending isotope uses to experimental biology has attracted many aspiring graduate students to his laboratories. Both at Stockholm and at Copenhagen—for he commutes between these centers—Professor Hevesy is a member of the partnership of physicists, chemists, and physiologists whose work in the biological borderlands has been a subject of Rockefeller interest since the days of the International Education Board. Currently, a grant to Copenhagen is supporting an intensive exploration of the biological uses of isotopes, a study projected under the joint direction of Niels Bohr and P. B. Rehberg with the collaboration of Hevesy. There are at least a dozen other places where grants have financed various applications of the isotope technique.

The fields of classical biology which have been cultivated through the Natural Sciences program lie chiefly within the areas of physiology, genetics, and embryology. Grants by the Foundation under this section of the program aided the distinguished embryological studies of George W. Corner at Rochester University, Viktor Hamburger at Washington University in St. Louis, and Frank R. Lillie at Chicago; the tissue studies of Ross G. Harrison at Yale and George B. Wislocki at Harvard; and the cytological research of Leonard Huskins at McGill and Wisconsin and of Torbjörn Caspersson at the Karolinska Institute, Stockholm—to name a few representative workers among the score who were assisted.

But the classical field which has received the largest measure of support is genetics. An accounting in 1950 showed that assistance had been given to fifty-three universities and other institutions, and the training of forty-six geneticists had been aided directly through Rockefeller Foundation fellowships in addition to those assisted by National Research fellowships. Altogether, up to that time, approximately two and three-quarter million dollars had been contributed to genetics research through the Natural Sciences division. In addition, more than a million dollars had been given through the Medical Sciences division, mainly for studies of hereditary factors in disease and other medical problems of human genetics. The Natural Sciences program in genetics has been directed more specifically at unraveling the fundamental phenomena of heredity and variation, the structure and composition of chromosomes, the nature of the gene and the secret of its control over the body's chemistry, growth, and development.

When Dr. Morgan requested aid in 1933, genetics was in the process of broadening its scope.

> The gross structural features of inheritance are today fairly well known [he wrote], and the workers are turning to the physiological aspects of heredity. Here we are endeavoring to bring our genetic group into closer contact with the physiological group. The success of this effort will depend in large part on the presence of progressive and thoughtful men familiar with the most recent advances in cell physiology. The geneticists stand ready to cooperate.[5]

The fact that genetics was in the expanding stage described by Morgan appealed strongly to Weaver and his associates, and it was recognized at once that here was a rich field offering untold opportunities for development. Immediately, grants began to go to genetics projects with a physiological approach. In addition to Morgan's research with fruit flies, the work at Jackson Memorial Laboratory, Bar Harbor, where mice were the subjects of a study of inheritance in mammals, and the research at Cornell University with maize as the experimental material, attracted support. From these early projects, the program has multiplied into a variety of genetical bypaths. While corn, flies, and mice continue to be the mainstays as experimental material, research projects in recent years have turned to other organisms, as well as to tools like X-rays, ultraviolet rays, and chemicals, and have opened trails which geneticists are hopefully prospecting.

In England, Foundation grants have supported projects in mathematical genetics at London University and the University of Birmingham. In France, aid has gone to the genetics laboratory of the Rothschild Foundation at Paris and the recently established French Institute of Genetics at Gif. But, to a greater extent than in any other biological science, the bulk of the appropriations for genetics went to American researchers. The research-team idea has found its finest embodiment in the United States, and the Foundation is proud to have been a co-worker with such groups as the Muller-Sonneborn-Cleland triumvirate at Indiana University, the Dunn-Dobzhansky group at Columbia, and the Morgan-Sturtevant-Beadle succession at the California Institute of Technology.

V

All this activity, whether in classical biology or in the newer fields on the borderline, has been in pure research—the clean, clear urge to gain new knowledge, the unimpeded reach of imaginative scholarship even when its results seem remote and unrelated.

And yet these pure science projects in biology often turn out to be the most practical of all research. An example is the work of the Department of Physical Chemistry in the Harvard Medical School. Its laboratory was established in the early 1920's and soon attracted Rockefeller support, first from the General Education Board and then from the Foundation. Indeed, the Foundation had a part in training its director, for one of that initial group of thirteen National Research fellows appointed in 1919 was Edwin J. Cohn. When Dr. Cohn returned from three years of fellowship study in Europe, during which he worked with Arrhenius in Sweden, Sørensen in Denmark, and Hopkins in England, he had resolved to concentrate his efforts on proteins. He gathered about him a team of specialists in various aspects of protein chemistry, and the Harvard Medical School laboratory became widely known for its investigations of protein structure, protein shape, protein properties and behavior. It was supremely a place for pure research.

And yet, when the Second World War came, and advisers to the government felt the need of a study of blood to guide transfusion practices, it was to this laboratory that they turned. Within a short time, Cohn and his co-workers switched from their theoretical researches to the urgent medical problem of separating blood plasma into its various components, such as albumin, used in the treatment of shock, and the protein factors which are responsible for clotting or the coagulation of blood. What they did, of course, was to put their theoretical knowledge to use, and perhaps they were better able to do this because they approached the practical problem from the broad base of fundamentals. Before the war ended, the processes worked out in the university laboratory were being applied on a large scale by pharmaceutical and other industrial establishments, and today plasma fractionation is a regular part of the American Red Cross's blood-bank service.

Since 1930, the Foundation has given Harvard more than half a million dollars toward support of this laboratory, and the assistance was continued during the war when its blood-fractionation program was receiving large subventions from the government. "I have prized the Rockefeller support because it has always been undesignated," said Dr. Cohn. "I could use it for whatever problem was uppermost at the time, and in this way it made possible our most fundamental research."[6]

Cohn's work is not the only instance in which research sponsored through the Natural Sciences program turned up results of therapeutic value. Some of the vitamin studies and other nutritional investigations were followed by human applications, and of course hormones and isotopes are spectacular for their usefulness to medicine. A small grant to Oxford University in 1936 presents an example of another kind. The grant was given in response to the application of a professor of pathology who explained that he had recently engaged a German refugee biochemist to collaborate with him on problems of "chemical pathology" and needed £250 with which to purchase laboratory equipment. The professor was Howard W. Florey, the refugee biochemist was Ernst Chain, and the eventual outcome of their research was the purification of penicillin and the proof of its clinical value. Oxford University furnished by far the greater part of the support—the Foundation in its succession of grants was a very minor partner—but it is interesting that a proposal which the Natural Sciences division accepted as an opportunity in pure biochemistry should have produced a result so promptly, so importantly, and so directly useful to medicine.

Utilitarianism, however, was never the yardstick. Projects were not espoused or rejected according to the degree with which they promised an immediate practical result. The test was knowledge: Is the proposed study likely to add to man's understanding of the living world of which he is a part? As light increases, the darkness recedes to greater distances; similarly, the increase of fundamental knowledge spreads in all directions and carries the power to illumine many problems. That was the faith in which, in the early 1930's, the Foundation entered upon its plan to advance experimental biology. An annual report of the period, as though to point up the humanly significant implications of basic research, listed, among others, the following questions as pertinent to the Natural Sciences program:

> Can we unravel the tangled problem of the endocrine glands and develop a therapy for the whole hideous range of mental and physical disorders which result from glandular disturbances?
>
> Can we develop so sound and extensive a genetics that we can hope to breed in the future superior men?
>
> Can we solve the mysteries of the various vitamins, so that we can nurture a race sufficiently healthy and resistant?
>
> In short, can we rationalize human behavior and create a new science of man?[7]

These questions were posed in 1933; and since then the Foundation has appropriated thirty million dollars for work in the natural sciences, of which approximately 80 per cent went for experimental biology. Quite recently, in a restatement of the objectives of his division, Weaver concluded his summary thus:

> The century of biology upon which we are now well embarked is no matter of trivialities. It is a movement of really heroic dimensions, one of the great episodes in man's intellectual history. The scientists who are carrying the movement forward talk in terms of nucleo-proteins, of ultracentrifuges, of biochemical genetics, of electrophoresis, of the electron microscope, of molecular morphology, of radioactive isotopes. But do not be misled by these horrendous terms, and above all do not be fooled into thinking this is mere gadgetry. This is the dependable way to seek a solution of the cancer and polio problems, the problems of rheumatism and of the heart. This is the knowledge on which we must base our solution of the population and food problems. This is the understanding of life.[8]

Clearly, the same principles and purposes which activated the program at the beginning are still guiding it, as it moves into its third decade.

CHAPTER XIV

TOOLS OF RESEARCH

AN EMINENT PHYSICIST HAS REMARKED that "a man with an idea can always borrow a cyclotron"[1]—which is another way of saying that in terms of importance to scientific research, the man with an idea ranks first. Cyclotrons may be useful to test ideas, to extend or develop them experimentally, but without adventurous thinkers there will be no ideas, and without ideas there will be no need for cyclotrons or any other research apparatus.

But after all, it is essential that there be a cyclotron for the man with an idea to borrow, since modern science, in practically all fields, has become so greatly dependent on precise and elaborate instruments. Indeed, backing brains often means providing a scientist with the equipment necessary for his work, and this is increasingly the case in our day.

The laboratory men of fifty or even thirty years ago were able to improvise much of their experimental apparatus, building it themselves out of pieces of glass tubing, sealing wax, metal plates, and string or wire. The historic equipment with which the first of the subatomic particles were discovered was largely homemade. But such simple and inexpensive measures are seldom able to meet the requirements of present-day research. Not only the physics and chemistry laboratories, but the outposts of biology have become highly specialized workshops employing instruments whose design and development is a profession in itself. A sizable proportion of the funds appropriated by the Foundation for the advancement of the natural sciences has gone to provide research workers in many lands with these precision instruments, including sometimes the buildings to house them and the auxiliary apparatus to service them.

II

In biochemistry, and particularly in the study of proteins, a primary problem is the separation of substances out of the natural mixtures in which they occur; beyond this are the problems of determining their molecular weights, sizes, shapes, and chemical compositions. Some of the new tools which perform these tasks have already been mentioned in passing, but a few words regarding their nature and usefulness may be helpful.

The ultracentrifuge and the electrophoresis apparatus are devices for separating molecules out of a solution or suspension. The ultracentrifuge does it by centrifugal force, electrophoresis by harnessing electrical properties. Both are used by biochemists to obtain pure fractions of substances, and the ultracentrifuge also serves as a weighing machine to determine the molecular weight of viruses, antibodies, enzymes, and other proteins, while electrophoresis reveals their electrical characteristics. Still another instrument has been helpful in measuring molecular shapes, especially those of long, slender structure such as the fibrinogen of blood.

In addition to molecular weights, sizes, and shapes, the biochemist needs to know the chemical composition of living matter, and the structural arrangement of the atoms in its molecules. An important reliance for determining composition is spectroscopy. The spectrograph, often using infrared or ultraviolet rays, not only reveals what compounds and elements are present, but from its record one can infer the relative quantities of each. Colorimetry and chromatography are two additional techniques of chemical analysis, sometimes used in connection with the spectrograph, sometimes independently. Other means of identifying elements in tissues or secretions are the isotope detectors: Geiger counters for radioactive isotopes, mass spectrographs for the stable ones.

X-ray diffraction and electron-diffraction methods spot the positions of atoms in a molecule. The practice of bombarding a substance with X-rays and measuring the angles at which the rays bounce off, has made it possible to measure the minute distances between the constituent atoms and to map out the architecture of some of the simpler organic molecules.

But all these techniques and devices work in the dark, so far as the human observer is concerned, and deliver their findings in the indirect form of pointed readings on a scale, plotted curves, shadow figures, or diagrams. Another one of the important new tools, the electron microscope, has the great advantage of visibility. It brings to view actual images and shows in tremendous enlargement details which the observer through the other instruments can only infer. To be sure, the electron microscope is not without some limitations of its own, but despite these it has become indispensable to many researches, especially those of the molecular biologist.

There are other mechanical, optical, electronic, and chemical aids to experimental biology, but perhaps the ones mentioned are sufficient to illustrate the nature and value of the current tools, most of which have come into use within the lifetime of the Foundation.

The development of some of these new tools has been especially assisted by the Foundation. The ultracentrifuge is an example. This high-speed rotating device was introduced as an instrument of precision by the Swedish biochemist, Svedberg. His work on it impressed Dr. Rose and his associates and was the occasion for an appropriation from the International Education Board in the twenties. Since then, the Foundation has made a succession of grants to the University of Upsala on behalf of Professor Svedberg's researches with the oil-driven ultracentrifuge which he developed, and a grant to the University of Wisconsin provided the only university installation of this type in the United States. Similarly, assistance has been given for the experiments of J. W. Beams at the University of Virginia, where compressed air—and later a most ingenious magnetic suspension and electric drive—was applied to ultracentrifuge propulsion. Further progress has been contributed by members of the Foundation staff working in the New York Laboratories of the International Health Division: J. H. Bauer and E. G. Pickels improved the stability of the driving mechanism and made other improvements which adapted the instrument to virus research; and John C. Bugher added an electronic control, regulated by time signals from the Bureau of Standards, which has markedly improved the steadiness of the rotational speed. The total effect of these various improvements has been to increase the reliability of the ultracentrifuge as a molecular sorting and weighing device.

"Now that we have instruments which give quantitative data, there just isn't any sense in trying to guess, estimate, or approximate the measurements," remarked a prominent European biochemist now resident in the United States. "There are plenty of other problems in biology for which one must depend on the imagination, but it is foolish to imagine when measurements are possible, and I simply will not engage in research without these precision tools."[2]

The Foundation's practice of equipping biologists with tools to do the job dates back to its first institutional grant in the natural sciences, half a million dollars to the Marine Biological Laboratory at Woods Hole in 1924. Since then, further grants have been made by both the Foundation and the General Education Board, and the total of Rockefeller funds now invested in this Marine Biological Laboratory is approximately triple the original grant. In addition, the Foundation appropriated three and a half million dollars for building, equipping, and endowing an independent but related outpost, the Woods Hole Oceanographic Institution, in the same Massachusetts village. Several other research centers in oceanography and marine biology have been assisted with buildings or equipment: the Marine Biological Laboratory of Plymouth, England, the Bermuda Biological Station, the University of Washington Oceanographic Laboratories at Seattle, the Scripps Institution of Oceanography at La Jolla, and the Hopkins Marine Station of Stanford University.

Dotted over many parts of Europe and the Americas are biological laboratories which were built and equipped either wholly or in large part with Foundation funds. These include the Institute of Experimental Biology at the University of Stockholm, the Biochemical Wing of the Dyson Perrins Laboratory of Organic Chemistry at Oxford, the Institute of Experimental Pathology in Iceland, the Genetics Laboratory at the University of Missouri, the Yerkes Laboratories of Primate Biology at Orange Park, Florida, and the Institute of Biological Investigations at Montevideo, Uruguay. Postwar grants to the University of Wisconsin and the Massachusetts General Hospital provided equipment for their enzyme research, and an equal gift to the University of California bought precision instruments for its Institute of Virus Research. Cornell was assisted in establishing its Electron Microscope Laboratory at Ithaca, and other grants for electron microscopy have gone to the Massachusetts Institute of Technology, Stanford University, the University of Washington, and the University of Glasgow.

There was a marked trend toward equipment grants in the years immediately following the Second World War, especially in grants to institutions abroad. In many laboratories, work had been at a low ebb, with little or no addition to facilities; and almost everywhere, it seemed, scientists were handicapped by the scarcity of modern tools. The unbalance in monetary exchange was also a factor. Governments and other local agencies were able to provide funds for laboratory salaries and the expenses of research in most of the countries where scientific work was being done, but the shortage of dollar exchange was such as to make it almost prohibitive for them to buy specialized equipment from abroad. During the period 1945-1950, more than sixty grants were made to European institutions and a score to Latin America for laboratory apparatus; and in a large number of instances the equipment was bought directly by the Foundation's purchasing department with United States dollars and shipped to the recipient. In this way, dozens of physical and chemical instruments, including ultracentrifuges, spectrographs, spectrometers, and X-ray tubes, were distributed among biological laboratories in a score of countries.

III

The cyclotron, invented by Ernest O. Lawrence, a former National Research fellow, and the electrostatic generator, invented by Robert J. van de Graaff, a former International Education Board fellow, are two types of high-voltage accelerators. Primarily, they are tools of the physicist, for both were originally designed as artillery with which to bombard the nuclei of atoms. As a result of these bombardments, in which the projectiles were charged particles accelerated to high velocities, the nuclei were not only compelled to yield up the secrets of their hidden structure, but their atoms were transformed into radioactive isotopes. The artificially produced isotopes immediately became useful to biologists, both for research with the tagged-atom technique and for experiments in cancer therapy; and thus these high-voltage tools of the nuclear physicist found early applications in biology.

It was the biological utility of the accelerators that attracted the attention of the Foundation and influenced its first grants in this field in 1937. One grant went to the University of Minnesota to finance the construction of a van de Graaff generator and provide support of isotope research at the university and the affiliated Mayo Foundation. A second grant was given the University of Copenhagen to enable it to build a cyclotron, again to produce isotopes for medical and other biological research. There was still another cyclotron grant made that year: it went to Paris, where the Collège de France, the Institute of Physical Chemistry at the Sorbonne, the

Rothschild Foundation, and the Radium Institute had joined forces for studies with radioactive isotopes.

Since then, funds to assist the construction and operation of high-voltage accelerators have been given to half a dozen universities: i.e., to California, Rochester, Washington (St. Louis), and Stockholm for cyclotrons; to Massachusetts Institute of Technology for an electrostatic generator; and to the University of São Paulo, Brazil, for a betatron. The betatron is a third type of accelerator, so named because it uses beta particles as projectiles, but like the others it bombards atomic nuclei and transforms them into radioactive isotopes.

The grant to the Massachusetts Institute for an electrostatic generator is of particular interest, for the purpose here was to enable Professor van de Graaff to build a perfected model of his invention. He had been called on during the war to supervise the construction of a number of high-voltage machines needed in various defense projects and hospitals, and in fulfilling these demands had assembled a team of physicists, electronic engineers, and mechanics who were experts on this type of apparatus. When hostilities ceased, van de Graaff wished to get back to his research in nuclear physics, but requests came from several laboratories abroad asking him to supply generators embodying his latest design. It was finally decided that he would hold his construction team together long enough to build one thoroughly engineered apparatus for his own use and as a prototype for subsequent copies. It would incorporate all the improvements developed during the wartime period of quickened experimentation, and thus provide the top research implement in the particular field for which it was adapted. At the same time, it was agreed, blueprints of the new design would be supplied, without charge, to other laboratories wishing to duplicate it. The Foundation's action supplied funds for construction of this master generator.

Similarly, the assistance given the University of California was to back up the work of the inventor of the cyclotron. Beginning in 1930, with a small-scale model with a diameter of only four inches, Professor Lawrence, aided by pioneering grants from the Research Corporation, had progressively increased the size and power of his machine until, in 1938, he was engaged in building one of sixty inches in diameter. It was designed to be the most powerful accelerator of its day, capable of speeding particles to energies exceeding twenty-five million electron volts. Because of this voltage, special precautions were required to shield operators against radiation effects, and the Foundation's first grant was $30,000 to provide these protective devices. An additional $50,000 was given in 1939 to support basic medical and biological research with the new machine.

Even before the 60-inch cyclotron was completed, Lawrence began drawing plans for a giant with a diameter of 184 inches. Its calculated energy output was to be within the range of 100,000,000 to 300,000,000 electron volts. Particles impelled by such energies should be capable of slugging out of atomic nuclei the mysterious subatomic particles now known as mesons which had been discovered among cosmic rays. Physicists believed that these mesons, which were intermediate in mass between the lightweight electrons and the heavyweight protons, had something to do with the binding forces which hold nuclei together. The study of mesons was therefore of top importance to nuclear physicists. In any event, the 184-inch cyclotron would provide man with his most penetrating tool for reaching into the atomic nucleus, that unexplored world within the invisible core of the atom.

It was on this basis that Professor Lawrence and his associates at the University of California appealed to the Foundation. No one could then be sure that biological or medical research required such a high-powered implement. Sixty-inch and even smaller cyclotrons were presumably adequate for producing isotopes for tracer or therapeutic use. But atomic investigation called for the heaviest possible artillery. It was purely as an instrument of basic research, to obtain new knowledge, to explore the little-known realm of spinning particles and mighty forces which constitute the atomic nucleus, that its sponsors proposed the construction of the 184-inch cyclotron. The estimated cost was $1,400,000. The Foundation voted $1,150,000, the University of California to raise the balance; and so, in 1940, work began at Berkeley on this unprecedented tool. As the president of the Foundation wrote in his annual report: "It is an adventure in pure discovery, motivated by the unconquerable exploring urge within the mind of man. . . . It is a mighty symbol, a token of man's hunger for knowledge, an emblem of the undiscourageable search for truth which is the noblest expression of the human spirit."[3]

The giant cyclotron was designed and its construction proposed before the outbreak of Hitler's war in Europe, and in supporting the project there was no thought in the trustees' minds that it would have military value, nor was this argument ever advanced. But, as events turned out, the project provided a key tool for the research which produced the atomic bomb. It was not the cyclotron itself that served as this tool. What proved so useful to the National Defense Research Committee, which was in charge of the early investigations looking to the development of atomic weapons, was the cyclotron's huge and powerful electromagnet. It was designed to be the largest in the world, measuring 184 inches in pole diameter and weighing 4,200 tons. When the Japanese struck at Pearl Harbor in December of 1941, the magnet was still under construction, scheduled to be completed the following November. It was then proposed that the job be put immediately on a twenty-four-hour basis, with three shifts of workers. Such a schedule, it was argued, would cut the time to less than half. Sixty thousand dollars would be required to finance the stepped-up work, and although this was a trifling sum compared with other amounts which the National Defense Research Committee was spending, that Committee hesitated for policy reasons to allot government money to build equipment which would be the property of an outside agency, the University of California.

In this dilemma, Professor Lawrence applied to the Foundation. He asked for a supplemental grant "for expediting the construction of the giant cyclotron, and for the purchase of certain associated equipment." Security reasons made it impossible to tell the trustees of the Foundation the real background of the request, for at that time the bomb project was the deepest of military secrets. Trustees who wondered why the University of California was coming back so soon for additional help were assured that the need was urgent but could not be stated in specific terms, and so the $60,000 was voted as a matter of faith. This was in January of 1942, and nothing was heard of the project until August, 1945, when the explosion of the atomic bomb was publicly announced by President Truman. Then, being free to speak, Professor Lawrence addressed a letter to Warren Weaver:

> At long last I have the very real pleasure of writing you, and through you the president and trustees, something of the vital part played by The Rockefeller Foundation in the development of the atomic bomb. I shall never forget how you and President Fosdick responded so promptly to our need for additional funds to expedite the completion of the giant magnet, and I am so glad that there is now a story to tell that is in a measure a recompense for your extraordinary support.[4]

What had been happening, behind the scenes, was this. The magnet had been used experimentally to increase the yield of the pure, fissionable U-235; and while the electromagnetic method was the last to be started in development, it was the first to get into large-scale production of material. As Lawrence stated in his letter: "I believe it is true that it was the assurance in 1942 that this method at least would 'pan out' that gave Dr. Bush and Dr. Conant final confidence in recommending the necessary large-scale expenditure of funds."

Lawrence's letter was received by the trustees with mixed emotions. They were naturally gratified that the Foundation had been of some recognized assistance in the war effort, and they noted that twenty-three of the leaders of the atom-bomb project had received part of their specialized training on fellowships provided by Rockefeller funds. In this list were such names as Oppenheimer, Lawrence, Fermi, Allison, Smyth, and Arthur Compton. But in the whole history of the Foundation, no grant had ever been made for a destructive purpose, let alone such a lethal weapon as this; and like all thoughtful people the world over, the trustees were abruptly awakened to the tragic irony that when man has been most successful in pushing out the boundaries of knowledge, he may, at the same time, have most endangered the possibility of human life on this planet. The pursuit of truth has at last led him to the tools by which he can himself become the destroyer of his own institutions and all the bright hopes of the race.

The difficulty is that there is no way of foreseeing the use to which knowledge will be put. We are driven back to a question of human motives and desires. There is scarcely a scientific formula or a process or a commodity or an instrument which cannot be used destructively if that is what we elect to do with it. We are ethically unprepared for the responsibilities of vast physical power. Men are discovering the right things, but in the wrong order.

Meanwhile, the giant cyclotron at the University of California has been turned to problems of basic nuclear research. The earlier speculation as to whether or not it would be capable of smashing mesons out of nuclei led to experiments that brought gratifying results in 1948. It was shown that the bombarding beam did produce mesons. Prior to this, these subatomic particles of intermediate mass had been observed only in the debris resulting from the chance collision of a cosmic ray; but now it was possible to produce them at will in the laboratory, and to plan controlled experiments for their study. The pursuit of truth has not yielded to pessimism.

IV

Astrophysical research requires telescopes, spectrographs, photometers, thermocouples, photographic plates, and a variety of other specialized tools. The Foundation's equipment grants in this field number three: a joint fund given the University of Leiden and the Union Observatory at Johannesburg to purchase a telescope and auxiliary apparatus for a co-operative photographic survey of stars of the southern hemisphere; an appropriation to the University of Oslo for instrumenting its Institute of Astrophysics; and $550,000 to the California Institute of Technology to complete the construction of the 200-inch telescope for which the International Education Board gave six million dollars in 1928.

The 200-inch telescope enlisted the services of scores of highly trained specialists in many fields. Astronomers and astrophysicists laid out the specifications of what they wanted and proceeded to design the instruments. But in addition it proved necessary to call in physicists, geophysicists, glassmakers, metallurgists, optical experts, electrical experts, architects, and engineers to contribute their specialized knowledge and skills. Although many men were involved in the later stages, the idea of this huge eye to peer through a thousand million light-years originated with one man, George Ellery Hale, and at the dedication in 1948 the instrument was appropriately named the Hale Telescope.

Dr. Hale was a great astrophysicist, discoverer of the magnetic nature of sunspots and other solar phenomena, but he will probably go down in astronomical history as the great telescope builder. Before he projected this largest of his undertakings, Hale had already launched two world centers of astronomical research—the Yerkes Observatory of the University of Chicago in the early 1890's, and the Mount Wilson Observatory of the Carnegie Institution, in the early 1900's. At Yerkes he built the world's largest refracting telescope, with a lens of 40-inch diameter, and at Mount Wilson the largest reflector, with a mirror of 100-inch diameter. When the 100-inch had shown that it could penetrate five hundred million light-years into space, bringing to view celestial bodies which had never before been seen or photographed, Hale began to dream of a still more powerful telescope. He discussed these dreams with a few associates at Mount Wilson and soon had an enthusiastic band of fellow dreamers. They began to sketch plans for a telescope with a 200-inch aperture, and then for one with an aperture of 300

John D. Rockefeller, Sr.

John D. Rockefeller, Jr.
President of the Foundation: 1913-1917; Chairman of the Board: 1917-1940

Frederick T. Gates
One of the chief organizers of the Foundation (Photo by Frederick Bradley)

Jerome D. Greene
Secretary: 1913-1917; Trustee: 1913-1917, 1928-1939

DR. SIMON FLEXNER
Director: Rockefeller Institute for Medical Research—1903-1935

WICKLIFFE ROSE
Director: International Health Division—1913-1923; President: General Education Board—1923-1929

WALLACE BUTTRICK
General Director: China Medical Board—1914-1918; Secretary and President: General Education Board—1903-1923 (Photo by Underwood & Underwood)

GEORGE E. VINCENT
President: 1917-1929 (Photo by Underwood & Underwood)

DR. RICHARD M. PEARCE
Director: Division of Medical Education —1919-1929

ABRAHAM FLEXNER
Secretary: General Education Board—1917-1925; Director of Studies and Medical Education—1925-1928

DR. FREDERICK F. RUSSELL
Director: International Health Division —1923-1935

MAX MASON
President: 1929-1936

WALTER W. STEWART
Chairman of the Board—1940-1950 (Photo courtesy *Life*, copyright Time, Inc.)

MARY BEARD
In charge of nursing education—1925-1938 (Photo by Harris & Ewing)

EDMUND E. DAY
Director: Division of Social Science—1930-1937 (Photo by Harris & Ewing)

DR. WILBUR A. SAWYER
Director: International Health Division—1935-1944

inches. This dreaming and sketching went on for three or four years, and then one day in February of 1928 Dr. Hale wrote a letter to Wickliffe Rose. He outlined the advantages that might accrue to science from a giant telescope and asked if Dr. Rose would consider "the possibility of making a grant to determine how large a telescope mirror it would be feasible and advisable to cast?"[5]

Rose replied at once: "It is a matter that interests us. We shall be very glad to discuss it with you,"[6] and some weeks later, during a trip to the West Coast, he stopped off at Pasadena and spent a day with Hale. That was a fruitful day for astronomy. For at its end Rose was filled with enthusiasm for the project, which by now had grown far beyond the original request for an exploratory grant. Hale and his associates decided that a mirror of 200 inches was the logical next step beyond the existing 100-inch at Mount Wilson, and were confident that a construction of this magnitude was feasible. So the project now was not merely one of prospecting the possibilities; it was that of designing and building such a telescope.

What institution would be the most suitable trustee for this superlative tool of research? In his February letter, Dr. Hale had raised this issue, suggesting that the telescope might be given either to the Carnegie Institution of Washington, for operation in connection with its Mount Wilson Observatory, or to the National Academy of Sciences, for operation under a joint committee of astronomers and physicists. A later suggestion was that an independent board be set up to own the instrument. At the same time, Dr. Hale called attention to the California Institute of Technology. Its prestige as a center of graduate education was an argument in its favor, for the advantage of linking research with teaching is well recognized. Moreover, the proximity of the Institute to the Mount Wilson Observatory would make possible the closest sort of co-operation between the two. The final choice fell on the California Institute of Technology, and to it the International Education Board made its appropriation of six million dollars.

Dr. Hale had estimated that from four to six or more years would be required to design, build, and install the telescope and auxiliary equipment in suitable observatory housing. Accordingly, the Board made its appropriation in the form of a commitment, from which funds would be allotted to the California Institute as rapidly as the work required. Actually, a war intervened and twenty years elapsed between the authorization of the project in 1928 and the dedication of the Hale Telescope on Palomar Mountain in 1948.

Meanwhile, both Rose and Hale had died and the International Education Board had long since liquidated its affairs and terminated its existence; but the General Education Board assumed responsibility for completing the financial obligations of the pledge as they fell due, and the Natural Sciences division of the Foundation served the boards as technical adviser on the project. After the war, with both labor and material costs higher, it was apparent that the original appropriation would be insufficient to complete the construction. Moreover, when the mirror had been hauled to the peak of Palomar and set in its steel mounting, the support system encountered certain minor unanticipated difficulties. There was further delay and expense in correcting and adjusting the supporting mechanisms. The Rockefeller Foundation made its supplementary grants to care for these additional costs and expenses, and finally, in January of 1949, the instrument was placed for the first time on a regular schedule of observations. Thus all three Rockefeller boards participated in the twenty-year project and contributed a total of $6,550,000.

This money was not spent on the telescope alone, for a 200-inch reflector without auxiliary equipment, housing, service facilities, and other requisites for successful operation would be a white elephant indeed. Part of the fund went to build the great dome—about the same size as the Pantheon in Rome—and to provide other buildings for housing the observatory. Part went to construct the three smaller telescopes of the Schmidt type which serve as feeders to the 200-inch. The Schmidts are really wide-angle cameras capable of photographing broad areas of the sky, and from these photographs the astronomers select particular objects to be investigated with the 200-inch. Without the Schmidts, smaller, but wide-eyed, to scan the heavens for it, the 200-inch would be greatly handicapped. The full operation of the 200-inch telescope also calls for spectrographs and other subsidiary instruments, all of which were provided as part of the Palomar Observatory installation.

Before he was willing to recommend the telescope project to his Board, Dr. Rose assured himself that it would have the full co-operation of the Carnegie Institution of Washington. He did not wish to launch a rival to Mount Wilson Observatory. The co-operation was assured in advance and has been loyally and generously available, both in the planning, designing, and supervising of the construction and in the subsequent operation of the 200-inch. In fact, as the great instrument neared completion, the California Institute of Technology and the Carnegie Institution of Washington joined in an agreement to merge the two observatories under one director and operate them as a single astronomical research agency. Certain problems can best be tackled with the 100-inch and lesser telescopes of Mount Wilson, whereas there are other problems for which the greater light-gathering power of the 200-inch makes it the indispensable instrument. The unified plan of operation gives the surest promise that the incomparable resources of both Mount Wilson and Palomar, their teams of scientists as well as their teams of instruments, will be utilized to their full, with no duplication of effort or waste of precious observing time. It presents also an impressive example of that collaboration between free men which is the very life of science.

Superficially, the 200-inch telescope and the lesser projects in astronomy which have received Foundation aid would seem to be far removed from the main interest of the Natural-Sciences program. What possible relationship can there be between the stars and experimental biology? And is there anything more foreign to human values than astrophysics? The answer to such queries lies in human history. The stars were man's first teachers of the orderliness of nature. It was through his observations of the cycle of day and night, the sequence of the seasons, the phases of the moon, and the wanderings of the planets among the stars, that man derived his first glimmering concept of the reign of law in nature. On that concept rests the whole magnificent structure of such civilization as we have attained—a faith in the universal interrelatedness of things, in the unity and integrity of nature.

There is another human aspect to astronomy. It was pointed out by Vannevar Bush in his address at the dedication of the Hale Telescope:

In no other discipline—not even, I dare say, in those whose field is life itself—do men confront mystery and challenge of the order of that which looms down upon the astronomer in the long watches of the night. The astronomer knows at first hand, and places all the rest of us in his lasting debt by translating to us, how slight is our Earth, how slight and fleeting are mankind. But more than that, he senses more closely than can we, I think, the majesty which resides in the mind of man because that mind seeks in all its slightness to see, to learn, to understand at least some little part of the mysterious majesty of the universe. No calling brings more sharply into focus the seeming disparity between man and the cosmos. And yet, no calling reflects more steadily the fact, both prideful and humbling at once, that the reaches of the intelligence of man are vast and that his will strives to encompass even the fabulous reaches beyond the stars. It is in the humility thus engendered that men recognize their individual insufficiency, and recognizing it join as free spirits in cooperation and collaboration.[7]

The great telescope on Palomar is more than a superb tool of astrophysical research. It is also a mighty symbol of human aspiration and collaboration in confronting the unknown, a sign and token of the inquiring mind whose never-ending search for truth is man's unique distinction among living things.

CHAPTER XV

AGRICULTURE

AGRICULTURE IS ONE OF THE OLDEST interests of the Rockefeller boards. Back in 1903, the newly organized General Education Board undertook a survey of the educational needs of the South. It had no thought of an agricultural program; it was interested only in schools. But the officers had not proceeded far before they realized that the improvement of school systems supported by taxation was inextricably interrelated with the improvement of economic conditions, and since agriculture was the principal source of the South's livelihood, little could be done about the interest in education until something was done about agriculture.

The Board's survey was therefore extended to include this field, and Dr. Buttrick spent almost a year visiting agricultural colleges not only in the South, but in various parts of the country. It was while he was in Texas that he learned of the work of Seaman A. Knapp.

Texas at this time was the chief battleground in the fight against the boll weevil, a pest which had recently crossed over from Mexico and was devastating the cotton fields. Dr. Knapp, a staff man of the United States Department of Agriculture, had established a demonstration farm in the infested region to show farmers how, despite the boll weevil, they could produce satisfactory crops. By such measures as careful seed selection, deep plowing in the autumn, wide spacing of plants, intensive cultivation, systematic fertilization, and rotation of crops, Dr. Knapp had stepped up the normal yield in his demonstration farm substantially, and farmers who went back to their fields and applied his methods were increasing their yields too. Dr. Buttrick was deeply impressed. "If the demonstration method paid in dealing with a pest-ridden farm, was there not every reason to suppose that it would pay still more handsomely where no handicap existed?" he reasoned. "In Dr. Knapp's farm demonstration work, limited at that time to combatting the boll weevil, the General Education Board found the answer to its search for a method of delivering the existing knowledge of effective agricultural processes to present farmers."[1]

A co-operative arrangement was worked out. The United States Department of Agriculture agreed to carry on the demonstrations in weevil-infested states and the General Education Board agreed to provide funds for extending the work to other states, both programs to be under Dr. Knapp's direction. This joint effort, launched in 1906 in a few rural centers in six states, rapidly multiplied until the entire South was dotted with nearly one hundred thousand demonstration farms. Later, the program was extended to Maine and New Hampshire. Each demonstration farm served its surrounding territory as a practical seminar in scientific agriculture, showing hundreds of farmers how to engineer a crop to a successful yield. From cotton, the program was expanded to embrace corn and other crops, and it played an important part in the movement for crop diversification.

By 1914, the General Education Board felt that the practical value of the work had been established and its continuance could be left to others. The Board had invested close to a million dollars in the farm demonstrations, the United States Department of Agriculture had invested double that amount, and, significantly, the Southern people themselves had put more than a million dollars into the effort. The demonstration farms paved the way for the development a few years later of the nation-wide agricultural extension service, supported by public funds and administered jointly by the Department of Agriculture and the land-grant colleges.

When Dr. Rose and his associates of the International Education Board were planning their dual program for the advancement of the natural sciences and of agriculture, as related in Chapter XII, this earlier experience of the General Education Board stood them in good stead. Indeed, in Dr. Rose's preliminary memorandum of 1923, listing the various possibilities which were being considered by the International Education Board, the first item was "farm demonstration." And the first project in agriculture actually undertaken by the Board was a plan for co-operation with Denmark in farm demonstration work—a movement that soon was extended to Norway and Hungary.

The agricultural program of the International Education Board was, as we have seen, directed by Albert R. Mann, who had been borrowed for the purpose from the New York State College of Agriculture at Cornell. Dr. Mann spent two years in Europe on this assignment, visiting all its important agricultural regions west of Russia, becoming closely acquainted with the agricultural problems of each, and developing a program which reached into more than a score of countries.

The principle of seeking out the most promising youth and assisting their development was applied in the International Education Board's agricultural program as it was in its natural-science program. Altogether, 233 young people in thirty-one nations were given fellowships in agriculture, to prepare them for posts in teaching, research, and administration. Aid was also given to a number of centers of agricultural education and research. Notable among these was the College of Agriculture of the University of Sofia, the Department of Research in Animal Breeding at the University of Edinburgh, and co-ordinated laboratories of agriculture, botany, zoology, and physiology at Cambridge University. The grant on behalf of Sofia enabled the university to complete its agricultural building, those on behalf of Edinburgh and Cambridge provided equipment and support as well as buildings.

In addition to the projects in Europe, the International Education Board sponsored a joint undertaking between Cornell University and Nanking University for the improvement of agriculture in China. This improvement was promoted through research in plant breeding and through the training of young Chinese in its principles and techniques. The central experiment station was a farm near Nanking, but missionary colleges and other institutions in several areas became interested, and eventually there were eleven co-operating stations. This research and training program was kept close to the soil. As rapidly as superior strains of cereals, beans, and other crops emerged from the experiments, a plan was worked out for distributing the seed to the farmers.

As the International Education Board's ventures in agriculture had been guided by the General Education Board's experience, so The Rockefeller Foundation benefited by the earlier work of the International Education Board in the Far East. For the Foundation's first efforts to help agriculture were centered in China—a program of rural reconstruction initiated in 1935 under the direction of Selskar M. Gunn. Dr. Gunn found that the earlier pioneering in plant breeding at Nanking provided a useful starting point for the rural reconstruction movement. Indeed, the department of agricultural economics at Nanking University became one of the principal centers of the Foundation's China program, and closely related to its work there were projects in animal husbandry and veterinary medicine at the nearby National Central University, as well as projects in the control of insect pests at the National Agricultural Research Bureau.

The China program enlisted the additional co-operation of Yenching University, Nankai University, Peking Union Medical College, the Chinese Mass Education Movement, and other institutions and organizations. It embraced, in addition to agriculture, such related interests as sanitation, preventive medicine, marketing, rural economy, rural administration, and community works. All the projects were integrated with the central idea of improving the lot of the 85 per cent of the Chinese people who lived by agriculture. Several hundred young Chinese received training on fellowships, a few in the United States and other foreign lands, but most of them in the homeland and on local projects associated with rural reconstruction.

The China program was frankly an experiment. Primarily, it was an attempt to awaken the Chinese universities and other native authorities to the means of national reconstruction that were available through improvement of the rural economy. To make any noticeable impact on a vast human aggregate represented by the hundreds of millions of rural Chinese required time and patience, and the trustees of the Foundation realized that decades would doubtless pass before the effort would bear conspicuous fruit. Even so, in the few years of its operation, the program yielded many tokens of its value. One result was the co-ordination of several fragmentary native efforts into a united movement to improve the lot of the Chinese peasant. Another was the discovery of leadership material among the youth. The Foundation had put more than a million dollars into this ambitious venture when, in 1939, the engulfment of war forced a curtailment of the effort. Fragments of the work were continued in after years, but like many another war-blasted project, its eventual appraisal must await the verdict of time.

II

Meanwhile, a wholly unique program in agriculture was being developed in Mexico. Its genesis was a casual comment to the writer of this history in 1941 by Henry A. Wallace, then Vice-President of the United States, who had just returned from a visit to that country. He remarked that if anyone could increase the yield per acre of corn and beans in Mexico, it would contribute more effectively to the welfare of the country and the happiness of its people than any other plan that could be devised.

This idea was discussed with the Foundation staff and with the trustees, and as a result Dr. E. C. Stakman of the University of Minnesota, Dr. Paul C. Mangelsdorf of Harvard, and Dr. Richard Bradfield of Cornell were enlisted as an advisory committee to explore the situation. It was on the recommendation of these three eminent agricultural scientists, after they had spent several months on a reconnaissance tour of Mexico, that the Foundation voted to embark upon a special program of agricultural research and development in that country. The Mexican Department of Agriculture officially invited the co-operation of the Foundation, and early in 1943 a formal agreement was entered upon between the two for a joint program to be organized within the Department and be operated by the Foundation.

The proposed program was indeed a new venture. All previous Rockefeller undertakings in agriculture—those of the General Education Board, of the International Education Board, and of the Foundation in China—had been distributive programs. That is to say, the responsibility in each of these earlier projects was limited to the providing of funds. Grants were made to universities and other institutions, but beyond that the Foundation did not enter into any of the scientific or technical details involved in the actual carrying out of the operation. The formulation, direction, and conduct of the projects were left entirely to the recipients. In Mexico, in contrast, the Foundation agreed not only to provide assistance in financing, but also in direction and operation. This meant the employment of a staff of agricultural scientists and active participation in the planning, organization and conduct of agricultural research. It was the sort of program that the Foundation had long been engaged with in hookworm, yellow fever, and other public health projects through its International Health Division; but never before had it attempted an operating program in any of the natural sciences.

Dr. J. George Harrar, who had had previous experience in Latin America, was engaged to head the work as the Foundation's field director for agriculture; and the brilliant success with which this new type of activity has met is in no small degree due to his character, judgment, and distinguished capacity for leadership. The Mexican Department of Agriculture created the *Oficina de Estudios Especiales* as a division to embody the joint undertaking, and it appointed Dr. Harrar chief of Special Studies. For several months of 1943, Harrar was the sole scientific member of the *Oficina,* and most of the time he spent in the field getting acquainted with Mexico. On horseback, by automobile, by train, and by airplane, he covered thousands of miles of rugged terrain, from the lush tropics of Vera Cruz to the rich plateaus, arid plains, and austere mountains farther north, frequently accompanied by Mexican colleagues from other bureaus. On these trips he began to collect seeds for later appraisal.

Harrar is a plant pathologist, and before the end of the first year a geneticist was added to the staff. Then came a soil scientist, later an entomologist, and as rapidly as the work grew, other experts were added, until by 1950 the staff numbered eleven American scientists, in addition to more than sixty Mexican associates. Since the establishment of the *Oficina,* administrative headquarters have been in one of the buildings of the Mexican Department of Agriculture in Mexico City; but its chief research center is a special laboratory built for the purpose on the grounds of the National College of Agriculture at Chapingo, a few miles outside Mexico City. In addition to this modern laboratory and adjacent greenhouses, 250 acres of the college fields are used in the researches. Outside of Chapingo, experimental plantings are made on farm plots scattered all over Mexico.

The investigations carried on by the *Oficina* have included experiments with soil management, fertilizers, insecticides and fungicides, conservation measures, irrigation, the use of labor-saving farm machinery, and, basic to all, the selection and development of superior plant varieties. Beginning with Harrar's initial tour of Mexico, there has been a continuous search for native varieties of corn, and more than two thousand different strains have been collected and tested. The tests showed that sixteen of these native maizes were superior. They differed in time required to mature, in size and shape of grain, in adaptation to different altitudes and latitudes, in resistance to diseases. Some that gave good yield in an arid region were poor in the humid tropics, but each had qualities which recommended it. The sixteen varieties were sown for seed increase, and, following extensive yield tests, six were offered to Mexican farmers for planting. One of these chosen varieties, tried out in the relatively rich soil of the Valley of Mexico, has repeatedly yielded 25 per cent more crop than the best hitherto grown in that region.

But plant breeders are not satisfied with merely identifying and distributing the best native varieties. They know that by controlled crossing of two or more stocks it is possible to produce hybrids and synthetic varieties which are better crop yielders than any strains found in nature. Therefore, while the more promising of the natural varieties were being released, to give farmers the benefit of their increased yields, geneticists were carefully crossing selected strains of the natural stocks. There were crossings, not only between strains of native Mexican varieties, but between these and promising varieties collected from other lands of North and South America. Through five years of such experiments, the *Oficina* developed eight acceptable stocks of hybrid corn. By 1950, enough seed had been obtained from the improved stocks to plant approximately 1,500,000 acres of Mexico's total corn acreage, or nearly 8 per cent of the national production. At this rate of acceleration, with the distribution of seed wisely controlled by the Mexican government, and with the continuing co-operation of the farmers, it is only a matter of time before the improved varieties and hybrids will completely supplant the less productive native stocks.

Soon after the corn-breeding program was launched, a plant pathologist was assigned to begin a study of Mexico's wheat, a crop which has had little success in that country. The problem here was to find or develop varieties which would resist the rust and other destructive fungus diseases. Mexico's principal wheat-growing regions are Sonora, the northwestern state which fronts on the Gulf of California, and the great inland plateau known as the Bajio. During the summer and fall, which are the rainy seasons, it was traditionally impossible to mature wheat in either region, because the rust flourishes in a moist atmosphere. Therefore wheat farming was attempted only in the winter. Even in winter, Sonora was occasionally swept by fog from the sea which enveloped its fields for weeks with continuous humidity and rendered the growing wheat an easy prey to rust.

Following the example of the corn breeders, the wheat researchers combed the hemisphere, and indeed such other distant regions as Australia and New Zealand, for contrasting varieties of their cereal. Hundreds of strains were collected, many long cultivated in Mexico, but a number from outside countries. Selection tests and inter-breeding produced twelve varieties which proved to be rust-resistant and well adapted to the Mexican climates. As a consequence of these developments, Mexican farmers in 1948 saw high-yielding, high-quality wheat growing normally in the rainy season. During the winter of 1948-1949 an epidemic of rust swept Sonora, with losses so complete that many farmers burned their crops to rid fields of the infected plants. But those who had ventured to try the rust-resistant varieties discovered that it was largely immune to the disease, and some harvested even larger crops than usual. It is reported that one enterprising farmer obtained from forty-five to fifty bushels per acre from the new seed despite the epidemic of rust, whereas even in favorable years his yield from the native variety rarely averaged thirty bushels.

What has been done with corn and wheat indicates the pattern of research that is being directed also at beans, sorghums, and other food crops. Thus, 45,000 acres of sorghums were planted in 1950, and 3000 acres of soybeans, where such crops had hardly existed in Mexico before. The over-all objective is to develop an all-round program for increasing Mexico's food supply. In 1948, for the first time in thirty-five years, aided both by these improved varieties and by a favorable growing season, Mexico did not have to import corn. In 1950 it planted to the newly improved wheat the largest acreage in its history—1,200,000 acres, or 60 per cent of the national production. Mexican ecologists look forward to the time when the native farms will produce grain in such abundance that there will not only be a sufficient supply for all the people but a surplus for feeding livestock, thereby improving the quality and quantity of native meat and milk.

The Mexican agricultural program is also a project in education. Indeed, the training program forms the basis of the project and is the foundation on which its ultimate future must rest. Each year, the Mexican Department of Agriculture assigns a number of young men from its School of Agriculture to serve the *Oficina* as research assistants, thereby promoting the development of a group of native scientists. To the end of 1950 a total of seventy-nine young Mexican agriculturists had been associated with the project in this way. The Foundation additionally aids the training by later appointing the more promising of these boys to scholarships which give them a year or more of postgraduate study in the United States. In the first seven years of the *Oficina*, seventeen of its Mexican research assistants studied on these scholarships in such places as the Universities of California, Kansas, Missouri, Minnesota, and Cornell. During the same period, eleven other Mexicans were given Foundation fellowships in agriculture for still more advanced study in the United States.

But the influence and service of the program has not been confined to Mexico. Beginning in 1945, the Natural Sciences division began to use the Mexican project as a training outpost for its agricultural fellows from other Latin-American countries, particularly those from Colombia and Brazil. The project provided, in a *milieu* in which Latin Americans were completely at home, a demonstration of what can be accomplished by capable scientists with modern yet relatively modest equipment. With this purpose in view, the Foundation made grants to agricultural colleges located in other Latin-American countries to enable them to send a few of their top students to Mexico for further training. In addition, the policy was developed of routing Foundation agricultural fellows from other Latin-American countries through Mexico, requiring them to spend several weeks working at Chapingo before going on to the United States for their principal postgraduate study. In some instances, the fellows on their return trip stopped for a final month or two in Mexico.

Viewed in perspective, it is clear that the training activities are not merely incidental to the Mexican agricultural program but constitute perhaps its most fundamental and significant feature. Through them, the program builds its future on a permanent basis, and also extends its influence to other countries. Speaking of these activities in 1950, Harrar said:

> Invariably those who have passed through the training period have gained not only additional technical knowledge but a broader view of Mexico's agricultural problems. Without exception the seventy-nine individuals commissioned to the program since its inception in 1943 are today rendering real service to agriculture through research and through the teaching of still younger scientists. The Mexican government is making a special effort to increase opportunities for well trained agriculturalists, stimulating them to pursue useful careers in agriculture. This growing body of eager, young, competent scientists forms the vanguard of future agricultural progress in Mexico. And the association of young scientists from several different American countries is bound to be of help in solving international agricultural problems.[2]

III

News of this co-operative undertaking spread rapidly to other countries. It traveled by word of mouth from the returning fellows, visiting professors, and others who had personal contact with the project, and by the printed word of technical papers and other publications reporting the results of the researches and their application to crop improvement. Eventually, inquiries began to come from other Latin-American countries, pointing to opportunities for similar programs in their lands and inviting The Rockefeller Foundation to collaborate.

The first collaboration outside of Mexico was undertaken in 1949, when the Foundation accepted an invitation from Colombia to inaugurate a program in corn and wheat. During the preceding nine years, it had been cultivating agricultural opportunities and agricultural education in Colombia through fellowships and grants in aid, and a sound basis had been laid for co-operative research. Early in 1950, therefore, two members of the scientific staff in Mexico were assigned to Colombia, a geneticist and a field agronomist, to become the nucleus of a Colombian research group. The National University set apart space at the School of Agronomy in Medellín to provide experimental plots and laboratory facilities, and additional facilities were furnished at the Federal Experimental Station near Bogotá. By the end of 1950, the first plantings had been made, the first seed harvested, and the program was actively under way.

Because of the prior experience in Mexico, the Colombian project started abreast of the Mexican, at least as far as wheat breeding is concerned; for several of the wheat varieties tested, crossed, and developed in Mexico during the 1940's appear to be well adapted to the soil and climate of Colombia. It is also significant of the widening influence of the Mexican program that a number of Colombian agricultural scientists are former fellows or scholars who were trained in Mexico. Some of these are actively associated with the Foundation scientists in the Colombian program.

By 1950, therefore, The Rockefeller Foundation was actively engaged with its own staff in conducting agricultural research and development in two countries, Mexico and Colombia. At that time, applications were in hand from four other Latin-American governments, exploring the possibilities of initiating similar joint efforts in their agriculture. It is as yet an open question as to how much further the Foundation will consider it desirable and possible to expand this work.

In many quarters, the Mexico project has been cited as an example of what President Truman's Point Four program could do on a larger scale. The undertaking also attracted the favorable attention of officials of the United Nations Food and Agricultural Organization. But already the influence of the work has ranged even farther. Reports from Asia indicate that accounts of what was done in Mexico have circulated there. The research findings and applications have been pointed to as evidence of what the export from Western countries of agricultural skill and technology might accomplish for hungry nations of the Far East. Essentially, it is only putting into practice the old principle of helping neighbors to help themselves.

From its inception to the end of 1950, the Mexican program had involved an outlay of roughly a million and a half dollars by the Foundation and substantial additional sums by the Mexican government. Weighed against the results accomplished, the money expenditures have been trifling. Adventurous ideas have been set in motion which have the power to affect the welfare and happiness of millions of human beings.

CHAPTER XVI

THE PROBLEM OF THE SOCIAL SCIENCES

PUBLIC HEALTH AND MEDICINE, EVEN WHEN supplemented by the biological sciences and pointed toward a fuller understanding of human behavior, do not constitute a rounded program for an organization whose concern is the well-being of men. The goal of health, physical or mental, is not sufficiently broad; something is missing from the equation. One of the missing factors is, of course, a knowledge of human relationships. How can the social adjustment of millions of human beings be arranged with less frustration and inequity? What are the principles on which nations and groups can live together in peace? What forms of organization or economic arrangement most effectively enhance the dignity and freedom of the individual? Public health has great social usefulness—and so has medical and biological research—and money spent in their development is devoted to a basic purpose. But unless we can find successful solutions to some of the intricately complex and fast-growing problems of human relationship, we run the risk of having a world in which public health and medicine are of little significance. A foundation, broadly concerned with the welfare of men, must therefore support the effort to make knowledge available for social purposes, and widen the area of understanding concerning those institutions and processes by which the relationship of human beings is organized and expressed.

The Rockefeller Foundation was admittedly slow in entering the field of social studies. The first attempt—in industrial relations—

ended, as we have seen, in disillusionment. Although Jerome Greene, the Executive Secretary of the Foundation in its early days, was keenly interested in this type of research, his efforts to enlist the support of the trustees were generally unsuccessful. For this result, Mr. Gates bears a large share of the responsibility. He had what might be called an almost mystic belief in the promise and potency of medical research; to him it was the open road that led to a better future, and few other avenues were worth exploring. In his unpublished autobiography he made this revealing comment: "As medical research goes on, it will find out and promulgate, as an unforeseen by-product of its work, new moral laws and new social laws, new definitions of what is right and wrong in our relations with each other. Medical research will educate the human conscience in new directions and point out new duties."

Moreover, Gates had a profound distrust of research in economics. "When you come to investigate these things," he wrote to Mr. Rockefeller, Jr., "you are not acting on inert matter or even on animals. Your material is the activities and organizations of business. Can you command this material as you can command the material of investigation in medical science? I fear not."[1] When, in 1914 the trustees of the Foundation appointed a committee of economists under the chairmanship of Professor Edwin F. Gay of Harvard "to make a selection of problems of economic importance which could be advantageously studied," Gates was vigorously opposed. "The fundamental principles of economics are well known," he said, ". . . I believe it would be possible for us, with one-tenth the labor and trouble that we are proposing to spend on this investigation, to find out ways that will put a few fundamental economic facts into every home in the land."[2] Today, thirty-five years later, Gates' argument, and particularly the illustrations which he used to point it up, seem like reflections from another world. Nevertheless, he succeeded in persuading the trustees to his point of view, and the proposals of Mr. Gay's committee were tabled. However, Greene's influence resulted in the allocation of substantial sums to create and support the Institute of Government Research, later merged with the Brookings Institution, and other appropriations were made by the Foundation in this same general field. But by 1920 the Foundation had to all intents and purposes been captured by the doctors, and while some grants were made in the following years for biology and cultural anthropology, the doors, although still ajar, were for the time being closed against practically everything except public health and medicine.

In 1923, the decision of The Laura Spelman Rockefeller Memorial to make the social sciences its chief objective furnished another and conclusive reason for the Foundation's disinclination to enter the field. The Memorial had a capital fund of $74,000,000. Established, as we have noted, by Mr. Rockefeller as a memorial to his wife, to support certain welfare activities in which she was interested, it had encountered some difficulty in finding a field of operations, not already pre-empted by the Foundation, in which its generous funds could advantageously be placed. In 1922, Beardsley Ruml, a young man in his late twenties who had been associated with Dr. James R. Angell, president of the Carnegie Corporation, and who had been trained in psychology, was appointed director of the Memorial. The appointment was considered as perhaps a temporary arrangement, since the idea of consolidating the Memorial with the Foundation had already been tentatively suggested.

Ruml, however, was not a man to remain inactive in the face of opportunity. In October, 1922, shortly after taking office, he submitted a memorandum to the trustees containing a bold plan to move the Memorial bodily into the field of the social sciences—economics, sociology, political science, and the related subjects, psychology, anthropology, and history.

> An examination of the operations of organizations in the field of social welfare [he said] shows as a primary need the development of the social sciences and the production of a body of substantiated and widely accepted generalizations as to human capacities and motives and as to the behavior of human beings as individuals and in groups. . . . All who work toward the general end of social welfare are embarrassed by the lack of that knowledge which the social sciences must provide. It is as though engineers were at work without an adequate development of physics and chemistry, or as though physicians were practicing in the absence of the medical sciences. The direction of work in the social field is largely controlled by tradition, inspiration and expediency.[3]

Ruml was under no misapprehension as to the herculean task involved in his proposal. He admitted that the social sciences were very young, that the facilities for the collection and tabulation of data were meager, that university classroom instruction limited the possibility of contact with social phenomena, and that the research carried on by the universities was "largely deductive and speculative, on the basis of secondhand observations, documentary evidence and anecdotal material." He admitted, too, that the subject matter of the social sciences was infinitely difficult. "It cannot be brought into the laboratory for study," he said. "Elemental phases are almost impossible to isolate; and important forces cannot be controlled and experimented with, but must be observed if, when, and as operative." But he insisted that "unless means are found for meeting the complex social problems that are so rapidly developing, our increasing control of physical forces may prove increasingly destructive of human values."[4]

Alva Johnston said of Ruml that he had "a creative ignorance which prevents him from seeing the No Thoroughfare, Keep Off the Grass, Don't Trespass, and Dead End Street signs in the world of ideas."[5] Certainly, in the forbidding field of the social sciences, Ruml proceeded with vigor and shrewdness to implement his ideas. He set out to find strategic undertakings for financial support as well as opportunities for dramatizing the importance of social studies. It must be admitted that for this activity the environment of 1922 and 1923 was propitious. The social sciences had been given considerable impetus by the First World War. Mobilization for war had shown the need for economic intelligence, for reliable statistics on all sorts of subjects, for information, insofar as it could be obtained, about the amount, source, and composition of the national income so that the scope of war activities could be planned. It also became necessary to know what the economy could produce. Were there limits on productivity beyond which a country could not go even in an emergency? Answers to such questions as these, which had been found essential to the conduct of war, were seen to be important also for peace. Organizations like the Brookings Institution and the National Bureau of Economic Research were beginning to function, and new ideas and new tools were in the making.

Ruml concentrated on two main approaches: the creation of facilities for research and the increase in the number of able men working in the field. He believed that the facilities could most effectively be developed in the university. He was impressed by the stability of the university as an organization, by the presence there of a wide range of professional opinion, and by the existence, however inadequately developed in the social sciences, of scholarly and scientific standards of work. But means must be devised, he insisted, for securing a far more intimate contact of the social scientist in the university with concrete social phenomena. "The impingement of the phenomenal world on the observer," he said, "is the beginning of things scientific."[6]

Consequently, the grants which the Memorial made in its early days to support university research were focused on the idea of bringing together the various disciplines of the social sciences—economics, sociology, and political science—in a systematic investigation of concrete social problems. Thus funds were given to the University of Chicago for a study of its own urban community; to Harvard and Radcliffe for economic and legal research in international relations; to the University of North Carolina for social, economic, and governmental research in the South; to the University of Wisconsin for studies in rural tenancy and land ownership. In all these cases—and in a score of others—the funds given by the Memorial were not for buildings or new courses of instruction; they were for traveling expenses, leaves of absence, statistical and clerical assistance, or whatever facilities were necessary to place the investigator in the desired relationship to his problem.

In addition to furnishing this opportunity for realistic studies, the Memorial's plan had the incidental advantage of inducing a degree of collaboration between various academic departments within the university. Ruml had a layman's impatience with the traditional and essentially artificial departmental divisions of university organization, and under his leadership the Memorial sought to bring about a synthesis of the various relevant disciplines in a united attack on social problems. Perhaps its most ambitious undertaking in this direction was its participation, along with the General Education Board and The Rockefeller Foundation, in financing the Institute of Human Relations at Yale, involving an attempt to co-ordinate and invest with a certain physical unity a number of more or less scattered programs, i.e., the activities of the University's Institute of Psychology and its Psycho-Clinic for child study, the University's work in mental hygiene, the developments in psychiatry at the School of Medicine, and the related contributions of the social sciences fostered in the School of Law and the Graduate School. In the evolution of this project, the three Rockefeller boards ultimately appropriated sums in excess of six million dollars. It must be admitted that in terms of its original declarations the hopes of the Institute were not realized. It was planned in an era of expansiveness and was handicapped not only by the latitude of its title but also by its inability to merge conflicting personnel and policies into a workable relationship. A unified and integrated program of research does not develop automatically from physical propinquity under a single roof. In more recent years, under new leadership, and with a program reduced to feasible dimensions, it has made a significant contribution in psychiatry, psychology, and anthropology.

The development of major university centers of research, both in the United States and abroad, became the most important part of the Memorial's program. Chicago, Harvard, Columbia, Yale, Virginia, Texas, North Carolina, Stanford, Vanderbilt, the London School of Economics, the Deutsche Hochschule für Politik in Berlin, the University of Stockholm, and many others were assisted in developing rounded centers of social-science research. This frequently involved fluid research funds appropriated to the university to be used in its own discretion; aid to university presses; the provision of special sums for publication; grants to enable a number of the centers to experiment with different types of training; emergency assistance to university libraries in continental Europe whose books and periodicals in the social sciences had been depleted or destroyed by the war; and various other devices for stimulating and encouraging the development of techniques and teaching in the social studies. Approximately twenty million dollars was appropriated for these general purposes, and during the seven years of the Memorial's operation in this field it can be said without exaggeration that notable progress was made in securing recognition from university administrators and from trustees and officials of other foundations that research facilities and opportunities are essential for the social sciences, that such research is costly in terms of both time and money, and that the nonacademic world is eager to profit by the results of scholarly investigation.

As the work progressed, Ruml realized that it could not be confined strictly to university departments. Research without application is barren; it must be harnessed to the processes by which the results of research are given practical effectiveness. This proposition, as far as the social studies is concerned, leads at once in the direction of social technology—or social engineering—with its recognized divisions of business, law, public administration, and social work. Ruml believed that such schools should be included in the program of the Memorial, and a number of appropriations of this type were made, particularly to schools of social work. Five such schools were aided—the Atlanta School of Social Work, the New York School of Social Work, the schools at Tulane University and the University of Chicago, and the National Catholic School of Social Service. A total of more than one and three quarter million dollars was appropriated for this purpose by the Memorial and later by the Foundation; and the strategic value of the investment was demonstrated in the decade following the depression, when the federal government, in its greatly enlarged social service program, demanded and secured the type of professionally trained personnel which these schools were helping to develop.

Moreover, special research agencies were coming into existence which were not directly connected with particular universities, but which were playing a part whose significance could not be overlooked. Perhaps the most immediately important example—and one with the creation of which Ruml was himself actively identified—was the Social Science Research Council. Organized in 1923 to correlate and stimulate research in the social sciences, and modeling its plans on the successful activities of the National Research Council in the physical sciences, it became the most important instrumentality in America for furthering intercommunication between students of social problems and sponsoring co-operative research among the several disciplines. The grants which the Memorial made to this council were extensive, and the same pattern of support was maintained during the twenty-year period which in 1929 followed the consolidation of the Memorial with the Foundation.

The Brookings Institution, the Institute of Pacific Relations, and the National Bureau of Economic Research were also among the special agencies which were substantially aided by the Memorial during the brief span of its existence. Here, too, a relationship was established which was followed in later years by the Foundation.

II

Concurrently with this development, Ruml was addressing himself to his second objective: the increase in the number of able men working in the field of the social sciences. In this program he relied to a large extent on a systematic provision of fellowships which, as he said, "will tend to place the social sciences in a more equal relation to the physical sciences."[7] The Memorial's fellowships in the United States were administered by the Social Science Research Council; overseas the program was carried on by the Memorial itself with the aid of "national advisers" in various countries including England, France, Germany, Austria, Czechoslovakia, Italy, Holland, Norway, Sweden, Denmark, and Australia. Ruml was anxious to effect what, with Rose, he called "cross-fertilization"—to promote the easy flow between institutions and across frontiers of men and ideas in the social sciences. In addition, therefore, to fellowships which frequently took men from one country to another, the Memorial appropriated funds for traveling professorships, conferences, international congresses, scientific journals, and other ends that underscored the opportunity and need of intercommunication between specialists in various parts of the world who were working on the same general problems.

In developing his two major objectives by methods which closely integrated the Memorial with universities and university personnel, Ruml kept in mind the necessity of what he called "the-feet-on-the ground policy." In the final report of the Memorial, written after its consolidation with the Foundation, he made this observation:

> Each program was dominated by a practical motive, to achieve concrete improvement in the conditions of life and to contribute realistically to the public welfare. That scientific research occupied an important place in each program was the consequence of the belief that the practical attack on social problems is the scientific attack broadly conceived, that more understanding was needed than could be obtained from an appeal to tradition, expediency, or intuition. The Memorial had no interest in the promotion of scientific research as an end in itself; its motive was not sheer curiosity as to how various human and social phenomena came to be and are; the interest in science was an interest in one means to an end, and the end was explicitly recognized to be the advancement of human welfare.[8]

As we have seen, the Memorial operated in the field of the social sciences for only seven years. Something like $41,000,000 was spent, inclusive of separate programs in child study and interracial relations, but exclusive of final appropriations of $17,500,000 for a number of permanent memorials to Mrs. Rockefeller and a grant of $10,000,000 for the establishment of the Spelman Fund of New York. The Memorial under Ruml's leadership was criticized in some quarters for lavish spending, but as Ruml said in his report to the trustees in 1922, when he first presented the prospectus for the social sciences: "The problem of policy for the Memorial is not the problem of a single year's activities; it is rather the problem of determining the work for a period of years, perhaps a decade." And he figured on the income of a decade, plus contributions from principal, in laying his plans.

When the Memorial was merged with the Foundation in 1929, Ruml retired as Director, and his place in the new division of the Social Sciences of the Foundation was taken by Edmund E. Day, professor of economics at Harvard and later dean of the School of Business Administration at Michigan, who had been associated with Ruml in the work. Ruml was a layman and an administrator. He always insisted that his job was with social scientists rather than with social science. The sums which, under his leadership, were used to stimulate scientific investigation were perhaps not large in comparison with aggregate expenditures for social sciences, but they represented a new margin of resources, and they were employed dramatically at a strategic moment. Chancellor Hutchins of the University of Chicago, speaking in 1929, summed up the verdict in words which a longer perspective will probably not overrule: "The Laura Spelman Rockefeller Memorial in its brief but brilliant career did more than any other agency to promote the social sciences in the United States."[9]

III

The Memorial's program was not developed without occasional misgiving and question on the part of the trustees. The field of the social sciences presented perplexing difficulties which did not attach to any other broad activity which the Rockefeller boards had hitherto undertaken. It was a new field and it involved serious possibility of public misunderstanding. Still vivid in the minds of some of the trustees was the recollection of the Congressional investigation and the bitter criticism which had followed the Foundation's attempt, ten years earlier, to make some approach to the problem of industrial relations. In 1924 the Executive Committee of the Memorial was requested by the trustees to make a study of certain troublesome questions of policy and to discuss them with four men outside the board who had their complete confidence: Dr. Vincent, Dr. Rose, Dr. Buttrick, and Dr. Abraham Flexner. These questions involved the wisdom of supporting research in so-called "controversial" issues, and the trustees themselves had been unable to come to an agreement as to a definition of the adjective. As a result of this study, a memorandum which met the views of all concerned was prepared and adopted as a statement of official policy. The principles which it laid down seem even today to provide a conservative basis for foundation activity in the social-science field, and for that reason the gist of it is presented in the following paragraphs.

The present memorandum proposes to indicate principles which affect the ability of the Memorial to become associated with projects in the field of social science. Certain principles would seem to make association undesirable. It appears advisable:

1. Not to contribute to organizations whose purposes and activities are centered largely in the procurement of legislation.
2. Not to attempt directly under the Memorial to secure any social, economic, or political reform.
3. Not to contribute more than a conservative proportion toward the current expense of organizations engaged in direct activity for social welfare.
4. Not to carry on investigations and research directly under the Memorial, except for the guidance of the Memorial.
5. Not to attempt to influence the findings or conclusions of research and investigations through the designation of either personnel, specific problems to be attacked, or methods of inquiry to be adopted; or through indirect influence in giving inadequate assurances of continuity of support.
6. Not to concentrate too narrowly on particular research institutions, incurring thereby the danger of institutional bias.

Certain principles would seem to make assistance from the Memorial desirable. It appears appropriate:

1. To offer fellowships to students of competence and maturity for study and research under the supervision of responsible educational and scientific institutions.
2. To contribute to agencies which may advance in indirect ways scientific activity in the social field.
3. To make possible the publication of scientific investigations sponsored by responsible institutions or organizations through general appropriations to be administered in detail by the sponsoring agency.
4. To contribute toward the expenses of conferences of scientific men for scientific purposes.
5. To make possible, under the auspices of scientific institutions, governmental agencies or voluntary organizations, demonstrations which may serve to test, to illustrate or to lead to more general adoption of measures of a social, economic or governmental character which have been devised, studied and recommended by responsible agencies.
6. To support scientific research on social, economic and governmental questions when responsible educational or scientific institutions initiate the request, sponsor the research and assume responsibility for the selection and competence of the staff and the scientific spirit of the investigations.[10]

In 1928, a second statement of policy by the trustees of the Memorial contained, in addition to the foregoing points, another point of significance which had not been elaborated in the first.

Subjects of a controversial nature cannot be avoided if the program is to concern itself with the more important aspects of modern social life. In fact, successful treatment of issues of a controversial sort would be so important a contribution to the fundamental objectives of the program that the existence of militant differences of opinion cannot be thought to preclude the promotion of inquiry under appropriate auspices.[11]

These statements of policy were officially adopted by the Foundation at the time of the consolidation with The Laura Spelman Rockefeller Memorial.

IV

When the Foundation took over from the Memorial in 1929 the responsibility for the social sciences, it took over a well-articulated program; and in the next two decades, under the successive administrations of Mr. Day, Miss Sydnor Walker, and Joseph H. Willits, the policy, with frequent modifications and shifted emphases, was a projection of the beginnings made under the Memorial. This new period coincided with an era of revolutionary change not only in the United States but around the world. Hardly had Day's administration begun when the financial crash of 1929 shattered the complacency of businessmen and economists. The depression with all its abnormal concomitants was followed by the Second World War, so that the two decades of work in the social sciences by the Foundation spanned a period of swiftly mounting change.

Day's main emphasis, like Ruml's, was on the university and university research. He believed that the university centers of advanced training constitute the source of the stream of competent personnel and scientific standards which are often so conspicuously lacking in the social studies. He was under no illusion as to the difficulties to be faced. "Practically all the sciences have sprung initially from philosophy," he said. "The introduction of laboratory methods enabled the natural sciences to make a rather complete separation, and the medical sciences made the same break later. The social sciences are still in the process of establishing their independence. . . . We have thus virtually to break an academic pattern. We have to establish a new academic mold."[12]

Consequently, under Day's brilliant and challenging leadership, Foundation aid was concentrated on high-grade university centers selected on a regional basis both in the United States and abroad, and Ruml's program in this direction was expanded and developed. In addition to the extensive use of fellowships, one of the principal techniques employed was the encouragement of social-science committees or councils at various universites which would control and administer the fluid research funds given by the Foundation, thus determining for themselves the fields and projects to which they would devote their attention. This device, in the years between 1929 and 1934, resulted in the appropriation by the Foundation of over two million dollars. In addition, three major fields of special interest were laid out for intensive support—international relations, economic stabilization, and public administration. These fields are briefly discussed in the following paragraphs, although certain aspects of them are reserved for a later chapter.

International relations. Some support in this area had been given by the Memorial, but because of the critical nature of the times it was stepped up under the Foundation in the early thirties. Substantial grants for research, conference, and publication were made to a great variety of organizations, both in the United States and abroad, including the Foreign Policy Association, the Council on Foreign Relations, the Institute of Pacific Relations, the Fiscal Committee of the League of Nations, the Royal Institute of International Affairs (London), the Graduate Institute of International Studies (Geneva), the Centre d'Études Politiques Étrangères (Paris), the Notgemeinschaft der Deutschen Wissenschaft (Berlin), the Institute of Economics and History at Copenhagen, and a dozen others. As will be noted later, this type of support was continued by the Foundation during the following two decades.

Economic stabilization. In the early thirties, the conditions prevailing around the globe gave overwhelming evidence of the importance of scientific study of the intricacies of economic stability. No other problem that faced the world at that time offered so supreme a challenge to available resources of scientific method and personnel. "That any early solution of the problem can be found is altogether unlikely," wrote Day, "but that every effort should be made to deal constructively with it as expeditiously as possible cannot be seriously questioned."[13]

Two lines of interest were recognized: (1) the improvement of the statistical record of cyclical change and sharper identification of the causal factors involved; (2) the encouragement of studies designed to develop and perfect appropriate practical measures for minimizing the damaging effects of economic instability. Toward these two interests, in the early thirties, and extending throughout the decade into the next, extensive grants which ran literally into millions of dollars were appropriated by the Foundation to research organizations around the world, such as the National Bureau of Economic Research, the Financial and Economic Intelligence Section of the League of Nations, the Social Science Research Council, the Brookings Institution, the Austrian Institute for Trade Cycle Research, the Dutch Economic Institute, the London School of Economics, and many others. One of the large grants, of $325,000, financed an international study of the history of prices and wages, carried on simultaneously in leading European countries and in the United States. The study was planned by Professor Edwin F. Gay of Harvard and Sir William Beveridge of the London School of Economics with the idea of providing a framework for subsequent surveys of economic and social development and giving statistical data of a dependable sort for measuring numerous phases of fundamental change.

An interesting side light on the mood prevailing among some of the trustees of the Foundation in the early thirties is shown by an appropriation of $1,500,000 that was made with the idea of expediting the search for some solution of the miseries and suffering caused by the financial depression. The expenditure was placed in the hands of a special committee of the trustees. Bread lines were everywhere and the collapse had reached unprecedented proportions. The world economy was desperately sick, and it was obvious that something was fundamentally wrong with a society in which raw materials were plentiful, workers were eager to apply their productive capacity, adequate industrial plants and equipment were at hand, and yet the whole enterprise was halted, and millions were out of work.

It cannot be said that any startling results came from this emergency appropriation. It was based on hopes that were far too sanguine. There was no quick and easy remedy for the malady; there was not even the possibility of swift and accurate diagnosis. Under this appropriation, grants were given for research and study of current phenomena to organizations like the Brookings Institution, the Social Science Research Council, the American Municipal Association, the American Public Welfare Association, and the National Association of Housing Officials. In other words, it was a continuance of the same kind of work on which the Foundation was already engaged. The trustees discovered that economic maladjustment is a long-term problem, and that there is no short cut to a cure. Two years later, the unexpended balance of this appropriation was returned to the general fund, and the activity was merged with the regular work of the Social Sciences division.

Public administration. This program, which fringed out into the broad area of community planning, had as its core the idea of adequate training for government personnel, particularly in the federal services. The rapid expansion of government activities in the thirties, with the attendant problems of recruitment, called for new methods and techniques of training, and the universities seemed to provide the best means of supplying the need. Accordingly, the Foundation made grants for this purpose to the Universities of California, Chicago, Cincinnati, Harvard, Minnesota, Virginia, and the American University in Washington, D. C. The grant to Harvard helped to organize the activity in public service training on a graduate level, and the work was the forerunner of the Graduate School of Public Administration established later through the generous gift of Lucius N. Littauer. At the American University in Washington, other pioneer work was undertaken. The Federal Administration had charged the Civil Service Commission with the task of formulating plans for providing career positions in the federal service, and for improving the level of competence, both through recruitment and in-service training. Since it was believed that there was a definite advantage in having this program carried on outside Government circles, the experiment was inaugurated at American University.

Foundation assistance also went to the National Institute of Public Affairs, which directed in Washington the recruitment of college graduates as interns in practical career-service training in various federal departments and agencies. Further Foundation aid was given to the Public Administration Committee of the Social Science Research Council in its efforts to study and reduce to usable form the experience that was accumulating as the government faced new problems and expanded its administrative activities.

It is perhaps significant of the interest of the Foundation in this field of training for government service to note that over three decades it appropriated approximately eleven million dollars for this purpose.

The Foundation's largest grant in the general area of public administration—$3,000,000—was made to the Spelman Fund, which, as we have seen, had been created in 1928, at the time of the consolidation of The Laura Spelman Rockefeller Memorial with The Rockefeller Foundation, and had been given a principal fund by the Memorial of $10,000,000. The purpose for which the Spelman Fund was established was to carry on certain programs which at the time of the consolidation did not seem to fit in with the plans of The Rockefeller Foundation. Among these programs was the direct co-operation with organizations like the Council of State Governments and the American Municipal Association for the improvement of public administration. The Foundation's program in this same general area involved a more indirect approach, largely through universities and research agencies.

The great contribution of the Spelman Fund under the guidance of Charles E. Merriam, Beardsley Ruml, and Guy Moffett, was the creation and financing of the Public Administration Clearing House, located at 1313 East Sixtieth Street, Chicago, and associated with the University. The building and the experiment, now widely known as "1313," have served to bring together in close co-operation twenty-one organizations of public officials which represent functional operations of government, such as welfare, finance, public works, personnel, and city management. Through these organizations—such as the International City Managers' Association, the American Public Works Association, and the Civil Service Assembly—officials are kept in touch with the results of administrative experience and of research in their respective fields. In other words, the main objective of "1313" is to help associations of public officials to provide for their members much the same kind of service that lawyers or doctors expect from their professional societies, or businessmen from their trade associations—the general improvement of standards, the exchanges of ideas, and the development of *esprit de corps* and stricter codes of ethics.

These associations were further aided by the Spelman Fund in studies and research in connection with important demonstration projects and administrative experiments. For example, the Municipal Finance Officers Association has developed uniform accounting classifications and terminology and model forms for municipal accounting and budgetary control. The American Public Works Association has produced standard specifications for public works construction.

The assets of the Spelman Fund were inadequate to carry this creative program to completion, and the Foundation's appropriation supplied the necessary means. As we have noted, the Spelman Fund has now been liquidated, but in "1313" it has left behind it a monument of permanent usefulness.

V

Such in barest outline was the Foundation's program in the social sciences during the early and middle thirties. Its ramifications were so extensive that it is difficult to discuss them without getting lost in a sea of detail. One is tempted to single out certain special items like the financing of the *Encyclopedia of the Social Sciences,* or the extensive support given to the Committee on the Costs of Medical Care which, under the chairmanship of Dr. Ray Lyman Wilbur, wrote a report that constituted a landmark in the long struggle to bring modern medicine to the people who need it. But most of the emphasis throughout this period was on institutional research, and the philosophy behind it, as we have seen, was based on the belief that the understanding and control of human phenomena lie in the scientific analysis and appraisal of facts. The techniques of social studies had lagged so far behind those of the natural or laboratory sciences that concentrated efforts were necessary to break down the old classical methodology and give impetus to a new kind of realism in social research.

In 1934, a committee of the trustees of the Foundation, after an extended study, expressed the belief that the time had come for a shift of emphasis. The committee felt, perhaps in an excess of optimism (the author of this history was its chairman), that the attempt of the Foundation to try to establish in the universities an empirical basis for the social sciences had been reasonably successful. "It seems to your committee," said the report, "that we now have the opportunity to see whether we cannot assist in applying to concrete problems of our social, political and industrial life some of the ideas and data which research all over the world is rapidly developing. This would not mean, of course, the relinquishment of research as a method. It would mean that we have no interest in the promotion of research as an end in itself. We are interested in it as a means to an end, and the end is the advancement of human welfare. . . . The mere accumulation of facts, untested by practical application, is in danger of becoming a substitute rather than a basis for collective action."[14]

The committee took particular exception to the fluid research funds granted by the Foundation to the universities to be used for research projects in their discretion and judgment, and it called attention to the fact that these projects ranged over wide fields from the study of the constitution of classical Greek cities to the social life of the Navaho Indian. The committee complained of the "lack of any systematic integration or concentration by the universities in administering the funds," and went on to make this comment:

From such inquiry as we have been able to make, we are not convinced that within some of the universities aided considerations of faculty politics do not occasionally play a part in determining the distribution of these blanket research funds. Consequently the best and most promising research projects do not always find support. Certainly in such a vast array of projects as is financed by our social science grants, it cannot always be true that the best judgment is shown or the best brains employed.

On the other hand, the fluid fund in the social sciences has served the purpose for which it was devised. It has helped to build up and stabilize the habit and desire in university faculties to do research work. However faulty critical judgment and discrimination may have been in the administration of these funds by university authorities, the impetus toward a realistic type of research has been genuine.*

As a result of this report, that part of the older program which concentrated support behind the idea of building up general university research was largely abandoned, and the emphasis was shifted to more specific fields of research and application "in the hope of making a realistic contribution to contemporary problems." In other words, the new program, if such it could be called, was centered, although by no means exclusively, on specific problems like international relations and social security which had already been extensively developed in the work of both Ruml and Day. The university, however, and its facilities for research, continued to be one of the main supports of the Foundation in putting this new program into effect, and even the program itself had to be modified by the necessities of the coming years.

In 1937, Day resigned from the Foundation to take the presidency of Cornell University, and after a year in which Miss Sydnor Walker served as acting director of the Social Sciences division, Joseph H. Willits, who had been head of the Wharton School of Finance and Commerce of the University of Pennsylvania, was appointed to the vacancy. Day's final appraisal of the developments that had occurred

* The best analysis of the experience of these social-science research committees which any university has made and published was that done for Columbia University by Professor James Bonbright. It states their strength and weaknesses in a constructive and judicial manner (*Report on the Work of the Columbia University Council for Research in the Social Sciences, 1925-1938*).

in the attitude of the universities toward the social sciences is significant:

During the past decade [he said] notable changes have taken place in institutional centers of research in the social sciences. The universities now recognize the importance of realistic training and research and are assuming the responsibility for providing them. The social scientist is relied upon to an increasing extent in American public life; his opportunities to participate in the handling of complex contemporary problems are numerous, and sometimes too insistently presented by laymen who are over-sanguine as to the results to be achieved by the application of scientific knowledge. Continued study in the university and in the community outside should in time enable the social scientist to meet these expectations.[15]

CHAPTER XVII

THE SOCIAL SCIENCES IN A TIME OF CRISIS

THE SOCIAL SCIENCES CAME TO MATURITY —or at least left their adolescence—at a singularly inhospitable time in history. Two cataclysmic world wars, with an equally cataclysmic depression sandwiched in between, and a future that is black with uncertainty, have swamped these freshly arrived sciences and techniques in a flood of newly created and insistent problems. It is as if, in the medical sciences, the doctors were struggling with a constant stream of new diseases for which there was no time for diagnosis and research, one strange and unexplained set of symptoms piling on another, and filling our hospital beds with unfamiliar and unidentified maladies. Moreover, as the new diseases break out, the existing diseases become vastly more complicated. Under conditions in some degree comparable, the social sciences have struggled over these last decades in an atmosphere of mounting complexity with problems developing far faster than they could be solved, and under the added handicap of having to work, not with rational material, but with the rational and irrational conduct of man.

In 1939, when Willits assumed the leadership of the Foundation's Social Sciences division, the Second World War was just on the threshold. An intellectual black-out seemed to be closing down on human life everywhere. To speak of research in the field of international relations, for example, appeared almost a jest—and a bitter jest at that. The president's review of the Foundation's work for that period reflected the anxiety and disillusionment of the time.

Everywhere reason is on the defensive [he said], and we live in danger that mass hysteria will completely overwhelm it at a time when it is most needed as a safeguard. If there have always been wars and rumors of wars, never before has there existed the possibility of such material havoc and cultural disintegration. It may be that this arid period in which we are living is the watershed between two forms of civilization, and that the future beckons to a Promised Land more pleasing than we dream. This optimism is creditable, but for the moment at least the world is facing a cultural crisis in which reason is everywhere in retreat.[1]

Willits brought to his new task a high courage and a sturdy faith. He insisted that intelligence must fight to make itself heard above the noise of marching feet, that objective and competent study must be employed to help men comprehend themselves and their relations to their fellow men. "When complexity multiplies," he said, "and problems pyramid, lack of effective support for competent intellectual effort can be as fatal to democratic process as lack of freedom."[2] With the world being torn apart by hate and violence, he recommended that the Foundation's program in international relations should be broadened and strengthened. With the question uppermost in men's minds whether an intermeshed economic civilization would not break apart at the seams under the impact of a second world war, he went ahead with long-range plans for a wider understanding of the nature of our myriad economic processes and of the means by which their health and productiveness could be conserved. And yet he was careful to say to the trustees: "All proposals should be scanned most severely, as the obvious danger is that the depth of our desire to aid may so easily lead to doing things that are futile and are endorsed only by their fine hopes."[3]

II

Some time after he assumed his new post, Willits wrote down for the guidance of his division a number of general objectives which he wanted to keep in mind in recommending grants in the social sciences. Among them were these:

1. Though the degree of social need is always pressing toward grandiosity, modest work will, in the long run, be most effective.
2. In recommending grants officers should try to anticipate the future—never merely ride the coat-tails of an already discernible trend.
3. The Social Sciences division has no "nostrums" to sell. In choosing the objects of grants the guiding tendency should be not to pronounce

answers but to discover truth—not to manipulate new forces but to understand them—not to choose society's path but to illuminate it.[4]

In broad outline, Willits' approach was based on that of Ruml and Day. The fellowship program was maintained at its former high level, and support was continued for research in universities and in central over-all agencies like the National Bureau of Economic Research, the Brookings Institution, and the Social Science Research Council. While the Foundation had certain fields of special interest, such as international relations and economic stability, its main endeavor was, as Willits expressed it, to discover the coincidence of the able mind, the significant lead, and the vital relation to reality.

Nor did the Foundation overlook the necessity of building strength in the individual research institution. This principle was unmistakably shown in its long relations with the National Bureau of Economic Research. Founded thirty years ago, this organization is one of the world's leading institutions seeking to lay a more adequate basis for objective thinking and research in economics. Beginning in 1920 with investigations of the amount and distribution of national income, the program of the Bureau was gradually broadened to include studies in business cycles, employment, wages, and prices. In the next two decades, investigation in production and productivity trends as well as in finance and fiscal policy was added. By entering new fields gradually and at the same time continuing work in old fields, following leads whenever results were promising, the various investigations constitute a significant beginning in the scientific measurement of the realities of economic change.

Dr. Wesley Mitchell, the leading spirit in the creation of the National Bureau, had a conception of research in economics that was daring and at the time perhaps somewhat unfashionable. This conception rested on two beliefs: (1) that the rich capacity of economists to produce imaginative hypotheses was not adequately balanced by efforts at verification and inductive research; (2) that with the facilities now available, it should be possible to supplement theoretical conjecture with scientifically measured fact and relation and, thereby, to work toward the substitution of tested conclusion and definitely measured knowledge for guesswork and dogmatic hypothesis.

So long as economics consisted chiefly of an effort to think out what would happen under certain conditions which a theorist set up in his imagination [said Dr. Mitchell], an economist needed merely a closet in which to think, some books and a little clerical aid. Now that economics is endeavoring to analyze actual experience, an investigator requires extensive facilities for making observations of his own and analyzing the observations of others.[5]

From the very beginning, two sharply defined criteria governed the National Bureau in its choice of fields of research:

> The subject must be socially significant. The National Bureau has been founded, staffed and supported by men who hope that it will promote social welfare. All its scientific work, however technical, has that ultimate aim.
>
> The subject must be susceptible of scientific treatment. To us this means first that the problems involved can be formulated definitely; second that we know or can learn the necessary techniques; third that reliable data have been collected by others or can be collected by us.[6]

The activity of the Bureau over the years is evidenced by its extensive publications, 133 to date, dealing with such technical subjects as business cycles, transportation, inventories, wages, productivity, and employment. In the field of financial studies, there are volumes on urban mortgages, farm mortgages, and corporate bond issues; and in public finance and fiscal policy, volumes dealing with such problems as capital-gains tax, federal grants-in-aid, and tax-exempt securities. These many books and publications do not lie idly on library shelves. As will be seen in the next chapter, they influence to an increasing degree the policies and decisions of governmental and business bodies, and their objectivity and thorough scholarship have won them an almost unique position in the practical management of our economy.

Throughout the Bureau's history, The Rockefeller Foundation has been the largest single contributor to its work. Including sums given by the Memorial, the Foundation's appropriations have amounted to nearly $5,000,000.

III

The Social Science Research Council is another example of an independent research agency which the Foundation has assisted over the years. Representing all the social sciences, it illustrates in its organization the remark of a former president of the American Political Science Association: "The problem of social behavior is essentially one problem, and while the angles of approach may, and should, be different, the scientific result will be imperfect unless these points of view are at times brought together in some effective way so that the full benefit of the multiple analysis may be realized."[7]

The Council concerns itself primarily with research projects which cut across two or more fields of knowledge, leaving largely to other auspices the support of projects which fall entirely within a single discipline. Nor are projects limited in scope to the fields commonly termed the social sciences; enterprises which require assistance from legal science or from the medical or natural sciences are also supported.

The promotion of research is the objective of all Council activities, but to this end the planning and appraisal of projects are recognized as essential. Advisory committees in several fields—such as finance and industry, migration, agricultural problems, industrial relations, public administration, and international relations—not only evaluate individual projects, but formulate plans for the development of research and for the recruiting and training of competent personnel in the particular field. The Council does not think of itself as a coordinating agency in any compulsive sense. It is rather a facilitating agency, and serves individual scientists, research institutions, universities, foundations, the government, and the public in such varying capacities as a planning agency, clearinghouse, liaison agent, advocate, critic, a source of support for strategically selected projects, a source of advice on personnel, and at times as an operator of urgent projects for which no other suitable sponsor can be found.

The Foundation has contributed substantially not only to the general budget of the Social Science Research Council, but also to the wide range of special projects of research which its committees have guided, including, among others, the following:

International Relations
Social Security
Study of the Tennessee River Valley
Government Statistics and Information
Inquiry on Nationalism and Internationalism
Population Studies
Public Administration Studies
Public Opinion Measurement (Joint Committee SSRC and NRC)
Housing Research
Economic History

This type of support is illustrated by the grant of $300,000 which the Foundation made to the Social Science Research Council in

1940 for research in the economic history of the United States. For genuine understanding of the causes, course, and significance of the processes of change in the economy of the country, it is important to study the long flow of social and economic events, so that light may be thrown upon gradually developing structural and secular modifications. In ten years of work, this activity has resulted in substantial progress in establishing economic history as a recognized discipline; a group of competent younger scholars has been developed in this neglected field; and some authoritative and influential volumes have been published.

In addition to these research functions, the Social Science Research Council has been an advisory and administrative body of great assistance to the Foundation, conducting many special types of research in which the Foundation was interested, and awarding its American fellowships and many of its grants-in-aid. The total appropriations made by the Foundation to the Council—including those made by the Memorial—amount to over $8,000,000. The Foundation over a period of years has also made substantial grants to the Canadian Social Science Research Council, organized for the same purposes and functioning in the same relationship as its sister agency in the United States.

Another over-all research organization with which the Foundation has had long relations is the Brookings Institution, created in 1927 through the amalgamation of three existing organizations: the Institute of Government Research, the Institute of Economics, and the Robert Brookings Graduate School of Economics and Government. Its research covers broad ranges of the social sciences, particularly in the field of economics, government, and international relations, and its publications, which are widely used, have gained for themselves a reputation for objectivity and balance. Over the years, the Memorial's and the Foundation's appropriations to Brookings, both for its general budget and for special researches, have amounted to roughly $2,300,000.

Other special research institutes have also been given assistance. The Food Research Institute of Stanford University furnishes a significant example. Established for fundamental studies of the problems relating to the world's food, it has centered its attention on a wide variety of basic questions, such as international commodity agreements, agriculture and business cycles, the relation between prices and government policy, and world developments in the food situation as a basis for relief plans and nutritional policies. Appropriations to this Institute begun by the Memorial were continued by the Foundation.

Support was also given to the economic section of the Institute for Advanced Study at Princeton. Scholars from this country and abroad sought out this institution because they felt that it presented perhaps the best combination of stimulus and freedom for truly advanced work that existed anywhere in the world. That the Institute thus served as such a powerful magnet was due to the quality of insight, wisdom, and experience represented in its staff.

IV

During these war years and in the postwar period, although substantial sums were given to special institutes of research, there was no tendency to neglect the universities. Except in one or two special cases, the fluid-research-fund device had been abandoned, but interest in the university as a natural center of research and as the source of the stream of the social scientists of the future was constantly maintained. "The universities are places of infinite hope and infinite despair," wrote Willits, "but they are the West Points where social scientists are germinated and their educational and professional standards determined."[8] Later he said:

> No indictment of university standards of graduate teaching in the social sciences would be fair which did not acknowledge the debt to many able and perhaps obscure men and women who, under discouraging conditions, are doing an excellent job. With integrity and competence, and too often without public understanding or appreciation, they are feeding into our society through their students the standards of mind and spirit toward the study of social problems that a civilized society needs. But the total situation is more likely to produce the mediocrity of today than it is to create the excellence which tomorrow requires. In the social sciences, the universities have not yet won the reputation as hosts for excellence that they have for the natural sciences, for medicine and even for the humanities.[9]

In undergraduate work, the Foundation was able to do very little, although occasional grants were made for experimental courses or to provide opportunities for realistic research. But first things had to come first, and the primary need was to build a foundation of basic knowledge upon which good teaching, both graduate and undergraduate, could rest. This had been true in the development of medicine, for example; until research established the essential facts of anatomy and its related subjects, the medical schools were forums of dogma and untested opinion. In the social sciences, the need for such a fundamental substructure was even greater, and the work of the Foundation in the universities was therefore devoted almost exclusively to the promotion of research at the graduate level.

The pattern of this type of support is almost bewildering in its variety, and it is possible in this chapter to mention specifically only a few of the grants that were made. The Foundation worked on an international basis, and as far as the war and its aftermath permitted, efforts were made to develop the research resources of universities abroad as well as at home. Thus, at Oxford, support was given to the Institute of Statistics for research on the empirical and quantitative side, and to develop additional research facilities at Nuffield College. At Cambridge, the Foundation's funds went toward the general budget of the Department of Applied Economics. "Cambridge influences teaching and policy on economic questions in Britain more than any other university," said the docket of the Foundation meeting at which the appropriation was voted. "The study of applied economics has been gaining ground in England, research in this field has developed rapidly, and the value attached to it in government circles and in industry has greatly increased."[10] Of the activities at the University of Manchester, where support was given for the Economics Research Section, the Foundation's officers reported: "The work in economics at Manchester is not surpassed, either in tradition or in promise. It combines theory and empirical testing in an extraordinary way."[11] In Paris, the Institute of Economic and Social Research (the Rist Institute) received substantial funds after the war, as it had before, and the hope was expressed that the grants would "reinforce the efforts of the French economists who are seeking to break the grip of tradition upon the social sciences in France and particularly upon economics."[12]

For these same general purposes, and with this desire to promote an empirical approach to the social sciences and help build a substructure of tested fact and relation, grants were made abroad to a wide range of institutions including, among others, the University of Glasgow, the London School of Economics, the University of Oslo, and the Dutch Economic Institute.

In the United States, the list of the Foundation's grants to universities is so extensive that it can only briefly be summarized. Columbia University may perhaps be used for illustration. In 1942, the Foundation gave funds for a study at that institution of the economic aspects of public finance. In 1945, it financed a study of group tensions under Professor Robert MacIver; and in 1947 its funds were used for three special studies by the Bureau of Applied Social Research of Columbia. At the University of Chicago, the Foundation financed research in the fields of sociology, social anthropology, and psychology; it gave funds for studies in price controls as well as for the general research program of the Social Science Research Committee of the University; it supported a program in education, training, and research in race relations; and it made grants to the Cowles Commission for Research in Economics, affiliated with the University —a group that is doing original work in the statistical testing of economic theories, the measurement of economic relations, and the explanation of business fluctuations.

Similarly, the Foundation made contributions to the University of Pennsylvania for an investigation of the distributive system as measured by the service it renders to the American consumer, and for the Industrial Research Department, which includes among its varied activities studies of wages, commodity prices, and many phases of the functioning of the Philadelphia labor market. To Yale, the Foundation contributed funds for a study of the labor market structure and wage determination; to the Massachusetts Institute of Technology, for research by the Industrial Relations Section in the economics of technological change; to the University of Minnesota, for an analysis of the distribution of family and individual income; to the University of Iowa, for a study of the social and cultural factors of child development; to Harvard, for research centered around the far-flung questions of the utilization and allocation of national economic resources, with particular reference to the changing structural characteristics of the American economy.

In all these types of activity, the university occupies a key position. We are living in such a partisan-minded world, with research viewed merely as a means of implementing partisan objectives, that the vigor and effectiveness of universities as independent research centers would seem essential to a long-run social policy.

V

During these critical years, the Foundation maintained as far as it could its work in international relations. With war overrunning vast areas of the world, certain curtailments were inevitable, and it was found impossible to carry on with the sweep and range of Day's broad program. There is a sense, of course, in which the Foundation's entire work in all fields has been aimed at the single target of world peace. Whether the activity has been the control of malaria in Sardinia, or the extension of our knowledge of human behavior through research in psychiatry, or the promotion of the interchange of students of philosophy between North and South America, the objective has been a humane and rational world in which peace among men could be secured. The preparation of the soil for a social order in which peace can permanently grow requires the maturing processes of time; and while some may doubt whether our civilization is going to be accorded this necessary factor of time, unless we take the completely defeatist attitude we have to proceed on the assumption that the world of the future will still be a free world in which reason rather than force will control.

Meanwhile, the direct approach to the overwhelming crisis of our generation cannot be neglected, and it was in this spirit and against this background that the Foundation in the forties carried on its activities in international relations. The establishment of the Russian Institute at Columbia University in 1946, with an initial grant of $250,000 is illustrative of the Foundation's approach. The relations of the Western world with Russia are too immediately important, too freighted with all sorts of possibilities, to be left to the mercy of uninformed emotion. What is required is a determination to be accurately informed, to see things as they are. In our generation, it may not be possible to throw any bridges across the ideological chasm, but certainly a wider and deeper knowledge on our part of Russian ideas and motivations is basic to fundamental policy and essential to self-interest. The Institute, which has become a leading center in the Western world for advanced training and research in the field of Russian studies, provides courses and seminars in the history, ideology, economic system, political institutions, literature, and foreign relations of Russia. Its aim is to train students as broadly based specialists who understand Russia and the Russians and who thus prepare themselves for careers of authority and influence. The number of students is limited and only the best of those who apply can be admitted. Among the students are also officers on active duty, assigned by the Army, Navy and the Air Force; others are foreign-service officers, similarly assigned by the Department of State. The nongovernment students come from most of the states of the Union, as well as from Canada, Great Britain, Belgium and Norway. Some forty of its graduates are teaching at institutions like Yale and Michigan, and a dozen others. Graduates have taken positions with journals and magazines like *Time* and *Newsweek,* or are in government service. Several former students are employed by the United Nations or by UNESCO and other specialized agencies. Whatever the hazards we face in our relations with Russia—and no one would minimize them—the work of this Institute at Columbia and of other research agencies points the way to more intelligent judgment than would otherwise be available.

Another strategic move was the support given to the Council on Foreign Relations for its so-called "war and peace studies." Experience has shown that the policy-making officers of the government are not only desirous of knowing what the intelligent citizen thinks ought to be done but are eager to have the analysis and judgment of outside experts whose help is prompted by disinterested motives. With this in mind, the Council, on the outbreak of the war in Europe in 1939, extended to the government an offer to assemble groups of experts who would analyze and make recommendations on the problems that would face the United States as a result of the conflict. The State Department accepted this collaboration but in doing so avoided, of course, making anything in the nature of an exclusive arrangement. On its side, the Council maintained its complete independence, received no subsidy or financial help from the government, and carried on its work throughout as a private agency. The assignment involved a long series of studies carried on by the best experts obtainable, and the results were forwarded privately to the government, where they were employed not only in the State Department but in the War, Navy, and Treasury Departments as well. The project, which throughout its course received cordial support in Washington, was in effect an active mobilization of the intelligence of the country in aid of foreign policy.

During this difficult period, also, the Foundation gave substantial help to organizations like the Foreign Policy Association; the Institute of Pacific Relations; the Canadian Institute of International Affairs; the Economic, Financial and Transit Department of the League of Nations, which during the war carried on its highly significant studies at Princeton, New Jersey; the Royal Institute of International Affairs (London); the Geneva Graduate Institute of International Studies, which continued the nucleus of a research program despite the comparative isolation of Switzerland; and the Swedish Institute of International Affairs (Stockholm), which not only maintained its level of activity during the war, but enlarged its work.

Another organization to which the Foundation gave extensive aid during this period was the Institute of International Studies at Yale, established in 1935 for the purpose of research and training in the international field. The Institute set out to do three things: (1) to make careful historical investigations of situations out of which wars might grow; (2) to develop some generalizations about the particular behavior of nations; and (3) to apply the knowledge so gained to the clarification of questions of American foreign policy. Over the years, the Institute has brought together a strong nucleus of scholars on regular appointment, supplemented by other scholars on leave of absence from their normal work. Not only have the publications of the Institute had wide influence, but the stress which has been laid on a broad and well-rounded program in education and training has resulted in a creative faculty and a promising student body. All in all, it is today one of the best institutes of its kind in any American university.

The Brookings Institution also began a broad program in research and education in international relations which was supported by the Foundation. Under able leadership, the Institution has centered its attention on both the immediate problems which face the United States, and, more particularly, the problems that are likely to emerge in the foreseeable future. In many fields, Brookings has repeatedly demonstrated its capacity to carry through its undertakings in time to be of constructive aid in the formulation of national policy. Its program in the international field represents one of the few attempts to project analytical methods of the social sciences into the study of the future, to examine the research techniques which are applied in the study of future policy decisions, and to spread the understanding of these procedures of analysis to several hundred key persons working in international relations.

In all this work, as in its other fields of activity as well, the Foundation was guided by a single criterion: to support the institutions or groups where able men were working fruitfully and intelligently on significant issues. Other than that criterion, the Foundation was guided by no aim or method in its work for world peace. It was interested in no device. It had no nostrum to sell.

VI

Following the line of his predecessors, Willits believed that while it was important to choose certain areas for primary research, it was also necessary to retain flexibility of program to meet unanticipated opportunities and to keep up with the ramifications of modern social concern. Consequently, projects and areas of interest were frequently supported which are not easily classifiable under any of the traditional fields of Foundation activity. For the sake of convenience, some of these projects and general topics are discussed in the following paragraphs.

Demography. The size and distribution of the population of the world are changing rapidly, and the spread of modern technology is giving these changes new political and social meaning. As a result, many of the terms in which both national and international problems are stated have altered in the last quarter of a century. What does it mean that the population of the West is approaching the end of its period of expansion or is even facing decline? What does it mean that the populations of Eastern Europe, the Soviet Union and Asia seem destined for a period of rapid expansion, ranging from a few decades to several generations, similar to that through which the West has been passing in the two centuries just concluded? What do these diverse trends mean in terms of international trade, international migration, international agreement or the frictions which lead to war? What do they mean internally in the regional adjustment of population to resources, in ability to improve levels of living, in cultural advance or degradation? In the United States, what does the shifting age composition of the population mean to such problems as full employment, social security and political power?

These are insistent questions which press for answer, and beginning in 1944 the Foundation made several grants, some of them of substantial size, to promote studies in demography, a science which is attempting to plot the curves and interpret the significance of these past and coming changes. The chief of these grants went to the Office of Population Research of Princeton University under Professor Frank W. Notestein, and to the Scripps Foundation for Research in Population Problems of Miami University, Ohio. In 1948 the Foundation appointed a mission of four experts in public health and demography, headed by Professor Notestein, which made an exploratory reconnaissance in Japan, Korea, Java, Formosa and the Philippine Islands to secure materials, contacts and ideas as a basis for long-range work.

Atomic Energy. Our generation is face to face with a force which can be used beneficently for human welfare or can be employed as a weapon conceivably capable of destroying civilization itself. It is not a matter which relates alone to the physical sciences; atomic energy has social and economic bearings which cannot be ignored. For a series of preliminary studies in this area grants were made by the Foundation to Cornell, Chicago, and the Committee on Social Implications of Atomic Energy of the Social Science Research Council. The work of this committee is carried on in consultation with the National Research Council, natural scientists as well as social scientists being included in its membership.

Japanese Resettlement. The forced migration and resettlement of the Japanese population in California as a war measure presented many social and economic problems such as inevitably attach to the involuntary, mass uprooting of a minority group. One hundred and twenty-seven thousand people, of whom 80,000 were American citizens, were torn from their homes and means of livelihood and herded behind barbed wire in guarded stockades. The doctrine of inherited racial enmity—"once a Jap always a Jap"—was invoked by the military to justify this startling abridgment of civil rights.

The University of California, in 1942, with a nucleus of sociologists, political scientists and psychologists, under the leadership of Professor Dorothy Thomas, began an on-the-ground study, financed by the Foundation, of this dramatic and often tragic episode, covering the entire situation from the period of evacuation into government-controlled camps to the final dispersal of individuals at the end of the war, and recording the intimate story of group incidents, individual experiences, and the resulting adjustments and maladjustments. The reports of the group constitute a contemporary record almost unique in the annals of social science.

Civil Liberties. Throughout history nations have faced the dilemma presented by the conflicting claims of national security and civil liberty. Wars or economic crises or fear of national calamity lead governments to curb the normal freedoms in order to safeguard the state. The present efforts of the United States government to eliminate disloyal or subversive persons from the federal service represent a modern phase of this old conflict.

In 1948, with the aid of a Foundation subsidy, a group of scholars under the direction of Dr. Robert E. Cushman of Cornell University began to study the impact upon American civil liberties of current governmental programs, both national and state, designed to insure internal security, a project which involved a number of published reports. In his introduction to the first volume of the series, Dr. Cushman made this explanatory comment:

No thoughtful person will deny or minimize the need for protecting, and protecting adequately, our national security. The right and duty of national self-preservation cannot be challenged. This protection of the national security requires in certain instances the restriction of some of our traditional civil liberties. We have, however, learned by hard experience that we can be made to sacrifice more civil liberty to the cause of national security than is really necessary. There is, therefore, sound reason for examining with objective care the appropriateness and effectiveness of any particular governmental action sought to be justified as a defensive measure against disloyal or subversive persons or conduct.[13]

Histories. In the decade of the forties, and particularly after the war, the Foundation made a number of grants for certain strategic histories of social consequence, so that the record of past successes or failures might be available for the guidance of the future. Thus a grant was made to the Royal Institute of International Affairs of London to enable Dr. Frank Walters to write a history of the League of Nations. Another grant was given to the Council on Foreign Relations for a history of American foreign policy from 1939 to 1946, to be prepared under the leadership of Dr. William Langer of Harvard. A similar grant was made to the Royal Institute in London for a history of international relations during the decade following 1939, to be written by Arnold Toynbee. Another appropriation enabled the Food Research Institute at Stanford University to prepare, in collaboration with experts from many countries, a history and appraisal of the world's experience in handling food and agriculture during the Second World War.

Moral and Ethical Problems. Beyond the questions of social fact lie the questions of social value, of morals and ethics. With the problems of mankind calling for perspective and vision, our social scientists cannot be merely analyzers and computers. There are desires in the world today that cannot be satisfied by the production and consumption of goods. "God knows we need coal and food to survive," said a European delegate to the United Nations, "but unless America can take the lead in providing a vital faith, in giving us a song that mankind can sing, all her exports will merely postpone the day of reckoning, and the world will die anyway."[14] To expect that exact measurement and exhaustive definition in the natural and social sciences will relieve men of the necessity of ethical inquiry, or that the meaning and values of human life will somehow or other crystallize as physics crystallizes around the concepts of mass and energy, is nothing short of superstition.

Admittedly, this is a difficult field to which there is no easy entrance. It lies partly, if not largely, in the province of the humanities, and at no time has the Foundation been unaware of its vital importance. But as the decade of the forties drew to its ominous close, the trustees expressed a growing concern about the urgency of moral and ethical problems in modern society, and a determination to employ, if possible, Foundation resources in a more direct approach to these problems than had hitherto been made. At this writing the project is in its initial stages, but several grants have been made to mature social scientists who are capable of contributing to the synthesis of fact and value which is the essence of moral philosophy, and the discussion of the subject has been stimulated at a number of institutions.

VII

Willits placed his main emphasis, as did Ruml and Day, on first-class men. "I would break any rule in the book for a chance to gamble on talent," he said. "May we never invest in the reproduction of mediocrity!"[15] Consequently, the fellowship program for the discovery and development of able personnel was pushed with determination. "Scouting for talent, just as the big leagues do," Willits called it. "The Social Science Research Council and the officers of the Social Sciences division of the Foundation," he wrote in 1950, "are deluged with calls from government, the United Nations and other agencies which need men trained in the social sciences. The demand far outstrips the supply. The danger is that the large sums being spent on surveys and other investigations will be partly wasted because competent and objective workers are far too few."[16]

The details of this program are discussed in a later chapter. It is important here merely to underscore the significance of this phase of the program in the development of the social sciences during the forties. The interchange of mature scholars was also an integral part of the strategy, just as it was and always had been in the other divisions of the Foundation's operations. The list is much too long to give in full, but illustrative of the program were the grants made to bring to the United States men of the caliber of Arnold Toynbee, Sir Alexander M. Carr-Saunders, Sir Hector Hetherington, Sir Henry Clay, Professor John Jewkes, French economists from the Institute of Applied Economic Science in Paris, as well as scholars from China, Holland, Belgium, Finland, Yugoslavia, Italy, and the Scandinavian countries. Similar grants were employed in reversing the process by sending many eminent American scholars abroad. The old practice which back in 1914 Rose called "cross-fertilization" continued to be one of the essential devices in the Foundation's handling of the social sciences.

CHAPTER XVIII

THE GROWTH OF THE SOCIAL SCIENCES

A FOUNDATION THAT HAS SEEN THE measurable consequences of its work in fields like medicine and the biological sciences is bound to experience some difficulty in adjusting itself to the social sciences. To bring under control world-wide diseases like hookworm and yellow fever, to give psychiatry a new impetus, to help in the development of a drug like penicillin, with its swift and dramatic consequences, to see giant corn growing on thousands of acres in Mexico where such corn never grew before—these tangible returns, and the sense of accomplishment they bring, do not prepare the trustees of a foundation for the discouragingly tortuous and glacierlike movement and pace of the social sciences.

Perhaps one of the difficulties is that our generation expects too much from the social sciences, forgetting that many of the predicaments of mankind do not lend themselves to scientific solution, but are the responsibility of all the moral and intellectual agencies of society, public and private alike. The economists and political scientists must help us, but so must the teachers, the parents, the philosophers, the poets, the novelists, the preachers, and the prophets.

Another obvious difficulty is the use of the word *science* to describe the social studies. They are not sciences in the sense in which the word is used in relation to physics and chemistry, for example. The two sets of disciplines parallel each other for part of the distance but not for the whole distance. The extent to which they do parallel each other is important; the improvements in tools and methods which are being made in the social sciences are perhaps as significant as those which, over the last three hundred years, have been made in the natural sciences. But for the rest of the way, social science deals not only with value judgments but with a host of variables with which the physicist and the chemist are not confronted. It is as if the crystals which Pasteur studied were involved in the same process of constant change as the phenomena investigated by Adam Smith. These variables handicap the possibility both of controlled experiment and of dependable interpretation, with the result that the obstacles to productive research in the social sciences are infinitely more real than any which the physical scientist has to encounter.

This situation, and the fact that the social sciences are still in an early stage of development, give the critics an opportunity to draw up a devastating indictment. They point to the disparity between expenditure and product, to the widely inaccurate prognoses of many of our economists, to the pontification on the basis of unverified hypotheses or of a few hand-picked facts which still parades, in many circles, as social science. Unfortunately, much of this indictment is valid. The very nature of the problems to be solved, the character of the data, the less mature development of tools and methodology, the pressure and incentives of immediacy or of partisan interest which push social students to jump to conclusions or to come to particular conclusions—all these make the broad area of the social studies the harbor for work that is often superficial and specious, and sometimes even dishonest. Moreover, the depth of much of our public discussion of social issues is determined by the advertising mind, the slapdash journalist, the man with an ax to grind or a panacea to offer, the politician with an election to win, with the result that the social acceptance of ideas formulated with integrity and sound method is handicapped, and progress commonly lags behind what even an immature social science has to offer.

Foundations working in this field are not unaware of these weaknesses; indeed, officers and trustees alike live with them so intimately that they do not always escape the feeling of frustration and impatience, and the nostalgic desire to return to areas of activity which promise more immediate and measurable rewards.

But this is a defeatist attitude which turns its back on the overwhelming problems of our time. Those problems lie in the realm of man's relation to man, in human behavior and social organization. Unless our generation, through cynicism and apathy, takes the position that human intelligence is powerless to plan a more rational life for mankind, it is bound to support the attempt, faltering as it may be in many of its approaches, to build depth and integrity into the study of social issues, and make scientific analysis and empirically tested fact available for social purposes.

The point must be kept in mind that there is no dramatic short cut, no penicillin, no sulfa drugs, that can be discovered to cure the ills of society. We are misled by our own analogies. The answers to complex political and moral problems do not come quickly, nor can they be confirmed by laboratory experiment. Social maladjustments can be relieved only by the slow accumulation of knowledge and wisdom influencing policies and decisions at myriad points. These influences work for the most part silently, with low visibility. They are seldom spectacular; they are never automatic; the structure has to be built brick by brick. While it is true that the vast undertaking can perhaps be divided into long-term and short-term programs, and that day-to-day efforts can be made to lessen the tensions and dissolve the suspicions that riddle our society, the crux of the problem is ignorance and prejudice and moral inadequacies which do not yield to quick and simple solutions. Social issues cannot be clearly defined and understood except on the foundation of patient, long-sustained, and painstaking work. Disciplined minds are needed, and the high integrity of objective scholarship; and the flow of first-class talent into these fields must be continuous and uninterrupted. As Mr. Justice Hughes expressed it: "If notwithstanding the apparent confusion and welter of our life, we are able to find a steadiness of purpose and a quiet dominating intelligence, it is largely because of the multitude of our people who have been trained to a considerable extent in scientific method, who look for facts, who have cultivated the habit of inquiry, and in a thousand callings face the tests of definite investigations."[1]

II

As a matter of fact, if we use as a measuring rod what has happened in the social sciences over a period of fifty years, or even of twenty-five years, there is little occasion for pessimism. In spite of the confusion of the last two decades, those who look behind the headlines can perceive the solid progress which has been made. The encouraging factor is the universal ground swell of interest in the direction of greater emphasis on the social sciences—an interest that is developing in colleges and universities everywhere, as well as in foundations and public bodies. This interest is heightened by the proof, which recent years have afforded, that the objective investigation of problems of human relations can produce results of high practical value, when properly trained research workers, imbued with scientific detachment and integrity, are given an opportunity to carry on their activities with adequate resources. Even as far back as fifteen years ago, The Rockefeller Foundation began to notice the change. Day, writing in 1935, made this comment:

> Much more than heretofore, social science in the universities is realistic in the sense that it now recognizes the enormous complexity of the problems under study. There is less abstract theorizing, less dispute as to method, more reasoning on the basis of extensive evidence regarding real situations. Rigorous theoretical training is now more securely upheld by a richer supporting documentation. This change in the character of research activity is reflected in the research training of the oncoming generation. They are better equipped technically at no apparent loss of basic theoretical training.[2]

This emphasis on personnel has been central in the work of The Rockefeller Foundation. The fellowship program, as we have seen, has over the years been one of the cornerstones of its activities. Thirty years ago, competent men in the social sciences were few, and even those men, with an occasional exception, were not adequately equipped according to the standards of today. Experience during the crisis of the Second World War and its aftermath is eloquent testimony to the part which Rockefeller Foundation fellowships and grants played in the development of competent workers. Of the literally hundreds of such fellowships in the social sciences, awarded either directly or through the Social Science Research Council, a few outstanding cases may profitably be cited. John Jewkes, formerly Senior Professor of Political Economy at the University of Manchester, now of Merton College, Oxford, was in charge of planning in the British Ministry of Aircraft Production during the war. Robert Marjolin is Secretary General of the Organization for European Economic Cooperation. Ralph J. Bunche, Nobel Peace Prize winner in 1950, is director of the Trusteeship Division of the United Nations. Peter Lieftinck is Minister of Finance in The Netherlands. Gunnar Myrdal, who formerly was a member of the cabinet of the Swedish government, is now Executive Secretary of the Economic Commission for Europe of the United Nations. Mrs. Alva Myrdal is director of the United Nations Department of Social

Affairs. Luigi Einaudi, an adviser rather than a fellow of the Foundation, is President of Italy. Sir Douglas B. Copland is Vice-Chancellor of the National University of Australia. Philip E. Mosely is director of the Russian Institute at Columbia University. Eric Roll and Arne Skang served as ministers to the Organization for European Economic Cooperation for Great Britain and Norway respectively. Hugh Gaitskell, at this writing, has just been appointed as the new British Chancellor of the Exchequer.

A review of the records of the men and women who over the last quarter of a century have received fellowships in the social sciences from Foundation funds shows gratifying results. Today they are occupying positions of importance and distinction in nearly every country of the world. They are on university faculties; they are connected with research institutions; they hold strategic governmental posts. Some of them, as is indicated by the above list, have gained outstanding recognition. It would be foolish, of course, to assume that their leadership and their contribution to social thinking are the results solely of their fellowship experience. Doubtless, many of them would have gained eminence without this experience or would have obtained the experience in other ways. But it is a satisfaction to record the subsequent success of highly promising men and women, picked largely from the younger generation, whom the Foundation was able to assist.

III

The growth of trained personnel in the social sciences has been paralleled by the growth of institutions for advanced work and teaching. One has only to review the record of the last three decades to obtain a measure of the development that has occurred. Before 1920, there was no National Bureau of Economic Research, no Brookings Institution, no Social Science Research Council, no Council on Foreign Relations, no Foreign Policy Association, no Royal Institute of International Affairs, no Public Administration Clearing House, no Food Research Institute at Stanford, no Industrial Research Department at Pennsylvania, no Russian Institute at Columbia. Today, these, and other centers, in universities and elsewhere, constitute public assets of immeasurable importance. They have provided increased accessibility to materials; they have aided group effort, group criticism, and group morale; they have facilitated the making of comparative studies. On the forge of their broad activities in research and teaching, the basis for a better understanding of social and economic issues is being steadily shaped.

The National Bureau of Economic Research can be used as an illustration. As was noted in the preceding chapter, its publications do not gather dust on library shelves. Its findings are cited in scientific and professional journals, treatises, and official documents. They are used by businessmen, legislators, labor specialists, and academic economists. They have been mentioned in Supreme Court decisions. They are constantly employed in government agencies like the Department of Commerce and the Bureau of the Census. Increasing use is being made of them by practicing economists in business, by editorial writers in the daily press, and by economic journalists in this country and abroad. Practically all of the current textbooks in either general economics or dealing with specific economic problems draw a great deal of their material from the publications of the Bureau or from the data available in its files. It can be truly said that without the National Bureau our society would not be nearly so well equipped as it is for dealing with the leading economic issues of our times.

Another illustration of the growing contribution of special institutes and groups to current social needs is to be found in the activity of the Public Administration Clearing House. As we have seen in a previous chapter, twenty-one organizations of public officials share with the Clearing House its building on the campus of the University of Chicago—organizations like the Governors' Conference, the Council of State Agencies, the Federation of Tax Administrators, and the National Association of State Budget Officers. Out of this intimate physical contact, wide consequences have developed, consequences which have influenced the upgrading of government services at many technical points—in the improvement of budgetary and personnel systems, for example, and the reform of state and local tax structures.

The National Bureau of Economic Research and the Public Administration Clearing House are merely two examples of concrete advance in institutional work in the social sciences. In this same general connection, one could comment on the activities of organizations like the Brookings Institution, or the Food Research Institute at Stanford, or the Social Science Research Council, or any one of a dozen institutions to which The Rockefeller Foundation has contributed over the last two decades. They are influencing practical action; they are paying off in the ultimate test of measurable achievement; they are gaining a firmer grasp upon fundamental conceptions and a greater mastery over methods. The progress, as we have seen, is not rapid, but it is gathering momentum. Modesty as to its pace should involve no discouragement. Along this road, if it is persistently followed, lie the possibilities of ultimate social intelligence—the kind of intelligence that can redress the dangerous imbalance of our present cultural development.

IV

Not only men and institutions, but the tools of knowledge as well, and even knowledge itself and its application to concrete situations, show signs of steady growth when measured over two or three decades. For example, thanks largely to Dr. Simon Kuznets and his associates at the National Bureau of Economic Research, we know much more about our national income than we did a quarter of a century ago—its size, its distribution, and the changes that occur in its character. Exhaustive investigation by groups of experts has brought within reach basic, articulated, quantitative information concerning the entire economy of the nation. This information has influenced public policy at a dozen points. It was one of the chief tools in planning our war production programs in the Second World War, and in determining what weights our economy could sustain. It underlies our analyses of federal budgeting and tax proposals and projects like the Marshall Plan. This same type of research has now spread to other countries, so that international comparison of the total net product and distribution of the economy of individual nations is increasingly possible.

The subject of business cycles furnishes another illustration. Because of the work of Wesley Mitchell and Arthur Burns, we know today far more about the problem and its setting than was known twenty-five years ago. Instead of starting from a dreamland of equilibrium or from a few simple assumptions suggested by "common sense," these investigators based their assumptions on concrete, systematic observations. It cannot be claimed that the research to date has an immediate relevance to economic policy, but it has at least provided a kit of tools by which new and deeper knowledge can be obtained.

Still another example is to be found in the improved methods used in population studies. For many years, estimates of future population were based on the application of Malthus' crude formula of population growth. This worked fairly well in the United States until late in the last century; but the new analytic methods developed by Thompson and Whelpton of the Scripps Foundation for Research in Population Problems at Miami University, Ohio, so revolutionized the basic principles of prediction that they were immediately adopted by the Census Bureau and are now employed in all its official population forecasting. In other words, ultimate population forecasts are based on far more adequate analysis of the specific processes determining future population than was ever before attempted—processes like immigration, emigration, and the birth and death rates of the different age groups of each of the segments of the population whose rates differ significantly.

Attention should also be called to the many important improvements in methods and techniques associated with the rapidly developing field of opinion and attitude research. Advances in sampling methods, interviewing procedures, questionnaire construction, and the design of problems for study have been notable. The work of Rensis Likert illustrates the practical use to which these new tools can be put. During the depression, he built up the Division of Program Surveys in the Department of Agriculture. By using the latest sampling and interviewing techniques, this organization was able to provide Department officials with far more accurate and specific knowledge of the problems and attitudes of farmers in different sections of the country than had ever before been possible. Indeed, this organization demonstrated so impressively its usefulness in obtaining information needed for guiding the development, application, and modification of the government's agricultural programs that it was increasingly called upon for similar services for other departments and agencies. During the war, it was repeatedly used by the Treasury Department to provide information on war-bond buying practices, intentions, and motivations of individual purchasers throughout the country. Knowledge so derived led, among other things, to the emphasis which was so successfully placed on payroll-deduction plans and other schemes utilizing personal solicitation and group pressure. The organization, which has now moved to the University of Michigan, is today used by the Governors of the Federal Reserve Board to conduct annual surveys of the behavior and intentions of the American people with respect to individual buying, saving, investment, and related matters. Many other governmental, industrial, and business agencies are utilizing its services—or those of similar organizations—to obtain a wide range of basic information.

No review of the concrete results of research in the social sciences—even a necessarily compressed one—could fail to include the contributions made by specialized knowledge, skills, and techniques to the armed forces and various defense agencies during the Second World War. The Office of War Information, for example, established a Survey Research Section to collect the opinions and major complaints of the defense workers and other civilians on the subject of the country's war effort. Many of the nation's policies were guided by the knowledge provided by these studies. Similarly, the Army created a Research Branch, staffed by sociologists, psychologists, and anthropologists, to study troop activities and the factors that make or break morale. These studies had far-reaching consequences in the handling of troops in the field. They provided, for example, the basis for the point system that determined the order in which troops were discharged after V-E Day, an order that was supported by the overwhelming belief of the troops in the fairness of the system. Studies of the plans and expectations of the members of the armed forces concerning what they would do after the war provided information used by Congress in designing and appropriating for the various veterans' aid programs.

These are only a few examples—at best a random sampling—of positive contributions resulting from the application to practical problems of social-science research techniques. With much, although not all, of this work The Rockefeller Foundation has had some relationship, either through direct support or through the training of personnel. The pattern which emerges shows a progress which, if not dramatic, is encouragingly real. The actual construction of a genuine science of human behavior still lies largely in the future; but the new directions in which effort is increasingly being expended provide significant and measurable manifestations of advance. Those who look for quick results, for a rapid reorganization of human behavior, will find little encouragement in what the social scientists are doing today. The impatient analogy between the spectacular progress of public health and medicine and what could conceivably be accomplished by the social sciences is basically unsound. Human emotions and prejudices, unlike human diseases, do not yield easily to rational solutions. We can look forward to no mechanistic answers which will automatically solve the problems of human adjustment. The assumption has to be made that there is time for intelligence to take hold, and students of society have to presuppose the opportunity for long-maturing work. Of course, social science cannot escape its obligations to the emergencies of the moment; but its main concern must inevitably be related to those results in terms of human welfare which are gained from patience, tenacity, research, and adequate and continuing support.

This, with few deviations, has been the faith of the trustees of The Rockefeller Foundation, and before them, of the trustees of The Laura Spelman Rockefeller Memorial; and over a period which now exceeds a quarter of a century they have backed up their faith by appropriations in the field of the social sciences which as of this writing approximate $100,000,000.

The twentieth century is the century when man became the student of man to a degree that is not fully realized. The approach, as we have seen, is on three main fronts—psychiatry, biology, and the social sciences. Its course has not yet been run, and it is bound to prove a tremendous force.

CHAPTER XIX

THE HUMANISTIC STUDIES

THE WORLD HAS PROVED OVER AND OVER again that men do not live by bread alone. Even if the social sciences were adequately developed and a substantial measure of rational control were introduced into the complex mechanism of the twentieth century, the total result, without the contributions to cultural development which the humanities must make, would still be distorted and incomplete. There is a hunger in the world which economists and political scientists cannot relieve. As they have in all ages, men turn today for their ultimate satisfactions to humanism—to the philosophers, the teachers, the historians, the artists, the poets, the novelists, the dramatists—all those who fashion ideas, concepts, and forms that give meaning and value to life and furnish the patterns of conduct. It is they who really construct the world we live in, and it is they who with sensitive awareness of human perplexity and aspirations can speak effectively to a distracted age. Every creative contribution of the physical and social sciences to the problems of society is to be welcomed; but to expect those sciences to meet the spiritual hunger for hope and belief and beauty and permanent values is a form of superstition as withering as any which humanity has thus far outlived.

Insofar as this principle has been reflected in the work of The Rockefeller Foundation, it is a development only of the last two decades. In 1913, when the Foundation was being organized, Jerome D. Greene, the executive director, listed the "fine arts" as among the fields which could profitably be entered. As we have seen, however, public health and medicine dominated the early years of the Foundation, and except for a single grant to the American Academy in Rome which Greene later described as "staking a claim for the fine arts,"[1] more than a decade and a half elapsed before the Foundation became formally identified with any work in this general area.

In the meanwhile, the General Education Board, in 1924, began a series of tentative grants to encourage the development of the humanities in the universities. The aim of this new program, as stated by the officers, was "to preserve the proper balance of our educational activities,"[2] and Abraham Flexner, the secretary of the General Education Board, was the driving force behind it. The initiation of this development was in part due to a dramatic speech which Edwin R. Embree, director of the Division of Studies of the Foundation, had made a year earlier at a joint meeting of the trustees of the Foundation and the General Education Board.* He warned that medicine and public health are not

> the only fields in which such organizations [foundations] could do notable work. In fact, may there not be some danger that the promotion of these subjects by so many rich and influential organizations may tend to throw out of proportion general consideration of the whole range of human affairs? . . . In this country . . . it being known that funds can often be matched with a contribution from these foundations toward medicine, a belief is reported to exist that in certain instances university presidents are deflecting to medicine and hygiene outside funds which might otherwise go to other departments. . . . Of what good is it to keep people alive and healthy if their lives are not to be touched increasingly with something of beauty?[3]

The first appropriation of the General Education Board in the field of the humanities was a seven-year grant, totaling $780,000, to the Oriental Institute of the University of Chicago to train the archaeologists needed for its large and expanding program. Training was also stressed in the gift of half a million dollars to Harvard for the Fogg Art Museum—a laboratory for students in the fine arts. Gradually this program, under Flexner's direction, began to concern itself with the humanities at the university and postuniversity level. Grants whose total exceeded $2,250,000 were given to

* Mr. Embree later became president of the Rosenwald Foundation.

the University of Virginia, Vanderbilt, Princeton, Chicago, Yale, Columbia, Harvard, and Michigan for endowment of work in the humanities or for fluid research funds on a term basis. An appropriation was also made to the American Council of Learned Societies, a federation of organizations devoted to humanistic studies, and a pattern of support was developed which was to be faithfully followed by the Foundation in later years.

The International Education Board, of which Flexner was the director of educational studies, soon joined its sister organization in entering the humanistic field. The charter of the General Education Board, as we have seen, limited its activities to the United States, and the International Board stepped into the breach to carry the activities overseas. Among its grants were a million dollars to the American Academy at Rome, half a million to the American School of Classical Studies in Athens, and over eight millions to the Oriental Institute of the University of Chicago, largely in connection with its archaeological work in Egypt and the Near East.

In reviewing the history of this early work in the humanities, before The Rockefeller Foundation came into the picture, one gathers the impression that it was colored by traditional concepts, centering largely in archaeological excavations, in scholarly research in ancient cultures, and in research centers in this country for classical humanistic studies. Even at the time, this type of activity did not escape the criticism of some of the trustees. Thus Anson Phelps Stokes, in 1927, wrote to Flexner: "The emphasis throughout [your] memorandum seems to me mainly on ancient history, ancient languages and archaeology," and he protested that the word "humanities" should be more broadly interpreted.[4] Years later, David H. Stevens, director of the Foundation's division of the Humanities from 1932 to 1950, made a trenchant comment on this early period: "How was this program a credit to us? In having a sense of magnitude. In what way a discredit? By buttressing scholasticism and antiquarianism in our universities."[5]

II

When the Rockefeller Foundation, in the reorganization of 1928, took over the humanistic studies from the General Education Board and the International Education Board, it created a division of the Humanities of which Professor Edward Capps was the first director. By training and tradition he was a classicist, and in the brief period in which he held the post, the program continued largely along the lines laid down by the other boards, centering to a great extent in archaeological interest, although branching out into some significant work in bibliography. At his retirement, no director was immediately appointed, and the resignation of one of the trustees, Mr. Stokes, who had frequently insisted before the board that "science is not dangerous if the humanities are also cultivated,"[6] was prompted, in part at least, by his disapproval of the delay. In 1932, Stevens, who had been Professor of English at the University of Chicago and vice-president of the General Education Board, was elected to the vacant position, and a new emphasis in the program began to assert itself. The agenda for a trustees' meeting in the spring of 1933 put the matter this way:

> The past twenty years have seen a continuous rise in the material valuations of life which should make possible and indeed demand a corresponding rise in its spiritual and cultural values. The humanities should contribute to a spiritual renaissance by stimulating creative expression in art, literature, and music; by setting and maintaining high standards of critical appreciation; and by bringing the intellectual and spiritual satisfactions of life within the reach of greater numbers. Beyond such benefits to the individual, the humanities should exert national and international influence for a reduction of racial prejudice. Ignorance of the cultural background of another people is at the root of many misunderstandings that are as harmful internationally as political and economic differences. That ignorance can be steadily lessened by an interchange of cultural values, by discovery of common origins for diversified national ideas and ideals and by the interpretation of one cultural group to another.[7]

This shift of emphasis from traditional humanistic research—a shift to interpretation rather than preservation—was a graduated process, and it was not until the mid-thirties that it began radically to affect the expenditures of the Foundation. During this interim period, the greater part of the appropriations went for fluid research funds in a selected group of universities as well as in the American Council of Learned Societies. Through these funds over two hundred humanistic scholars received direct assistance. It was a fortunate time for historians, linguists, and editors of texts and manuscripts. Many older men who had been handicapped by lack of funds for work abroad completed their life-long studies of particular themes and undoubtedly inspired their students to productive activity in their special fields. Several co-operative projects of large scale were formulated and put into action. Support was given to such enterprises as the *Dictionary of American Biography,* largely financed from other sources; the *Dictionary of American English*; critical texts of Spenser and Chaucer; and archaeological expeditions in Egypt, Greece, and Syria. The *Dictionary of American Biography*, a monolith of American scholarship, was completed by scores of workers inside and outside the universities; and field work for the *Linguistic Atlas of New England* brought together large stocks of unique data.

The aristocratic tradition of humanistic scholarship to which we have referred undoubtedly had its values. The manipulation of the substances of literary and linguistic history vitalized graduate studies and brought new interests to the fore; it stimulated pioneer work in many directions. Few will question, for example, what Breasted's work in Egypt has done in making humane for us a culture that we only dimly knew, or what results would flow if we could break through the system of communication locked in the Mayan glyphs. But basically this was not the kind of program which the trustees of the Foundation supported with unquestioning enthusiasm. Jerome D. Greene, now one of the trustees, and deeply interested in the humanistic studies, felt that the humanities were suffering from "what might be called the snobbishness of the classical tradition."[8] So much of the work seemed oblivious of the present; it was based on the idea that what was in the past humane remained so today. A report of a special committee of the trustees in 1934 asked this question:

> What does all this activity accomplish in stimulating aesthetic appreciation except in a limited number of highly specialized students? . . . It frankly appears to your committee that a program in the humanities, based on a cloistered kind of research, is wide of the goal which the Foundation should have in mind. It is getting us facts but not necessarily followers. We have more detailed information about a great number of rather abstruse subjects, but that does not logically mean that the level of artistic and aesthetic appreciation in America has been measurably raised.[9]

This same note was struck by the president of the Foundation (the present writer) in his annual review a year or two later:

> From being aristocratic and exclusive, culture is becoming democratic and inclusive. The conquest of illiteracy, the development of school facilities, the rise of public libraries and museums, the flood of books, the invention of the radio and the moving picture, the surge of new ideas—and above all, perhaps, the extension of leisure, once the privilege of the few—are giving culture in our age a broader base than earlier generations have

known. . . . New interests are in the making—an adventurous reaching out for a fuller life by thousands to whom non-utilitarian values have hitherto been inaccessible. . . . Any program in the humanities must inevitably take account of this new renaissance of the human spirit.[10]

In 1935, therefore, the trustees decided, in addition to maintaining certain older interests, to strike out experimentally in new fields, and in a formal resolution they authorized the officers to develop projects in the general area of libraries and museums, drama, radio, and moving pictures, the collection and interpretation of native cultural materials, and the improvement of international communication through the development of language teaching, particularly with relation to Latin America and the Far East.[11] This emphasis on the relevancy of humanistic study to contemporary life is one which has been maintained for the last decade and a half. Experience has modified the items in the original program, and the diversification has frequently been shifted and altered to meet the unforeseen exigencies of the fourth decade; but the redirection of Foundation support from traditional humanistic research toward activities which would conceivably bring the values of the humanities more directly into contact with daily living has been the constant policy of the division.

III

The interest of the Foundation in libraries and library techniques stemmed from the older program in the humanities. Back in the twenties, the International Education Board made an appropriation of £250,000 for the building and endowment of a new library at Cambridge University in England, located on a site already purchased by the University. At Oxford, the Bodleian Library, founded in 1598, is not only the University's central library, but a national repository, containing a comprehensive record of three centuries of British life. Under the copyright act, it receives, as Cambridge does, a copy of every book printed in England. The scope and scholastic values of its collections, attracting scholars from all over the world, has made Oxford a leading center in humanistic research. The University's problem at the end of the twenties was how to preserve the traditional and historic value of the Bodleian and at the same time maintain Oxford's prestige as a "home of living research" by keeping it abreast of modern library requirements.

In 1929, at the invitation of the Foundation, a commission from the University, in an attempt to find a solution, visited libraries in

Rome, Paris, Geneva, and other continental centers, and in sixteen American and Canadian cities. As a result of the study, a plan was outlined providing for the continuance of the historic Bodleian, mainly as an enlarged range of reading rooms, and for the erection of a new building adequate for the housing of five million volumes. For this purpose the Foundation made a grant of $2,300,000, and the new facilities, long delayed by the war, were formally opened by King George VI in 1946.

Concurrently with this development, the Foundation gave assistance to the National Central Library in London, which had been established to supplement the library facilities of the provincial universities and act as a clearinghouse for the distribution of books to individuals and schools. Aid was also given in the establishment of a library training center in London.

Out of the earlier humanities program, too, came the Foundation's interest in developing adequate tools for library research—an interest which continued through the thirties. An appropriation was made, for example, to place the complete card catalogues of the Library of Congress, relating to nearly 2,000,000 books, in the fifty leading libraries of the world. By a photographic process, these cards were reduced to 167 volumes, eighteen cards to a page, and it was these sets that were presented to libraries ranging all the way from Australia, Tokyo, and Calcutta to Oxford, Edinburgh, and the Vatican.* Grants were also made for three extensive cataloguing projects in Europe: the catalogue of printed books in the British Museum, the general catalogue of the Bibliothèque Nationale in Paris, and the union catalogue of the Prussian State Library in Berlin, which embraced not only its own collections but also those in the ten Prussian university libraries, in the State Library of Bavaria, and in the National Library of Vienna. Support was given, too, to the Library of Congress in a number of exploratory fields where, because techniques were untried and results were uncertain, public funds could not readily be obtained to blaze the trail. Thus, grants were made to enable the Library to gather source material in American history by obtaining photographic copies of materials in libraries abroad. Another grant was for the purchase of equipment for the collection of

* In naming five American librarians who had carried the load of detail of this vast enterprise, the preface to Volume I made this acknowledgment: "They have done far more for the enduring life of their country than many whose first names and photographs are familiar around every wood-burning stove in the United States."

American folklore at a time when the Library was beginning to work in that field. Grants were also made toward the development of a catalogue and the organization of bibliographical services for the Hispanic and Slavic materials in the Library. Finally, the Foundation contributed toward the expenses of equipping and operating for an initial period a laboratory of microphotography, to enable the Library to make its materials easily available in that efficient and economical form.

In this movement to adapt microphotography to library use the Foundation was deeply interested. The advantages of microfilm are obvious: reduction of storage space, preservation of fragile materials, simplification of interlibrary loans, and the development of collections of facsimile copies of rare documents at small expense. Over a twelve-year period, the Foundation assisted thirty-eight microfilm projects in twenty-one libraries and other institutions, both in the United States and abroad. Early in the Second World War, with widespread bombing on the increase, rapid work was necessary in England to protect from complete loss the records of civilization that existed only in unique books and manuscripts. With Foundation aid, microfilms of these treasures were produced as fast as possible and were stored in duplicate both in Britain and in the United States. Plans and photographs of historic British buildings were also made, so that in case of destruction, a record would remain, and with it the possibility of rebuilding.

Fellowships in library administration also constituted a significant part of the program. These fellowships were administered on an international scale, and the plan embraced nineteen countries, not only in Europe, but in Latin America and the Far East. The purpose of the appointments, forty-eight in number, was to give to younger librarians, marked for early promotion to key positions in libraries important for international service, training in methods, bibliography, and book purchasing in countries other than their own.

The Foundation's work in the field of museums was largely limited to experiments in training personnel and in testing methods of display. At a number of museums in the United States, groups of "internes" were appointed, each chosen for his knowledge of some particular phase of museum practice, such as classifying, lighting, display arrangement, or the preparation of catalogues. At the end of their service, these internes either went on to other museums which wished to benefit by their knowledge, or returned to the museums from which they had been recruited, some of them in other countries.

In a few other cases, grants were made to particular museums like the New York Museum of Science and Industry and the Museum of Modern Art for experimentations with new and original methods of display and educational presentation. As in the work with libraries, the fellowship device was widely used both to train younger people and to keep museum personnel in contact with new methods and ideas in other centers.

IV

Foreign scholars in the humanities, as well as scholars here in the United States, occasionally show some impatience with what they think is the overemphasis of American students on the tools of research. In our preoccupation with the gadgets of indexes and dictionaries and good library methods, we have little time for the task of interpretation and valuation which is the basic function of humanism. In our interest in the technology, we miss the content.

This criticism is perhaps not completely fair. The development of adequate tools and methods is important. Without them, scholarship would be thwarted and handicapped. And where is the line that can be sharply drawn between technology and content? Nevertheless, there is enough truth in the criticism to suggest the necessity of a better perspective. Humanistic study needs imagination, creativeness, and a clear objective as much as it needs microfilming machines and photostat copies. It needs, too, as we have indicated before, an ability to communicate with the general public, to make the values which it represents an integral part of the life of people. As Howard Mumford Jones said: "Unless learning is socially relevant, learning is, and remains, antiquarianism."[12]

This was the reasoning behind the decision of the Foundation to move tentatively into the field of radio and motion pictures. Here were active mediums of communication that were shaping and molding the social ideas and aesthetic standards of people. Could a constructive contribution be made in this area by finding out, for example, what the public wanted and whether its wants could be met? It must be admitted that the trustees of the Foundation took this step with some misgiving. The problem was extremely complex, and the hope of any substantial degree of success seemed dim. However, as an exploratory operation a beginning was made.

In radio, a series of grants was given to the World Wide Broadcasting Foundation, which operated a short-wave station in Boston.

The idea was to make possible experimentation with the production of educational programs on a financial basis which would insure superior quality without need of commercial subsidy. Through the use of other languages than English, the programs of this station helped to bring the United States into cultural contact with people in many countries, and as an example of the maintenance of high standards it has undoubtedly served a useful purpose. During the war, its facilities were widely used by the government and are employed today in helping to broadcast the *Voice of America*.

Another experiment was a co-operative undertaking in Chicago involving three universities and four local stations. After five years, the project, which had done some significant work in educational broadcasting, had to be abandoned; but a residue remains in the programs of the Chicago Round Table, which supports weekly discussions of ideas and events. Still another experiment along regional lines laid the groundwork for the Rocky Mountain Radio Council, embracing the states of Colorado and Wyoming. The programs of this Council have now become a regular service to the forty-four educational and public organizations which constitute its membership, to most of the thirty-seven radio stations operating in the two states, as well as to the people of the region.

Along somewhat similar lines, the Foundation gave aid to the Library of Congress for a program of popular education, in the belief that the Library had unusual facilities, both in material and personnel, for interpreting American life and tradition. These facilities, which the commercial companies lacked, included 20,000 recordings in its Archives of American Folk Song, source materials in its Division of Manuscripts, and reports of the Federal Writers Project, which covered local and regional folklore and history. Programs were given on a wide variety of subjects, and some interesting pioneer work was done in previously unexplored techniques. It became evident, however, that during the war years public money could not easily be obtained for such a project, and when the experimental period of the Foundation's grant came to an end, the program was discontinued.

An undertaking of perhaps deeper promise was the support given to the School of Public and International Affairs of Princeton University toward a study of the role that radio plays in the lives of the listeners. Organized under Dr. Paul F. Lazarsfeld, it attempted to answer such questions as these: What individuals and social groups listen to the radio? How much do they listen and why? In what ways are they affected by their listening? The radio industry had, of course, been concerned with determining the size and distribution of its audience as prospective purchasers for products advertised over the air. To learn what it could of the listener as an individual and as a member of society, the Princeton study, quite literally, began where the industry left off. This same type of study was later supported at Columbia University, also under Dr. Lazarsfeld. The research by the two institutions not only gave a detailed and accurate portrait of the American listening public, but also developed new methods of inquiry applicable to forecasting and testing the response of untried programs; and the reports which grew out of the studies have been widely used in the radio industry. Dr. Lazarsfeld's office was increasingly consulted as a source of expert and impartial advice. Inasmuch as analysis of public opinion lies on the fringes of the humanities, with parts of it reaching into sociological problems, later support by the Foundation for this type of work was transferred to the Social Sciences division.

Out of this interest in studies of radio broadcasting grew another project which had wide public implications. In 1940, the Princeton School of Public and International Affairs, with the help of the Foundation, began to record and analyze short-wave broadcasts dealing with the war and beamed to America from Europe. At the same time, a similar station, located at Stanford University in California, began, also with the assistance of the Foundation, to monitor short-wave broadcasts from across the Pacific. Some of this broadcasting was news, much of it was propaganda. The results of the analysis in both institutions were made available in the form of bulletins which were sent to students of communication and international affairs. When the United States entered the war, the need became apparent for a full-scale governmental agency to monitor and analyze broadcasts from abroad. The Federal Communications Commission therefore established at Washington the Foreign Broadcasting Monitoring Service, with the Princeton director in charge, and with four members of his staff as his assistants. Additional listening posts were created in Puerto Rico and on the West Coast, with facilities for immediate reporting to Washington by teletype, and with a staff that was expanded from the original ten or fifteen to over four hundred. The initial federal budget for this essential purpose was $800,000, in contrast to the Foundation's priming grant of something like $45,000 which had launched the Princeton and Stanford experiments in basic methods and trends.

The activities of the Foundation in the motion-picture field were limited to half a dozen diversified experiments. One interesting project was the assistance given to the Museum of Modern Art in New York in establishing its now celebrated film library. The purpose of this library, organized in 1935, was to meet a growing demand for a comprehensive knowledge of all types of films. Its two main functions were to serve as a repository for films and printed materials important for understanding the development of motion pictures, and to exhibit as well as circulate these films and data to other educational organizations. The result has been that the film library has become a world storehouse—and one actively in use—of materials with historical significance relative to the development of this form of mass communication.

Another experiment, not quite so happy, was the assistance given to the American Film Center, an organization that was attempting to enter the field of educational motion pictures. The unanswered question at the time was whether the demand for such films was sufficiently large to justify production. The motion-picture industry is a costly business that lives on the returns of giving the public what it wants. In fact, the costs of production are such that the entire income of a foundation could be swallowed up by a relatively small production program, for there is as yet little assurance that what are thought to be better films would find a public demand that would bring returns. Obviously, therefore, it would be impossible for a foundation to embark on any large undertaking in this direction. The only course open would be the limited support at strategic points of influences or of agencies working toward a higher standard of films.

The American Film Center could not surmount the hurdles of public taste, the box office, and the high cost of production, and after several years of effort it was liquidated. Although the Foundation financed a number of interesting studies in motion pictures, it must be admitted that its record in this field was one of only limited success.

> One lesson is clear [wrote Stevens in 1947] . . . if grants of a size the Foundation could contemplate are to have real effect, the outcome must be strategically directed toward the practices of the broadcasting and motion picture industries. Only by change in their present practices, controlling as they do the facilities for communication, and commanding as they do the mass audiences, will a wider educational or cultural usefulness be achieved in film or radio.[13]

Perhaps a more substantial, although intangible, contribution in this general field of mass communication was made by the Foundation's fellowship program. Twenty-four fellowships in film studies and seventy-five in radio were granted during the decade when the Foundation was following this interest. Many of the men and women trained in this way have gained prominence both in the commercial and noncommercial aspects of film and radio; and although it is impossible to measure their influence and effectiveness, it may well be that their contribution of ideas and leadership has resulted in an appreciable advancement in their fields.

V

"Nationalism cannot resist the force of powerful intellectual curiosities that carry individuals beyond all borders to common sources of knowledge."[14] This generalized statement which Stevens made to the trustees in 1933 was the starting point of the Foundation's interest in modern languages. In a world whose ties are increasingly interwoven and interrelated, it is not enough to have the barriers of language breached by only a handful of cloistered scholars. If cultural interests are to be given a wider currency, and if the imperative need of mutual understanding between races is to be met, something must be done to break down the insularity created by ignorance of other languages.

This was the argument of the trustees eight years before Pearl Harbor. At the moment, they were thinking primarily of the Far East. America had never developed a school for the study of Oriental languages and cultures, although such schools had existed in Europe over many years. There was the School of Oriental and African Studies of the University of London, the École Nationale des Langues Orientales Vivantes in Paris, and the Enukidze Institute of Oriental Languages in Leningrad. Similar schools existed in Prague, Warsaw, Rome, Leyden, and other cities. These schools combined the practical teaching of Oriental languages to diplomats, businessmen, and scholars with a high type of specialized study of the cultures themselves.

In the early thirties in this country, instruction in Far Eastern languages was limited to a few older professors teaching Japanese and Chinese. In 1933, through the instrumentality of the American Council of Learned Societies, the Foundation made an appropriation designed to strengthen the Library of Congress as a center for students of Japanese and Chinese languages. Beginning in 1934, with Foundation aid, a series of summer institutes was inaugurated at Harvard, Columbia, California, and Cornell for the quick induction of younger scholars into the languages and cultures of Japan, China, and Russia. The movement began to spread and by 1941 twelve institutions had special courses in one or more of these three languages. As the work progressed, new techniques of language instruction were developed which were quite distinct from the traditional methods of college courses. For example, the Foundation financed an experiment at Yale in the teaching of Chinese which demonstrated that an initial command of that language in writing and in speech could be gained in two nine-week full-time courses. Similar intensive courses were supported in other institutions; and when Pearl Harbor arrived with its insistent demand for knowledge of the Far East and its languages, there was a substantial basis on which to build.

In the extraordinary development which followed—a development guided largely by the American Council of Learned Societies—the Foundation played an important role. Its grants paved the way for the material, methods, and personnel which constituted the nucleus of the United States Army language training program. Funds were given for the production of translations, vocabularies, grammars, dictionaries, primers, bibliographies, and glossaries of technical terms. Financial support was advanced to expedite courses not only in the Chinese, Japanese, and Russian languages, but in Turkish, Arabic, Persian, Hindustani, Malayan, Burmese, Tibetan, Siamese, Pidgin English, and various regional languages of Africa. The number of institutions where this type of special course was being given rose from twelve to fifty-five. The demand was not for linguists of the scholarly research type, but rather for a large number of men with a ready conversational grasp of these strategic tongues. "The practical services rendered by the Humanities division during the war were of vital importance," wrote Stevens in a review of the period, "and surprised many skeptics who had insisted on thinking of the humanities as a useless luxury."[15]

During this period, too, the Foundation supported the development in the Far East and among foreign-born groups in this country of the system of Basic English. This system, developed by C. K. Ogden and I. A. Richards at Cambridge University, is a form of English in which 850 words, with certain additions for special purposes, will, for many practical situations, do the work of the 20,000 words in common use. As one commentator put it: "Why should a foreigner be taught to say that he has *disembarked* from the ship? Isn't it sufficient for him to say that he *got off*? And why should he be taught to say that he has *recovered* from the flu, or *escaped* the police, or *ascended* a stairway, or *boarded* a train, or *obtained* a job? Isn't it enough to say that he *got over* the first, *got away from* the second, *got up* the third, *got on* the fourth, and simply *got* the fifth?"[16]

Scores of books, among them the English Bible, have been put into the simplified vocabulary of Basic. But the Foundation had no thought of supporting Basic against other competing approaches. Simultaneously, it was giving aid to the very different work which Charles C. Fries was doing in the teaching of English at Michigan, as well as to Richards' work with the Harvard Commission on Language Teaching. It also helped to finance the University of Chicago study that sought to evaluate these and other methods of acquiring a second language. In all this activity, the aim of the Foundation has been to assist in the exploration of the field, to try to find some feasible path through the barriers of unfamiliar languages which divide the world.

As the work developed after the close of the war, stress was placed not only on languages but on cultures—the history, the literature, the philosophy, the ideas of Oriental civilization—and the Foundation made extensive grants for library development and staff appointments. Among the places aided were the University of Washington, the University of California, the Hoover Institute of Slavonic Studies at Stanford, Pomona College, the University of Chicago, Yale University, and the Library of Congress. The study of Slavic and Chinese cultures and institutions was especially emphasized. Similar grants were made abroad, notably in England, Holland, and Sweden. A balanced program of Indic studies was initiated at the University of Pennsylvania under favorable circumstances. The heavy concentration within the United States of all this activity was a by-product of war and postwar conditions; certainly it was not based on any illusion that internationally acceptable interpretations of the world's cultures can be achieved by American workers alone.

It can hardly be questioned that the language program of the Foundation has had a major influence on the character of academic work in this field. It has played a major role in creating the present interest in area studies, and in more intensive language instruction. The men and women trained under Foundation fellowships are now the leaders in many of the centers of Far Eastern research in the United States; and between 1943 and 1948 this country moved into a forward position among Western countries in Oriental and Slavic studies. A new pattern has been established, a new awareness of other corridors that lead, like our own, into the vast amphitheatre of blending cultures into which we have now come.

CHAPTER XX

HUMANISM AS AN INTERPRETER

THE HUMANIST IS OFTEN PICTURED AS A scholar preoccupied with the past; but for true humanism there are no visible frontiers between past, present, and future. It is the timelessness of his materials which accounts for the humanist's concern with them. Indeed, to release men from the bondage of time is one of his major functions. Not the past alone, but its projection into the present and future is important.

This, as we have seen, was the emphasis which the Foundation in the early thirties began to put upon its work in the humanities. In these years before the war, the new ideas in progressive education were bringing to the fore such terms as "participation" and "self-expression." The recognition given in modern schools to precepts like "learning through doing" and "doing with a purpose" brought fresh vigor to the humanities, for these are also the principles underlying creative work in the arts. If in our schools and colleges today the humanities mean more to more people—including the scholars—it is due in part, at least, to the recognition of the value of individual participation and self-expression in cultural activities.

Another significant change in public appreciation of the humanities came about through apparent accident. It was a logical sequence to the economic depression and its relief measures. "Art for the masses" came within the plans of the government for relief, and communities which had previously had no opportunites to take part in creative outlets, whether handicraft, music, or drama, began to feel a new stimulus. Although Europe had long had its national drama and music festivals reflecting year-round activities of native populations, before 1929 the United States had little encouragement toward such vital expression in the arts.

It was in this atmosphere that the Foundation began work to encourage wider participation in humanistic projects, especially in drama. Later, as we shall see, some of this broadening interest was focused, through Foundation effort, on the characteristics of various regions in the United States. During this period, too, south of our borders, assistance was given in countries where the zeal of refugee scholars from Old Spain combined with the enthusiasm of Latin-American humanists, especially in Mexico, to stimulate imaginative work. In postwar years, the Foundation gave aid to ventures, both here and abroad, in literary criticism and creative writing. This, briefly sketched, was the emphasis of the Foundation's program in the humanities during the later thirties and the greater part of the forties, and it was based on the belief that an organization concerned with the well-being of men can scarcely evade the attempt to make people free to share intelligently their cultural inheritance. Above all, this chance should be available to those original minds capable of interpreting their own times to their own contemporaries and to all who come after them. These broad objectives, as in every aspect of the Foundation's program, were out of all proportion to its means. Its hope was that its appropriations might contribute strategically rather than quantitatively to significant trends.

II

In any plan to increase general interest in the humanities, the Foundation felt that drama had a high place, not only for the actors but for the audience. "Acted drama," said Stevens, "evokes active sharing in experience to a greater degree than any other form of expressive art, making each spectator in his own way a participant in the realities of the illusion."[1] Once the decision was made to enter this field, the Foundation again turned to the universities. Following the lead of Professor George Baker, first at Harvard and subsequently at Yale, one American university after another was making provision for the study of drama, both for graduates and undergraduates, by establishing departments of drama, with special facilities for playwriting and production, and with a large measure of freedom from traditional academic restraints. Moreover, a few strong community theaters were demonstrating that regional values in drama were as significant to American life as metropolitan recognition of exceptional abilities. The Foundation therefore began its work in these university and community centers by making grants to foster playwriting, to train directors and other specialists, and to develop techniques. At Yale, for example, funds were given for research in such matters as stage lighting, as well as for bringing together a master collection of photographs showing the settings of European and American plays from the year 1500 to the present day. Nearly sixty thousand photographs, gathered in the United States and from ten European countries, were arranged and documented for use.

At the University of Iowa, Foundation funds aided the completion of a theater building of advanced design, and brought new staff members to the department. In North Carolina, where the university was doing work of high standard throughout the state, the Foundation helped to increase its extension programs in drama for high schools and for two community centers. Community pageants and state folk festivals were organized, and dramatic study became a fully recognized credit course in the high schools. On Roanoke Island, the summer training courses of the university ran for a full nine-week period concurrently with the production of Paul Green's pageant *The Lost Colony,* commemorating the 350th anniversary of the landing of the first English settlers in this area. Produced with the co-operation of the Playmakers, the Federal Theatre, and community residents, this pageant was so enthusiastically received that it has been presented for several years to audiences that totaled 75,000 people each season, the State of North Carolina assuming all the expenses not met from admission fees and other sources.

In Cleveland, Ohio, the Foundation found conditions ripe for the parallel development of university and community drama. Western Reserve University, where graduate work of excellent quality had been developed, was providing advisory service to high schools, social settlements, and other groups. The Cleveland Play House, one of the most successful community theaters in the country, had a large subscribing membership to support its full-time repertory company. The Foundation first took the exceptional step of helping the Play House to remove a mortgage, so that the income thus saved could be applied to teaching. This benefited the thirty-five apprentices who came to the Play House each year from all parts of the country, and opened up wider facilities to the advanced students of the University. At the University, Foundation funds were given first to strengthen the staff, and later to provide the faculty with adequate workshops as well as a theater for their teaching.

Sums were also given to other universities for strengthening the teaching staffs—both for equipment as well as for projects—in order to demonstrate the effectiveness of university drama in state programs of secondary education. The principle of the wide use of plays in education through traveling companies has now been definitely accepted; and in many parts of the country high-school audiences as well as the general public are seeing—often for the first time—performances of Shakespeare and other classic and romantic productions. Thus, in the State of Washington in a single year, audiences totaling nearly seventy thousand saw *The Comedy of Errors* and *No More Frontiers,* and the experiment was hailed in the realms of both the theater and education as one of the most significant developments in the field of either in a generation.

In carrying on its work in this area, the Foundation utilized the services of two organizations interested in drama, The National Theatre Conference and The Authors League of America, both of which were active in aiding young playwrights and directors. The Conference is a co-operative group, made up of the directors of community, college, and university theaters; the League, through its subsidiary organization, the Dramatists' Guild, has had wide influence in effecting better relations between the commercial and noncommercial theatrical fields. To the National Theatre Conference the Foundation gave long-continued help which enabled it to extend to schools, colleges, and community groups its services in developing educational and creative values through drama. During the years of this support, interchange between professional and nonprofit theaters steadily increased, and new plays were frequently released simultaneously in both types. Mutual help was derived from the interchange of personnel for special projects, and the educational standing of drama was improved in colleges and universities.

To both the National Theatre Conference and the Authors League of America the Foundation made extensive grants for fellowships, supplementing its own work in this direction. Over a period of fifteen years, the three organizations together awarded nearly one hundred fellowships—most of them to younger men and women of promise who needed a year in which to put to application in writing the outcomes of their formal training, or a final period of apprenticeship in direction or stage design. The appointments included men who subsequently won conspicuous success—Tennessee Williams, for example, and Lemuel Ayers, the stage designer, and E. P. Conkle, best known for his *Prologue to Glory,* and the late Thomas Job, author of *Uncle Harry*. Former Rockefeller fellows in drama are also to be found today in the departments of a dozen American universities and in many of the community theaters. It is this investment in young people which has helped to bring vitality and imagination to American dramatic writing and to the American stage.

III

The history of our own culture and institutions here in the United States has been for many years a relatively neglected field. Whole areas of American life and tradition are only now beginning to be explored at all adequately, areas such as our economic, social, and intellectual history, the history of our science, medicine, and technology, as well as of our art, music, and drama. As yet, only a beginning has been made in the study of the rich, regional cultures which nourish whatever national culture today exists in the United States and Canada.

No nation which does not understand its past can manage its future. Study is needed of the bases of our American habits and traditions—a wider knowledge of who we are and where and what we came from, a fuller interpretation of American life to enable us to comprehend what we possess today and on what our tomorrow can be built. An interest of this kind involves no narrow nationalistic aim. The culture of one world in the making is necessarily compounded of the diverse contributions of many peoples. Until a nation understands itself in relation to its own culture, it cannot intelligently harmonize and integrate its life into the larger pattern.

Beginning in 1942, on the initiative of the Foundation, a series of conferences was held of scholars, writers, critics, and journalists to test the feasibility and validity of this general thesis. Each of these conferences represented a special region, such as the Connecticut Valley, the Great Plains, and the maritime and industrial areas of Northeast Canada and New England. The aim of these meetings was to elicit ideas and collaboration in an approach to a deeper and more general understanding of our local cultures, an approach which would give vitality to public education and a sense of significance to American studies among scholars. It was hoped, too, that through regional studies new source materials might be uncovered and a new impetus developed for constructive, genuinely interpretative pictures of American life. The conference on the Great Plains area brought together professors of history from the Universities of Alberta, Saskatchewan, Manitoba, Minnesota, Texas, and Wisconsin, professors of English from the Universities of Oklahoma and Texas, as well as journalists and local writers. The one thing that all had in commom was a deep interest in their region. One of the journalists later wrote a review of a conference he attended in which he said:

> We must preserve every scrap of our history in which is recorded the story of how we came to be what we are. We must encourage every interpreter of that history, for outside of our borders (and even within them) there is a strange lack of information about its details, a stranger lack of comprehension of its meaning. We must acknowledge the dignity and importance of what the artist, the playwright, the poet, the musician is doing when he takes his theme from some perhaps small aspect of American life with which he is familiar. We must value the folk arts and handicraft which people from other countries have brought to us and which we have in the past been inclined to reject.[2]

It was this spirit which launched the Foundation on its program in regional studies. For the most part, it concentrated its support on interpretative studies which tend to lend form and relevance to what is known. Thus, a sum was given to the Texas State Historical Association to enable that organization to make grants-in-aid to men and women working on the interpretation of the Southwest. Another grant, to the University of Wisconsin, contributed toward studies of the process of the transformation of Wisconsin from "a wilderness lightly tied to Western civilization" to a highly developed and integrated segment of American life. Still another grant, to the University of Oklahoma, provided for a system of fellowships, administered by the University, as a stimulus to academic and nonacademic writers on regional subjects. An appropriation was also made to the Huntington Library of Pasadena for studies of the culture of the Pacific Southwest region, including Southern California, Nevada, Utah, Arizona, and New Mexico. The spirit in which this grant was administered is indicated by the set of principles adopted by the Library staff: "First, the study shall not be parochial, provincial or antiquarian in character; second, it shall provide the basic materials for an understanding of the contemporary economic, social and cultural development of the Southwest; finally, it shall seek to show the place of the Southwest in the life and service of the nation."[3]

The Foundation also made appropriations, among others, to the

University of Utah for studies of the Mormon area; to the University of Alberta for interpretations of the traditions of Canada's youngest province; to the University of Saskatchewan for work in Western Canadian history; and to the University of New Brunswick for interpretative studies of its own area.

An appropriation of $100,000 which the Foundation made to the Library of Congress enabled that organization to give grants-in-aid to workers in the field of biography, folklore, and historical interpretation who were not sponsored by universities or other educational or scholarly institutions. Similar grants to the Newberry Library of Chicago and to the University of Minnesota served the purpose of creating centers to which gifted students of Midwestern culture could turn for timely aid. That these studies produced more than books may be illustrated by the remark of a listener following an address by the director of the Newberry Library: "I never knew history was like that. I never knew that the Midwest had a history. I thought history was Bunker Hill and Plymouth Rock and George Washington."[4]

Assistance to American studies was by no means limited to the regional approach. Some subjects have an interpretative significance broader than any particularized area, and this significance was recognized by the Foundation in a number of major grants, as for example, those to support the research of Dumas Malone on the biography of Thomas Jefferson, or to the Abraham Lincoln Association to produce a definitive text of the works of Lincoln. Throughout this period, too, the Foundation sought opportunities to support the development of American studies in colleges and universities. At Princeton, for example, aid was given to an interdepartmental approach to an understanding of American tradition and American contemporary life —an approach which involved the departments of art and archaeology, economics, politics, English, history, and philosophy. Similar work was undertaken in other institutions.

As might be expected, the immediate result of this wide and varied support in American studies has been a flood of books—literally scores of them—factual and interpretative, many of them original and imaginative, based on the ingredients of our cultural history. A few of them have found their way to "best seller" lists; most of them have thrown new light on the significance and meaning of American tradition and outlook in the life of today and tomorrow. It would be invidious to single out the achievement of any one of these writers for special praise, but perhaps the following list of a few titles will serve to indicate the high quality of the product: *Midwest at Noon* by Graham Hutton; *America's Daughter* by Era Bell Thompson; *The Old Northwest* by R. C. Buley; *William Allen White's America* by Walter Johnson; *Small Town Renaissance* by Richard Waverly Poston; *Frontier Justice* by Wayne Gard; *The Indians of the Southwest* by Edward Everett Dale; *Oklahoma, Footloose and Fancy-Free* by Angie Debo; *America's Heartland: The Southwest* by Green Peyton; *Dixie Frontier* by Everett Newfon Dick; *Wisconsin Is My Doorstep* by Robert E. Gard; *Maria, the Potter of San Ildefonso* by Alice Marriott.

It is a significant fact that interest in American history and culture is developing in European institutions. Late in the forties, the Foundation made provision for visits to the United States and Canada of a number of foreign scholars responsible for North American studies in their universities. In addition, grants were made to Cambridge, Oslo, Upsala, and Munich for working collections of books needed by these scholars and their students. That the inauguration of American studies abroad may in turn have a salutary effect upon such studies in the United States is not beyond the limits of possibility.

IV

The years following 1937 were marked by a new interest in Latin-American studies. Not only was the United States Government encouraging cultural relations with countries to the south, but scholars in many of our universities were anxious to extend their interests beyond the narrow limits of anthropology, archaeology, and colonial history which had largely monopolized their established courses. In line with this movement toward the consideration of Latin America as an area, a lively interest was developing in the current art and literature of our southern neighbors; and the Foundation's program was launched on a favorable tide.

The work began with a survey by the American Council of Learned Societies whose committees, over the past thirty years, have broken ground in some of the most important activities undertaken in the field of humanities. The participation of the Foundation took the form, at first, of encouraging the programs of Latin-American studies in some of the universities in the United States as well as in centers like the Pan American Union and the Hispanic Foundation of the Library of Congress. This support included the allocation of funds for accumulating the necessary materials of research and was followed by a wide extension of fellowships both to American and Latin-

American scholars, sending the former to the Southern Hemisphere and bringing the latter to the north. Some of these fellowships helped to develop teachers of methods in learning English and Spanish—not teachers of the languages, but specialists in method. Other fellowships and grants served to introduce modern library administration and archival reform in Argentina, Chile, Brazil, Peru, Colombia, Mexico, Venezuela, Cuba, and Puerto Rico. Through minor grants and fellowships, museums were also assisted in Rio de Janeiro and Bahia, two in Mexico City, and one in Guatemala—the new National Museum.

But it was in Mexico that the Foundation made its most extensive Latin-American grants in the humanities to support the basic work of two outstanding centers: the National Institute of Archaeology and History and the College of Mexico, and to help the development of philosophy at a third: the National University. The Institute is a semi-autonomous federal agency, charged with the custody of the nation's pre-Columbian and colonial monuments. It has become a center of international training in research, and its work in archaeology and anthropology, generously supported by the government, has given it a distinguished position in the Western Hemisphere. The Foundation's association with the Institute was confined to its educational and research functions, supplying fellowships to enable students from other Latin-American countries to come there, assisting in the development of the library and archives, and providing for visiting professors in anthropology and related subjects. "Even more important," wrote Stevens in 1947, "are the international effects that are following the close collaboration among the countries now benefited by the work of the Institute. It has made their common possession of Mayan, Aztec and contemporary Indian cultures a means of intellectual cooperation."[5]

The College of Mexico, founded in the thirties of this century, is a research center for the development of specialists in history, literary criticism, language, and economic studies. It has demonstrated the intellectual allegiances of Old Spain and the New World, first by using distinguished refugee scholars, and then by joining with the Institute of Archaeology and History to give a balanced training in both Spanish and Latin-American literatures. The Foundation's support was for fellowships, historical studies, and Latin-American linguistics.

The modest grants in philosophy which the Foundation gave to the National University were stimulated in part by the presence of refugee scholars and by the fact that philosophy is an active discipline in Latin America. The resulting publications have influenced the program of the newly organized Inter-American Philosophical Association, which had been effective in securing co-operation among philosophers of North and South America.

In all this activity, it must be recognized that historically and culturally Latin America has closer ties with Europe than with the United States. There is a very genuine basis, however, for a wider common understanding. Not only do North, Central, and South America occupy one hemisphere, but all of the peoples in that hemisphere have recently faced, or are still facing, pioneer conditions. All of them are inheritors and trustees of fresh lands and vast natural resources. Compared with the older European civilizations, the nations of the Western Hemisphere are perhaps freer from tradition and readier for new experiments in cultural living. In any event, the opportunity for interchange between the nations of North and South America is obvious, and the possibilities that may come of this development in terms not only of sympathetic understanding but of a new and more vital cultural life seem to be real and tangible.

V

A frequent criticism of current humanistic study is aimed at its preoccupation with factual research—new fields of facts to conquer, new puzzles for scholarship to unravel, new opportunities to correct a text or discover a parallel. Henry Seidel Canby in an address before the Modern Language Association described the humanistic scholar in these words:

> Unconsciously he has left the difficult and doubtful ranges of interpretation, of appreciation, of valuation, all involving the never-to-be-entirely-calculable human spirit, and has thrown the emphasis more and more on fact-finding, on the material background of human experience, upon the search for the last detail of accurate knowledge. . . . He has become more accurate and more knowledgeable than his predecessors, and this is good, but somehow, somewhere, the precious and nourishing liquid of literature has been spilled from the ever more carefully moulded goblet.[6]

While Mr. Canby's comment was directed largely to literature, it is undoubtedly applicable to other disciplines, and its validity, in some respects at least, must be recognized. In the two decades of its operation in the humanistic field, the Foundation, through its fellowships and grants-in-aid, has attempted, insofar as possible, to meet the situation by a careful screening of personnel. During this period, its fellowships have been awarded to more than five hundred men and women selected by officers of the Humanities division. In addition to these, 735 fellows were appointed by outside institutions, notably the American Council of Learned Societies, with funds provided by the Foundation. For these two types of fellowships, more than $2,500,000 was appropriated. The scholars who had this support have worked in literature and philology, Oriental studies, history, archaeology, philosophy, art, architecture, and a dozen other subjects. Probably some of their work has been profitless—a piling of fact upon fact, with little relation to the values needed by our times. But who can tell in advance the scholar from the pedant? Or who can determine the kind of intellectual and cultural soil out of which creativeness, imagination, and great teaching will spring? Meanwhile, it can be recorded that of the scores of scholars who received support from the Foundation, not a few have become the interpreters of their generation, bringing to life in contemporary language what is relevant in the stream of human culture.

A more direct and ambitious attempt to stimulate the creative spirit in the field of literature was made by the Foundation in financing, in 1945, the Atlantic awards, administered by the University of Birmingham in England to help promising young British writers, dislocated and exhausted as a result of the war, by giving them a year or two of freedom from the pressure of making a living. As of this writing, forty-seven men and women have received this type of aid: twenty-seven novelists and short-story writers, seventeen poets, and three dramatists. It is perhaps too soon to assess the ultimate value of this project, but in a recent statement the Birmingham committee of awards reported that "several of them [the authors] are building up for themselves a high reputation." And the committee added this interpretation of the project:

> The war killed many men, and with them, no doubt, many good books. That loss is irretrievable; but help can be given, in time of peace, to those young writers who are threatened by inimical forces which, if less immediately apparent and less tangible, are as likely as war itself to stultify and ultimately to destroy their talents.[7]

A similar purpose was implicit in an action taken by the Foundation with relation to young American writers. Instead of fellowships, however, the Foundation made grants to three periodicals which encourage literary excellence and provide media for the publication of new writings: the *Kenyon Review*, the *Sewanee Review*, and the *Pacific Spectator*. The funds were given to enable these periodicals to raise their rates of payment to authors from the starvation scale called "nominal" to a scale that was regarded as "reasonable." In effect, the grants were subsidies to younger writers who established their claim to such assistance by securing the publication of their material in magazines that maintain superior literary standards.

Of course, the maintenance in a society of creative work of high level involves much more than the support of the writer or artist himself. His apparent problems are really the problems of the role and acceptance of humanism in a civilization—problems that no single organization, least of all a foundation, can effectively solve, although single organizations can help in small ways in establishing more favorable conditions.

VI

The Foundation's program in the humanities, like the programs of other divisions of its work, was purposely kept elastic and flexible in order to meet unanticipated needs and opportunities. Consequently, some projects are not easily classifiable under the headings of the regular program and are therefore mentioned in the paragraphs which follow.

Philosophy. A familiar passage in Bacon's *Advancement of Learning* refers to "the three parts of man's understanding, which is the seat of learning: history to his memory, poesy to his imagination, and philosophy to his reason." In our times, philosophy needs recognition and fortunately is beginning to receive it. If there can be a return to reason, from which, in Hogben's phrase, man is in retreat, the other parts of Bacon's definition can take their accustomed places, and contribute to our understanding, each in its own way.

As we have seen, philosophy is an active discipline in Latin America, and the Foundation facilitated the visits of several scholars to the United States, where they exchanged views with their American associates and lectured at various colleges and universities. Aid was also given to the American Philosophical Association for a series of public forums in seven cities to discuss with teachers, ministers, lawyers, and other laymen the meanings of philosophy in modern times, and its place in American life and institutions. Out of these forums came the book *Philosophy in American Education: Its Tasks and Opportunities*. A summer session in philosophy and an international congress of philosophers, designed to promote the exchange of ideas between East and West, were assisted in 1948 by the Foundation through a grant to the University of Hawaii.

The Foundation aided directly a number of outstanding scholars in philosophy of whom perhaps three may be mentioned as examples: Dr. Hu Shih, to enable him to continue his history of Chinese philosophy; Dr. Charles Morris of the University of Chicago, whose books *Signs, Language and Behavior* and *The Open Self* have given him a leading place in American philosophy; and Dr. Baker Brownell of Northwestern University, whose book *The Human Community: Its Philosophy and Practice for a Time of Crisis* started as a project in the Foundation's program in regional studies, but developed into an outstanding analysis of the relation of philosophy to the contemporary world.

Another grant by the Foundation to the Aspen, Colorado, congress for the Goethe Bicentennial Celebration was made with the primary aim of bringing Albert Schweitzer from his African responsibilities to a place where his unique personality and point of view could be more widely appreciated. The impact of his extraordinary career as philosopher, musician, and spiritual leader is already beginning to influence the thinking of this generation.

The Berkshire Music Center. The Foundation never developed a program in music for two reasons: it had no staff qualified for activity in this field, and in the second place, other organizations, designed for this particular purpose, were doing effective work. An exception was made in connection with the Berkshire Music Center, established by the late Dr. Serge Koussevitzky, the brilliant conductor of the Boston Symphony Orchestra, in connection with the annual Berkshire Music Festival. The Center, which was launched by a grant from the Foundation, is a training school for musicians, with courses for orchestral conductors, composers, and singers. The faculty consists mainly of the first-desk players of the Boston Orchestra, and the six weeks' session includes, at the end, the three weeks of the festival, attendance at which is the privilege of all the pupils of the Center. Three excellent young conductors, Thor Johnson, Leonard Bernstein, and the Brazilian, Carvalho, now successfully launched in their profession, are already the fruit of Dr. Koussevitzky's teaching; and Berkshire has become established as an internationally recognized musical center of high importance.

The American Council of Learned Societies. No adequate story of the Foundation's work in the humanities could fail to mention the significant part played by the American Council of Learned Societies. Organized in 1919, and patterned on the National Research Council, its membership includes the foremost learned societies concerned with humanistic studies, such as the American Historical Association, the American Philosophical Society, the Modern Language Association of America, and the American Academy of Arts and Sciences—to mention only four out of twenty-three. The Council's activities embrace a wide field, including major projects like the *Dictionary of American Biography* and the *Linguistic Atlas of the United States and Canada;* assistance to individual scholars through fellowships and grants-in-aid; and the stimulation through special committees of experts of new areas of study. Thus, committees have been established not only in major cultural areas—Chinese, Japanese, Indic and Iranian, Arabic and Islamic, Slavic, and Latin-American—but on subjects such as musicology, the history of ideas, American culture, and Negro studies.

With all this activity The Rockefeller Foundation has been closely identified. In much of its work, as, for example, in the handling of part of its fellowship and grant-in-aid programs, the Council has been the agency through which the operation has been channeled. In addition, the Foundation has contributed to many of the projects of the Council and has made substantial appropriations to its general budget. The relationship has been one of mutual advantage; certainly without the advice and rich resources of the Council the Foundation's program in the humanities would have been seriously handicapped.

Although late in entering the field of the humanities, the trustees of the Foundation have felt increasingly that in a world where the values by which men have guided and still guide their lives are in constant danger of being submerged, no area of activity has greater significance. Like the social sciences, it is an area of imponderables, and, even more than in the social sciences, satisfactory methods of measuring results cannot easily be established. Moreover, it is a difficult area to cultivate, and the determination of what is relevant to the deep needs of our time is often a baffling task. The choices of approach by any one organization are by no means infallible; mistakes are inevitable and disappointments are not infrequent. But for over two decades the Foundation has maintained its faith in this general line of attack, and has supported it with substantial appropriations.

CHAPTER XXI

INVESTMENT IN LEADERSHIP

WICKLIFFE ROSE USED TO SAY THAT HE was primarily interested in "backing brains." Since 1914, when the system was initiated, the award of fellowships on an international basis has constituted in The Rockefeller Foundation the most important single device for the training of competent personnel for intellectual leadership. It has been an investment in ability, a gamble with promising talent; and as we have already seen in earlier chapters, it has had consequences which cannot easily be measured. A fellowship is in one sense an uncontrolled experiment. What kind of career the man in question might have had without assistance can never be determined. Thus it would be wholly unwarranted to attribute to the fellowship itself the notable record made by many hundreds of Rockefeller Foundation fellows. The testimony of the men themselves, however, is convincing evidence that fellowship experience, wisely planned and coming at a critical juncture in a student's career, can play a significant role.

Over a period of thirty-five years, the Foundation has awarded some ten thousand fellowships, either directly or through intermediate agencies like the National Research Council, the Social Science Research Council, or the American Council of Learned Societies. The total cost of all these separate fellowships has approximated $28,000,000, and the trustees of the Foundation have repeatedly affirmed their belief that funds thus placed behind intellectual capacity and imagination are never misspent.

The ten thousand fellows have come from approximately seventy-five different countries, and have represented many races, languages, backgrounds, and branches of scholarship. Their fellowships have enabled them to obtain, in so far as it has been humanly possible to devise it, the best training open to them anywhere in the world, at the time when that training was most useful. As a group, although scattered around the globe, they have had a common experience; spiritually, if not linguistically, they speak a common language. Although not the primary purpose of the fellowship program, one of its important by-products has been its tangible contribution toward keeping the high-roads of the world open to the transportation of ideas. Today the Rockefeller fellows occupy positions of importance and distinction in nearly every country in the world. They are on university faculties, in medical schools, in research institutes and laboratories. They are carrying on significant and productive work in wide fields of knowledge, from sanitary engineering to Shakespearian scholarship. Some of them, indeed, have gained outstanding recognition; fourteen have been awarded the Nobel prize. Others hold, or have held, strategic governmental positions, or have found opportunities for creative careers in fields like journalism, drama, and radio. The total results of the program in terms of intellectual leadership and constructive achievement have been gratifying beyond anything that was contemplated when the fellowship system was inaugurated.

In general, the fellowships supported by the Foundation have been limited to those students who have not only finished their graduate work but have in addition proved their capacity for productive scholarship through several years of experience in their chosen fields. The application does not come from the candidate himself, but from his superior who has had an opportunity to gauge his work. One of the usual conditions of the fellowship is the assurance that a post will be waiting for the candidate in his own country upon his return. In other words, the Foundation has tried to guard against the danger of allowing the fellowship experience to expatriate the fellow.

While he holds a fellowship, the student works and studies in whatever country and in whatever institution is best fitted to his needs. In the years when war conditions did not prevent it, this resulted in a migration of students across frontiers not unlike that, perhaps, which characterized the Middle Ages, but on a much broader geographical scale. The criss-crossing lines of this globe-wide movement of scholars form an involved and intricate pattern. French and German students worked at the School of Biochemistry at Cambridge University, while British students went to the Pasteur Institute in Paris or the Technical Institute at Zurich. American scholars worked in the laboratories of the University of Sheffield and the Karolinska Institute of Sweden, while European scholars came to the California Institute of Technology or the University of Wisconsin. Chinese nurses were trained in midwifery in England and Scotland; French, Rumanian, and Bulgarian nurses went to the National School of Nursing in Warsaw; and malariologists from Southeast Asia came to Johns Hopkins or the Istituto Superiore di Sanita in Rome. American and Canadian doctors received specialized training in Edinburgh, London, Paris, Vienna, Berlin, or half a dozen other medical centers; South American agriculturalists studied at Chapingo in Mexico as well as at Cornell and the University of Minnesota; Japanese, Australian, and Indian students were brought to Europe or the United States. Institutions like the London School of Economics, Niels Bohr's Institute of Theoretical Physics at the University of Copenhagen, the Johns Hopkins Medical School, the National Bureau of Economic Research, Oxford University—to mention only a few out of dozens—became the centers of advanced training for students around the globe.

It must again be emphasized that in all this activity the Foundation had but one aim: to place the student in the institution where he could obtain the best possible training in the work for which he showed definite promise, no matter where the institution was located. In other words, the Foundation was not interested in one training center as against another, or in one country as opposed to another. It had no desire to bring students to the United States unless the quality of instruction in a particular American institution offered more than could be obtained elsewhere. Its outlook was truly international; through its officers it was in close touch with the world of scholarship, and it was guided by no parochial interest or concern.

As the work in fellowships developed over the years, it is interesting to note how often the fellows who sat at the feet of the revered masters in the earlier period themselves became the masters to the succeeding generations. For example, Dr. Harvey Cushing, one of the great neurological surgeons of his day, was Surgeon-in-Chief of the Peter Bent Brigham Hospital in Boston from 1912 to 1932. During that period, eighteen Rockefeller fellows studied under him. One of them was Dr. Hugh Cairns of Australia, who at the time of his appointment was Assistant Surgeon at the London Hospital. Cairns' subsequent brilliant promise on his return from Boston to London justified the Foundation in making an appropriation to develop the field of neurosurgery at the London Hospital, and under Cairns' leadership it became a center for another generation of neurosurgeons, with Rockefeller fellows coming from as far away as Australia and Portugal. Dr. Cairns, now Sir Hugh Cairns, is at present Nuffield Professor of Surgery at Oxford.

A further illustration relates to Dr. Ernest O. Lawrence, whose work at the Radiation Laboratory of the University of California has been described in an earlier chapter. Part of his advanced training was received on a fellowship supplied by the Foundation through the National Research Council. Today, another generation of students is working under Lawrence at Berkeley. Prominent among them recently was Cesare Lattes, the brilliant young Brazilian, who, under a fellowship from the Foundation, carried on an epoch-making experiment in the production of mesons from atoms, and who is now, at the age of twenty-five, a full professor on the faculty of the University of São Paulo.

II

In addition to the regular training fellowships, awarded by the different divisions of the Foundation, special systems of fellowships were occasionally employed to meet particular situations. The establishment of the Welch fellowships, named in honor of that wise and beloved leader in American medicine, Dr. William H. Welch, is a case in point. An appropriation of $168,000 was made to the National Research Council to support a plan for senior fellowships in internal medicine, offering long training and adequate stipends to carefully selected men from thirty to forty years of age. In tenure and terms of appointment, these fellowships resemble the Trinity College fellowships of Cambridge University or the Beit fellowships in Great Britain; and the appointments are made at the discretion of the Council up to a total term of six years for each fellow. Fellowship holders are free to move to the clinics best equipped to train them, and their clinical and teaching experience as well as their opportunities for research equip them for university posts in medicine. Indeed, it was in the hope that this mechanism would provide a more adequate supply of highly qualified teachers that the Welch fellowships were instituted.

Another illustration of special fellowships, or rather, perhaps, fellowships handled by an unusual technique, has to do with the grants which, for over a quarter of a century, the Foundation has made to the British Medical Research Council to enable that organization to send abroad each year a picked group of British students for advanced training in the medical sciences. Over this period, the Foundation has appropriated approximately half a million dollars for the purpose, but the appointment of the fellows, the selection of the institution in which they take their training, and all other details of the program are cared for by the Council, of which Sir Walter Fletcher and Sir Edward Mellenby have, in succession, been the distinguished directors. The list of appointees contains many notable names, including Sir Howard Florey, Nobel laureate of 1945; Dr. J. C. Bramwell, the celebrated cardiologist of the University of Manchester; Sir John Conybeare, physician to Guy's Hospital; Dr. A. A. Moncrieff, Nuffield Professor of Child Health at London University; and Dr. C. H. Waddington, Professor of Animal Genetics at the University of Edinburgh.

Still another device which arose out of the exigencies of the Second World War brought to America in 1941 and 1942 a carefully selected group of predoctoral British medical students whose training had been interrupted by the derangement of conditions for thorough and adequate teaching. Chosen by a committee of vice-chancellors of British universities, these students, provided with two-year scholarships, found welcome in twenty-three medical schools in the United States and Canada, from Harvard west to the University of California and from Toronto south to Tulane. In many ways, it was an extraordinary experiment which made possible the continuation of a high standard of training for young men who were chosen to represent the future of British medicine at a time when the present looked ominously black. Moreover, it bound together by even closer ties the unity that has always characterized British and American medicine. The following sprightly letter, written by one of the visiting students and published in the London *Lancet,* is quoted as indicative of the spirit of co-operation which underlay this enterprise:

In the last months I have heard Toscanini, Heifetz, Rachmaninoff and Horowitz, and have seen a production of Macbeth that left as little to be desired as any production could; I have driven to Chicago and back, and seen something of the little towns that go to make the Mid West, without realizing that it was as if I had been from London to Warsaw in two days; I have acquired an old blue jalopy which rears at a traffic light; I have grown fat eating irradiated oats, polyvitamin chocolate bars, and aseptic hot dogs; I have almost essayed to jitterbug, but find the cut of English trousers rather a handicap; I have shouted at football games, but still can't fathom why; I have made many friends, both students and faculty, in my own and other universities; I have got engaged to be married. I like America.[1]

III

The Second World War, of course, sharply contracted the regular fellowship program, and in many instances the fellows were uprooted from the work for which they had been trained. Numbers of them perished in concentration camps or gave their lives in defending the principle of intellectual freedom. A letter received by the Foundation in 1946 from a former Hungarian fellow movingly portrayed, in its uncertain English, the faith and spirit that sustained these men of scholarship during this tragic period:

> Seven years had passed away since I came home from America. Seven terrible years full with unspeakable sufferings, troubles and griefs. Humanity, altruism and love have disappeared of one part of mankind. . . . Now that all is over, one may ask whether the . . . work achieved by human benevolence was it all in vain, when all could be destroyed utterly by human wickedness? I survived all the sufferances of the past seven years, and now I try to give an answer to this question. I think the influences and impressions of my fellowship years contributed a great deal to see always the way of truth in that chaos of ideas and to be sure of their issue. I could remark also that between all Hungarian Rockefeller fellows there was an unspoken, but obvious spiritual connection, that could be considered as a basis, remained solid among the ruins, and on which the future of mankind can be reorganized. So the work was, and will not be, in vain.[2]

The exigencies of the war necessitated considerable modification in the fellowship system. It became almost impossible to appoint fellows in European countries, and the number of such fellowships dropped from 141 in 1939 to 4 in 1943. On the other hand, Latin-American fellowships over the same period rose from 47 to 107. A large part of this increase was in the field of the natural sciences, with agricultural fellowships predominating. As the war drew to a close, the Foundation began the development of a fellowship plan designed to aid the most promising American students who were in the armed forces and whose work in the universities had been interrupted by the war. Many of them had assumed responsibilities which made their return to research or to a life of scholarship exceedingly difficult, and there was substantial indication that the verdict "thin quality," which had been passed upon the generation of students coming out of the First World War, would be repeated in relation to the students in the postwar period of the late forties.

To help in meeting this contingency, the Foundation undertook, in four of its divisions—the Medical Sciences, the Natural Sciences, the Social Sciences, and the Humanities—a series of emergency measures. Training in medicine was particularly hard hit. Under the pressure of military necessity, not only were the usual four years of medical school telescoped into three, but the periods normally devoted to interneships and residencies in hospitals were sharply curtailed. In ordinary times, those medical students who survive the successive screening tests are given a postgraduate period of about five years to gain experience, to mature in knowledge of medicine, and to prepare for specialization. It is this period that sifts out and identifies the best men, the men who will be the teachers of the next generation. Under the wartime emergency, this five-year period was cut to less than a year, and men were rushed into the Medical Corps of the Army and Navy before they had a chance to ripen into the well-rounded scientists who constitute our top group in medicine. Those who came back from the war were older, many of them with family obligations, and their natural inclination was to accept whatever professional opportunity seemed most attractive.

To try to meet this challenge, if only in a limited way, the Foundation made grants totaling $508,000 to enable twenty-one leading medical schools in the United States to offer the most promising of the returning doctors, who had graduated from their institutions, residencies paying stipends from $4,000 to $8,000 per annum. In this fashion, more than a hundred young men were given an opportunity to complete the rounded training which the war had cut off.

In the field of the natural sciences, many of the students of exceptional promise were not in military service, but had been deferred for work in war laboratories. This was especially true of physicists and mathematicians, and to a lesser extent of chemists, biologists, and engineers. But the men returning to civilian life from the wartime laboratories had had their careers as seriously interrupted as if they had been with the armed forces. Although they had been assigned to work in the fields of science, their duties had in most instances been highly specialized, precluding any opportunity for broad, basic training. Many of them had fulfilled most of the requirements for the doctorate when they were called away to these emergency laboratory jobs. Some were just beginning their postgraduate studies and had two or three more years of training ahead.

Without some encouragement, it seemed likely that many if not most of these young men would be tempted into the more lucrative fields of engineering and industrial work, and that the universities would be left with scant material from which to select their future teachers of science and leaders of research. To help meet this situation, as far as limited funds could meet it, the Foundation made appropriations of approximately $600,000 to the National Research Council which provided for 200 predoctoral fellowships for a carefully selected group.

The war migration of social scientists into government service, civilian and military, was also a movement of generous dimensions. A minority of these students in anthropology, economics, government, administration, sociology, statistics, and related fields worked on scientific tasks; but the majority were in administrative or military posts. Many of them had not finished their postgraduate training when the war interrupted their preparation; and as in medicine and the natural sciences, the question was how these young men could resume their studies and complete their qualifications as teachers and researchers in their special fields. To help meet this problem, the Foundation made a series of "demobilization awards" to the Social Science Research Council in a total amount of $400,000. Under these awards, 164 scholars received assistance, of whom 112 were in the predoctoral category.

The same sort of wartime interruption of training and dispersion of personnel affected linguists, historians, writers, and other workers in the humanistic field; and the Foundation made appropriations totaling $250,000 to salvage some part of this loss. Unlike this activity in the other divisions, this special fellowship program was administered directly by the Foundation, but the aim was the same: to find the exceptional person whose failure to return to his chosen career would constitute a permanent loss in the generation ahead. The fellows were chosen on the recommendation of leading teachers and scholars who knew of their work and promise. "Oh happy post-war world!" wrote a marine captain from the Iwo battlefront where he received a letter from his sponsor asking him if he would accept a fellowship. And he added: "You will never know what a bolt from the blue your letter was. Thousand pound bombs sound like cap pistols by comparison. That such things can happen in a world such as this is still something of a mystery to me. But of course the answer is a thunderous yes. I can't remember consciously praying for this, but certainly it must have been an answer to an unbreathed petition."[3]

Under this emergency program in the humanities, exactly one hundred fellowships were awarded. Among the recipients, by way of illustration, were J. Leslie Hotson, the Elizabethan scholar, who was a captain in the Signal Corps; Edwin M. Wright, a Middle Eastern expert, who was an army captain; and Frederica de Laguna, an archaeologist attached to the University of Pennsylvania Museum, who was a lieutenant in the Waves.

IV

In addition to the fellowships customarily given for postgraduate training, but modified occasionally, as we have seen, to include predoctoral work, the Foundation awarded what were known as "special fellowships" to mature, outstanding scholars, not as a means of training, but to enable them to obtain, through travel or otherwise, a wider perspective in relation to the work in which they were interested. These special fellowships took many forms, including travel grants and other types of aid, and their terms were adjusted to the circumstances of each individual case. Thus, health officials were enabled to visit public health activities in states and countries other than their own; or economists from Europe came to the United States to get ideas from an institution like the National Bureau of Economic Research; or scientists in American laboratories exchanged ideas face to face with their fellow researchers in the laboratories of Great Britain or the Continent; or Latin-American scholars worked in the Library of Congress or the Bodleian to obtain materials related to their special interests.

Often the purpose of the special fellowship or grant was not the advantage that might accrue to the particular scholar, but rather the impact of his special knowledge or point of view on his associates in another country. Thus, Sir Howard Florey came to the United States in the crucial days of 1941 to explain to American scientists the experience of the Oxford Laboratory in the production of penicillin; Sir William Beveridge (now Lord Beveridge), author of the widely acclaimed Beveridge Report, was welcomed in the United States by government officials, students, and many others interested in the problems of social security; on his visits to Mexico and Colombia, Dr. E. C. Stakman, professor of plant pathology at the University of Minnesota, brought fresh impetus to scientific agriculture.

Anything that promotes the exchange of creative ideas across boundary lines contributes to the welfare of mankind; and the device of special fellowships which the Foundation has employed in over seven hundred cases in the last thirty-five years has obviously served a significant purpose.

Another technique should be mentioned in this connection, a technique classified in the Foundation's terminology as a grant-in-aid. Initiated in 1929, it developed out of an older device of a developmental aid or laboratory aid fund employed mainly by the division of Medical Sciences. In its newer form it consists of blanket funds voted by the trustees and used in the discretion of the officers of all the Foundation's divisions to support small projects in amounts up to $7,500* and for terms not in excess of three years. The funds are employed for two general purposes: (1) to facilitate the completion of a minor but worth-while project in fields in which the Foundation has a recognized interest; and (2) to enable the officers to maintain close contact with the development of personnel and problems, and to test and explore, under small expenditures, those projects which are possible candidates for larger and more extended support through appropriations by the trustees. Another important use of the technique is the follow-up of a fellowship experience by a small amount of aid to the research activities of a returned fellow.

The award of a grant-in-aid follows no set form. Usually it is made to an institution, or to the department of an institution, for the benefit of an individual; and sometimes to an individual either for his own work or for the work of those who are associated with him. The amount granted may be as small as $50; the average is approximately $3,000. It may be directly applied to salary in order to free a man for some significant research; it may be applied to the salaries of his assistants; it may be devoted to publication or to the purchase of books or apparatus or expendable material or experimental animals. It is in a real sense the Foundation's hedge against the evils of bigness, and it has made possible a flexibility that would otherwise be difficult to achieve, as well as a promptness which sometimes is of strategic importance.

Although not related to the fellowship device in any organic way, the grant-in-aid supplements that device, and over the years has proved so useful a tool that the trustees have appropriated sums in excess of $10,000,000 to support it.

* This figure has now been changed to $10,000.

V

Another technique which was not precisely similar to the fellowship device (and is therefore not included in the total figures above given) was the Foundation's work in rescuing refugee scholars from Europe. The displacement of scholars for political and racial reasons began in Germany with the advent of Hitler. Subsequently, this abuse spread to Spain, Italy, Austria, Czechoslovakia, and then, country by country, marched with the advancing armies until nearly all the Continent of Europe was affected. Thousands of university and research teachers were dismissed, among them some of the most distinguished in the world. Not only were they debarred from teaching and research, but, as the fury grew, they found themselves frequently in peril of their lives. Many eminent scholars, indeed, died for no cause but their race, their religion, or their intellectual integrity. Many others escaped to friendly countries. Hundreds of these, as the German armies plunged forward, were forced to flee again; scholars who thought they had found haven in Austria or France were obliged to move on to England or America. There is even today no accurate estimate of the extent of this vast disturbance. The evidence, however, strengthens the conclusion that as a mass migration of scholarly personnel it was unprecedented in history.

The Rockefeller Foundation program for European refugee scholars began in 1933 and ended, with the cessation of hostilities, in 1945. Altogether, the Foundation expended nearly a million and a half dollars for this purpose and aided 303 individual scholars. Many of the men thus assisted found satisfactory posts in America and became American citizens; others were accommodated temporarily in Europe or Latin America until the close of the war, or, enabled to continue their productive work in American universities during the hostilities, returned later to European positions.

During the first seven years of the program, or until 1940, the Foundation took no initial responsibility in the selection of the scholar; all actions were taken at the instance of some institution in the United States or Europe. In 1940, however, with the invasion of Scandinavia, the Lowlands, and France, and the intensification of the war on England, a new type of problem developed. In the previous program, the refugee scholars, in general, were already in America when requests were received. In this new crisis, the scholar, caught at his post, was unable to escape without outside assistance.

With the consent of the State Department, therefore, and in cooperation with the Institute of International Education, the Emergency Committee in Aid of Displaced Foreign Scholars and the New School for Social Research, a special program was initiated. Under this program, American institutions, with the aid of grants from the Foundation, endeavored to reach the distressed scholars by cable, offering them teaching contracts for two years and traveling expenses to the United States. The Foundation's temporary office in Lisbon was used effectively in making travel arrangements, and in many instances considerable ingenuity was required to effect the rescue. But aside from this, the Foundation's participation was limited to supplying a portion of the funds required. If it had not been for the leadership of Dr. Stephen Duggan, chairman of the Emergency Committee, and the devotion and resourcefulness of Dr. Alvin Johnson, director of the New School, the program could not have been successful.

Of the total of 303 scholars aided by Foundation funds, 191 were German; 36, French; 30, Austrian; 12, Italian; 11, Polish; 6, Hungarian; 5, Czechoslovak; 5, Spanish; 2, Danish; 2, Belgian; 2, Dutch; and 1, Finnish. They represented a great variety of academic disciplines. Of the total, 113 had been trained in the social sciences, 73 in the natural sciences, 59 in the humanities, and 58 in the medical sciences.

The enrichment of American scholarship as a result of this migration can scarcely be overstated. Seven of the refugee scientists were already Nobel prize winners; two later became prominent in connection with the evolution of the atomic bomb; several are now heads of departments in American universities; many occupy important professorships, some in subjects hitherto relatively undeveloped in the United States, notably in mathematics. To use this particular discipline as an illustration, one may cite the brilliant faculty in mathematical research which had been developed at the University of Göttingen, ironically enough with funds supplied by the International Education Board in 1926, and which was dispersed in the thirties almost en masse. If Hitler had set out with benevolent intent to build up America as the world's great mathematical center, he could hardly have achieved more successfully the result which his ruthlessness accomplished. Welcomed in the universities of the United States, a substantial proportion of the members of this faculty, together with other refugee mathematicians, have made a contribution in mathematical theory and applied mathematics which can scarcely be measured, but which had high practical usefulness in the development of war effort in the Second World War. In the same way that many countries were enriched by the Huguenot immigration that followed the revocation of the Edict of Nantes in 1685, so the United States and other countries as well have greatly profited by the scholarship driven out of central Europe through the self-defeating blindness of an intolerant ideology.

The twentieth century has witnessed a vast international movement of scholars. Some of it has been forced by tragic circumstances; some of it stimulated with deliberate intent. Its effects have been incalculable. Francis Bacon in his *New Atlantis* in 1627 drew a shadowy sketch of the development. It will be remembered that according to his plan two delegations of fellows from Solomon's House were to go on missions every twelve years for terms of study. These two missions, each of three members, were to stay abroad until, at the end of their twelve years, returning ships picked them up after leaving new missions elsewhere for the acquisition of the materials of knowledge and invention. This, in Bacon's mind, was the way to develop man's most important international trade which, he said, was "not for gold, silver, or jewels, nor for silks, nor for spices, nor for any other commodity of matter; but only for God's first creature which was light."

Bacon's ships were never more than mythical, but this imagery of three hundred years ago outlined a movement which in our time reached proportions he doubtless never dreamed of.

CHAPTER XXII

"THROUGHOUT THE WORLD"

"UNIVERSALITY AND DEATHLESSNESS"—these were the words with which Mr. Gates christened The Rockefeller Foundation shortly after its birth in 1913.[1] The second attribute was qualified almost at the start. The idea, never precisely formulated, of extending the life of the Foundation to some indefinite period by spending only from income was abandoned in the early years in spite of Mr. Gates' attempts to maintain it. But the first attribute—universality—was, as we have seen, written indelibly into the charter of the Foundation: "the well-being of mankind throughout the world"; and its effect on subsequent policy has been incalculable. It made itself evident in the very first action taken by the trustees in projecting around the globe the hookworm work of the old Rockefeller Sanitary Commission, which had been limited to the Southern States. Gates wrote the resolution to effect this purpose—evidently with deep emotion. "I felt," he said years later, "as if it were a response to the same entreaty which had greeted St. Paul: 'Come over into Macedonia and help us.' "[2]

Wickliffe Rose, in spite of his Huguenot inheritance, had little of Gates' evangelical fervor. He believed in Gates' objective, but he never would have expressed himself in this idiom. He had the mind of a general, and he wanted a broad area in which to maneuver, because anything less than that would be ineffective. He thought of the world as a field of strategy in the conquest of disease or the extension of knowledge. Whether it was hookworm or yellow fever or the development of mathematics, he followed it across oceans and continents. "Keep your eye on the objective," he used to say; "never mind the incidentals." And his word "incidentals" included nationalisms, geographical frontiers, and political differences and difficulties. With this spirit he imbued his staff; and one of the stories which has become part of the folklore of his era relates to an incident that occurred during a revolution in a Central American country where the Foundation was engaged in a study of yellow-fever control measures. Dr. Emmett Vaughn, who was in charge of the work, determined to continue his research. Every morning, with a flag of truce, he crawled through the barricades to collect his mosquitoes on one side of the fighting line, and in the afternoon he crawled back again to gather up his specimens on the other side. He was molested by neither army. Both sides thought him somewhat crazy —a man who, when great issues of human destiny were being fought out, spent his time catching mosquitoes. Today in that Central American country the revolution has been largely forgotten, but Dr. Vaughn is remembered as the man who helped to stamp out an age-long pestilence.

President Vincent was also an important influence in building this tradition of universality. In his annual reports as well as in his public addresses, he based his argument on Pasteur's dictum that knowledge is the patrimony of humanity. "This ever-growing common fund," he said, "is reviewed, rectified, reorganized and augmented by thousands of investigators in university and industrial laboratories, botanical and zoological gardens, agricultural experiment stations, hospitals and research institutes of many kinds in almost all the countries of the world."[3] It is not American medicine or American public health measures that the Foundation is trying to introduce to the world, he argued. No country has a monopoly on excellence. In many respects, America has more to learn from other countries than they have to learn from us. All that the Foundation is attempting to do, with its relatively limited resources, is to help establish a common front against disease, drawing on the resources and talents of all countries. Whether it is malaria or cholera or plague or tuberculosis or whatever the disease may be, the nations of the world face these enemies of mankind, not as isolated groups behind boundary lines, but as members of the human race projected suddenly into a frightening propinquity.

This point of view, too, was reflected in Dr. Pearce's work in medical education. Like Rose and Vincent, he was endowed with what might be called a planetary consciousness, and he thought instinctively in global terms. He believed profoundly that modern medicine could be employed to weave a pattern of unity into the society of mankind. A decade and a half later, during the Second World War, this same idea was illustrated in the annual review of the President of the Foundation (the author of this history):

An American soldier wounded on a battlefield in the Far East owes his life to the Japanese scientist, Kitasato, who isolated the bacillus of tetanus. A Russian soldier saved by a blood transfusion is indebted to Landsteiner, an Austrian. A German soldier is shielded from typhoid fever with the help of a Russian, Metchnikoff. A Dutch marine in the East Indies is protected from malaria because of the experiments of an Italian, Grassi; while a British aviator in North Africa escapes death from surgical infection because a Frenchman, Pasteur, and a German, Koch, elaborated a new technique.

In peace as in war we are all of us the beneficiaries of contributions to knowledge made by every nation in the world. Our children are guarded from diphtheria by what a Japanese and a German did; they are protected from smallpox by an Englishman's work; they are saved from rabies because of a Frenchman; they are cured of pellagra through the researches of an Austrian. From birth to death they are surrounded by an invisible host—the spirits of men who never thought in terms of flags or boundary lines and who never served a lesser loyalty than the welfare of mankind. The best that every individual or group has produced anywhere in the world has always been available to serve the race of men, regardless of nation or color.[4]

II

It was this general point of view that brought the Foundation, in the twenties and early thirties, into touch with the technical work of the League of Nations. Writing in 1922, Rose said:

Modern life is rapidly overflowing national boundary lines. Governments are finding themselves confronted more and more with situations which no nation acting alone can meet, and are being drawn into responsibilities no single nation can assume. Functions that are essentially international in character will in the end be recognized as such, and will be organized on an international basis. Having been called into existence to safeguard world peace, the League is now being recognized as a convenient agency through which national governments may act in concert in dealing with other common interests as they arise.[5]

The branch of the League's work which interested Rose was, of course, its Health Organization, one of the outstanding accomplishments of the twenties. Handicapped by lack of funds in its early days, it asked the Foundation to supplement its budget in respect to certain proposed activities which it was unable to finance. The first activity was the interchange of public health personnel, through study tours or institutes attended by representatives of many countries. Thus, in 1924—to use a single year as an example—three such interchanges occurred in Great Britain, Denmark, and Switzerland, each averaging about two months, and bringing together for the period ninety-nine public health officers from twenty countries. In addition, there were interchanges of specialists, the tuberculosis group spending a hundred days in eight countries and school medical officers dividing forty-two days of study between three nations.

Another activity of the League's Health Organization to which the Foundation made substantial contributions was its Epidemiological Intelligence Service, created to compile in a uniform manner the vital statistics of European countries, including a method for classifying joint or contributory causes of death, the classification and statistical treatment of stillbirths, a standard million population for the adjustment of crude death rates, and age and sex classification. Until the Second World War interrupted its operation, this new uniform system of epidemiological intelligence proved of substantial value, not only as a practical guide to health officers, but in pointing the way to the possibility of larger rallying points of unity, around which men of different faiths and cultures could profitably combine.

For over a decade, the Foundation also helped the League's Health Organization to maintain at Singapore, a regional headquarters for the more prompt and accurate reporting of epidemic and other disease conditions in the Far East. As Rose said: "A competent agency constantly on the watch-tower, with dependable working relations with all countries, giving definite and reliable information concerning these great plagues when they first show themselves and before they get out of hand, can make an invaluable contribution to the health of the world. And this, it may be pointed out, is a task which no national government can undertake."[6]

Altogether, the Foundation gave approximately $2,000,000 to the League's health work.* Indeed, at one point after 1920, Rose hoped that the League's Health Organization, if adequately financed by its constituent members, could take over all the work which the International Health Division of the Foundation was carrying on. Very

* The $2,000,000 to build and endow the library of the League of Nations was given not by the Foundation, as is widely stated, but by Mr. Rockefeller, Jr.

reluctantly, he came to the conclusion that this hope could not be realized, at least in his lifetime. There were three principal obstacles. The Health Organization was not adequately financed, and in the growing economic crises of the twenties and early thirties its budget was necessarily reduced below a level that could effectively maintain its broadening work. In the second place, because it was a government organization, subject to the red-tape procedures which seem to be an inseparable adjunct of public operations, it could not act with the speed and decisiveness which the nature of its work often demanded. Thirdly, in spite of its able leadership, it was frequently and inescapably thwarted by political considerations such as a private agency does not have to face. The unembarrassed ease with which Rose could choose his staff and marshal his forces against a public health problem almost anywhere in the world led him to the conclusion that, although his own funds were relatively limited, there was still a place for an uninhibited private organization, not only to meet challenging opportunities in the field of public health, but also to demonstrate what could be done on an international scale by free imagination and constructive intelligence.

III

As we have already seen in earlier chapters, the example of Rose and Pearce in developing their programs on a world-wide basis was eagerly followed by the other divisions of the Foundation as they began their activities after the reorganization of 1928. The details of many of these activities have already been considered; in all cases they were motivated by the single phrase in the charter: "the well-being of mankind throughout the world"; and they were predicated on the conception that civilization and the intellectual life of men represent a co-operative achievement, and that the experience of the race can be pooled for the common good. It is an ironic circumstance that this objective should have had to run the gauntlet of two world wars with their hideous aftermaths, when behind closed frontiers, rigidly sealed off from contact with the ideas and opinions of other nations, vast populations have suffered from mental undernourishment and starvation. Intellectual malnutrition can be as stunting to human life and character as the absence of calories and vitamins. The influences that in normal times flow freely across boundary lines, the uninhibited stream of ideas coming from all corners of the world, are, in this modern society of ours, a corrective and stabilizing factor in the lives of men, bringing strength and fertility to soils that would otherwise become sterile and dry. "Speech is civilization itself," says Thomas Mann. "The word, even the most contradictory word, preserves contact—it is silence that isolates."[7]

This was the philosophy behind much of the work that the Foundation attempted to do in the discouraging atmosphere of the Second World War. As in the early twenties, emphasis was placed on filling the gaps in the periodicals and books of libraries shut off from contact with the rest of the world. With funds supplied by the Foundation, the American Library Association purchased and in some instances microfilmed approximately three hundred and fifty of the scholarly journals of the United States—journals like the *American Economic Review, Cancer Research,* the *Art Quarterly,* the *American Journal of Surgery*—storing them in warehouses until conditions made possible their distribution to the libraries of Europe and Asia. Funds were also given to the Royal Society, London, to assist in the publication of British scientific journals; and grants were made for the support of similar journals in India and for an interchange of material between American and Chinese libraries. Sets of reference books of five hundred titles each—books which a first-class library would normally buy, but which the foreign libraries missed because of the war—were purchased and held in reserve for future distribution.

When the war closed with the surrender of Germany, the Foundation made a determined effort to see what could be done to get research started again and to tie together the threads that connect Europe's intellectual life with the rest of the world. All five divisions of the Foundation participated in an effort which had two purposes: first, by grants, necessarily modest in character, to provide equipment or support to a few of the universities, libraries, and research centers; and second, to create, as far as physical conditions made possible, methods of communication by which these institutions, isolated by war, could establish contacts with each other and with the rest of the world. In the natural sciences, for example, grants for fundamental research were made to the universities of Upsala, Oslo, Utrecht, Leeds, and Oxford, the Karolinska Institute in Sweden, the Carlsberg Foundation in Denmark, and the Eidgenossische Technische Hochschule in Switzerland. The sum of $250,000 was given to the Centre National de la Recherche Scientifique in Paris for equipment and supplies in thirty-five of the leading research laboratories of France. A grant of $100,000 was made to this same organization for a series of international conferences in such fields as chemical genetics, protein structure, enzyme chemistry, and cellular physiology. Another appropriation made possible the meeting of the International Astronomical Union in Copenhagen, to which delegates came from all over the world.

In the medical sciences, a series of appropriations was made to support basic research and teaching in the universities of Zagreb, Zurich, Brussels, Cambridge, and London. Another grant made it possible to publish in English and French, for wide distribution, many of the excellent studies in clinical and laboratory work produced in France between 1939 and 1945. Funds were also given for a union catalogue of medical periodical literature published in England during the war years, with provision for supplying the medical libraries of Europe with microfilm copies of outstanding items.

In the field of the humanities, appropriations for books included funds to the National Central Library of London to replace as far as possible the destroyed collections of Great Britain; and an appropriation was made to help in the purchase of books for the ten leading libraries of Poland, where war losses had amounted to nearly 1,500,000 books. It was through its division of the Humanities, too, that the Foundation made extensive grants to the American Book Center for War Devastated Libraries, and its successor, the United States Book Exchange.

In the social sciences, substantial grants were made to British and Continental institutions to enable them to pick up the threads of their research in economics and international relations. A special appropriation made possible the purchase and distribution in the leading libraries of Europe of sets of books on the social sciences, each set containing from 300 to 350 titles, representing the more recent publications.

In the field of public health, emergency grants for equipment and supplies were made to institutes of hygiene and other health activities in countries on the Continent, including Poland, Holland, Norway, and Yugoslavia. Fellowships and travel grants were stepped up in all the Foundation's divisions, and in the year and a half following V-J Day, 240 such awards were made to Europeans, distributed as follows: public health, 84; medical sciences, 77; natural sciences, 21; social sciences, 32; humanities, 26. Of this total, 212 came to the United States and Canada for study, while 28 went to various countries on the Continent.

Altogether, something like six million dollars was appropriated for this emergency work in Europe, but the sum was pathetically inadequate. The situation was far beyond the capacity of private funds. Such funds could ameliorate some of the difficulties, but the need was so universal and overwhelming that it could be met, if at all, only by governments. Meanwhile, a new kind of intellectual fog was beginning to settle down over the world, a fog so dense and general as to cripple the limited effectiveness even of private funds that were trying to carry on their work across boundary lines.

IV

In various aspects of its activity over nearly four decades The Rockefeller Foundation established contacts with ninety-three countries, territories, or political divisions of the world.* Sometimes these contacts were more or less tangential—a few fellowships or grants-in-aid to create, if possible, a favorable soil for more substantial work. Often, as we have seen, they resulted in close and long-continued collaboration.

The one large country with which the Foundation never established a satisfactory relationship was Russia. The outbreak of the First World War, a year after the Foundation was organized, followed by the upheaval of the Bolshevik revolution, necessarily postponed any possibility of visiting the country in the early days, even had there been occasion to do so. As a matter of fact, the diseases with which Rose was grappling in that pioneer period were not those particularly characteristic of Russia, and in the chaos of the country in the years following the close of the war it was felt that more promising opportunities for effective mechanisms in public health existed elsewhere. This was strongly the opinion of Dr. Russell during his leadership of the International Health Division. The same thing could be said of the work in agriculture of the International Education Board. No attempt was made to extend it to Russia, because the disturbed conditions of the country were inimical to experimentation. Moreover, foreign ideas even at that time were generally unwelcome.

However, in the early twenties, The Laura Spelman Rockefeller Memorial appropriated $785,000 to the American Relief Administration and to its affiliate, the Student Friendship Fund, for food and clothing for teachers and students in Russian universities. During a period of unprecedented famine, the funds at the disposal of these

* These areas are listed in Appendix III.

organizations were employed to establish feeding kitchens for 20,000 students at universities in Leningrad, Moscow, Kiev, Odessa, Ekaterinoslav, and other centers, where food was served of sufficient caloric value to maintain effective work.

As far as the Foundation was concerned, Russian medical schools were included in the list of similar European institutions to which medical periodicals were systematically sent in the twenties and early thirties. Dr. Gregg of the Foundation's Medical Sciences division visited the medical schools in Leningrad and Moscow in 1927. By Western standards, their condition was unsatisfactory and little could be done except to provide a few training fellowships and some laboratory equipment. Ten years later, in 1937, he made a similar trip, and was impressed by the tremendous improvement in the organization and equipment of the schools that had occurred during the decade. However, due to the great purge of the middle thirties, a pall of fear and anxiety had settled on university personnel, and the presence of a foreigner, to say nothing of any assistance from a foreign organization, was obviously embarrassing. In the meantime, representatives of the International Health Division had visited the Soviet Union, but nothing materialized beyond two or three fellowships, and some laboratory equipment for their schools of hygiene.

With the outbreak of the Second World War, the Soviet Union was practically cut off from the rest of the world, and opportunity for cultural exchange on any effective basis declined almost to the vanishing point. Early in 1944, the Foundation, with the approval of the State Department, suggested to the cultural attaché of the Russian embassy in Washington the possibility of establishing at the close of the war a series of exchange fellowships in such subjects as agriculture, forestry, epidemiology, public health organization, and library methods. The proposal was referred to VOKS in Moscow, and, as was the case with similar suggestions from other American and Western European institutions, no answer was ever received. Indeed, shortly thereafter it became impossible for representatives of the Foundation to obtain visas to enter Russia, and in the course of the next two or three years conditions blocked the satellite states, including Poland and Czechoslovakia, with which, particularly in the fields of medicine and public health, the Foundation for nearly three decades had had friendly and constructive relations. An impenetrable barrier was stretched across the world, reinforced by fear and hate. A new era had dawned, black and ominous, an era which Gates and Rose, long in their graves, would not have understood, and which happily they did not live to see. Gates' doctrine of universality, derived from the New Testament, and Rose's serene belief in the power of human reason which he drew from Aristotle and Hegel, have been eclipsed in the dark clouds that hang over the face of this generation.

We have to reconcile ourselves to the grim necessities which today's problem of security brings to all of us. But perhaps it is not too much to hope that some new pattern will evolve, some internal regeneration among the people of the Soviet Union, which will open their doors and windows to the stimulus of ideas from without, and through which the inspiration of the Tolstoys, the Tschaikovskys, the Metchnikoffs, the Pavlovs, can again come like a clear breeze to refresh the spirits and minds of men. For in a deep and ultimate sense, it is still one world, one human race, one common destiny. That was the high faith that lay behind the creation of the Foundation, and on that faith the future must depend.

CHAPTER XXIII

THE EVOLUTION OF PRINCIPLES AND PRACTICES

IT IS NOW NEARLY FORTY YEARS SINCE The Rockefeller Foundation was launched on its far-flung work. During this period, principles and practices have evolved, methods have been shaped by experience, and techniques have developed from trial and error. Some of these principles and ideas have their roots in the years of association of Mr. Rockefeller and Mr. Gates, long before the Foundation was created. Others represent a gradual evolution, based on new conditions and a changing social environment.

Because The Rockefeller Foundation was one of the pioneers in the field, and in point of age is one of the oldest institutions of its kind, it may be of value to outline some of the principles and practices which, although often modified, have guided its work. There is here no implication that these concepts are necessarily applicable to other foundations established under different conditions or for different purposes. They merely represent the accumulated experience and viewpoints developed over years of operation by a single organization.

I

A foundation is not only a private philanthropy; it is affected with a public interest and is in a real sense a public trust. Exempt from taxation, it enjoys a favored legislative status. The grants which it makes are matters of public concern, and public confidence in the foundation as a social instrument must be based on an adequate understanding of its purposes and work. A foundation, therefore, cannot escape the responsibility, moral if not legal, for giving the public—preferably at regular intervals—complete information of its activities and finances.

This is a principle which The Rockefeller Foundation has followed practically from the beginning of its work. As early as 1913, Jerome D. Greene, the executive secretary, was writing about "the accountability of The Rockefeller Foundation to the people of the United States," and was trying to devise a systematic method by which the Foundation's activities could obtain the benefit of "public scrutiny, criticism and publicity."[1] By its creators the Foundation was regarded as a co-operative enterprise; not a dominating or patronizing force in carrying forward a particular program, but a single factor, and not the controlling factor, in joint undertakings for the advancement and diffusion of knowledge and understanding. "An extra engine put on to help the train over a stiff grade"—this was Dr. Buttrick's homely description of the function of a charitable trust.[2]

To create the necessary atmosphere for the development of this conception, the Foundation initiated a system of annual reports, which as the years went by became increasingly comprehensive. Today, they not only contain the entire record of all appropriations and payments, but they give the complete financial picture of the Foundation, including a list of securities held, with ledger and market values, all transactions during the year related to invested funds, and the balance sheet with income and expense account. In no lesser way can the essentially public nature of the responsibilities of a foundation, as evidenced by its exemption from taxation, be adequately discharged.

Great advantage accrues from an elastic charter which gives the trustees full responsibility for the operation of the organization and the use of funds. This was Mr. Rockefeller's unique contribution to the foundation which he created. He trusted the future. He did not think that benevolence and wisdom were confined to his time, and he had a healthy skepticism of the ability of one generation to foresee the needs and requirements of the next. He left to future trustees the interpretation of the general objective of the charter: "the well-being of mankind throughout the world," realizing that the interpretation would change from decade to decade as human problems changed. Because he mistrusted organizations set up in perpetuity, he gave the trustees full power to spend the principal as well as the income of the fund. "Perpetuity is a pretty long time," he dryly remarked.[3]

In the four decades of its operation, the trustees have appropriated approximately $125,000,000 from principal, as challenging opportunities presented themselves which could not easily be avoided. This does not necessarily mean that this same policy will be continued in the future, because the board of trustees is always free to adjust its practices to new situations and new points of view. But in the world of sweeping change and insecurity in which we live at the present time—a world which Mr. Rockefeller did not live to see—the essential wisdom of the completely elastic and flexible charter he gave the Foundation seems abundantly clear.

The grants of a foundation should not be tied up to rigid and unchangeable purposes. A charitable trust should not serve as an instrument to aid an outmoded past in imposing itself on a new kind of future. Unfortunately, the history of charitable trusts contains too many tragic spectacles of large masses of property settled to unalterable uses. In endowing what they thought was of permanent importance, earlier generations made wrong guesses which embarrass us today. How can we assume that our guesses have any greater validity or are made with any clearer foresight?

This was the philosophy behind the action taken by the trustees of The Rockefeller Foundation in 1937 under which recipients, past and present, were advised that it was the desire of the Foundation that the gift, "whether the income only is spent or the principal as well, shall always be regarded as available for use in the broadest way, so as best to promote the general purpose for which it was made." This liberalizing act relating to all future grants for endowment, and also, as far as permitted by law, to past gifts, contained the following provisions:

(1) Ten years after the date of the gift, the income from it may be used in whole or in part for some purpose other than that for which the gift was made, such purpose to be as reasonably related to the original purpose as may be found practicable at the time, having regard to intervening changing conditions.

(2) Beginning five years after the date of the gift, 5 per cent of the principal of the fund may be used each year for any purpose for which income may then be used.

(3) After the expiration of twenty-five years, any part or the whole of

> the principal may be used for some other purpose, the new purpose—as in point one—to be as reasonably related to the original purpose as may be found practicable at the time, having regard to intervening changing conditions.[4]

These liberalizing provisions represent an attempt to free the future from frozen funds and "tired" endowments, in the belief that the wisdom of this generation cannot be substituted for the wisdom of the next in the solution of problems hidden from our eyes.

"Money is a feeble offering without the study behind it which will make its expenditure effective." This is a sentence which Mr. Rockefeller wrote nearly fifty years ago, after a lifetime of experience in what he called "the difficult art of giving."[5] The sentence is profoundly true, in relation both to individuals and institutions. Dr. Henry S. Pritchett of the Carnegie Foundation expressed the idea in even more vigorous terms: "Somebody must sweat blood with gift money, if its effect is not to do more harm than good."[6]

No article in the creed of The Rockefeller Foundation has been more fully substantiated in the four decades of its experience. Without unstinted expenditure of time, investigation and expert competence, nothing permanently constructive can be accomplished merely by the use of money. Effective philanthropy, especially in the main intellectual fields, is by no means a simple and artless affair which any one with good intentions can handle. Rather it is a highly specialized, arduous and complex business. This was the principle that Gates learned from Mr. Rockefeller, and Buttrick and Rose from Gates; and it has been passed on to later generations of officers and trustees. "It requires just as much effort to give away a thousand dollars as it does to give away a million dollars." This dictum, stemming far back in the history of the Foundation, has set the pattern of its work and organization—a pattern based on highly trained personnel, chosen for their knowledge and competence in the various specialized fields into which the Foundation has gone.

In the beginning the Foundation's organization was small. As the program grew it was necessary to expand the staff, and today some thirty officers, aided by various secretarial, clerical, and special services, are employed in the task of maintaining close contact with ideas and personnel at the frontiers of the various fields of knowledge in which the Foundation is working. In addition to this central staff, eighty-five men and women are employed in the laboratories and field activities of the Foundation's operating programs in public health and agriculture.

Through rigorous schedules of study, travel and interviewing, these men and women keep the trustees informed of opportunities related to the Foundation's broad objectives, report on progress of efforts currently supported, and mature for consideration specific proposals upon which the trustees take action.

Human judgment is fallible, and no organization can hope for a record unspotted by mistakes. Some causes are exceptional, many are worthy, but the majority, although often inspired by the best of motives, are commonplace. To distinguish between the exceptional and the commonplace, to discriminate between promising and pedestrian ideas, to discover where talent lies in terms of human ability—this almost unattainable objective requires patient, meticulous and conscientious investigation, and nothing can take its place.

Once grants are made to responsible groups or institutions, no degree of control over the operation of the grants should be exercised by a foundation. "Cut the strings when the gift is made." This has been the evolving policy of The Rockefeller Foundation. The unwisdom of any other course lies in the patent fact that control of a vast number of projects becomes centralized in one institution, with consequences that are practically inefficient and embarrassing, as well as socially unhealthy. If adequate care has been taken in the study and preparation of the project, it is far better to trust the recipient institution to carry it out in good faith than to attempt any type of alien control.

Every social agency, including a foundation, carries within itself not only the seeds of possible decay, but a tendency to exalt the machinery of organization above the purpose for which the organization was created. As Dr. Pritchett pointed out years ago, business concerns are subject to exactly the same tendencies, but in a business organization there is an ever-present test of efficiency lacking in those agencies that deal with intellectual and social products. A business enterprise is established primarily to make money, and when dividends cease, search is immediately made to determine what is wrong. No such automatic criterion exists to test the efficiency of a social organization. It is always difficult to know whether such an organization is really paying dividends or not.

The necessity of constant self-examination, the need of adaptability to changing conditions, have always been present in the thinking of The Rockefeller Foundation. Indeed, on few other principles has so much emphasis been placed. If the work is to be kept out of ruts, if the organization is to avoid frustration and stagnation, programs and methods must be elastic, fresh, alive, and open-minded. This was the point which Mr. Rockefeller, Sr., and his son constantly stressed. Writing to the author of this history in 1925, Mr. Rockefeller, Jr., said:

> Any human institution tends . . . to confuse motion with progress, and to exalt machinery and organization above work and objectives. This is certainly true in the business world and it is equally true in philanthropy. We get so used to following a particular line of activity that the routine and machinery by which it is accomplished takes on a certain sanctity. . . . There is nothing sacred or inviolate about any type of organization. Machinery and personnel are merely the instruments by which objectives are reached, and unless we keep ourselves clear-eyed and fresh and keep the machinery elastic, we run the risk of dry rot.[7]

Anyone who thumbs over the old records of the Foundation will come across constant expression of this point of view as well as frequent resolutions like the following, passed by the trustees in President Vincent's administration in 1925:

> RESOLVED, that the officers be requested to keep in mind the importance of constant vigilance in the appraisal of work already in progress, in withdrawal from projects as soon as these are in a position to develop independently, in the termination of administrative units, whether Boards or Divisions, when conditions justify, and in the consideration of new opportunities whether these are closely related to present activities or extend into other fields.[8]

Nevertheless, the trustees of the Foundation were always aware that flexibility can degenerate into capricious variation. A foundation which shifts its emphasis too often jeopardizes its work. Anxiety about results can undermine the patience necessary in the maturing of long-range plans and ideas. A reasonable compromise has to be established between the principle of elasticity on the one hand and on the other hand the kind of tenacity essential to stability.

II

The proper objective of a foundation, unless created for a particularized purpose, is to prime the pump, never to act as a permanent reservoir. Its work is in the field of demonstration, and it cannot wisely, in most cases, assume the burden of permanent support. It should make sure that there will be some well-established agency to carry on the activity that it has initiated or assisted. The proportion of a budget which it provides should not be so large as to discourage support from other sources. Its contributions should not dry up the springs of popular giving. On the other hand, when a foundation withdraws from a project, its withdrawal should not be so precipitate as to wreck the enterprise. A tapering down of contributions over a period of years will, under ordinary circumstances, give an organization a chance to build up stable support from its own natural sources.

In undertaking a new line of work, it is better to begin in a small way and progress by trial and error to larger ends. This principle was derived from Mr. Rockefeller's personal experience. "Nothing great as great begins." The Rockefeller Institute for Medical Research was started with a pledge of only $20,000 a year. Late in his life, Dr. Buttrick, appraising the early days of his institution, wrote these revealing sentences: "I think it was extremely fortunate for the General Education Board that at the beginning it had very little money. If we had had a lot of money, I am afraid we would have made many more mistakes, and perhaps never have seen those little germinal ideas which have led us into larger relations."[9]

It must be obvious that The Rockefeller Foundation has not always followed this principle. Sometimes, a unique opportunity for public welfare has seemed to justify another approach. But, by and large, it can fairly be said that the general pattern of the Foundation's appropriations, modified as conditions demanded, has been based on modest beginnings, followed by increasing support as the record of accomplishment has justified it. Scores of instances could be cited to illustrate the procedure, particularly in the development of scientific leadership. A repeating pattern is this: a fellowship, a modest one-year grant-in-aid, a second grant-in-aid for perhaps two years, a somewhat larger but still modest appropriation for three years, and then one or more substantial grants in support of an established research project. Some of the outstanding scientific work both in the United States and abroad has been developed by this process.

A foundation that operates on a national or international basis cannot wisely concern itself with local charities. The burden should be carried by each community for itself, or as Mr. Rockefeller said years ago, "by the people who are on the spot, and who are, or should be, most familiar with local needs." Mr. Rockefeller was interested in the more fundamental question. "To help the sick and distressed appeals to the kind-hearted always," he said. "But to help the investigator who is striving successfully to attack the causes that bring about sickness and distress does not so strongly attract the giver of money."[10] This was written early in the century and would of course have to be qualified today. But it stresses a principle which the Foundation has consistently followed. Two lines of policy were open to the trustees: one was to engage in projects which were remedial and alleviatory; the other was to try to select problems which lie at the root of human difficulties, and which require for their solution, or for any approach to a solution, patience, tenacity, research, careful planning, generalship, and adequate and continuing funds. Because projects of this latter type are always difficult to discover and manage, the temptation is to take the easy road, to do the obvious thing, even if it is something which, because of its popular appeal, other agencies might support, or which ultimately would be taken care of in some other way. The difference between these two courses has always seemed to the trustees of the Foundation to be the difference between the less important and the fundamental, between a policy of scattered activities and a policy of relative concentration.

For over thirty years in its annual report appeared this sentence: "The Foundation does not make gifts or loans to individuals, or finance patents or altruistic movements involving private profit, or contribute to the building or maintenance of churches, hospitals or other local organizations. . . ." This is the negative side of an affirmative policy, the policy being one of concern for the determining causes of human well-being.

A foundation easily falls into the habit of frittering away its funds, in an extensive series of small grants. Years ago, Mr. Gates used to thunder against what he called "the iniquity of retail giving," and in more recent years, others have scored the policy of "living in the thick of thin things." The argument has been that a foundation capable of making large grants for significant purposes should not scatter its funds thinly over a wide area.

With this argument there can be little quarrel. On the other hand, it is exceedingly questionable whether a rigid line can be drawn against the small gift. Often, a promising development can be brought to fruition with just a few thousand dollars. Sir Howard Florey's successful pioneering with penicillin required very little initial financial assistance. The opportunity was ready, and all that was needed was extra laboratory facilities. The best that a foundation can aim to do is to find the strategic opening. This requires a degree of wisdom and imagination, and mistakes are inevitable. In furthering the advance and application of knowledge, bold strokes involving large sums are frequently part of the strategic approach; but sometimes the small gift, rightly placed, can powerfully affect the future.

A foundation with wide and intimate contacts can perform a useful function in serving as an unofficial clearinghouse for ideas and plans in many fields. Certainly this has been true of The Rockefeller Foundation. Its officers are in continual touch with promising developments and personnel around the world. The most effective projects it has supported have been developed in the field. These projects have come from close acquaintance with scientists and laboratories, from days and weeks spent on university campuses, from hard journeys on horseback and riverboat to discover the breeding places of disease or the prospects for a new type of corn. The officers thus develop a point of view that is both cumulative and comparative.

Consequently, the Foundation has become a center to which research students and universities turn for information; and much of the time of the officers is spent, not on questions of financial support, but in discussing with eager inquirers the developments in their fields in other institutions and in other countries. As the late President Keppel of the Carnegie Corporation said: "Much of what one university learns about another is learned in foundation offices."[11]

The quality of a foundation's work depends as much on the quality of its trustees as it does on the quality of its officers. Officers require initiative, imagination, curiosity, and an ability to present to the trustees objectively and fairly their findings and recommendations. Trustees have the responsibility not only for the selection of officers, but also for the determination of policy and program. It is their function to maintain balance and proportion, to think in terms of the whole institution and its social consequences rather than its separate parts, to "brood"—in Mr. Rockefeller, Jr.'s, happy word—over the performance and aims of the organization against the total background of human need and opportunity.

This requires ability of a high order—a judicious type of temperament, an impartial approach. One of the rigidly observed rules of The Rockefeller Foundation is that any trustee personally connected with an organization or institution which is being considered as the recipient of a grant leaves the board room during the time that the project is under discussion.* Objectivity, perspective, and an ability to see things in the large are indispensable faculties in the equipment of a foundation trustee.

Modesty becomes foundations because the question of financial support in all circumstances requires tact and good taste. One of the surest ways of losing credit and gratitude is to lay claim to them; many institutions, including governments, have this lesson to learn. A thoughtful critic of foundation procedure wrote this comment, which foundation executives might well ponder: "Nothing is so repugnant as the arrogance of those who presume to impose cultural norms upon a society on no basis or warrant other than their pecuniary success under the dispensation of a competitive economy."[12]

When Dr. Rose in 1909 wrote out what he called the "Principles of Administration" of the Rockefeller Sanitary Commission, at the very top of the list he put this sentence, of which mention has already been made: "The Commission will seek to hide itself behind its work and to keep to the front the local agencies through which the work is being done."[13] This could well be the motto and spirit of philanthropic foundations.

* This rule is written into the by-laws.

CHAPTER XXIV

PERSPECTIVE

IN ATTEMPTING TO FORM ANY ADEQUATE estimate of the work of The Rockefeller Foundation in its first four decades—and such an attempt is probably premature—one qualifying circumstance needs to be stressed: almost from its birth it was plunged into the cataclysmic years of the twentieth century. Within a few months after it was launched came Sarajevo and the First World War. It was five years after the Armistice in 1918 before anything like a normal world evolved from the chaos. The great depression following 1929 had a profound effect on the character of the Foundation's work, and even before the immediate impact of the catastrophe had dissipated, the nations were swept into the Second World War. Of all the years during which the Foundation has operated, scarcely six or seven could by any kind of measurement be called normal. It has carried on its work under a leaking roof, and in retrospect much of its activity seems to have been a patch-and-repair job.

One looks back on some sections of the record with a feeling akin to dismay. Not that the things done were unwisely conceived or unnecessarily undertaken; but so often they were far removed from the "germinal ideas" which Gates and Rose and Buttrick used to discuss in the early days of the Foundation; they did not represent the imaginative, creative things that could have been done in even a relatively well-ordered world—the kind of world, for example, that existed in the two or three decades prior to the establishment of the Foundation. In this sense, an organization dedicated to the welfare of men could scarcely have been launched in a more unpropitious hour. One thinks of the vast feeding programs which the Foundation launched in Europe during the famines of the First World War; of the fight on the widespread epidemic of tuberculosis in France which grew out of the ravages of war; of the millions of books and periodicals distributed to libraries decimated by both wars; of the promising research projects that were disrupted and often crippled as doctors and scientists were drawn into war services; of the creation of public health institutes on a battle-scarred continent only to have them wiped out or depleted in the second war; of the assembly of the finest mathematical faculty in the world at Göttingen which was scattered by Hitler's terrorism; of the health institute in Tokyo which became a military headquarters; of a physics institute in Madrid standing isolated and unused; of the sums spent to protect the priceless cultural heritage of Europe—paintings, books, manuscripts, architecture—from devastation and loss.

Again the point must be emphasized that all these projects were undoubtedly worth while, and the Foundation has reason to be proud of its part in them. What we are faced with is the fundamental antithesis between humane ideas and organizations on the one hand and on the other hand the deepening tragedy of the twentieth century. The Foundation was a child of the era in which it was born, and it has been shaped by its environment.

II

In spite of this limiting circumstance, the contributions of the Foundation to the intellectual life of the world and the well-being of men can scarcely be questioned. It was one of the early experiments in the voluntary diversion and organized application of great wealth to social ends; and it has met with a measure of success which even its hopeful friends in the beginning scarcely anticipated. "We built better than we knew," said Mr. Rockefeller, Sr., writing to Mr. Gates in 1924, and he went on to speak of "the beneficent results which are so far in advance of our fondest dreams."[1] In fields like public health and agriculture the Foundation has demonstrated the merit of new ideas—so completely, in fact, that its programs have frequently been taken over by governments, and people have voted to tax themselves to maintain the demonstrations. In medicine, psychiatry, and the biological sciences it has been an invigorating stimulant, aiding materially in the wide advance of knowledge and application which have characterized these subjects in the last thirty years. In the social sciences, it has helped to build integrity and scientific standards into research, pioneering in basic techniques hitherto relatively unexplored. In the humanistic studies it has been one of the influences which have assisted in bringing to a broader public not only the traditional values inherited from the past, but new interpretations of value adapted to a new age.

It can be said, too, that the Foundation has won a place for itself in the confidence and respect of many people in many lands. This could be demonstrated by scores of illustrations, but perhaps a single incident will serve. Two victims of the Hitler persecutions, who met their deaths in concentration camps, left wills naming The Rockefeller Foundation as a principal beneficiary. As far as can be discovered neither of these men had been in contact with the Foundation. They did not know each other. One, a Frankfurt physician, died probably of malnutrition at the Theresienstadt camp. The other, a Hungarian industrialist, was executed in the gas chambers at Auschwitz. He left the Foundation nearly $100,000 in a New York bank and other lesser funds in institutions located in Geneva, London, Cairo, and Johannesburg. It would seem that in both cases the donors looked upon The Rockefeller Foundation as perhaps the one stable and enduring organization worthy of their final trust.

All this on the credit side can truly and objectively be said about The Rockefeller Foundation without in any way detracting from the myriad efforts of hundreds of other agencies working toward the same ends. The age-old task of weaving an adequate pattern of human welfare is of course a vast, conjunctive effort, and the Foundation has been merely a single thread in a mighty skein.

Obviously, there is another side to the picture. No institution is exempt from mistakes and shortcomings, and surely a foundation whose expenditures have run into hundreds of millions of dollars can scarcely be expected to produce a spotless record. No one knows better than the writer, much of whose life has been spent with foundations, how profitless some of the research is, how wide the gap between expenditure and product, how often the promising project ends in nothing but intangible or insignificant generalities. Sometimes the fault lies with the research group or institution; just as often, perhaps, it reflects the faulty judgment or misguided enthusiasm of the foundation. One of the great temptations that face foundations is to seek for immediate returns, to judge their activities by standards of quickly maturing results, forgetting that in many fields growth is a slow process which requires a favorable soil. Dr. Buttrick said, years ago: "We may plant a germinal idea and water it and fertilize it, but God, or the nature of things if you please, must give the increase."[2] Foundations are particularly exposed to the evils of immediacy, and too often their work is handicapped by what might be called the lack of a sense of depth in time.

A corollary difficulty in the management of foundations, as far as their programs are concerned, relates to their fear of being overreached or imposed upon. This can be a creditable attribute, but it is a handicap when it becomes a chronic state of mind masquerading as caution. Sometimes foundations resent the necessity of giving support to an idea or an institution beyond a predetermined and rather optimistically reckoned date. Estimates of how long new developments in underprivileged countries may take to become self-supporting, naïve assumptions about the prospects of men returning from training fellowships, disappointed expectations of the results of surveys and demonstrations, all these suggest a lack of tenacity, a poor sense of timing, and an anxiety lest the foundation has been victimized. This anxiety frequently inclines foundations to cut down the periods of grants and to increase the number of projects which seem worth while "as a trial run." The end result has not infrequently been that men with valuable ideas whom the foundations are trying to aid worry themselves into nonproductive anxiety about financial uncertainties because of an excess of caution or fear on the part of their supporters. To quote Dr. Buttrick again—and his mellow philosophy about foundations is as pertinent today as it was a quarter of a century ago when he died: "The quality which a foundation needs almost above everything else is tenacity of patience and purpose."[3] Or as Dr. Rose used to say: "Remember we are not in a hurry."

Of course, a foundation needs knowledge and imagination, too. And mistakes are inevitable because human judgment is frail. Perhaps the mistakes are due in considerable degree to lack of what might be called a clairvoyant kind of imagination. So often a new germinal idea runs completely contrary to accepted opinion; it violates all the canons of current scientific thinking; or it is lodged in some remote and hidden corner. One wonders what would have been the answer of a foundation to Louis Pasteur if he had applied for aid in the development of his strange conception that the process of fermentation and the process of infection are related. Or what assistance from any responsible foundation could Madame Curie have obtained during those years when with her own hands she shoveled tons of pitchblende in that old shed in the Rue Lhomond? One of the most mysteriously imaginative minds that ever pondered on the deep relations that exist between numbers was to be found, not so many years ago, in the delicate and diseased body of a humble civil servant in India; and at the turn of the century it was a patent examiner in Zurich who was beginning to see, with amazing clarity and insight, relations between time and space that were presently to revolutionize all scientific thought.

To detect genius when it appears, to distinguish between fundamental ideas that are struggling to be born and those that have already safely arrived, to be able to discriminate between the significant and the trivial—this is the difficult, indeed the almost impossible, standard by which foundations must measure themselves.

These comments and criticisms relate to foundations in general, but in part at least they represent points of view which the trustees and officers of The Rockefeller Foundation, in moments of self-examination—and there have been many—have frequently discussed. No one can claim that these and other difficulties attending the management of a great philanthropic enterprise have all been eliminated from the Foundation; but the organization throughout its history has been sensitive to the subtle dangers and weaknesses inherent in the very nature of its responsibilities, and has tried as best it could to avoid them.

How far it has succeeded in this ambition is probably not for the present writer to judge. But this much can be said with assurance: the organization has outlived the evil prophecies which attended its birth. Then the emphasis—particularly in the days of the Walsh investigation—was on the irresponsibility of great wealth in the hands of a few trustees, and the temptation to employ this power for unsocial purposes. Fears were frequently expressed that The Rockefeller Foundation would be used to crush labor unionism, or warp education for capitalistic ends, or foster religious strife, or undermine the aims of progressive legislation in promoting forward-looking social practices. The criticism was also made, then and later, that the Foundation was little more than the donor's personal giving, incorporated, that the trustees were not really independent, and that their actions were determined by a small group responsible to the donor's family.

Time and the persuasive argument of performance have answered most of these charges. To one who was associated with the Foundation for nearly three decades, their absurdity is evidenced by the character and high integrity of the trustees. One recalls Charles Evans

Hughes with his cool logic and his almost majestic probity; or William Allen White with his massive common sense; or Ray Lyman Wilbur with his challenging directness and incisiveness. One remembers, too, men like John W. Davis, Owen D. Young, Martin A. Ryerson, Anson Phelps Stokes, Frederick Strauss, Jerome D. Greene, Thomas I. Parkinson, Walter Stewart of the Institute for Advanced Study, Ernest Hopkins of Dartmouth—to mention arbitrarily only a few—men who brought great gifts of detachment and judgment to the deliberations of the board. One thinks of the scrupulousness and high sense of right and honor of Thomas M. Debevoise, who was counsel to the trustees for nearly two decades and a half.* One recalls with special vividness the modesty and statesmanship of John D. Rockefeller, Jr., who served as chairman of the board for twenty-three years, presiding over its deliberations with an impartiality, a mastery of the relevant, and an unfailing courtesy which brought him the respect and affection of the long line of trustees and officers who were associated with him.†

These were the men who guided the destiny of the Foundation and gave balance and perspective to its program. An organization with such trustees is not necessarily endowed with final wisdom or protected from the human frailty of making mistakes; but neither is it vulnerable to the charge of irresponsible management or disingenuous motives.

III

The foundation, in its modern sense, is almost exclusively an American phenomenon of the twentieth century. During the whole of the nineteenth century, only seven persons of wealth established foundations in the United States for philanthropic purposes. In the first decade of the twentieth century, approximately a dozen new foundations were established, and at least twenty-two in the second decade; since 1920, it is estimated, new foundations have been created at the rate of over ten a year. An intelligent critic, not too friendly to foundations, some years ago made a statement which would probably go unchallenged: "Very few important cultural projects of any size," he said, "are consummated in this country without

* The counsel to The Rockefeller Foundation is not a trustee, but he attends all meetings of the board and of the executive committee.

† The complete roster of the trustees is given in Appendix I; and of the principal officers in Appendix II.

having experienced either the direct or indirect impact of foundation philosophy and influence."[4]

The question is, of course, whether the philosophy and influence of foundations are healthy ingredients in American life. Is the stimulus which they undoubtedly bring to many branches of intellectual effort offset by the evils which are frequently urged against them? Perhaps the most common of these allegations is that foundations are obsessed by "illusions of omniscience or omnipotence or both," to use the words of President Keppel of the Carnegie Corporation,[5] and that they are destined by their very nature and personnel to be instruments of an outmoded past. This charge has been raised before, and doubtless will be raised again. Any attempt to answer it is embarrassed by the fact that the phenomenon of the modern foundation is of so recent an origin. As a human institution, it is still relatively young and untested, and an appraisal of its total assets and liabilities, its contributions and weaknesses, is bound, at the present moment, to lack perspective.

Perhaps without presumption, however, the writer may set down two general principles or guiding marks, based on long experience, which seem to him to determine, in part at least, whether the attitude of the foundation toward the society of which it is a part is soundly and healthily conceived.

In the first place, a foundation should be a pioneering institution rather than a regular source of support for tried and established activities. Its capital is venture capital, and it should be used adventurously. Indeed, its business is to take risks. Its primary obligation is to blaze trails, to find new methods, to explore new ideas, to keep its work, in John Dewey's phrase, "close to the growing edge of things," to experiment in areas where public funds cannot readily go, to be prepared for intellectual adventure in developing, for example, an untried therapeutic agent like penicillin, or in making a fresh approach to the teaching of languages.

A foundation fulfills its unique promise when it works on the frontiers of knowledge and experience, rather than in the more settled areas behind. Moreover, frontiers are never stationary; sooner or later, they will themselves be settled, and the line will move forward once again. There is no such thing as the *status quo* in medical research, for example, or in any other kind of research. Facts march. There are no areas of human thinking around which magic circles can be drawn to protect them against possible obsolescence. In physics, chemistry, mathematics, biology, and also in the social sciences, each generation, with new light thrown by better instruments of precision or by more delicate apprehension, corrects the mistakes of its predecessors and makes a few of its own. Hypotheses serve their purpose and are then given honorable retirement when better ones appear. In the field of science, and in human relations as well, the problem is never finally solved; the last word is never said. Knowledge, like life itself, is dynamic and not static. An understanding of what might be called the biological inevitability of change, and a broad sympathy with intellectual adventure, must be the basis of any organization whose sincere objective is the welfare of men, particularly when one of its main approaches is through the extension of knowledge.

In the second place, promising men and creative ideas are basic and fundamental; and they are far more important than money. The best that a foundation can aim to do is to put its support in the right place at the right time. The most that it accomplishes is to expedite the development of ideas, which, without help, might be retarded.

There is a common fallacy—and even some foundation executives may not be entirely immune from it—that money can create ideas, and that a great deal of money can create better ideas. Nothing could be wider of the mark. The bottleneck is always men—imaginative men with fertile ideas related to the future. For them there is no substitute; without them, the money of a foundation will purchase nothing but motion and futility. The point is pertinent because of the age-old tendency of wealth to think of itself in terms of exaggerated importance. It can be of great and strategic assistance, but it is only a means to an end—and often, as history shows, a not indispensable means; and the end is creditable or otherwise, depending on the idea and the man behind whom the support is placed.

In this respect, the writer believes, The Rockefeller Foundation has been singularly fortunate. The trustees and the officers have reason to be grateful first to the founder and his clear-sighted advisers for the opportunity which they made possible. But for such success as the Foundation has achieved, they have to thank the vision, the competence, the integrity, the wisdom, the skill, the tenacity, and the selflessness of those whose work they have sought to aid.

APPENDICES

APPENDIX I

TRUSTEES OF THE ROCKEFELLER FOUNDATION

(1913-1950)

NAME	SERVED AS TRUSTEE	
	BEGINNING DATE	TERMINAL DATE
Agar, John G.*	February 25, 1920	Retired November 9, 1928
Aldrich, Winthrop W.	April 10, 1935	Retired June 30, 1951
Angell, James R.*	November 9, 1928	Retired April 15, 1936
Arnett, Trevor	November 9, 1928	Retired April 15, 1936
Barnard, Chester I.	April 3, 1940	
Buttrick, Wallace*	January 24, 1917	Died May 27, 1926
Claflin, William H., Jr.	April 5, 1950	
Compton, Karl T.	April 3, 1940	
Davis, John W.	February 24, 1922	Retired April 5, 1939
Dickey, John S.	April 2, 1947	
Dodds, Harold W.	April 7, 1937	
Douglas, Lewis W.	April 10, 1935	Resigned April 2, 1947
	December 6, 1950	
Dulles, John Foster	April 10, 1935	
Edsall, David L.*	May 25, 1927	Retired April 15, 1936
Eliot, Charles W.*	January 21, 1914	Resigned May 5, 1917
Flexner, Simon*	May 22, 1913	Retired April 16, 1930
Fosdick, Harry Emerson	January 26, 1916	Resigned February 23, 1921
Fosdick, Raymond B.	February 23, 1921	Retired June 30, 1948
Freeman, Douglas S.	April 7, 1937	
Gasser, Herbert S.	April 7, 1937	
Gates, Frederick T.*	May 22, 1913	Resigned July 2, 1923
Gifford, Walter S.	April 15, 1936	Retired April 5, 1950
Greene, Jerome D.	May 22, 1913	Resigned January 24, 1917
	November 9, 1928	Retired December 6, 1939
Hadley, Herbert Spencer†	February 23, 1927	Died November 4, 1927

* Deceased.

† Died, never having attended a meeting.

NAME	SERVED AS TRUSTEE	
	BEGINNING DATE	TERMINAL DATE
Hepburn, A. Barton*	March 18, 1914	Died January 25, 1922
Heydt, Charles O.	May 22, 1913	Resigned January 24, 1917
Hopkins, Ernest M.	November 9, 1928	Retired December 2, 1942
Howland, Charles P.*	November 9, 1928	Died November 12, 1932
Hughes, Charles E.*	January 24, 1917	Resigned February 18, 1921
	November 6, 1925	Retired November 9, 1928
Judson, Harry Pratt*	May 22, 1913	Resigned February 27, 1924
Kellogg, Vernon L.*	February 24, 1922	Retired April 11, 1934
Loeb, Robert F.	April 2, 1947	
Lovett, Robert A.	May 20, 1949	
Mason, Max	January 1, 1930	Resigned June 30, 1936
McCloy, John J.	March 3, 1946	Resigned June 11, 1949
Moe, Henry Allen	April 5, 1944	
Murphy, Starr J.*	May 22, 1913	Died April 4, 1921
Myers, William I.	April 2, 1941	
Parkinson, Thomas I.	April 10, 1935	Retired December 31, 1946
Parran, Thomas	April 2, 1941	
Richards, Alfred N.	April 7, 1937	Retired April 2, 1941
Rockefeller, John D.*	May 22, 1913	Resigned December 4, 1923
Rockefeller, John D., Jr.	May 22, 1913	Retired April 3, 1940
Rockefeller, John D., 3rd	December 16, 1931	
Rose, Wickliffe*	May 22, 1913	Retired June 30, 1928
Rosenwald, Julius*	January 24, 1917	Retired April 15, 1931
Rusk, Dean	April 5, 1950	
Ryerson, Martin A.*	January 26, 1916	Retired December 3, 1928
Smith, Geoffrey S.	April 5, 1950	
Sproul, Robert G.	April 3, 1940	
Stewart, Walter W.	April 15, 1931	Retired December 6, 1950
Stokes, Anson Phelps	November 9, 1928	Resigned April 12, 1932
Strauss, Frederick*	January 26, 1916	Retired April 15, 1931
Sulzberger, Arthur Hays	April 5, 1939	
Swift, Harold H.	April 15, 1931	Retired April 5, 1950
Trowbridge, Augustus*	November 9, 1928	Died March 14, 1934
Van Dusen, Henry P.	April 2, 1947	
Vincent, George E.*	January 24, 1917	Retired December 31, 1929
Whipple, George H.	May 25, 1927	Retired December 1, 1943
White, William Allen*	February 21, 1923	Retired April 10, 1935
Wilbur, Ray Lyman*	February 21, 1923	Retired December 4, 1940
Woods, Arthur*	November 9, 1928	Retired April 10, 1935
Young, Owen D.	November 9, 1928	Retired December 6, 1939

* Deceased.

APPENDIX II

LIST OF CHIEF OFFICERS OF THE ROCKEFELLER FOUNDATION

(1913-1950)

Chairmen of the Board of Trustees

John D. Rockefeller, Jr.	1917-1939
Walter W. Stewart	1939-1950
John Foster Dulles	1950-

Presidents

John D. Rockefeller, Jr.	1913-1917
George E. Vincent	1917-1929
Max Mason	1929-1936
Raymond B. Fosdick	1936-1948
Chester I. Barnard	1948-

Vice Presidents

Thomas B. Appleget	1929-1949
Edwin R. Embree	1927
Roger S. Greene	1918-1929
Selskar M. Gunn	1927-1941
Lindsley F. Kimball	1949-

Secretaries

Jerome D. Greene	1913-1916
Edwin R. Embree	1917-1924
Norma S. Thompson	1925-1947
Flora M. Rhind	1948-

Treasurers

Louis G. Myers	1913-1932
Lefferts M. Dashiell	1932-1938
Edward Robinson	1938-

Comptrollers

Robert H. Kirk	1915-1924
George J. Beal	1924-

INTERNATIONAL HEALTH DIVISION

Directors

Wickliffe Rose	1913-1923
Frederick F. Russell, M.D.	1923-1935
Wilbur A. Sawyer, M.D.	1935-1944
George K. Strode, M.D.	1944-

DIVISION OF THE MEDICAL SCIENCES

Directors

Richard M. Pearce, M.D.	1919-1930
Alan Gregg, M.D.	1930-

DIVISION OF THE NATURAL SCIENCES

Directors

Max Mason	1928-1929
Herman A. Spoehr	1930-1931
Warren Weaver	1932-

DIVISION OF THE SOCIAL SCIENCES

Directors

Edmund E. Day	1928-1937
Sydnor H. Walker (Acting)	1937-1938
Joseph H. Willits	1939-

DIVISION OF THE HUMANITIES

Directors

Edward Capps	1929-1930
David H. Stevens	1932-1949
Charles B. Fahs	1949-

APPENDIX III

AREAS OF ROCKEFELLER FOUNDATION ACTIVITIES

(1913-1950)

Europe

Albania
Austria
Belgium
Bulgaria
Czechoslovakia
Denmark
Estonia
Finland
France
Germany
Great Britain
  England
  Scotland
  Wales
  North Ireland
Greece and Crete
Hungary
Iceland
Irish Free State
Italy and Sardinia
Latvia
Lithuania
Netherlands
Norway
Poland
Portugal
Rumania
Spain
Sweden
Switzerland
U. S. S. R.
  Armenia
Yugoslavia

Africa

Algeria
Anglo-Egyptian Sudan
Nigeria
Uganda
Union of South Africa

The East

Afghanistan
Australia
British Borneo
  British North Borneo
  Sarawak
British Pacific Islands
  Solomon Islands
  Gilbert and Ellice Islands
  Tonga
Ceylon
China
Cook Islands
Cyprus
Egypt

Fiji
Hawaii
Hong Kong
India
Indonesia
  Java
  Sumatra
Iran
Iraq
Israel
Japan
Korea
Lebanon
Mauritius
New Hebrides
New Guinea
New Zealand
Pakistan
Palestine
Philippine Islands
Seychelles Islands
Siam
Straits Settlements and Federated Malay States
Syria
Turkey
Western Samoa

North America

Alaska
Bermuda
Canada
Mexico
United States

South America

Argentina
Bolivia
Brazil
British Guiana
Chile
Colombia
Dutch Guiana
Ecuador
Paraguay
Peru
Uruguay
Venezuela

Central America

British Honduras
Costa Rica
Guatemala
Honduras
Nicaragua
Panama
Salvador

Caribbean

Barbados
Cuba
Dominican Republic
Haiti
Jamaica
  Cayman Islands
Leeward Islands
  Antigua
  Montserrat
  St. Kitts
Puerto Rico
Trinidad
  Tobago
Virgin Islands
Windward Islands
  Grenada
  St. Lucia
  St. Vincent

TOTAL

Europe	28
Africa	5
The East	33
North America	5
South America	12
Caribbean	10
	93

NOTES

CHAPTER I

1. Letter Press Book of the American Baptist Education Society, 1891, pp. 467-473.
2. The author was present at the meeting and has checked his recollection with Dr. Alan Gregg who was also present.
3. *The Gates Papers:* Memorandum entitled "The Secret of Mr. Rockefeller's Character and Success." Undated.
4. *Random Reminiscences of Men and Events,* by John D. Rockefeller. (Garden City: Doubleday and Company, 1937), p. 117.
5. Gates: Manuscript autobiography.
6. *John D. Rockefeller,* by Allan Nevins. (New York: Charles Scribner's Sons, 1940), Vol. II, p. 287.
7. *Ibid.,* Vol. II, p. 665.
8. *Ibid.,* Vol. II, p. 291.
9. *Forbes Magazine,* September 29, 1917, p. 69.
10. Nevins, *op. cit.,* Vol. I, p. 43.
11. *Ibid.,* p. 226.
12. Rockefeller, *op. cit.,* p. 140-141.
13. *The Life of Andrew Carnegie,* by Burton J. Hendrick. (London: William Heinemann, Ltd., 1933), Vol. I, p. 349.
14. Nevins, *op. cit.,* Vol. II, p. 191.
15. *The Gates Papers, op. cit.*
16. Letter Press Book of the American Baptist Education Society, 1891, pp. 499-503.
17. Rockefeller, *op. cit.,* p. 156.
18. Gates: Manuscript autobiography.
19. University of Chicago, Minutes of the Board of Trustees, December 19, 1910.
20. *Remarks of the Retiring Chairman, Mr. John D. Rockefeller, Jr., at the Meeting of the General Education Board, April 6, 1939,* p. 3. The Rockefeller Foundation files.
21. Letter: J. D. Rockefeller, Jr., to R. C. Ogden, February 1, 1907. Mr. Rockefeller's files.
22. *Our Times,* by Mark Sullivan. (New York: Charles Scribner's Sons, 1926-1932), Vol. III, p. 327.
23. Rockefeller Sanitary Commission, Annual Report, 1914, p. 11.
24. Rockefeller, *op. cit.,* p. 148.

25. Gates: Manuscript autobiography.
26. Letter: Wickliffe Rose to the author from Paris. Undated.

CHAPTER II

1. Gates: Manuscript autobiography. The letter is dated June 3, 1905.
2. *Ibid.* The text of the June 3, 1905 letter as quoted in the autobiography differs slightly from the text appearing in *The Gates Papers.* I have followed the autobiography.
3. Letter: John D. Rockefeller, Jr., to John D. Rockefeller, Sr. December 31, 1906. Mr. Rockefeller's files.
4. *The Gates Papers:* an address given on the tenth anniversary of The Rockefeller Institute for Medical Research.
5. Hearing before Committee on the District of Columbia. United States Senate on the bill S.6888 to incorporate The Rockefeller Foundation, March 11, 1910.
6. Statement on the Proposed Incorporation of The Rockefeller Foundation, by Jerome D. Greene, March 15, 1912, submitted as part of Report No. 529 to the House of Representatives, April 11, 1912, p. 6.
7. *The Life and Times of William Howard Taft,* by Harry F. Pringle. (New York: Farrar and Rinehart, Inc., 1939), Vol. II, pp. 662-663.
8. *The Survey*, February 24, 1912.
9. *The Independent,* February 8, 1912.
10. *Washington Times,* April 11, 1912.
11. *Philadelphia Inquirer*, January 18, 1913.
12. *Chicago Inter-Ocean,* April 17, 1912.
13. Letter: J. D. Greene to W. P. Dillingham, March 3, 1913. The Rockefeller Foundation files.
14. Gates: Manuscript autobiography.
15. Letter: John D. Rockefeller, Sr., to The Rockefeller Foundation, June 14, 1913. Minutes of The Rockefeller Foundation, June 18, 1913, p. 1019.
16. Letter: Jerome D. Greene to John D. Rockefeller, Jr., March 9, 1940. Mr. Rockefeller's files.
17. Minutes of The Rockefeller Foundation, July 1, 1913, p. 1032.
18. *Random Reminiscences of Men and Events,* by John D. Rockefeller. (Garden City: Doubleday and Company, 1937), p. 177.
19. *Principles and Policies of Giving,* by Jerome D. Greene, October 22, 1913. A memorandum. The Rockefeller Foundation files.
20. *The Gates Papers:* A memorandum entitled "Philanthropy and Civilization."
21. Minutes of The Rockefeller Foundation, June 27, 1913, p. 1027.
22. China Conference of The Rockefeller Foundation. The China Medical Board, Vol. IV, Section 3, pp. 1-2. The Rockefeller Foundation files.
23. The China Medical Board, Vol. I, Appendix II, p. 357. The Rockefeller Foundation files.
24. Hearings of the United States Commission on Industrial Relations. February 5, 1915—64th Congress. Senate Documents, Vol. 27, p. 8228.
25. *Ibid.*, p. 8298.

26. George E. Vincent to the author personally.
27. *Demitasse,* by Alan Gregg. September, 1945. Unpublished memorandum. The Rockefeller Foundation files.
28. *The Gates Papers:* A memorandum entitled "Principles of Philanthropy as a Science and Art." 1923.

CHAPTER III

1. Rockefeller Sanitary Commission, Vol. III, Reports. The Rockefeller Foundation files.
2. Minutes of the Rockefeller Sanitary Commission, 1909-1914, p. 49.
3. Annual Report of the Rockefeller Sanitary Commission, January, 1915, p. 11.
4. First Annual Report of the Administrative Secretary of the Rockefeller Sanitary Commission, 1910, p. 4.
5. Annual Report of The Rockefeller Foundation, 1923, p. 88.
6. Minutes of the Rockefeller Sanitary Commission, 1909-1910, Appendix, pp. 1-2.
7. Address at the Memorial Services for Dr. Rose. February 25, 1932.
8. The Rockefeller Foundation: A Review for 1919, by George E. Vincent, p. 20.
9. Rose to the author and others.
10. *William Henry Welch and the Heroic Age of American Medicine,* by Simon and J. T. Flexner. (New York: Viking Press, Inc., 1941), p. 355.
11. "School of Public Health," by Wickliffe Rose, 1915. Manuscript. The Rockefeller Foundation files.
12. The Rockefeller Foundation: A Review for 1919, by George E. Vincent, p. 26.
13. Letter: Wilbur A. Sawyer to the author, August 31, 1949.
14. Address at the Memorial Services for Dr. Rose. February 25, 1932.

CHAPTER IV

1. Letter: G. E. Vincent to R. Cole, May 3, 1918. The Rockefeller Institute files.
2. Annual Report of The Rockefeller Foundation, 1925, p. 103.
3. The Rockefeller Foundation: A Review for 1928, by George E. Vincent, p. 47.
4. *Rats, Lice and History,* by Hans Zinsser. (Boston: Little, Brown and Company, 1935), p. vii.
5. Russell to the author.

CHAPTER V

1. Memorandum of Interview with General Gorgas by Wickliffe Rose. July 14, 1914, p. 4. The Rockefeller Foundation files.
2. Annual Report of The Rockefeller Foundation, 1916, p. 70.
3. Letter: Wickliffe Rose to General Gorgas, January 27, 1917. The Rockefeller Foundation files.

CHAPTER VI

1. "The Present Status of Anopheles Gambiae in Brazil," by Marshall A. Barber. *American Journal of Tropical Medicine*, Vol. XX, No. 2, March, 1940, p. 264.
2. The Rockefeller Foundation: A Review for 1928, by George E. Vincent, p. 34.

CHAPTER VII

1. *The Gates Papers:* "The China Medical Board." An undated memorandum.
2. *Ibid.*
3. *Ibid.*
4. *Some Roads Towards Peace,* by Charles W. Eliot. A report to the Carnegie Endowment for International Peace, 1912, p. 5.
5. "Present Educational Situation in China and Its Significance for Human Welfare and Progress," by Paul Monroe. Manuscript report for the China Conference of The Rockefeller Foundation, p. 25, January 19-20, 1914.
6. Record of the China Conference. The China Medical Board, Vol. IV, Section 3, p. 10.
7. Report of the Oriental Education Commission, November-December, 1909, Vol. 2, p. 399.
8. Report of the China Medical Commission, 1914.
9. Letter: H. P. Judson to R. S. Greene, November 20, 1914.
10. Address by Dr. Welch to the Members of the Saturday Club, Shanghai, October 30, 1915. The Rockefeller Foundation files.
11. Eliot, *op. cit.,* p. 22.
12. *New York Times,* February 16, 1916.
13. Letter: W. Buttrick to R. S. Greene, July 11, 1916.
14. Letter: W. Buttrick to F. T. Gates, May 8, 1916.
15. Welch, *op. cit.*
16. Report of the First Meeting of the China Medical Commission. August 18, 1915.
17. Address by Dr. Buttrick to the Missionary Conference, Garden City, January 11, 1916. The Rockefeller Foundation files.
18. *The Gates Papers: op. cit.*
19. The Rockefeller Foundation: A Review for 1947, by R. B. Fosdick, p. 25.
20. Release to newspapers by The Rockefeller Foundation, January 16, 1947.

CHAPTER VIII

1. *The Gates Papers:* Miscellaneous memoranda.
2. *A Half Century of American Medicine* by Simon Flexner. The Founders' Day Address, University of Louisville, April 3, 1937.
3. Minutes of the General Education Board, October 23, 1913, p. 201.
4. Letter: Dr. Welch to Dr. Buttrick, June 19, 1914. General Education Board files.

5. Memorandum regarding Mr. Rockfeller's gift for medical education in the United States, December, 1919. General Education Board files.
6. *The Gates Papers:* Mr. Gates' argument was developed in a memorandum entitled "Thoughts on the Rockefeller Public and Private Benefactions." December 31, 1926.
7. Letter: Abraham Flexner to H. S. Pritchett, November 1, 1922. General Education Board files.
8. *The Gates Papers:* Memorandum on the General Education Board, 1927.
9. Annual Report of the General Education Board, 1928-1929, p. 46.
10. Letter: Dr. Eliot to Dr. Buttrick, April 24, 1917. General Education Board files.
11. Letter: Dr. Buttrick to Dr. Eliot, May 16, 1917. General Education Board files.
12. Letter: A. P. Stokes to the author, August 23, 1924. General Education Board files.
13. Letter: A. Gregg to the author, November 20, 1950.
14. *I Remember* by Abraham Flexner. (New York: Simon and Schuster, 1940), p. 308.

CHAPTER IX

1. The Rockefeller Foundation: A Review for 1920, by George E. Vincent, p. 6.
2. *Demitasse*, by Alan Gregg. September, 1945. Unpublished memorandum. The Rockefeller Foundation files.
3. Memorial Address, by Dr. Vincent, April 15, 1930.
4. *Ibid.*
5. Annual Report of the General Education Board, 1920-1921, p. 18.
6. Diary of Richard M. Pearce, December 21, 1924, p. 212. The Rockefeller Foundation files.
7. The Rockefeller Foundation: A Review for 1925, by George E. Vincent, p. 26.
8. "Report on Recent Developments in Medical Education in London," by Richard M. Pearce. 1920.
9. Report of the Royal Commission on University Education in London, 1913, pp. 107-110. The Rockefeller Foundation files.
10. "Report on Recent Developments in Medical Education in London," by Richard M. Pearce. 1920.
11. *The London Morning Post*, June 12, 1920.
12. Letter: E. Hatch to G. E. Vincent, June 6, 1923.
13. Notes on University College, by R. M. Pearce, February 8, 1928.
14. Minutes of The Rockefeller Foundation, March 20, 1931, p. 31051.
15. Letter: Y. J. Pentland to G. E. Vincent, April 26, 1921.
16. Letter: G. E. Vincent to S. Flexner, July 2, 1924.
17. Letter: S. Flexner to G. E. Vincent, January 25, 1922.
18. Diary of Richard M. Pearce, December 1-3, 1924.
19. Minutes of The Rockefeller Foundation, May 27, 1925, 25154.
20. "Medical Education in Belgium," by R. M. Pearce, 1923.

21. Letter: G. E. Vincent to M. Ansiaux, December 28, 1928.
22. Letter: John D. Rockefeller, Sr., to The Rockefeller Foundation, December 18, 1919.
23. Letter: Bayard Dodge to R. M. Pearce, November 17, 1927.
24. Minutes of The Rockefeller Foundation, November 13, 1929, p. 29449.
25. Memorandum: Dr. S. M. Lambert, July 30, 1926. The Rockefeller Foundation files.
26. *A Yankee Doctor in Paradise* by S. M. Lambert. (Boston: Little, Brown and Company, 1941), p. 274.
27. These comments appear in the various documents relating to this episode. The Rockefeller Foundation files.
28. Letter: R. M. Pearce to Dr. W. S. Carter, November 17, 1925.
29. Letter: R. M. Pearce to A. Gregg, December 28, 1924.
30. Letter: A. Gregg to R. M. Pearce, October 31, 1929.
31. Minutes of The Rockefeller Foundation, November 13, 1929, p. 29442.
32. Notes on a conference with G. E. Vincent and E. Embree by Richard M. Pearce, April 19-20, 1922.

CHAPTER X

1. Letter: R. M. Pearce to Alan Gregg, December 28, 1925.
2. Minutes of The Rockefeller Foundation, November 6, 1925, pp. 25277-25279.
3. Letter: Alan Gregg to the author, December 26, 1950.
4. "Tentative Divisional Reports on the Postwar Program of The Rockefeller Foundation." June, 1944, p. 16. Mimeographed.
5. Memorandum regarding possible psychiatric developments, by David L. Edsall. October 3, 1930. The Rockefeller Foundation files.
6. Agenda for the Special Meeting of the Trustees of The Rockefeller Foundation. April 11, 1933.
7. "What Is Psychiatry," by Alan Gregg. Manuscript report. December 3, 1941, p. 1.
8. *Psychiatry in a Troubled World*, by William C. Menninger. (New York: The Macmillan Company, 1948), p. 342.
9. *Ibid.*, p. xiv.

CHAPTER XI

1. Report of the Interboard Committee on Reorganization, by R. B. Fosdick. May 22, 1928.
2. "Scheme for the Promotion of Education on an International Scale." A memorandum by Wickliffe Rose. 1923. General Education Board files.
3. Record of Special Meeting of the Board of Trustees. Princeton, New Jersey, October, 1930.
4. Report of Committee on Appraisal and Review, 1934.
5. *Ibid.*
6. The Rockefeller Foundation: A Review for 1946, by R. B. Fosdick, p. 29.

CHAPTER XII

1. *Autobiography* by Robert Andrews Millikan. (New York: Prentice-Hall, Inc., 1950), p. 213.
2. *Ibid.*, p. 184.
3. "Scheme for the Promotion of Education on an International Scale." A memorandum by Wickliffe Rose. 1923, p. 4.
4. *Ibid.*
5. R. B. Fosdick in his introduction to *Education on an International Scale*, by George W. Gray. (New York: Harcourt, Brace and Co., 1941), p. vii.
6. Annual Report of the General Education Board for 1924-1925, p. 7.
7. Annual Report of the General Education Board for 1925-1926, p. 5.

CHAPTER XIII

1. "Natural Sciences—Program and Policy." Extract from Agenda for Special Meeting of the Trustees of The Rockefeller Foundation, April 11, 1933, p. 76.
2. *Ibid.*, pp. 76-77.
3. *Ibid.*, p. 77.
4. "The Progress of the Natural Sciences," by Warren Weaver. Confidential Monthly Report to the Trustees, March, 1950, p. 21.
5. Letter: T. H. Morgan to Max Mason, May 15, 1933.
6. Record of an interview with Dr. Cohn by George W. Gray. May 9, 1950.
7. Annual Report of The Rockefeller Foundation, 1933, p. 199.
8. Letter: Warren Weaver to Mrs. J. M. H. Carson, June 17, 1949.

CHAPTER XIV

1. "Physics for Adventure." A speech before the American Physical Society, April 28, 1950 by W. V. Houston. Reprinted in *Physics Today*, June, 1950, p. 21.
2. Albert Szent-Gyorgyi to Warren Weaver in conversation.
3. The Rockefeller Foundation: A Review for 1940, by R. B. Fosdick, p. 41.
4. Letter: E. O. Lawrence to Warren Weaver, August 20, 1945.
5. Letter: G. E. Hale to W. Rose, February 14, 1928. General Education Board files.
6. Letter: W. Rose to G. E. Hale, February 21, 1928. General Education Board files.
7. "Palomar, June 3, 1948." The printed account of the dedication exercises.

CHAPTER XV

1. The General Education Board: An Account of Its Activities, 1902-1914, pp. 23-24.
2. *Mexican Agricultural Program,* by J. G. Harrar. The Rockefeller Foundation, New York, 1950, p. 36.

CHAPTER XVI

1. *The Gates Papers:* Letter, F. T. Gates to Mr. Rockefeller, Jr., March 19, 1914.
2. *Ibid.*
3. General Memorandum. October, 1922. The Laura Spelman Rockefeller Memorial files.
4. *Ibid.*
5. *The New Yorker:* Profile. February 10, 1945.
6. Address, "Recent Trends in Social Science," given at the University of Chicago, December 17, 1929.
7. General Memorandum. October, 1922.
8. Final Report of The Laura Spelman Rockefeller Memorial, 1933, p. 9.
9. Address at the dedication of the Social Science Research Building, University of Chicago, December 17, 1929.
10. Final Report of The Laura Spelman Rockefeller Memorial, 1933, p. 14.
11. "Principles governing The Laura Spelman Rockefeller Memorial program in the Social Sciences." December 12, 1928.
12. Record of Special Meeting of the Board of Trustees. Princeton, New Jersey, October, 1930.
13. Interim Report of Activities of The Rockefeller Foundation, December 13, 1933.
14. Report of the Committee on Appraisal and Plan, December 11, 1934.
15. Annual Report of The Rockefeller Foundation, 1935, p. 193.

CHAPTER XVII

1. The Rockefeller Foundation: A Review for 1938, by R. B. Fosdick, p. 42.
2. Memorandum: J. H. Willits to R. B. Fosdick, February 15, 1939.
3. "Notes on a Trip to Europe," by J. H. Willits, 1939.
4. "Plans for Future Work of The Rockefeller Foundation in the Social Sciences." November, 1944.
5. "The National Bureau's Work and Needs," 1939, p. 3. Manuscript report.
6. *Ibid.*, p. 6.
7. Presidential Address by Charles E. Merriam. Reprinted in the *American Political Science Review,* February, 1926, p. 9.
8. Memorandum: J. H. Willits to R. B. Fosdick, November 10, 1942.
9. "The Social Sciences in 1944. Analysis of Program," by J. H. Willits. October 20, 1943.
10. Minutes of The Rockefeller Foundation, January 18, 1946, p. 46004.
11. Minutes of The Rockefeller Foundation, September 20, 1946, p. 46307.
12. Base Record of The Rockefeller Foundation, December, 1937, p. 4.
13. *Security, Loyalty and Science,* by Walter Gellhorn. Cornell University Press, Ithaca, 1950, p. vi.
14. United Nations delegate in conversation with the author.
15. Memorandum: J. H. Willits to R. B. Fosdick, November 10, 1942.
16. The Program in the Social Sciences. A Statement by J. H. Willits. Confidential Monthly Report to the Trustees, June, 1950, p. 28.

CHAPTER XVIII

1. Address of Charles E. Hughes, "Some Aspects of International Cooperation," at the opening meeting of the American Association for the Advancement of Science, Washington, D.C., December 29, 1924. Reprinted in *Science,* Vol. LXI, January 9, 1925, p. 24.
2. Annual Report of The Rockefeller Foundation, 1934, p. 173.

CHAPTER XIX

1. Letter: J. D. Greene to R. B. Fosdick, January 25, 1944.
2. Minutes of the General Education Board, October 10-11, 1924, p. 108.
3. "Memorandum on the Conference at Gedney Farms," January 18-19, 1924. The Rockefeller Foundation files.
4. Letter: A. P. Stokes to A. Flexner, April 9, 1927. The General Education Board files.
5. "The Humanities in Theory and Policy," March 31, 1937. Manuscript report.
6. Minutes of the Meeting at Princeton, New Jersey, October 29-30, 1930.
7. Agenda for Special Meeting of Trustees of The Rockefeller Foundation, April 11, 1933.
8. "The Place of the Humanities in a Program of Human Welfare." A manuscript memorandum prepared at the request of a special committee of the Foundation. 1934.
9. Report of the Committee on Appraisal and Plan. December 11, 1934.
10. The Rockefeller Foundation: A Review for 1937, by R. B. Fosdick, p. 45.
11. Minutes of The Rockefeller Foundation, April 10, 1935, p. 35122.
12. "The Gay Science," by Howard Mumford Jones. *The American Scholar.* Autumn, 1945, p. 398.
13. "The Humanities Program of The Rockefeller Foundation, 1942-1947," p. 34. Manuscript report.
14. Agenda for Special Meeting of the Trustees, April 11, 1933.
15. "The Humanities Program of The Rockefeller Foundation, 1942-1947," p. 1.
16. Confidential Monthly Report for the Trustees, April 1, 1940, p. 14.

CHAPTER XX

1. "The Humanities Program of The Rockefeller Foundation. A Review for the Period 1934-1939," p. 54. Manuscript report.
2. *St. Paul Dispatch,* February 26, 1942.
3. "Westward the Course of Empire," by Robert G. Cleland. An address delivered on Founder's Day, February 28, 1944. The Huntington Library Quarterly, Volume VII, No. 4, August, 1944, p. 15.
4. Letter: Stanley Pargellis to D. H. Stevens. February 28, 1947.
5. "The Humanities Program of The Rockefeller Foundation, 1942-1947," p. 9. Manuscript report.

6. "The American Scholar and the War," by Henry S. Canby. *Saturday Review of Literature,* January 16, 1943, p. 10. This editorial was originally prepared as a speech to the Convention of the Modern Language Association which was not held on account of restrictions on travel.
7. *To the Aid of the Writer: Atlantic Awards in Literature.* A pamphlet issued by the University of Birmingham, 1950.

CHAPTER XXI

1. *The Lancet,* August 29, 1942, p. 256.
2. Letter: Emeric Toro to The Rockefeller Foundation, February 12, 1946.
3. Letter: French R. Fogle to his sponsor, Marjorie Nicolson. Cited in Confidential Monthly Report to the Trustees, June 1, 1945, p. 6.

CHAPTER XXII

1. *The Gates Papers.*
2. Gates in conversation with the author.
3. The Rockefeller Foundation: A Review for 1923, by George E. Vincent, p. 9.
4. The Rockefeller Foundation: A Review for 1941, by R. B. Fosdick, p. 10.
5. "Epidemic Control in Europe, and the League," by Wickliffe Rose. *Review of Reviews,* Vol. 66, July, 1922, pp. 77-80.
6. *Ibid.*
7. *The Magic Mountain, by* Thomas Mann. (New York: Alfred A. Knopf, Inc., 1928), Chapter 6.

CHAPTER XXIII

1. "Principles and Policies of Giving," by Jerome D. Greene, October 22, 1913, pp. 7-9. A memorandum.
2. Dr. Buttrick in conversation with the author.
3. Mr. Rockefeller, Sr., in conversation with the author.
4. Minutes of The Rockefeller Foundation, April 7, 1937, pp. 27138-27140.
5. *Random Reminiscences of Men and Events,* by John D. Rockefeller. (Garden City: Doubleday and Company, 1937), p. 147.
6. Annual Report of the Carnegie Corporation, 1922, p. 19.
7. Letter to Mr. Fosdick from Mr. Rockefeller, Jr., quoted from "A Statement by the President Made at a Meeting of the Trustees, February 24, 1926," by George E. Vincent. The Rockefeller Foundation files.
8. Minutes of The Rockefeller Foundation, February 25, 1925, p. 25029.
9. "Memorandum from Old Man Buttrick," January 17, 1924. Written from the Johns Hopkins Hospital. The Rockefeller Foundation files.
10. Rockefeller, *op. cit.,* p. 147.
11. *The Foundation,* by Frederick P. Keppel. (New York: The Macmillan Company, 1930), p. 98.
12. *Wealth and Culture,* by E. C. Lindeman. (New York: Harcourt, Brace and Co., 1936), p. 59.

13. "Principles of Administration of the Rockefeller Sanitary Commission," by Wickliffe Rose. 1910. The Rockefeller Foundation files.

CHAPTER XXIV

1. *The Gates Papers:* Letter: Rockefeller to Gates, January 9, 1924.
2. "Memorandum from Old Man Buttrick." January 17, 1924. The Rockefeller Foundation files.
3. Buttrick in conversation with the author.
4. *Wealth and Culture,* by E. C. Lindeman. (New York: Harcourt, Brace and Co., 1936), p. 20.
5. *Philanthropy and Learning* by Frederick P. Keppel. (New York. Columbia University Press, 1936), p. 174.

INDEX